DICTIONARY OF
FRENCH
SLANG
AND COLLOQUIAL EXPRESSIONS

SECOND EDITION

Henry Strutz

Formerly Associate Professor of Languages
State University of New York
Alfred State College of Technology

BARRON'S

All inquiries should be addressed to:
Barron's Educational Series, Inc.
250 Wireless Boulevard
Hauppauge, NY 11788
www.barronseduc.com

ISBN-13: 978-0-7641-4115-7
ISBN-10: 0-7641-4115-5

Library of Congress Catalog Card Number 2008938299

Printed in China
9 8 7 6 5 4 3 2 1

Contents

French Slang

Many researchers, including Einstein, have said that the urge to play is the source of all human creativity. Slang is playful in all languages. French slang is particularly playful, perhaps more gracefully playful than the rough play of some other languages. The French language is famous for its lucidity, elegance, and wit. Much French slang shares in those characteristics. The ancient Babylonians, Chinese, and Greeks sometimes used terms for fruits, vegetables, and animals to designate parts of the human body. Some of those same designations are still used today in many languages, including French, but French often adds a light touch and Gallic wit.

Language at Play

Slang is lively, dynamic language, language at play. Words often get shortened by chopping off the beginning (apheresis) or the end (apocope). Words perceived as insipid, pretentious, or pompous, are livened up or taken down a peg or two by adding slang prefixes, or, more frequently, suffixes. (See the entries **-aga; -ard; -arès; -caille; -da; -muche; -ouche; -ouille; -uche; -zig**.) The French enjoy having fun with their language and have created several playful slang systems and no less than twelve series of variations on the personal pronouns. (See the entries **javanais; largonji; louchébem; mézigue, verlan**.) **Verlan** (backslang) is in full flower, and new words are being coined all the time. There is even **verlan** of **verlan**. The best known of these coinages are included in this dictionary.

Almost all words can be **"verlanized"** *(backslanged)*. Just move the last syllable to the beginning and *voilà*—**verlan**. Some are easy to recognize, for instance: **deban (bande); jourbon (bonjour); fumpar (parfum); ouf (fou); tarcol (coltar)**. You might want to have fun and create some yourself. Don't feel limited by the original spelling, since pronunciation (often varying pronunciations), not spelling, is the determining factor, and vowels and consonants can change. For example, the **verlan** *(backslang)* versions of **femme; flic; gauche; mec;** and **paquet** are **meuf; keuf; cheug; keum; képa**.

Javanais, not as complicated or varied as **verlan,** forms slang words by inserting **av, va,** or **ag** after a consonant. For instance, **jeudi** becomes **javeudavi** and **chatte** becomes **chagatte.**

Largonji, is another slang system. Like **javanais,** it probably originated in former French Indochina. In this system, the first letter is replaced by "l" and the original first letter starts the last syllable that ends in an often fanciful suffix such as: **-é; -ès; em; ic; iche; -oque; -uche.** As is the case with verlan, the pronunciation, not the spelling of the original word, is what counts. Examples: **lamfé (femme); latronpem (patron); laubé/laubiche (beau); lauchem (chaud); linspré (prince).**

Many have pointed out that despite a multiplicity of rich cheeses (see the entries **Franchecaille** and **fromegi**) and sauces, obesity is not as prevalent in France as elsewhere, as in North America, for instance. Some claim a connection to wine drinking. Dr. Andrew Weil, a nutritionist, ethnologist, and philosopher, speculates that this paradox may be due to something unknown—in the food, the ambiance, whatever. Might not a playfulness, a lightness of spirit be partly responsible also? Life can be made more light-hearted, more amusing, even healthier, if approached playfully. There may be a correlation between lightness of body and the enlightened mind, the mind that delights in word play. France has long been devoted to the light, in both senses—whether striving to capture the light in constructing Gothic cathedrals, in creating the technique and language of ballet, or in the lightness of a soufflé or in **nouvelle cuisine.** The light of reason shone particularly bright in the **siècle des lumières,** the eighteenth century, when the *Encylopédie* was published in the face of obscurantist opposition. Fabled French light (of the **midi,** the **Île-de-France,** of Paris, the **Ville lumière,** and so on) has inspired painters. This lightness of spirit and body may, in part, account for the extent and variety of French slang. Traditionally, one function of slang, notably "thieves' cant," is to conceal. People involved in crime, drugs, nonconjugal sex, and such, want to keep outsiders in the dark about their activities. In a deeper sense, however, many slang expressions often cast light, and sometimes even a little sweetness, on what is otherwise dark and sinister.

Foreign Influences on Slang

Foreign languages are best studied in a spirit of openness, receptivity. Even more openness is desirable when studying slang. Over the centuries, French slang has been open to influences from its European neighbors and has borrowed generously from them, as well as from the gypsies, potentially everyone's neighbors. Arabic is also well represented, a reflection of France's former colonial presence in North Africa and the Middle East. Despite official attempts to discourage it, American slang is currently "in," especially in matters relating to drugs and rock music.

Speaking French

Speakers of standard French often elide vowels, especially **e,** and leave out **ne** in negatives. As you would expect, such omissions occur more frequently in slang, as in **t'inquiète.** This is true of English as well: "wanna" for "want to," and the omission of final "g," as in "gettin." For **je ne sais pas,** you will sometimes hear **j'sais pas** or even **sais pas. Il n'y a pas** becomes **n'y a pas** or **y'a pas. Tu as** is often pronounced **t'as.** Many of the sentences illustrating the entries make these omissions. By no means should you get the idea that slang parlance is the sole and exclusive province of ill-spoken "low-lifes" in inner city and suburban slums, although you will certainly find it there. Books on slang sell well in France. Most who buy them are not marginal people, those on the fringes of society, but literate, articulate individuals interested in all ranges of the splendid instrument that is the French language. Some of them call themselves **argotnautes** and are involved in **argotologie.** Many who scale the heights of "high culture," **haute cuisine,** and **haute couture** also want to check out linguistic "lower depths" and incorporate slang expressions in their speech and writing. This was true even in Proust's time. He complained that the determined pursuit of slang by some writers was an affectation. You should strive to recognize slang, but use it cautiously yourself until it comes naturally to you. Slang expressions are increasingly encountered in literature and prestige publications in our day and much "street French" is also heard in the **salon** and around the table.

Creating Slang

The **passé simple** is a literary tense and therefore rarely, if at all, used in the example sentences. Yet it isn't as dead on the street as usually alleged, since, as the entry for **rappeur** points out, there are rap performers who use it extensively. Young people are traditionally users and creators of slang. Each generation wants to assert its uniqueness, its identity, in language too, but older people have taken increasingly to slang, perhaps because they are still young at heart. Some slang, still in current use, goes back to Rabelais and Villon. Balzac, Zola, Céline, and many other famous authors have used and even created slang. Many slang words have entered popular speech and are no longer felt as slang. For most speakers of French, the distinction between colloquial speech and slang is anything but rigid.

The original, basic meanings of **chier, con, cul, foutre, merde, pisse,** and so on involve sex and/or elimination. They are still "strong stuff" and some—fewer and fewer—speakers of French will not use them in polite society. Yet language is a living, evolving thing, and these words have developed different, extended meanings and also given rise to families of words that are in use at all levels of society, words in which the originally sexual or excretory connection is only minimally perceived, or no longer felt at all. See the entries **chienlit; chier; con; cul; déconner; démerdard; emmerdeur; foutre; pisseux,** among many others. The verb **baiser** has moved in the opposite direction, and is no longer used for "to kiss." Language, like all else, is involved in processes of change.

Humor in Slang

Slang expressions often deal playfully with dysfunction—excessive eating and drinking, violence, disease, mortality, and other aspects of the human condition sometimes difficult to bear. Their burden can be made lighter by shedding linguistic light on them. Humor can put things in a different light and brighten up what is dreary or ominous. French slang often consummates a particularly felicitous marriage of the visceral and cerebral, of the older parts of the brain concerned with the basics of survival (eating, drinking, sex) and the higher perceptions and functions associated with later brain development.

Freud liked to quote the Roman playwright Terence's maxim: **humani nihil a me alienum puto** (I consider nothing human foreign to me). Human experience is complex and varied. Talking about it in varied, often humorous imagery, can provide insight into problem areas. Aspects of the human condition that are distasteful to some can be made more palatable, less "foreign," if playfully expressed. This dictionary, though far from exhaustive, will give a good idea of the playful possibilities in French, and when possible, in the English translations.

Even though slang is frequently used, it isn't much taught in school, and you may have stumbled in the dark when coming across it in the written or spoken language. I hope this dictionary will help you to play a better language game—in the light.

PREFACE TO THE SECOND EDITION

This second, expanded edition includes many new entries, notably in the area of **verlan** (backslang) and entries drawn from francophone areas on several continents. Particular attention has been given to French as spoken in Canada, especially Quebec. In France, the *cités des banlieues* (low-rent housing projects in the suburbs) are largely populated by immigrants from the country's former colonies. Young people there are particularly given to creating **verlan.** As mentioned in the preface to the first edition, **verlan** is in full flower. Yet flowers wither, grow seedy, lose their bloom. In the new edition, dated entries have been eliminated in favor of hardier perennials.

Shedding Light on Mud

Robert Chapman, in the preface to his *Dictionary of American Slang,* asserts that slang is involved with a *nostalgie de la boue* (yearning for mud, the primordial). Oscar Wilde's declaration, "We are all in the gutter, but some of us are looking at the stars" is a recognition of the *boue* (mud) within us. Slang is often an attempt to deal with *la boue en nous*, the mud in us. "Shit happens" is a popular vulgarism. When Iraq's now dead dictator Saddam Hussein had problems with revolting Shiites, a nationally syndicated newspaper cartoon taunted a harrassed Saddam with the caption, "Shiit Happens." Slang can be a fanciful, humorous (frequently gallows-humorous), irreverent reaction to "shit" when it happens. This should not be taken as a license to *foutre la merde partout* (spread disorder). Some behavior and some language is appropriate in certain places and situations, not in others.

To acknowledge the primordial, the basic in the world is to make the basic less "base," less "vile." It is a noble human trait to aspire to spirituality, to transcend the down-dragging forces. One way to rise above the law of gravity is with levity, with slang and its playfulness. French expressions like *un cul béni;* and *il ne se prend pas pour une petite merde,* and English ones like "he thinks the sun shines out of his ass" take down a few pegs the pompous, pretentious and Puritanical, those who refuse to recognize the *boue,* the basic, in themselves and in the world.

Men, Women, Social Classes

Apart from many notable exceptions such as Tallulah Bankhead, slang words relating to body functions, sex, and violence have long been associated with tough guys or those trying to be tough guys. Yet, just as slang has become "the unconventional speech of all the classes" (Partridge), males have, for some time, ceased to have a near monopoly on strong language. As Eleanor and Michel Levieux say when discussing *con* and *chier* in their book *Insiders' French* (1999), "Use of this category of language used to lie only within the male province.... Today (they) have become democratized, the casual property of all speakers, men and women alike, and are no longer edited out of interviews in the media."

Public Figures and Slang

The French media, however, haven't become as blasé as one might think. Prominent ecclesiastics, and presidents of countries, Nixon, Putin, and Sarkozy for instance, get much media attention when they use strong language considered inappropriate for the office they hold. Many in the media and the general public were shocked, or professed to be shocked, when French President Nicholas Sarkozy said, *"Casse-toi, pauvre con* (Beat it, dumb jerk!)" to an individual who had refused to shake his hand at an agricultural show in 2008. *Casse-toi* is inelegant, but not vulgar.

Religion and Slang

Some say religion, sex, and politics are taboo in polite, politically correct conversation. Others counter that conversations that exclude those subjects aren't worth having.

The sacred and the profane have long been linked in language, to the displeasure of religionists who enjoin against "taking the name of the Lord in vain." Most languages have "minced oaths," also known as "pseudo-profanities," or "euphemisms." To avoid saying "God," especially in bygone days, speakers of English came up with "gosh," "golly," "gad," and "gadzooks (God's hooks)," whereas the French have circumvented *dieu* with old-fashioned euphemisms such as: *morbleu, pardi, palsambleu, sacrebleu, ventrebleu.* On a less exalted level, "shoot" and "sugar," *miel, mince,* and *miette* are euphemisms for "shit" and *merde,* respectively.

In many languages speakers use religious vocabulary in secular situations. The driving force behind faith is often intensity of feeling. To express strong feeling people use strong language with expressions derived from religion. Speakers create euphemisms to avoid what some perceive as blasphemy.

Religious Slang in France

In France, Christianity and pre-Christian nature religions cohabited relatively peacefully for some centuries until the church took on overwhelming power. Many expressions used in France derive from a long Catholic tradition. Since the Revolution the clergy is no longer the "First Estate" and laws separating Church and State were enacted in 1905. The French, and their attitudes to religion, have, for the most part, mellowed. See GRAND-MESSE. *Spirituel* means both "spiritual" and "witty" and expressions that seem a bit "blasphemous" at first blush are usually greeted with laughter, or a smile. See CRÈCHE 2; SIÈGE and many more. They can be taken as "blasphemous" or witty, depending on one's perspective.

Religion-related continental French slang is often worldly-wise or playfully sexual, whereas religious terms in Quebec slang frequently express exasperation, rage, or outrage in aggressive expletives. Many "pious ejaculations" (a term once widely used in prayer books) have metamorphosed into impious exclamations.

Religious Slang in Québec

As happened centuries earlier in France, the once enormous influence of the Catholic Church has declined dramatically in Quebec. Nevertheless, French, as spoken in Quebec, once part of *la Nouvelle France,* has seen a proliferation of religion-derived profanities. Many of them reflect a preoccupation with ecclesiastical accoutrements, rituals, and doctrines. See the entries *CALICE!*; *CIBOIRE!*; *SACRE 2*. They, and the euphemisms for them, are numerous. The most frequently used ones are: *câlisse, calvaire, ciboire, crisse, (h)ostie, sacrament,* and *tabernac.*

In today's European French the verb *jurer* is used for "to swear" and a *juron* is a "swear word." Francophones in Quebec, however, have recourse to the older terms, *sacrer* and *sacres*, ecclesiastically connected cuss words. When using the *sacres* Quebec francophones often intend blasphemy. They sometimes string them together to create a blasphemous barrage, or they make irreverent additions such as *hostie tostée, hostie au lard/au paprement* or *crisse qui pisse*. To avoid blasphemy the original spelling is changed or played with, thus producing a great many "minced oaths" or euphemisms known as *sacres doux* "mild swear words." The *sacres doux* derive from the *sacres durs* (strong cuss words). *Calvaire!* and *Ciboire!*, for instance, have at least seven variants each, loosely called "euphemisms," even though speakers still make the association with "Calvary" or "ciborium." Many languages, including English, use religion related vocabulary in oaths, exclamations, and interjections. Such vocabulary in slang is a striking phenomenon. Nowhere is it more striking than in Quebec.

Quebec, a Stalwart Defender of French

Most French people respect and admire Quebec, a francophone island surrounded by an Anglophone ocean, for its valiant battle to retain its French linguistic and cultural identity.

Not unsurprisingly, many French Canadians, and "Cajuns" in Louisiana, incorporate great chunks of English vocabulary into their language. Careful speakers of French in Quebec, however, have been active in the battle against *le franglais* and have shown great sensitivity to and respect for the French language by creating excellent new coinages such as, BRILLE-BRILLE, CLAVARDAGE, COURRIEL, and POURRIEL. French Canadians have also retained and extended the meanings of words no longer current in metropolitan French usage. See POGNER. All this means cultural enrichment.

This new edition provides an enlarged geographical perspective on the racier, snappier side of French. Slang broadens perspectives. "Under certain circumstances, profanity provides a relief denied even to prayer," declared Mark Twain. One can speculate as to which is more effective. Although we are not compelled to say either the prayers or the profanities, it is desirable to be familiar with the vocabulary of both. I hope this book will help you to achieve that goal.

BIBLIOGRAPHY

The following books, dictionaries, and web sites may be useful to you for further study.

Alliot, David. *Chier dans le cassetin aux apostrophes: argot des métiers du livre.* Horay, 2004.

Bélanger, Mario. *Petit guide du parler québécois.* Stanké, 2004.

Bergeron, Léandre. *Dictionnaire de la langue québécoise.* Typo, 1998.

Brunet, François and Declan McCavana. *Dictionnaire bilingue de l'argot d'aujourd'hui.* Pocket, 2004.

Burke, David. *Street French Slang Dictionary & Thesaurus.* New York, Wiley, 1997.

Caradec, François *Dictionnaire du français argotique et populaire.* Paris, Larousse, 2006.

Carrière, Jean-Claude. *Les mots et la chose.* Paris, Le Pré aux Clercs, 1991.

Cassagne, Jean-Marie. *Le grand dictionnaire de l'argot militaire.* LBM, 2008.

Colin, Jean-Paul and Jean-Pierre Mével. *Grand dictionnaire de l'argot et français populaire.* Larousse, *2006.*

Cormier, Yves. *Dictionnaire du français acadien.* Montréal, Fides, 1999.

DesRuisseaux, Pierre. *Dictionnaire des expressions québécoises.* Bibliothèque Québécoises, 2003.

Dontchev, Doncho. *Dictionnaire du francais argotique, populaire et familier.* Éditions du Rocher, 2000.

Edis, Genevieve. *The Complete Merde!* Harper Collins, 1996.

Lexik des cités. Fleuve Noir, 2007. (A collective work by young people from Évry, a Paris suburb. They are listed as: Alhassane and Alhousseynou Sarré, Boudia Sylla, Cédric Nagau, Cidy Azor, Dalla Touré, Franck Longepied,

Imane Rajef, Kandé Sylla, Marcela Pérez and Marie Mirline Azor.)

Levieux, Eleanor and Michel Levieux. *Insiders' French.* University of Chicago Press, 1999.

Merle, Pierre. *Mots de passe—Dictionnaire de la prostitution.* Lausanne: Favre, 2005.

———. *Nouveau dictionnaire de la langue verte. Le français argotique et familier du XXIe siècle.* Denoël, 2007.

Munier, Alexis and Emmanuel Tichelli. *Talk Dirty: French.* Adams Media, 2008.

Pickup, Ian and Rod Hares. *Streetwise French Dictionary.* McGraw-Hill Education, 2002.

Plourde, Michel, *Le français au Québec: 400 ans d'histoire et de vie.* Publications du Québec, Fedes, Quebec, 2000.

Thibault, André. *Dictionnaire Suisse Romand.* Éditions Zoë, 2004.

http://www.argodico.com/index.php?option=com_glossary &Itemid=33
http://www.languefrancaise.net/recherche/liste2.php ?PHPSESSID=81894707d0354d
http://argot.abaabaa.com/
http://www.lexilogos.com/argot.htm
http://pagesperso-orange.fr/mondouis/argot.htm

ABBREVIATIONS

abbr. = abbreviation
adj. = adjective
Ar. = Arabic
Bel. = Belgium
Brit. = British
Cf. = compare
cités = cités des banlieus (housing
          projects in the suburbs)
crim. = criminal
euph. = euphemism
Eng. = English
esp. = especially
f. = feminine
Fr. = French
Ger. = German
h.s. = herself/himself
hum. = humorous
invar. = invariable
It. = Italian
lang. = language
lit. = literally
m. = masculine
m.s. = myself
NW = Northwest
orig. = originally
o.s. = oneself
pej. = pejorative
qch. = quelque chose
qn. = quelqu'un
Que. = Quebec
rel. = related

s.o. = someone
s.t. = something
Sp. = Spanish
t.s. = themselves
y.s. = yourself

ABATS, *m., pl.* Male genitalia, "nuts" (lit. "giblets"). *Ils devaient montrer leurs abats au toubib militaire.* "They had to show their nuts to the army doctor."

ABATTAGE, *m.* Cutting down of trees; slaughter of animals. **Avoir de l'abattage.** To have get-up-and-go. *Ce député a beaucoup d'abattage et se fera réélire.* "That deputy's very dynamic and will get himself reelected." **Faire de l'abattage.** To turn tricks constantly. *Mon maq exige que je fasse de l'abattage.* "My pimp insists that I turn lots of tricks."

ABATTIS, *n., pl.* Arms or legs (lit. "poultry giblets"). **Numéroter ses abattis,** lit. "to count one's limbs." *Après l'accident on a numéroté nos abattis.* "After the accident we checked to see that we were still in one piece." *Tu peux numéroter tes abattis!* "I'm going to knock your block off!"

ABEILLE, *f.* Bee. **Avoir les abeilles.** To be fidgety. *Tu bouges sans arrêt; on dirait que tu as les abeilles.* "You keep moving around; you look like you've got ants in your pants." **Mettre les abeilles.** To annoy. *Cesse de me mettre les abeilles!* "Quit bugging me!"

ABONNÉ, -E, *m., f.* Subscriber. **Être aux abonnés absents.** To be dead drunk; be out of it. **Se mettre aux abonnés absents.** To tune out. *Je suis aux abonnés absents toutes les fois qu'il reprend ce sujet.* "I tune out every time he takes up that subject." *Pendant ses conférences la moitié des étudiants se met aux abonnés absents.* "During his lectures, half the students turn off."

ABORDAGE, *m.* Assault. See VOL À L'ABORDAGE.

ABOULER. To hand over. *Aboule tout le fric ou je tire!* "Hand over all the dough (money) or I'll shoot!"

(S')ABOULER. To come (over). *Aboule-toi, vite!* "Come over here, quick!"

ABRICOT, *m.* Female genitalia (lit. "apricot"). *Mon mari est dingue de mon abricot.* "My husband is nuts about my (apri)cunt."

ABUS, *m.* Abuse. **Il y a de l'abus!** That's going too far! *Le supermarché falsifie les dates limites. Il y a de l'abus!* "The supermarket fakes the 'use by' dates. Things are getting out of hand!"

ACCORDÉON, *m.* Extensive criminal record, *police,* (lit. "accordion"). *Avec un tel accordéon tu passeras le restant de ta vie en tôle.* "With a record like yours, you'll spend the rest of your life in the slammer."

ACCOUCHER. To confess (lit. "to give birth"). *Tu as qch.à me dire. Accouche donc!* "You've got something to tell me. Come on, spit it out!"

ACCRO, *m.,* from **accroché** (hooked). **1.** Junkie. *Peu à peu il est devenu accro.* "Little by little, he got hooked." **2.** Ardent fan. *Les accros du jazz viendront nombreux au spectacle.* "Jazz fanatics will turn out in force for the show."

ACCROCHER. 1. To hit it off (lit. "to attach"). *Nous accrochions tout de suite.* "We hit it off right away." **2.** To arrest. *Ce n'est pas la première fois qu'on l'accroche.* "It's not the first time she's been busted."

(S')ACCROCHER. To make a great effort. *Il s'accroche pour réussir dans son métier.* "He's going all out to succeed in his profession." **Tu peux te l'accrocher.** "You can forget it. Give it up."

ACCROCHE-TOI, JEANNOT! *joc.* "Hang in there, buddy! Show your stuff!"

ACCUS, *m., pl.,* from **accumulateurs** (storage batteries). **Recharger les accus. 1.** To recharge one's batteries (by eating, drinking, resting). *On avait grand besoin de recharger les accus.* "We really needed a pick-me-up." **2.** To set 'em up again. *"Patron, rechargez les accus," dit-il, en tapant son verre sur le zinc!* "'Bartender, hit us again,' he said, banging his glass on the bar."

(D')ACHAR, *abbr.* of **acharnement** (tenacity). **Lutter** or **travailler d'achar.** To fight; work assiduously. *Elle travaillait d'achar, pendant que les autres ne foutaient rien.* "She worked like all get-out, while the others didn't do a damned thing."

(D')ACHAR ET D'AUTO(R) (**autor** = **autorité**). Vigorously. *Elle fait tout d'achar et d'auto.* "She does everything intensely and well."

ACHILLE, *m.* **1.** Achilles (name). **2.** Knife, *crim. Il prétend posséder l'achille de Jack l'éventreur.* "He claims he owns Jack the Ripper's knife."

ACRAIS!/ACRÉ! Watch out! Cheese it! *Acré! Planque ta came—les stups sont là.* "Watch out! Hide your stash—the narcs are here."

À CROUME. On credit. *Ils ont tout acheté à croume.* "They bought everything on credit."

ACTER, show biz. To act. *Si tu veux acter dans un des mes films, ma petite, il faut que tu sois arrangeante avec moi.* "If you want to act in one of my pictures, little girl, you'll have to be nice to me."

ACTEUSE, *f.* Lousy actress. *Cette acteuse a des fans et même un fanzine.* "That lousy actress has fans and even a fanzine."

ADJA, *m.* or *f.* To scram [from Romani **dja!**—go!]. **Faire l'adja/mettre les adjas/se tirer des adjas.** *Si l'on ne fait* *pas l'adja, les poulets nous piqueront.* "If we don't disappear fast, the cops'll nab us."

ADJUDANT, *m.* **1.** Warrant officer. **Coucher avec la femme de l'adjudant.** To get sent to the stockade. *Après la bagarre, on les a envoyés coucher avec la femme de l'adjudant.* "After the brawl, they were sent to the guardroom." **2.** Authoritarian person. *Bien/oui, mon adjudant, tout comme mon adjudant voudra.* "OK, boss, just as you want."

ADJUPÈTE, *m., pej.* for **adjudant.**

ADO, *m., f. abbr.* of **adolescent(e).** *Il y a des cours de musique pour ados.* "There are courses in music for adolescents."

À DONF, youth, backslang* for **à fond.** Totally. *Pousse pas ta musique à donf ou tu deviendras sourdingue.* "Don't play your music at full blast or you'll go deaf."

AFANAF, *adv.* Fifty-fifty (from Eng. "half and half"). *Et si on faisait afanaf?* "How about our going Dutch?"

AFFAIRE, *f.* **1.** Affair. **La belle affaire!** Big deal!' *"Je n'ai rien à me mettre!" —"'Ah, la belle affaire!' lui répondit-il."* "'I haven't got a thing to wear.'—'So what!,' he said." **En faire une affaire d'état.** To make a federal case out of something. *Ce rien, il va en faire une affaire d'état.* "He's going to make a big to-do out of that little nothing." See LÂCHER L'AFFAIRE. **2.** Shady operation. *Le gangster a pu faire son affaire en donnant des pots-de-vin à la police.* "The gangster could do his thing after bribing the police." See FAIRE SON AFFAIRE À QN. **3.** Sexually proficient person. *Malgré sa beauté, ce n'est pas une affaire.* "Despite her beauty, she's no good in bed."

AFFAIRES, *f., pl.* Menstrual period. *Son amant aime lui faire l'amour quand elle a ses affaires.* "Her lover likes to make love to her when she has her period."

(S')AFFALER. To confess; inform, *crim.* (lit. "to collapse with fatigue"). *Si tu t'affales auprès des flics, je te casse la gueule!* "If you rat to the cops, I'll break your face."

---

* See explanation of **verlan,** page iv.

AFFICHE, *f.* **1.** Poster. **Être à l'affiche.** To be playing. *Qu'est-ce qui est à l'affiche ce soir à l'Odéon?* "What's on at the Odeon tonight?" **2.** Affected homosexual. **Faire l'affiche.** To camp up a storm. *Faire l'affiche te défoule, mais ce soir, sois discret.* "Camping it up relaxes you, but tonight, be discreet."

AFFICHÉ, -E. Published; displayed. **C'est affiché.** "It's a sure thing."

AFFICHER. To put up posters. **Afficher un sourire.** To put on a (phony) smile. *La tueuse à gages affichait un sourire avant de le tuer.* "The hired killer put on a smile before killing him."

(S')AFFICHER. To flaunt o.s. *En dépit des gens bien-pensants, Anna Karenina s'affichait avec son amant.* "Despite the hostility of the self-righteous, Anna Karenina appeared in public with her lover."

AFFRANCHI, *m.* Shady character. *C'est une bourgeoise qui ne fréquente que les affranchis.* "She's upper middle-class, but hangs out only with lowlifes."

AFFRANCHIR. 1. To put someone wise (lit. "to liberate"). *Je l'ai affranchie sur son jules, mais macache.* "I set her wise about her boyfriend but it was no use." **2.** To initiate sexually. *Casanova voulait l'affranchir, mais elle en savait plus que lui.* "Casanova wanted to initiate her sexually but she knew more than he did."

AFFREUX, *m.* Sinister person. *C'est un affreux, ton frangin!* "Your brother's bad news."

AFFREUX JOJO, *m.* Nasty brat; trouble-making individual. *Elle n'a pas de chance. Son mari et son gamin sont deux affreux jojos.* "She has no luck. Her husband and kid are two impossible creatures."

AFFURER. To make big money. *Ce magouilleur veut fait croire qu'on va affurer gros.* "That slick operator is trying to make us think we're going to make a killing."

AFFÛTER. To fine-tune (lit. "to sharpen"). Affûter la forme. To get into shape. *Il ferait mieux d'affûter sa* *forme que de cultiver sa graisse.* "He should work out instead of feeding his face."

AFFÛTIAUX, *m., pl.* Trinkets. *Elle avait sorti tous ses affûtiaux pour lui plaire.* "She got out all her baubles to please him."

AFNAF = AFANAF.

AGAÇANTE, *f. adj.* Sexually provocative (lit. "annoying"). *Elle se fringue de façon très agaçante.* "She's a very sexy dresser."

AGACE-PISSETTE, *f. Que.* Cockteaser. *Il cherche des vierges, pas les agace-pissettes.* "He's looking for virgins, not cockteasers."

AGACER LE SOUS-PRÉFET. To masturbate (lit. "to harass the sub-prefect"). *Il s'épuise en agaçant trop le sous-préfet.* "He wears h.s. out by flogging the bishop too much."

AGATES, *f., pl.* Peepers. *Je ne pouvais voir que les agates de la fatma.* "All I could see were the Arab woman's eyes."

AGITÉ, -E, *m., f.* Agitated person. **Un(e) agité(e) du bocal,** *idiom.* A loony. *Céline a appelé Sartre un "agité du bocal".* "Celine called Sartre 'a nutcase.'"

AGITER. To shake. **Les agiter.** To clear out. *Agite-les ou je te casse la gueule.* "Beat it or I'll knock your block off."

(S')AGITER. 1. To hurry up. *Si tu t'agites, tu seras à l'heure.* "If you step on it, you'll be on time." **2. Se l'agiter.** To masturbate. *Il se l'agitait longtemps sans pouvoir bander.* "He pulled at it for a long time but couldn't get it up."

AGOBILLES, *f., pl.* **1.** Burglars' tools. *Les poulets l'ont surpris, les agobilles en main.* "The cops caught him, burglars' tools in hand." **2.** Testicles. *Je ne peux m'imaginer ce gus aboulique avec des agobilles!* "That guy's so apathetic it's hard to believe he's got balls!"

AGRAFER. 1. To arrest (lit. "to fasten"). *Le commissaire a juré que le violeur serait agrafé sous peu.* "The commissioner swore the rapist would be arrested shortly." **2.** To hold up. *Le concierge me guette pour m'agrafer avec ses ragots.* "The concierge lies in wait to button-hole me with gossip." **3.** To steal. *Où qu'elle aille, Hedi essaye d'agrafer qch.* "Wherever she goes, Hedi tries to swipe something."

AIDÉ, -E. Pas aidé, -e. Not favored by looks or brains. *Elle n'est pas aidée mais a réussi à épouser un milliardaire.* "She's no beauty, but she managed to marry a billion-aire." *Il n'est pas aidé! Que fera-t-il donc dans la vie?* "He's not bright. What's he going to do in life?"

AIGUILLER. 1. To mark cards (lit. "to point"). *Il a triché en jouant avec des cartes aiguillées.* "He cheated by playing with marked cards." **2.** To have sexually. *Don Juan aiguillait les nanas et son valet les comptait.* "Don Juan laid the ladies and his valet kept score."

AIL, *m.* Garlic. **Bouffer/vendre de l'ail** (lit. "to eat/sell garlic"). To be a lesbian. *J'adore bouffer de l'ail mais parfois un mec comme dessert, ça me plaît.* "I love being a lesbian but once in a while I enjoy a guy for dessert." **Aimer, sentir, taper l'ail** (lit. "to like, reek of garlic"). To be a lesbian. *Ça sent l'ail chez elles, mais c'est leur affaire.* "There's a lesbian atmosphere in their house, but that's their business." See GOUSSE; MARCHANDE D'AIL.

AILE, *f.* Wing. **Avoir du plomb dans l'aile.** To have problems. *Ça fait longtemps qu'il a du plomb dans l'aile!* "He's been in a bad way for some time!" See BATTRE DE L'AILE; BATTRE DES AILES; COUP DANS L'AILE; ROGNER LES AILES.

AILES BRUNES/NOIRES/ROUGES, motorcyclist (Hell's Angels) slang for types of sex in which **ailes** may refer to "testicles." **Avoir ses ailes brunes.** To have anal sex. **Avoir ses ailes noires.** To have sex with a black girl. **Avoir ses ailes rouges.** To have intercourse with a girl during her period. *Avec sa Suédoise le motard a ses ailes tantôt brunes, tantôt rouges, mais avec son Ougandaise, il les a toujours noires.* "The motorcyclist sometimes browns his Swedish girlfriend or has her during her period, but with his Ugandan girlfriend, he always gets poontang."

AIMER. To love. **Va te faire aimer.** Get lost! Piss off! Fuck off!

AINF, *f., youth, cités.* Hunger (backslang of **faim**). *Ali a toujours ainf.* "Ali's always hungry."

AIR, *m.* **1.** Air. **Être en l'air.** To be without funds. *Dès les premiers tours de roulette au casino de Deauville j'étais en l'air.* "After the first few turns of the roulette wheel in the casino at Deauville, I was broke." **L'avoir en l'air.** To have an erection. *Il est à l'âge où il l'a toujours en l'air.* "He's at an age where he's always got it up." See BRASSER DE L'AIR; CHANGER D'AIR; CRACHER EN L'AIR; DÉPLACER DE L'AIR; (S')ENVOYER EN L'AIR; FOUTRE EN L'AIR (FOUTRE 3); (SE) FOUTRE EN L'AIR; JOUER (À) ...L'AIR; (NE PAS) MANQUER D'AIR; PARTIE...AIR; PISSER EN L'AIR; POMPER 1. PRENDRE DE L'AIR. **2.** Appearance. **Avoir l'air.** To look like. *De quoi aurais-je l'air en minijupe au milieu de ces robes longues?* "What will I look like in a miniskirt surrounded by all those evening gowns?" **Avoir l'air fin/con/couillon/cul.** To look like a real jerk/asshole. *Tu auras l'air fin si tu changes d'avis.* "You'll look like a real idiot if you change your mind." **En avoir l'air et la chanson** (a pun on meaning **3**, "tune"). To be what one looks like. *Ce con en a l'air et la chanson.* "That jerk is as dumb as he looks." **3.** Tune. See JOUER...AIR; JOUER...BAVEUSE; JOUER UN AIR...FLÛTE; (DE L')AIR! See DE L'AIR!

AIRBAGS, *m., pl.* **1.** Impressive breasts (lit. "air bags"). *J'aimerais poser ma tête entre ses airbags là!* "I'd like to rest my head between those splendid tits!" **2.** Individual endowed with large breasts. *T'as vu tous les airbags le long du bois de Boulogne?* "Have you seen all those big-busted gals all over the Bois de Boulogne?"

AISE, *f.* Pleasure; ease. **À l'aise/à l'aise, Blaise,** *adv.* Easily; no problem. *"On y va tout de suite?" "À l'aise."* "Can we go right away?" "No problem!"

AL, *youth, cités.* There (backslang of **là**). *Je serai toujours al pour toi.* "I'll always be there for you."

ALCO(O)LO, *m., f., adj.* and *n.* Lush. *Il a le pif d'un alcolo mais ne boit que du thé.* "He's got an alkie's schnozz but he's a teetotaler."

ALICAMENT, *m.* Therapeutic food (from **aliment,** "food" and **medicament,** "medicine"). *Ève, très écolo, prône les alicaments et rejette les OGMs (organismes génétiquement modifiés) et toute nourriture monstrueuse.* "Eve, very ecology-minded, extolls the virtues of therapeutic food and rejects GMOs (genetically modified organisms) and all Frankenfood."

ALIGNER. Les aligner. To pay up (lit. "to align them" [bank notes]). *Emma Bovary, ne pouvant pas les aligner, s'est suicidée.* "Emma Bovary couldn't come up with the money and committed suicide."

(S')ALIGNER. 1. To take on s.t. difficult. *Lors de la grève des dames-pipi il a dû s'aligner le nettoyage des chiottes du musée.* "During the toilet attendants' strike he had to clean the museum's toilets." **2. Pouvoir (toujours) s'aligner.** To have little chance. *Tu peux toujours t'aligner —ils n'en prendront que treize sur mille.* "You can forget it—they'll only accept 13 out of 1,000."

ALLÈCHE, *f., youth.* Poster (from **allécher,** "to tempt"). *Vise un peu l'allèche pour le concert rock.* "Take a look at that ad for the rock concert."

ALLER À LA CACASSE/AU CUL/RADADA. See CACASSE; CUL **3**; RADADA.

ALLER-RETOUR/ALLER ET RETOUR, *m.* A double slap in the face (lit. "round trip"). *Cesse d'aguicher les mecs, sinon tu auras un aller-retour.* "Stop coming on to guys or I'll box your ears."

ALLONGER. 1. To align. **Les allonger.** To fork over money. *Allonge-les ou tu auras affaire à mes potes!* "Pay up or you'll have to deal with my pals." **2. Allonger qqn.** To knock s.o. down. *L'auteur menaçait d'allonger*

le critique. "The author threatened to flatten the critic."
3. To bump off. *Le gangster voulait allonger tous ses rivaux.* "The gangster wanted to rub out all his rivals."

**ALLONGER UN COUP/UNE BEIGNE/CLAQUE/
TALOCHE/TARTE À QN.** To give s.o. a wallop. *Si tu continues à crier, je t'allonge une taloche.* "If you keep on shouting, I'll give you a good whack."

ALLONGÉS, *pl.* The dead (lit. "stretched out"). **Être aux allongés.** To be among the dead. *Le pauvre, il souffrait tellement qu'il est mieux aux allongés.* "The poor guy, he suffered so much, he's better off dead." **Boulevard/ jardin des allongés,** see JARDIN.

(S')ALLONGER. To own up. *Après trois heures d'interrogatoire il s'est enfin allongé.* "After three hours of questioning he finally spilled the beans."

(SE L')ALLONGER. To masturbate. *Portnoy ne pensait qu'à se l'allonger.* "All Portnoy thought about was jerking off."

ALOUETTE, *f.* Female traffic cop (lit. "swallow"). *Fais gaffe, dans une heure l'alouette te posera un papillon!* "Watch out, in an hour the meter maid'll give you a ticket."

AL(L)OUF, *f.* Match. *La gosse jouait avec la boîte d'alloufs.* "The little girl played with the matchbox."

ALLUMÉ, -E. Lit up (lit. and figuratively). *Ils étaient tous allumés lors du viol collectif.* "They were all high at the time of the gang rape."

ALLUMÉ, E, *m., f.* Drunkard. *C'est un allumé: il n'a plus son permis (de conduire).* "He's a drunk and no longer has a driver's license."

ALLUMER. 1. To excite sexually. *Avec sa jupe ras le pétard, elle allume tous les gus.* "In her miniskirt up to her ass, she turns on all the guys." **2.** To gun down. *Les mercenaires les avait tous allumé dans le village.* "The mercenaries gunned down everyone in the village." **3.** To reprimand. *Maman va t'allumer.* "Ma's going to give you a bawling out."

ALLUMER LES BOUGIES. To elucidate (lit. "to light the candles"). *Trêve de mystification; allumons les bougies!* "That's enough of a mystery. Let's have some light on the matter."

ALLUMEUR, *m.* Con man's sidekick. *Il ne voulait plus faire l'allumeur et pensait faire de l'arnaque seul.* "He didn't want to be the decoy anymore and planned some scams of his own."

ALLUMEUSE, *f.* **1.** Bar girl. *Il n'avait bu qu'un verre avec l'allumeuse et a été sidéré en voyant la note.* "He only had one drink with the B-girl and was floored by the bill." **2.** Hooker; cockteaser. *Longtemps allumeuse, elle cherche maintenant l'illumination dans l'Himalaya.* "A longtime hooker, she's now looking for illumination in the Himalayas."

ALPAGUER. 1. To buttonhole (lit. "grabbing s.o. by the collar of the alpaga (alpaca) coat"). *Je ne me laisse plus alpaguer par ce chronophage.* "I don't allow that time waster to buttonhole me anymore." **2.** To arrest. *Il s'est fait alpaguer par la flicaille.* "He got nabbed by the cops."

ALSACO, *m., pej.* Alsatian. *Ce titi parisien a pour parents des Alsacos.* "That Parisian kid's parents are Alsatians."

AMATEUR DE ROSETTE. See ROSETTE 2.

AMAZONE, *f., joc.* **1.** Horsewoman (orig. the legendary one-breasted female warrior). **Monter en amazone.** To ride sidesaddle. *Quand elle monte en amazone elle est très élégante.* "When she rides sidesaddle she looks very elegant." **2.** Prostitute who works out of her car. *Beaucoup d'amazones peuvent se payer des voitures de luxe.* "Many car-based prostitutes can afford luxury autos."

AMBIDEXTRE, *m.* Male bisexual (lit. "ambidextrous"). See BIMÉTALLISTE; VOILE.

AMERLAUD/AMERLO(T)/AMERLOCHE/AMER-LOQUE/AMERLUCHE, *m.* American. *Elle a épousé un Amerloque.* "She married an American."

AMI-AMI. See FAIRE AMI-AMI.

AMINCHE, *m.* Friend. *Tu me le présentes, ton aminche?* "Are you going to introduce me to your pal?"

AMOCHER. To bash (from **moche** ["ugly"; "rotten"]). *Lors de l'accident sa voiture et lui furent bien amochés.* "He and his car were badly banged up the accident."

AMORTI. Over the hill (lit. "depreciated"). *Pour les jeunes, on est amorti après trente ans.* "For the young, you're over the hill once you're thirty."

AMORTISSEURS, *m., pl.* Breasts (lit. "shock absorbers"). *Tâte-les, mes amortisseurs, c'est pas du faux.* "Feel my knockers and you'll see they're not fake."

AMOUR, *m.* **1.** Love. See BALAI D'AMOUR; FILER...AMOUR; GUEULE D'AMOUR; MARCHANDE D'AMOUR; PANIER D'AMOUR; PAPILLON D'AMOUR. **2.** Charmer; darling. *Sois un amour et passe-moi la confiture.* "Be a dear and pass me the jelly."

(À L')AMOUREUSE. Lit. "lovingly." Said of a prostitute who gives extras, without charging extra. *Les michés préfèrent Julie qui travaille à l'amoureuse.* "The johns prefer Julie who labors for love."

AMYGDALES, *f., pl.* Tonsils. **Se faire lécher les amygdales.** To get tongue kissed. *Lèche-moi les amygdales, mais ne me mords pas la langue!* "Give me a French kiss, but don't bite my tongue!" See (SE) CALER LES AMYGDALES. *Cf.* ROULER UN PALOT....

ANANAS, *m.* **1.** Hand grenade (lit. "pineapple"). *Ce groupuscule d'anars avait stocké des centaines d'ananas.* "That tiny group of anarchists had stockpiled hundreds of hand grenades." **2.** Breast. *J'aimais ses ananas fermes et tendres.* "I loved her firm and tender breasts."

ANAR/ANARCHO, *m.* or *f.,* from **anarchiste.** Anarchist. *Le fils aîné du président se veut anar.* "The president's eldest son claims to be an anarchist."

ANDEK! Watch out! (from Ar.). *"Andek!", cria le jeune beur en voyant les flics.* "Watch out," cried the young (Fr.-born) North African when he spotted the cops."

ANDOUILLE, *f.* Nerd (lit. "chitterling sausage"). *Espèce d'andouile! Tu t'es fait avoir.* "You dummy! You were had." **Faire l'andouille.** To act like a fool; horse around. *Ne fais pas l'andouille!* Quit acting like a jerk! See DÉPENDEUR.

ANDOUILLE DE CAL(E)CIF/À COL ROULÉ, *f.* Penis (lit. "sausage in the shorts; turtleneck sausage"). *Les gars ont comparé leurs andouilles de calecif.* "The young boys compared their sausages (peckers)."

ANGE, *m.* Angel. **Un ange passe, passa, a passé,** *idiom* (said when there is a lull in the conversation). *La discussion était animée; soudain un ange a passé.* "The discussion was spirited; suddenly there was an awkward silence." **Être aux anges.** To be in ecstasy. *Elle était aux anges d'avoir gagné.* "She was in seventh heaven when she won." See FAISEUR D'ANGES; VOIR LES ANGES.

ANGE GARDIEN, *m.* Pickpocket's lookout (lit. "guardian angel"). *Le tireur et son ange gardien entraient dans le métro à l'heure d'affluence.* "The pickpocket and his lookout went into the subway during rush hour."

ANGÉLINA, *f.* Passive homosexual. *C'est un bar frequenté par les angélinas.* "Passive gays hang out in that bar."

ANGLAIS, *m., pl.* Englishmen. **Avoir ses Anglais.** To have one's menstrual period (Eng. soldiers were known as "redcoats.") **Les Anglais ont débarqué; sont arrivés.** To begin to menstruate (lit. "the English have landed.") *Je me croyais enceinte, mais les Anglais ont enfin débarqué.* "I thought I was pregnant, but my period finally started."

ANGLAISER. To sodomize. *La marine anglaise était au port et les angélinas cherchaient à se faire anglaiser.* "The English fleet was in and the passive fags wanted to get fucked."

ANGLICHE/ANGLUCHE, *m., f., adj.* and *n.,* often *pej.* English/Brit./limey. *J'aime me baguenauder sur le Bvd. des Angliches à Nice.* "I like to stroll along the Boulevard des Anglais in Nice."

ANGOISSER. To harrass sexually (lit. "to distress"). *Max m'a angoissée mais je l'ai envoyé balader.* "Max came on strong to me but I told him to get lost."

ANGORA, *m.* Female genitalia (from the association with the Angora cat). *Mon mari adore mon angora.* "My husband loves my pussy." *Cf.* CHATTE; CHAGATTE; MINET 1; MINETTE 2; MINOU.

ANGUILLE DE CALEÇON/CAL(E)CIF. Penis (lit. "eel in the shorts"). *Son immense anguille de calecif n'était qu'un gode!* "His immense dick was just a dildo."

ANNEAU, *m.* **1.** Anus ring (lit. "ring"). *Pépé a de sacrées émeraudes à l'anneau.* "Grandpa has enormous hemorrhoids." **2.** Buttocks. *Il m'a donné un coup de pied dans l'anneau pour m'être moqué de lui.* "He gave me a kick in the butt for having made fun of him." See DÉFONCER… ANNEAU.

ANTIFLE, *f.* Church. *Malgré leurs familles, ils ont refusé de se marier à l'antifle.* "Despite their families, they refused to get married in church."

S'ANTIFLER. To get married. *Ni croyants ni pratiquants, ils se sont quand même antiflés à l'église.* "They neither believe nor practice their religion, but they got hitched in church anyway."

ANTIGEL, *m.* Hard liquor (lit. "antifreeze"). *Et si on prenait un petit coup d'antigel?* "How about our having a little snort?"

ANTIGRIPPE, *m.* Alcoholic drink; after-dinner drink. *Il a toujours sur lui sa petite bouteille d'antigrippe.* "He always has his little bottle of booze to keep out the cold."

ANTISÈCHE, *f.* Trot; pony. *Des étudiants essayaient de se servir de leurs antisèches à l'exam.* "Some students tried to use their ponies during the exam."

APÉRO, *m.* Aperitif. *C'est l'heure de l'apéro! Si on le prenait chez moi?* "It's aperitif time (happy hour). How about having it at my place?"

APPART(E), *m.* Apartment. *Son appart est dément!* "Her apartment is fantastic!"

APPE = APPART.

APPELER. To call. **Se faire appeler Arthur/Joseph/Jules.** See ARTHUR.

APPONDRE, *Swiss.* To add. **S'appondre à la tâche.** To set to work in earnest. *Plus vite tu t'appondra à la tâche plus vite tu seras libéré.* "The sooner you give yourself over to the job the sooner you'll be free."

APPUYER SUR LE CHAMPIGNON. See CHAMPIGNON.

(S')APPUYER. 1. To put up with (lit. "to lean on"). *J'aime tchatcher avec elle, même si je dois m'appuyer ses gamins.* "I enjoy gabbing with her even if I have to put up with her kids." **2.** To get stuck with s.t. *Pourquoi c'est toujours moi qui m'appuie la plonge?* "Why am I the one who always gets stuck with the dishes?"

APRÈM, *m., abbr.* for **après-midi.** Afternoon. *C't'aprèm j'suis libre.* "I'm free this P.M."

À PLUSS!/À PLUTE!, *abbr.* for **à plus tard!** *À pluss, mon pote!* "See you later, my friend."

AQUARIUM, *m.* **1.** Glass-enclosed office. *Si j'étais exhibitionniste, j'aimerais travailler dans cet aquarium.* "If I were an exhibitionist, I'd like working in this fishbowl." **2.** House or place of ill repute. *Ce n'est pas un aquarium ici; partez faire votre boulot ailleurs.* "This is no sleazy dive; go elsewhere to ply your trade." **Note:** In addition to the idea of "open display," many terms for "pimp" are types of fish, such as **maquereau, merlan, poisson,** and so on. *Cf.* FENÊTRIÈRE.

ARABI, *m., pej.* Arab. *Ton oncle ne semble pas aimer les Arabis.* "Your uncle doesn't seem to like Arabs."

ARAIGNÉE, *f.* **Avoir une araignée au plafond.** To have bats in the belfry (lit. "to have a spider in the ceiling"). *Parfois je crois que tu as une araignée au plafond.* "Sometimes I think you've got bats in the belfry." See FAIRE...ARAIGNÉE.

ARBALÈTE, *f.* Penis (lit. "crossbow"). **Filer un coup d'arbalète.** To screw. *Elle aimait les préliminaires, mais il ne voulait que lui filer un coup d'arbalète.* "She liked foreplay, but all he wanted to do was stick it into her."

ARBI/ARBICOT = ARABI.

ARBRE, *m.* Tree. See GRIMPER À L'ARBRE; GRIMPER AUX ARBRES.

ARCAGNASSES/ARCAGNATS, *m., pl.* Menstrual period. *La gosse était paniquée par ses premiers arcagnasses.* "The kid was frightened by her first period."

ARCAN/ARCANDIER, *m.* Hoodlum. *Ce quartier grouille d'arcans.* "That neighborhood is full of thugs."

ARCHE, *f.* Buttocks (lit. "ark"; "strong box"; poss. influence of Eng. "arse" or Ger. **Arsch**). **Fendre l'arche,** *idiom.* To be a pain in the ass. *Tu me fends l'arche.* "You're a real pain in the ass."

ARCHER/ARCHER DU ROI, *m.* Policeman (lit. "[king's] archer"). *Monsieur le commissaire, est-ce-que vos archers sauraient me protéger si j'accepte cette mission?* "Commissioner, will your men be able to protect me if I accept this mission?"

ARCHI-, *pref.* Extremely. **Archichiant.** Deadly dull. *Le film était archichiant.* "The movie was mind-numbing." **Archicon.** Unbelievably stupid. *Si tu crois ça, tu es archicon.* "If you believe that, you're a real idiot." **Archifaux.** Totally wrong. *Votre réponse est archifausse.* "Your answer is totally wrong." **Archifou.** Stark raving mad. *Tous les archifous ne sont pas à l'asile.* "Not all the crazies are in the asylum."

ARDILLON, *m.* Penis (lit. "prong"; "barb"). *Mon mari avait l'ardillon bien plus ardent avant!* "My husband's dick used to be much more passionate!"

-ARD. Frequently used suffix added to adjectives and nouns, usually pej., disparaging. See CORNARD; QUEUTARD; SALOPARD; TROUILLARD.

ARDOISE, *f.* **1.** Slate. See MOUILLER UNE ARDOISE; PRENDRE UNE ARDOISE À L'EAU. **2.** Debt (originally recorded on a blackboard). *Ce poivrot a des ardoises chez tous les cafetiers du coin.* "That drunk has run up a bill with all the local café owners." **3.** Toilet; "tearoom" (homosexual). *Tous les jours il drague dans les ardoises du parc.* "Every day he cruises the T rooms in the park."

-ARÈS/ARESSE. Slang suffixes that create invariable adjectives with only one form for the *m.*, *f.*, and *pl.* See BOUCLARÈS; DÉFONCARÈS; EMBALLARÈS; PLANQUARÈS.

ARÊTES, *f., pl.* Back; ribs (lit. "fishbones"). *Elle n'a rien à se mettre sur les arêtes.* "She's got nothing to wear (put on her back)."

ARGAGNASSES = ARCAGNASSES.

ARGOMUCHE, *m.* Street talk (from **argot** [slang] and suffix **-muche**). **Jacter/jaspiner l'argomuche.** To talk slang. *Dans la zone, on ne jacte que l'argomuche.* "In the slums, all we talk is slang."

ARGOUGNER = ARPIGNER.

ARIA, *m.* Operatic aria. **Faire des arias.** To make a song and dance. *C'est dans son caractère de toujours faire des arias.* "It's his nature to always make a fuss."

ARISTO, *m., f., abbr.* of **aristocrate.** *Ce resto est un nid d'aristos.* "Aristocrats hang out in that restaurant."

ARLEQUINS, *m., pl.* Leftovers; bits of this and that (from Harlequin's motley costume). *Elle sait faire un gueuleton avec des arlequins.* "She knows how to make a feast out of leftovers."

ARLO, *m.* Cheap knickknack. *Tu dis que ce n'était que de l'arlo, mais ma licorne en verre avait une grande valeur sentimentale pour moi.* "You say it was worthless, but my glass unicorn had great sentimental value to me."

ARMÉNOUCHE, *m.* Armenian. *Il y a beaucoup d'arménouches dans notre quartier.* "There are lots of Armenians in our neighborhood."

ARMOIRE, *f.* Closet. **Armoire à glace.** Strapping hulk (lit. "clothes closet with a large mirror"). *Les gardes du*

17

corps sont souvent des armoires à glace. "Bodyguards are often big bruisers."

ARNAQUE, *f.* Swindle. *Tu as vu les prix? C'est de l'arnaque!* "Have you seen the prices? It's highway robbery!"

ARNAQUER 1. To arrest. *Le dealer s'est fait arnaquer par les douaniers et leurs chiens.* "The drug dealer was nabbed by the customs officials and their dogs." **2.** To swindle. *Si tu veux te faire arnaquer, va manger dans ce nouveau restaurant.* "If you want to get ripped off, go eat in that new restaurant."

ARNAQUEUR/ARNAQUEUSE, *m., f.* Swindler. *Dans le film* L'arnaque, *Newman et Redford jouaient les maîtres arnaqueurs.* "In the movie *The Sting,* Newman and Redford played master con artists."

ARPENTER (L'ASPHALTE/LE BITUME). To be a streetwalker (lit. "to walk to and fro (on the pavement)"). *J'ai commencé à arpenter très jeune.* "I started soliciting when I was very young."

ARPENTEUSE, *f.* Prostitute. *Ce prof, un de mes meilleurs michés, me dit qu'il fait des recherches sur les arpenteuses.* "That professor, one of my best customers, tells me he's doing research on working girls."

ARPÈTE/ARPETTE, *m., f.,* often *pej.* Apprentice (from Ger. **Arbeiter** [worker]). *L'arpète du sorcier avait bousillé le boulot.* "The sorcerer's apprentice botched the job."

ARPIGNER. To grab. *Ce petit voyou a arpigné mon sac (à main).* "That little hood grabbed my purse."

ARPINCHE, *m.* Miser. *Tu n'auras pas un sou de cet arpinche.* "That miser won't give you a cent."

ARPION, *m.* **1.** Foot. *Il m'a foutu un coup d'arpion.* "He gave me a kick in the pants." See TAPER DES ARPIONS. **2.** Toe. *Le danseur s'est cassé le gros arpion.* "The dancer broke his big toe."

ARQUER. To walk (lit. "to bend a bow"). *J'ai tant couru que je ne peux plus arquer.* "I ran so much, I can't take another step."

ARRACHÉ, *m.* Snatching. See VOL À L'ARRACHÉ.

ARRACHER. 1. To rip out or off; grab. **Ça arrache!** "That really grabs you." *Ce calva, ça arrache.* "This apple-jack brandy is strong stuff. It really gets to you!" **2. En arracher.** To work hard. *Il en a arraché aujourd'hui!* "He worked hard today!"

ARRACHER SON COPEAU. To have an orgasm (lit. "to tear off a (wood) shaving"). *Le marin rêvait d'arracher son copeau avec une fille du port.* "The sailor dreamed of getting it off with a girl in port."

(S')ARRACHER. To run away; escape. *Je ne pensais qu'à m'arracher de chez mes parents.* "All I could think of was getting away from my parents."

ARRANGER. To beat up (lit. "to arrange"). *Après cette bagarre stupide, te voilà drôlement arrangé.* "Just look at you, all beat up after that stupid fight."

ARRÊTER. To stop; arrest. **Arrête tes salades!** "Cut the crap! Stop giving me a hard time!" See FRAIS.

ARRIÈRE-TRAIN, *m.* Buttocks (lit. "animal's hindquarters." *Tu as vu l'arrière-train qu'elle se paye?* "Have you seen the ass on her?"

(S')ARRIMER. To shack up together (lit. "to link up"). *Mimi aimerait avoir un gosse, mais ne veut s'arrimer à aucun bonhomme.* "Mimi would like to have a child, but she doesn't want a committed relationship with any male."

ARROSER. 1. To celebrate with a drink (lit. "to water"). See ÇA S'ARROSE; COURAGE ARROSÉ. **2.** To bribe. *Il fallait bien l'arroser pour avoir le contrat.* "His palm had to be well greased to get the contract."

ARSOUILLE, *m.* (Either from **souillon** ["slut"; "slob"] or from Eng. "arsehole.") **1.** Crook. *Cet arsouille a triché aux cartes.* "That crook cheated at cards." **2.** Tough. *Je l'ai connu arsouille, mais sa fiancée l'a civilisé et adouci.* "When I knew him he was a hooligan, but his fiancée has civilized and softened him."

(S')ARSOUILLER. 1. To get soused. *Il aimait chaque week-end s'arsouiller avec les copains.* "Every weekend he liked to booze it up with the boys." **2.** To live a life of debauchery. *Après le monastère il s'est arsouillé.* "After the monastery, he lived riotously."

ARTHUR. Se faire appeler Arthur. To get reprimanded. *Si tu sèches encore le cours, tu te feras appeler Arthur.* "If you keep cutting the course, you'll get called on the carpet."

ARTILLER. 1. To make fat profits. *Les initiés artillaient gros.* "The insiders made fat profits." **2.** To plug/bang sexually. *Les marins ne pensaient qu'à artiller les filles du port.* "All the sailors had on their mind was screwing the girls in the port."

ARTILLERIE, *f.* **1.** Loaded dice (lit. "artillery"). *Ce joueur porte toujours son artillerie sur lui.* "That gambler's always got his loaded dice on him." **2.** Plentiful, simple food. *J'aime la nouvelle cuisine; chez mes parents ce n'est que de l'artillerie.* "I like nouvelle cuisine; at my parents' it's just meat and potatoes." **3.** Male genitalia. *Cet exhibitionniste aime sortir son artillerie dans le métro.* "That flasher likes to take out his equipment in the subway."

ARTISTE, *m., f.* Counterfeiter. *Il est artiste de premier ordre et ses derniers billets étaient un travail d'artiste.* "He's a first-class counterfeiter and his most recent bank notes were a work of art." See TRAVAILLER EN ARTISTE.

AS *m.* Ace (cards; aviation). See AS DU VOLANT. **Être plein aux as.** To be loaded; filthy rich. *Son nouveau mari est plein aux as.* "Her new husband is filthy rich." **Passer à l'as.** To go down the drain. *Tous leurs projets sont passés à l'as.* "All their projects went down the drain." **Passer qch. chose à l'as.** Not to count something deliberately. *Le gangster a donné des pots-de-vin au juge qui a passé des preuves importantes à l'as.* "The gangster bribed the judge who suppressed important evidence."

AS DE PIQUE, *m.* **1.** Pope's/parson's nose (lit. "ace of spades"). *"Les derniers seront les premiers," disait-elle en* *mangeant l'as de pique.* "'The last shall be first', she said, eating the part that went over the fence last." **2.** Human posterior. **Être ficelé/fichu/foutu/fagoté comme l'as de pique.** To be dressed in an asinine manner. *Le modèle Line est souvent fagoté comme l'as de pique.* "The (artists') model, Line, often dresses grotesquely." **3.** Female genitalia. *Quand Line est à poil, les peintres admirent la splendeur de son as de pique.* "When Line is completely nude, the painters admire her big black bush."

AS DE TRÈFLE = **TRÈFLE.**

AS DU VOLANT, *m.* Top driver. *Il se prend pour un as du volant.* "He thinks he's a wonderful driver."

ASCENSEUR. Elevator. **Renvoyer l'ascenseur** (lit. "to send back the elevator"). **1.** To return a favor. *J'ai été déçue qu'il ne me renvoie pas l'ascenseur.* "I was disappointed at his not returning the favor." **2.** To get back to right away. *Je suis à la bourre et ne peux te renvoyer l'ascenseur.* "I'm in a hurry and can't get back to you now."

ASMEUK, *youth, cités.* Like that/this (backslang of **comme ça**). *Fais-le asmeuk.* "Do it like this." *Cf.* COMMACE.

ASPERGE, *f.* **1.** Tall, thin person (lit. "asparagus"). *Pour avoir de grands enfants, le petit roi d'Italie a choisi une asperge pour reine.* "To have tall children, the tiny king of Italy chose an asparagus as queen." **2.** Penis. **Aller/être aux asperges.** To engage in prostitution. *Je vais parfois aux asperges pour mettre du beurre dans les épinards.* "I do a little hooking occasionally to improve our financial situation." **Cultiver des asperges.** To work as a prostitute. *"Au lieu de cultiver ta flemme, va cultiver des asperges."* "Instead of loafing around, get to work (hooking)."

ASPHALTE, *m.* Pavement. **Arpenter/faire/polir/l'asphalte.** To be a hooker. *Avant le clandé j'ai longtemps poli l'asphalte.* "Before the whorehouse, I walked the streets for some time."

ASPINE, *m.* or *f.* Money. *Cet arpinche ne vit que pour son aspine.* "That miser lives only for his money."

ASSAISONNER. 1. To bash (lit. "to season"). *Ses copains de classe l'ont assaisonné.* "His classmates beat him up." **2.** To kill. *Aboule le fric ou je t'assaisonne.* "Hand over the dough or I'll rub you out."

ASSE. That (backslang of **ça**). *Pourquoi asse?* "Why that?"

-ASSE. *Pej. sl. suffix. Rika se dit comtesse—comtesse de mes fesses! Elle n'est qu'une comtasse.* "Rika calls herself a countess—countess, my ass! She's a bogus countess." See BLONDASSE; CONASSE; GROGNASSE; PUTASSE; POUFIASSE; VINASSE.

ASSEOIR. To flabbergast (lit. "to seat"; "establish"). *Sa stupidité nous assied.* "His stupidity flabbergasts us." **En rester assis.** To be dumbfounded. *Il a eu le premier prix; on en est resté assis.* "He got the first prize; we were knocked for a loop."

(S')ASSEOIR. To sit down. **S'asseoir dessus/sur qch.** To not give a damn about. *Ton choix c'est de la merde; je m'assieds dessus.* "Your choice is rotten; I don't care for it at all."

ASSIETTE AU BEURRE, *f.* Sinecure. *Il chôme car il ne cherche que l'assiette au beurre.* "He's unemployed because all he wants is a cushy job." **Avoir l'assiette au beurre.** To be rich and powerful; ride the gravy train. *Il rêve d'avoir l'assiette au beurre.* "He's dreaming of being on easy street."

ASSURER. 1. To know one's stuff (lit. "to assure"). *Il assure en tout, sauf en sciences.* "He's up on everything, except science." **2.** To look snazzy. *Elle a acheté une robe pour assurer dans son nouveau job.* "She bought a dress to look smart at her new job." **3.** To have well under control. *Dors tranquille, moi j'assure.* "Rest easy, I have the situation well in hand."

ASTAP(E). 1. Really funny (from **à se taper le cul par terre** ["to split one's sides laughing," lit. "to knock one's ass on the ground"]). *Elle raconte toujours des histoires astapes.* "The stories she tells are real thigh-whackers."

2. Till this afternoon! (Contraction of **à c't'aprème,** from a contraction of **à cet après-midi.**)

ASTICOT, *m.* **1.** Maggot. See ENGRAISSER LES ASTICOTS. **2.** Wimp. *On le traitait d'asticot, mais il nous a tous surpris.* "We called him a worm but he surprised us all."

ASTICOTER. To needle. *On dirait que tu te fais un vrai plaisir de m'asticoter.* "It seems you get a real kick out of bugging me."

(S')ASTICOTER. To bicker. *Ils ne s'arrêtent pas de s'asticoter.* "They never stop squabbling."

ASTIQUER. To polish. **Bien astiqué.** Spruced up. *Depuis son service militaire il est toujours bien astiqué.* "He's always well groomed since his stint in the military."

ASTIQUER LA BAGUETTE/COLONNE/GAULE. To jerk off. *On n'a pas de préso, mais au moins astique-moi la colonne.* "We haven't got a rubber, but give me a hand job at least."

ASTIQUER LE BOUTON. To stimulate the clitoris. *C'était le pied quand Luc, au resto, m'astiquait le bouton avec son gros orteil!* "It was mind-blowing when Luc's big toe tickled my clit in the restaurant!"

ATCHOUM! 1. Atchoo! (sneeze) *Hatchoum et tous les sept nains sont sympa.* "Sneezy and all 7 dwarves are appealing." **2.** Premature ejaculation. *Ce soir tu me fais pas d'atchoum!* "Don't come too fast on me tonight!"

ATOUT, *m.* Clout (lit. "trump"). *Il avait reçu tant d'atouts qu'on ne le reconnaissait plus.* "He was so bashed up that he was unrecognizable."

ATTIGER. 1. To beat up. *Les flics niaient l'avoir attigé.* "The cops denied having worked him over." **2.** To infect with VD. *Malgré le préso il s'est fait attigé.* "Despite the condom, he got VD."

ATTIGER/ATTIGER LA CABANE. To exaggerate. *Quand elle raconte ses histoires elle attige toujours la cabane.* "When she tells her stories, she really lays it on thick."

23

ATTRAPE-COUILLON *m.* Stronger version of **ATTRAPE-NIGAUD.**

ATTRAPE-NIGAUD. Sucker bait. *Que de l'emballage pompier, trompeur—du vrai attrape-nigaud.* "Nothing but flashy, deceptive packaging—real idiot bait."

ATTRIBUTS, *m., pl.* **1.** Attributes. **2. Attributs (virils).** Male genitalia. *Ce défroqué est écartelé entre les attributs divins, les virils, et les appas féminins.* "That defrocked priest is torn between the divine attributes (omniscience, ubiquity, and so on), male private parts, and feminine charms."

AUBERGE, *f.* Inn. **Ne pas être sorti de l'auberge.** Not to be out of the woods yet. *On a gagné le premier procès, mais on n'est pas encore sorti de l'auberge.* "We won the first trial, but we're not out of the woods yet."

AU BLACK/NOIR/SCHWARZ. Nondeclared (for tax purposes); under the table (Fr. **noir,** Ger. **schwarz** = "black"). *Il veut toujours être payé au black.* "He always wants to be paid under the table."

AUCHE, *youth, cités.* Hot; difficult; dangerous. (backslang of **chaud**). *Asse (ça) se fait auche ici.* "It's getting hot here."

AUGE, *f.* Plate (lit. "trough"). *Mon auge est vide.* "My plate is empty."

AUSSI SEC. Quick as a flash [from **aussitôt** ("right away")]. *Aussi sec elle lui a retourné une gifle.* "She immediately slapped him back."

AUTEL, *m.* Baker's oven (lit. "altar"). *Le boulanger basané ressemble à un ange blanc quand il prépare ses pains pour l'autel.* "The dark-skinned baker looks like a white angel when he prepares his loaves for the oven."

AUTOBUS, *m.* Occasional prostitute. *Personne ne pouvait soupçonner qu'elle jouait à l'autobus.* "No one could have guessed that she hustled occasionally."

(D')AUTOR, *abbr.* of **autorité.** With determination. *Si tu t'y mets d'autor, tu finiras le projet bien avant la date lim-*

ite. "If you really apply yourself, you'll finish the project before the deadline." See also (D')ACHAR ET D'AUTOR.

AUXI/AUXIGOT, *m.* Prison trustee (from **auxiliaire**). *Les auxigots jouissaient de privilèges.* "The trustees enjoyed privileges."

AVALER LA PILULE. To grin and bear it (lit. "to swallow the pill"). *Rien à faire, il faut avaler la pilule.* "No way around it, we'll have to bite the bullet."

AVALER SON ACTE DE NAISSANCE. To die (lit. "to swallow one's birth certificate"). *Tu parles comme si demain tu allais avaler ton acte de naissance.* "You talk as if you were going to cash in your chips tomorrow."

AVANTAGE, *m.* Advantage. **Faire un avantage à qn.** To be nice to s.o. *On m'a fait un avantage sur cette robe qui avait fait la vitrine.* "They gave me a discount on this dress that was in the window."

AVANTAGES, *m., pl.* Breasts. *Pour séduire, elle mettait ses avantages en valeur.* "To be seductive she showed lots of cleavage."

AVANT-POSTES, *m., pl.* Breasts (lit. "outposts"). *Elle se tenait très droite pour faire pointer ses avant-postes.* "She carried herself very erect so that her tits would stick out."

AVANT-SCÈNE, *f.* Breasts (lit. "proscenium"). *Avec une telle avant-scène elle ne peut faire que des ravages.* "With knockers like that, she can't help but break some hearts."

AVARO, *m.* Sad/bad happening (from **avarie,** "damage to goods in transit"). *Dans sa vie il n'avait que des avaros.* "His life has been a succession of kicks in the ass."

AVATAR, *m.* **1.** Mishap (orig. "manifestation of the God Vishnu [Hinduism]"). *Je vous souhaite un voyage avec moins d'avatars cette fois-ci. Que Vichnou, dans un de ses avatars nombreux, vous protège.* "I wish you a less problematic trip this time. May Vishnu, in one of his numerous manifestations, protect you." **2.** Virtual identity in cyberspace. *La vie de mon avatar est bien plus* *passionante que la mienne.* "My avatar's life is much more enthralling than mine."

-AV(E). Suffix or element found in many Romany (Gypsy) words. See: BICRAVE; BOUILLAVE; CHOURAVE; MARAVE; NATCHAV; PACHAVE; POUCAVE. When attached to non-Romany words, it adds a sinister connotation. See: POUR-RAVE; TIRAVE. Not rel. to **javanais** where "av" can figure in any and all words, e.g., lava gavare = *la gare.*

AVEC, *m.* Bonus. *Elle travaillait dur dans l'espoir d'un avec.* "She worked hard, hoping for a bonus."

AVIRON, *m.* Spoon (lit. "oar".) *J'ai bu ma soupe à même le bol parce que tu ne m'as pas donné d'aviron.* "I drank my soup right out of the bowl, because you didn't give me a spoon."

AVOINE, *m.* Oats. **Coller/filer/refiler une avoine à qn.** To beat s.o. up. *Il l'a mise dans une telle colère qu'elle lui a filé une avoine.* "He infuriated her so much that she gave him a sound thrashing."

AVOINER. 1. To beat; whip. *Le moine avoinait son cheval et s'avoinait plus tard.* "The monk beat his horse and flagellated h.s. later." **2.** To speed. *Il aime avoiner dans sa nouvelle Peugeot.* "He likes to tear up the road in his new Peugeot."

AZIMUT, *m.* Azimuth (magnetic angle used in astronomical calculations). **Dans tous les azimuts/tous azimuts.** Every which way; on all fronts. *On l'a cherchée dans tous les azimuts.* "We looked for her all over the place."

AZIMUTÉ, -E, *m., f., adj.* and *n.* Crazy. *C'est un azimuté; qui part toujours dans tous les azimutes.* "He's bananas, always riding off in all directions."

BA, *abbr.* of **bonne action** ("good deed"). *J'essaye chaque jour de faire ma BA.* "Every day I try to do a good deed."

BABA, *adj.* Dumbfounded. **Être baba; en rester baba.** To be knocked for a loop. *J'étais baba de sa forme après l'intervention.* "I was flabbergasted to see her in such good shape after the operation."

BABA, *m.* Rear end. **L'avoir dans le baba.** To be conned. *Je l'ai eu dans le baba, en payant cette merde beaucoup trop cher.* "I really got screwed by paying much too much for that junk."

BABA/BABA-COOL, *m.* Youth, 1970s. Hippy. *Il est baba-cool, respecte son gourou, et rejette la violence.* "He's a flower child, respects his guru, and rejects violence."

BABELUTTE, *f., Bel.* Candy, lollypop. *Ses mômes se gavent de babeluttes.* "Her kids stuff themselves on sweets."

BABILLARD, *m.* **1.** Book; newspaper (**babiller,** "to babble"). *Il aime lire chaque matin son babillard.* "He likes to read his newspaper every morning." **2.** Bulletin board. *Je dois consulter mon babillard électronique.* "I have to take a look at my electronic bulletin board (computer)."

BABINES, *f., pl.* Lips. **Se (pour) lécher les babines.** To lick one's chops. *Il se léchait les babines à l'idée d'une* *soirée strip-tease.* "He licked his chops looking forward to an evening of striptease."

BABOULES, *f., pl.* Testicles. *Je lui ai foutu un coup dans les baboules.* "I gave him a kick in the balls." *Cf.* RELIGIEUSES; ROUBIGNOLLES.

BAB'S = BABA/BABA-COOL.

BABTOU, *m., f.* White person (probably backslang of Ar. **toubab,** a variant of **toubib** [doctor] used in NW Africa, possibly from aWolof lang. verb meaning "to convert" [doctors and missionaries in colonial times were white] or from Brit. "two bob" [shillings], coinage once used in the Gambia). *Je connais des babtous bien.* "I know some nice white people."

BAC, *m., abbr.* of **baccalauréat.** High school diploma. *J'ai dû passer trois fois mon bac avant de l'avoir.* "I had to take the exam three times before getting my high school diploma."

BAC À SABLE, *m.* Territory (lit. "sandbox"/ "litter box"). *Je me tiens à mon bac à sable et je me fous du reste.* "I stick to my turf and don't give a damn about the rest."

BACANTES/BACCHANTES, *f., pl.* **1.** Bacchantes (devotees of the wine god Bacchus). **2.** Mustache; whiskers (from Ger. **Backe,** "cheek"). *Il aimait lisser de sa main ses belles bacchantes.* "He loved stroking his attractive mustache."

BACCARA, *m.* Hard luck. **Être en plein baccara.** To be in a jam; be bankrupt. *Au Sentier, beaucoup sont en plein baccara.* "In the garment district, many are having a hard time."

BÂCHE, *f.* **1.** bed sheet; cover (lit. "canvas cover"). **Piquer une bâche.** To hit the sack. *J'avais besoin de piquer une bâche.* "I needed to hit the hay." **2.** Cap. *Il ne se balade jamais sans sa bâche.* "He never goes anywhere without his cap." *Cf.* TOILES.

BACHOT, *m.* Variant of **bac.**

BACHOTER. To study hard. *Après avoir tant bachoté elle devrait réussir.* "After all that cramming she should pass."

BADA, *m.* Hat. **Faire porter le bada à qn.** To frame s.o. *Mes copains m'ont fait porter le bada.* "My friends set me up and I got a bum rap." *Cf.* CHAPEAU.

BADABOUM, *m.* Brawl. *La flicaille a mis fin au badaboum.* "The cops stopped the free-for-all."

BADIGEON, *m.* Heavy makeup (lit. "whitewash"; "paint"). *Avec tout ton badigeon tu ressembles à une pute.* "With all that war paint you look like a whore."

BADIGOINCES, *f., pl.* Lips. *Sers-toi de tes badigoinces et affiche un sourire!* "Use your lips and put a smile on your face!" See (SE) CALER.

BAFFE, *f.* Clout. **Coller/flanquer/foutre une baffe à qqn.** To hit s.o. *Il flanque des baffes à son chien pour le faire obéir.* "He whacks his dog to get it to obey."

(SE) BÂFRER. To stuff one's face. *Il aime se bâfrer chez les autres.* "He loves to pig out at other people's tables."

BÂFREUR, -EUSE, *m., f.* Glutton. *N'invite pas ce bâfreur.* "Don't invite that glutton."

BAGATELLE, *f.* Sexual relations. **Les bagatelles de la porte** (the idea is "little trifles before entering the gate"). Heavy petting; foreplay. *Les bagatelles de la porte l'avaient épuisé et il s'est endormi.* "Foreplay exhausted him and he fell asleep." **Être porté sur la bagatelle,** see CHOSE.

BAGNE, *m.* Sweatshop (lit. "prison"). *Ce boulot, c'est le vrai bagne.* "This place is a real salt mine/the pits."

BAGNOLE, *f.* Car. *Ma vieille bagnole a refusé de démarrer ce matin.* "My old jalopy wouldn't start this morning." **Quelle belle bagnole!** "That's some car! Quite a heap!"

BAGOUGNASSES, *f., pl.* Lips. *Essuie tes bagougnasses avant de m'embrasser.* "Wipe your lips before kissing me."

BAGOULER. To talk a blue streak. *L'entendre bagouler me fatigue.* "Listening to him rattle on wears me out."

BAGOUSE/BAGOUZE, *f.* **1.** Ring. *Elle aime couvrir ses doigts de bagouses tocardes.* "She like to cover her fingers with flashy rings." **2.** Anus. **Être/refiler de la bagouse.** To be a homosexual. *J'ai su tout de suite qu'il était de la bagouse.* "I knew right away he was gay." **3.** Luck. **Avoir de la bagouze.** To be lucky. *Il est temps qu'on ait un peu de bagouze.* "It's time we had a bit of luck."

BAGOUT, *m.* Glibness. **Avoir du bagout.** To have the gift of gab. *Ce camelot a du bagout.* "That street vendor's a smooth talker."

BAGUE = BAGOUSE.

BAGUETTES, *f., pl.* Thin legs (lit. "(chop)sticks"; "batons"). *Sa nana est une planche à pain juchée sur des baguettes.* "His chick's a bread board (flat-chested) perched on spindly legs."

BAHUT, *m.* **1.** Taxi. *Impossible d'avoir un bahut à l'heure de pointe!* "Impossible to get a taxi at rush hour." **2.** Small truck. *Son bahut est toujours en panne.* "His truck's always breaking down." **3.** School. *Chaque fin de semaine elle était heureuse de quitter le bahut.* "Every weekend she was glad to get out of school."

BAIGNER. To bathe. **Baigner dans le beurre/l'huile.** To go like clockwork. *Pourquoi t'inquiéter? Tout baigne dans l'huile!* "Why get upset? Everything's going great!" *Ça baigne!* "Everything's hunky-dory!"

BAIL, *m.* **1.** Lease. **Casser le bail.** To get a divorce (lit. "to break the lease"). *On a décidé de casser le bail, malgré les enfants.* "We've decided to get a divorce despite the children." **Ça fait un bail!** It's been a long time! *Ça fait un bail qu'on a dansé ensemble!* "It's been ages since we danced together!" **2.** Money (from Eng. "buy"). *As-tu besoin de bail pour le week-end?* "Do you need money for the weekend?"

BAILLE, *f.* Water (river, sea, and so on). *Ses copains l'ont mis à la baille.* "His friends threw him into the drink."

BAIN, *m.* Bath. **Être dans le bain. 1.** To be in the know. *Je préfère être dans le bain avant d'attaquer un nouveau projet.* "I prefer to be well informed before tackling a new project." **2.** To be implicated. *Elle ne savait pas que son fils était dans le bain.* "She didn't know her son was mixed up in it."

BAIN-MARIE, *m.* Bidet (lit. "double boiler" from an alchemical instrument named for Moses' sister, a supposed alchemist). *Elle ferait bien d'utiliser son bain-marie après chaque passe.* "She really should use her bidet after each trick."

BAISANT, -E. Really nice. **Pas baisant.** Nasty. *Il n'est pas baisant, ce mec là.* "That guy's a mean customer."

BAISEBEIGE. Hip variant of BCBG **2.**

BAISE, *f.* Sexual intercourse. *Pour lui, les femmes ne sont bonnes que pour la baise.* "For him, all women are good for is screwing."

BAISE-EN-VILLE, *m.* Overnight bag. *Il a plein de présos dans son baise-en-ville.* "He's got plenty of condoms in his overnight bag."

BAISER. 1. To have sexually; fuck (orig., but no longer, "to kiss," although the noun **le/un baiser** is still standard Fr. for "the/a kiss"). *Mon mec baise vachement bien.* "My guy's terrific in bed." See MAL-BAISÉ. **Se faire baiser.** To get screwed (in both senses). *Catherine la Grande aimait se faire baiser par une élite qu'elle sélectionnait.* "Catherine the Great enjoyed getting fucked by an elite she selected." *Nous nous sommes vraiment fait baiser.* "We really got shafted." **2.** To swipe. *Qui m'a baisé de ma montre?* "Who pinched my watch?" **3. Ne rien y baiser.** To understand nothing. *J'ai bien écouté, mais je n'y ai rien baisé.* "I listened closely but I didn't get it at all."

BAISER À LA BOURGEOISE. To copulate in the male superior position. *Elle s'est lassée de baiser à la bourgeoise.* "She got tired of the missionary position."

BAISER À LA PAPA. To copulate calmly. *Après des paroxysmes, ça fait parfois du bien baiser à la papa.* "After passionate bursts it's sometimes nice to have a good, slow screw."

BAISEUR, -EUSE, *m., f.* Sexy or horny person. *C'était un sacré baiseur, avant.* "He was a real stud, once."

BAISODROME, *m.* Brothel; place of frequent sexual encounters. *Ah, ce petit hôtel au fond du bois, c'est un vrai baisodrome.* "Ah, that little hotel deep in the woods, lots of screwing going on there."

BALADER. 1. To take for a walk. *J'aime balader mon chien.* "I like to take my dog for a walk." **Envoyer balader qn.** To send s.o. packing. *Il voulait de l'argent; je l'ai envoyé balader.* "He wanted money; I gave him his walking papers." **Envoyer balader qch.** To chuck; dump. *J'en avais marre, je voulais tout envoyer balader.* "I was fed up with it and wanted to pack it all in." **2.** To hoodwink. *Il m'a baladé avec toutes ses sornettes.* "He led me down the garden path with his tall stories." **3.** To defeat easily. *Elle a baladé toutes ses rivales au tennis.* "She had all her tennis competitors for lunch."

BALADEUR, -EUSE. Wandering. **Avoir la main baladeuse/les mains baladeuses.** To have roaming hands. *Je ne guinche plus avec lui, car il a les mains baladeuses.* "I don't dance with him any more because he paws me."

BALAI, *m.* Broom. See CON COMME UN BALAI; COUP DE BALAI; DONNER UN COUP DE BALAI; RAMASSER LES BALAIS; VOITURE.

BALAI À/DE CHIOTTES, *m.* Bristly mustache (lit. "toilet bowl brush"). *Tu te plains de mon balai à chiottes.* "You complain about my stiff mustache."

BALAI D'AMOUR, *m.* Soft mustache. *Avant tu aimais mon balai d'amour.* "You used to love my tender mustache."

BALAIS, *m., pl.* Years of age. *J'ai 95 balais, mais on me donne toujours moins.* "I'm 95, but people always take me for younger."

BALAISE. See BALÈZE.

BALANCER. 1. To swing. See BIEN BALANCÉ. **2.** To throw out. *Tous les jours je balance des quantités de magazines.* "Every day I throw out loads of magazines." **3.** To give. *Balance-moi un peu de fric pour le week-end.* "Give me some money for the weekend." **4.** To denounce. *J'ai été balancée par ma meilleure copine.* "I was denounced by my best friend." *Cf.* INDIC; POUCAVE.

BALANCER LE FOUTRE/POTAGE/LA SAUCE/ SEMOULE. To ejaculate. See SEMOULE. *Cf.* VENIN.

BALANCER UN COUP/UNE BEIGNE/UNE CLAQUE. See FILER UN COUP...À QN.

BALANCER UN PET. To cut a fart. *Arrête de balancer des pets.* "Quit farting." *Cf.* LÂCHER UN COILS...; LÂCHER MEDOR.

BALANCER UNE VACHERIE. See VACHERIE.

BALANCER UNE VANNE/DES VANNES. See VANNE.

(SE) BALANCER. To hurl o.s. (lit. "to rock"). *Il s'est balancé dans le vide avec son parachute.* "He bailed out over empty space."

(S'EN) BALANCER. To not give a damn. *Toutes ces histoires, je m'en balance!* "I don't give a damn about all that stuff."

BALANÇOIRE, *f.* Swing. **Envoyer qn. à la balançoire,** *idiom.* To tell s.o. to get lost. *J'avais envie de l'envoyer à la balançoire.* "I felt like telling him to get lost."

BALANÇOIRE À MICKEY/À MINOUCHE. Sanitary napkin. *Elle préfère les tampons aux balançoires à Mickey.* "She prefers tampons to rags."

BALAYETTE, *f.* Penis (lit. "whisk broom"). See DANS... BALAYETTE!

BALAYETTE INFERNALE. Very large penis. *Elle priait chaque fois qu'elle voyait sa balayette infernale!* "She prayed every time she saw his huge tool." **Une partie de balayette infernale.** A session of intense sex. *Après une partie de balayette infernale, nous étions pompés.* "After intense lovemaking we were exhausted."

BALCON, *m.* Balcony. **Il y a du monde au balcon.** "She's amply bosomed/stacked/got big tits" (lit. "the balcony is crowded").

BALEC! To hell with it! (Interjection formed from **je m'en bats les couilles.** See COUILLES.) *Tu me planques? Alors là, balec!* "You're dumping me? Well, I don't give a good goddamn!"

BALÈZE. 1. Brawny. *Il est balèze, ton jules.* "Your boy friend's a hunk." **2.** Brainy. *En manipulation de données, il est balèze.* "He's a whiz at data handling."

BALLET, *m.* Ballet. **Ballet bleu.** Sex with underage boys. **Ballet rose.** Sex with underage girls. *Selon les ragots le roi participe aux ballets bleus et roses. — Oui, l'union fait la force et il cherche à s'unir un max à ses sujets.* "According to malicious gossip the king participates in orgies with minors." — "Yes, there's strength in unity and he wants to join with as many of his subjects as possible."

BALOURD, *m.* Counterfeit (lit. "oaf"). *Tu croyais ton sac sorti de chez Vuitton mais c'est un balourd.* "You thought your handbag came from Vuitton, but it's a fake."

BALPEAU/BALLEPEAU, backslang of **peau de balle.**

BALTRINGUE, *m.* **1.** Good-for-nothing; outsider *Ton reuf, c'est un baltringue de première.* "Your bro's worthless." **2.** Coward; homosexual (in this meaning the feminine **une** is often used). *Il perd les boules comme une baltringue.* "He flips like a chicken liver."

BALTRINGUER. To flee. *La vipère l'a fait baltringuer.* "The viper made him clear off fast."

BAMBOU, *m.* Bamboo. **Avoir le bambou = avoir le bâton.** See BÂTON 1; COUP DE BAMBOU.

BAMBOULA, *m., pej.* **1.** Black person. *Lors de la fête, les Bamboulas dansaient dans la rue.* "During the holiday, the blacks danced in the street." **2.** *f.* Spree. *Mon fils ne pense qu'à faire la bamboula.* "All my son wants to do is party." (Both derive from **bambalon,** an African drum.)

BAMÉ, *m., f.* Spaced-out person. *Il y a une bande de bamés ce soir dans la boîte.* "There's a bunch of crazies in the place tonight."

BANANE, *f.* **1.** Banana. **Avoir la banane.** To have an erection. *J'ai la banane dès que je la vois.* "I get hard every time I see her." **Se prendre une (peau de) banane.** To fail. *Après ses grands tubes son dernier disque s'est pris une banane.* "Many of her songs were big hits but her last two records bombed." See PEAU DE BANANE. **2.** Military decoration. *Raconte comment tu as gagné toutes ces bananes.* "Tell us how you got all that fruit salad." **3.** Twin-rotor helicopter. *Beaucoup de bananes se sont écrasées au sol récemment.* "Many choppers have crashed recently." **4.** Fool. *Je te l'ai déjà souvent dit, banane!* "I've already told you many times, idiot."

(SE FAIRE) BANANER. To be conned. (*Cf.* BANANE **4.**) *Les veuves se sont fait bananer par l'escroc.* "The widows were swindled by the crook."

BANDANT, -E. 1. Sexually desirable. *Charlotte est la plus bandante de toute la classe.* "Charlotte is the sexiest girl in the whole class." **2.** Exciting. **Pas bandant.** Nothing to write home about. *Le film ce soir n'est pas bandant.* "Tonight's movie isn't very interesting."

BANDER. To get an erection (from "to bend; tighten a bow"). *Je suis en quête de dessous pour faire bander mon mari.* "I'm looking for undies that'll excite my husband." **Bander pour qn.** To turn on. *Je bande pour aucune d'elles.* "None of them turns me on." **Bander pour un mec/bander pour une fille.** To go for a guy/girl (both are now also used by women, the second one by a lesbian). *Elle savait qu'il était marié, mais elle bandait pour lui.* "She knew he was married, but she went for him."

BANDER FOULARD/MOU. 1. To be scared. *Quand son mari l'a menacé, il bandait mou.* "When her husband threatened him, he got scared." **2.** To have a flabby erection. *D'habitude il bande foulard, mais hier soir il m'a surprise.* "He usually has trouble getting it up, but last night he surprised me."

BANDER GUIMAUVE. To be impotent. *Malgré son grand âge il ne bande pas guimauve.* "Despite his advanced age, he's not impotent."

BANDEUR, -EUSE, *m., f.* Sexy. *C'est une petite bandeuse!* "She's a raunchy little sexpot!"

BANNIÈRE, *f.* Banner (flag). **En bannière.** In shirttails; shirtsleeves. *Il m'a reçue en bannière, à moitié nu; j'en étais choquée!* "He received me in shirttails, half-naked; I was shocked!"

BANQUER. To pay up. *Elle peut acheter des fringues haute couture; c'est son baron qui banque!* "She can buy high-fashion clothes; it's her sugar daddy who shells out for them."

BAPTÊME, *m.* Gang rape (lit. "baptism"). *"À cette garce, il lui faut un baptême," disait le gangster.* "'That bitch needs a gang bang,' said the gangster." *Cf.* TOURNANTE.

BAPTÊME! *Que.* Shit!; Hot damn!; Holy cow! *Baptême je t'attends plus!* "Goddammit I'm not waiting any longer for you." *See…*BÂTEAU! BATINS!; EN BAPTÊME…; ÊTRE EN BAPTÊME….; OSTENSOIRE!; SACRE 2.

BAPTISÉ AU SÉCATEUR. See SÉCATEUR.

BARAKA, *f.* Good luck (from Ar. for "blessing"). **Avoir la baraka.** To be on a roll. *À Las Vegas il a eu la baraka.* "He lucked out in Las Vegas."

BARBAQUE, *f.* **1.** Meat. *Les végétariens nous ont invités à un barbecue sans barbaque.* "The vegetarians invited us to a meatless barbecue." **2.** Flesh. *C'est une tribu de cannibales qui sait très bien assaisonner la barbaque.* "They're a tribe of cannibals very knowledegable in the seasoning of flesh." See MARCHAND DE BARBAQUE.

BARBE, *f.* **1.** Beard. **Se mettre une fausse barbe.** To practice cunnilingus (lit. "to put on a false beard"). *Mon mari n'aime pas se raser mais il adore se mettre une fausse barbe.* "My husband doesn't like to shave but he loves to eat hair pie." *Cf.* BARBU. **2.** S.t. annoying. **C'est la barbe! C'est la Sainte-Barbe! Quelle barbe!** What a drag! See LA BARBE!

BARBEAU, *m.* Small-time pimp (lit. "barbel" [fish]). *Son barbeau est celui qui porte des bagues tocardes.* "Her pimp's the one who wears flashy rings."

BARBER. 1. To bore; annoy. *Ce pitre me barbe.* "That clown bugs me." **2.** To trick. *T'as essayé de nous barber, couillon!* "You tried to put one over on us, dickhead!"

BARBILLON/BARBIQUET/BARBISET = BARBEAU.

BARBOTER. To steal, swipe (orig. "to splash about"). *La bande a barboté 5.000 euros.* "The gang stole 5,000 euros."

BARBOUSE/BARBOUZE, *f.* **1.** Beard. *Je t'aimais mieux sans barbouze.* "I liked you better without the beard." **2.** Secret agent. *Plusieurs films ridiculisent les barbouzes qui se mettent des fausses barbes.* "Many movies make fun of secret agents who put on false beards."

BARBU, *m.* Female pubic hair (lit. "bearded man"). See DESCENTE...BARBU.

BARCA! = BARKA!

BARDA, *m., Ar.* Gear. *J'en ai marre de trimballer tout ce barda.* "I'm fed up with lugging around all this stuff."

BARDER. To heat up. See ÇA VA BARDER!

BARGE/BARGEOT/BARJO/BARJOT, backslang of **jobard.** Crazy. *Il est barjot, ce motard; il roule sans casque.* "That biker's off his rocker; he rides without a helmet."

BARKA! "Enough! That will do!"

BARNAK!/BARNIK!/BATARNAK! *Que., euph.* for **tabernacle!/tabernak!** Sometimes spelled *barnaque/barnique/batarnak.* See SACRE **2.**

BARON, *m.* **1.** Accomplice. *Elle empochait les bijoux pendant qu'il faisait le baron.* "She pocketed the jewels while he acted as decoy." **2.** Sugar daddy. *Son baron faisait tout pour lui plaire.* "Her sugar daddy did everything to please her."

BARRE, *f.* Bar; rod. **Avoir barre(s) sur qn.** To be one up on s.o. *Il a tout fait pour avoir barre sur moi.* "He did everything to have an edge on me." **Avoir une/la barre avec qn.** To make a hit with s.o. *À son regard, j'ai vu que j'avais la barre.* "The way she looked at me told me that I'd hit it off with her." **Avoir une barre pour qn.** To have the hots for s.o. *Il a une barre pour moi, mais je le déteste.* "He's got the hots for me but I despise him." See COUP DE BARRE/POMPE; COUP DE FUSIL/BARRE; (SE) PRENDRE UNE BARRE; (À) TOUTE BARRE.

BARRÉ. Être bien/mal barré. To be well/badly positioned. *Dans cette affaire on est mal barré.* "We're not in a good position in this matter."

(SE) BARRER. To scram. *Je voulais lui parler mais il s'est barré.* "I wanted to talk to him but he beat it."

BARREUR, *m.* Nightclub doorman; bouncer (lit. "helmsman"). *Le barreur de la disco a évincé les skins.* "The disco bouncer threw out the skinheads."

BARRIQUE, *f.* Barrel. See ROND…BARRIQUE.

BAS-DUC/BAS-DU-CUL, *m., adj.* and *n.* Short(y). *Elle est trop bas-du-cul pour faire un mannequin.* "Her ass is too close to the ground to make it as a model."

BASKETS, *f., pl.* Sports shoes. **Être bien/à l'aise dans ses baskets.** To be relaxed/together. *Dans n'importe quelle situation, il est bien dans ses baskets.* "He keeps his cool, whatever the circumstances." **Faire baskets.** To take French leave. *Ils ont fait baskets dans beaucoup de restos.* "They left without paying in many restaurants."

BASSINER. To grate on; harass (lit. "warm with a warming pan"; "water"). *Arrête de me bassiner avec toutes tes lamentations!* "Quit bugging me with all your moaning."

BASTA! "That's enough of that!"

BASTON, *m. or f.* (usually *m.* today). Fight. *Y a eu du baston au bar.* "There was a fight in the bar." *Cf.* CHERCHER BASTON.

BASTRINGUE, *m.* **1.** Seedy dance hall. *Allons gigoter au bastringue du coin!* "Let's go shake our dancing legs at the local dance hall." **2.** Band. *Lui et ses copains ont créé un petit bastringue.* "He and his friends have formed a little combo." See (ET) TOUT LE BASTRINGUE. **3.** Din. *Impossible de dormir avec un tel bastringue!* "Impossible to get any sleep with that racket."

BATACLAN, *m.* Stuff. *Les enfants sont partis depuis longtemps mais leur bataclan est toujours ici.* "The kids moved out long ago, but their junk is still here." **Tout le bataclan!** The whole shebang. *Je veux qu'ils prennent tout: tout le bataclan!* "I want them to take everything, the whole works!"

BATEAU, *m.* Boat. **Mener en bateau.** To dupe, lead down the garden path. *Leur banquier les a menés en bateau.* "Their banker took them for a ride." **Un sujet bateau.** Trite subject. *Mon oncle ne peint que des sujets bateau.* "All my uncle paints are trite motifs."

BÂTEAU!/BATÊCHE/BATÉYE/BATINCE!/BATINS!/ BATINSSE! *Que., euph.* for BAPTÊME!

BÂTIMENT, *m.* Building; building trade. **Être dans le bâtiment.** To be in the building industry. *Son père est dans le bâtiment.* "Her father's in the building trade." **Être du bâtiment.** To be part of a particular group, profession. *Je ne sais pas si Guy est du bâtiment mais il ne sort qu'avec des mecs.* "I don't know whether Guy is one of them (gays) but he just goes out with guys."

BÂTON, *m.* **1.** Stick. **Avoir le bâton.** To have an erection. *Cette vieille fille croit que les hommes ont toujours le bâton et sont prêts à la violer.* "That old maid thinks men are always erect and ready to rape her." See MENER…

CHAISE. **2.** Leg. *Elle a cassé son bâton gauche en patinant.* "She broke her left leg skating."

BATTANT, *m.* Heart. *Il jure qu'il l'aime du fond de son battant.* "He swears he loves her from the bottom of his heart."

BATTANT, -E, *m., f.* S.o. with get-up-and-go. *C'est une battante; elle réussira.* "She's a go-getter; she'll succeed."

BATTRE DE L'AILE. To be in a bad way. *Son commerce battait de l'aile et il a dû fermer boutique.* "His business was on its last legs and he had to shut up shop."

BATTRE DES AILES. To flail one's arms about. *Il est pété et bat des ailes.* "He's high on s.t. and is flapping his arms about."

BAVARD, *m.* **1.** Telephone answering machine (from the adj. "talkative"). *Il n'y avait aucun message sur le bavard.* "There wasn't a single message on the answering machine." **2.** Lawyer. *Méfie-toi de ton bavard; c'est un escroc!* "Don't trust your mouthpiece; he's a crook."

BAVER. 1. To drool. **Faire baver.** To create difficulties. *Le maire m'en a fait baver.* "The mayor gave me a real hard time." **2.** To drool over. *Tes bijoux me font baver.* "Your jewels make me drool with envy." **3.** To speak. **Baver sur qn.** To speak ill of. *Il faut se méfier de lui; il bave sur tous.* "You've got to watch out for him; he dumps on everybody."

(EN) BAVER DES RONDS DE CHAPEAUX. To have a rough time of it. *Avant d'avoir l'autorisation j'en ai bavé des ronds de chapeaux.* "Before getting the authorization I really had to sweat it."

BAVETTE, *f.* **1.** Bib. **Tailler une bavette.** To chew the fat; shoot the breeze. *On se taillera une bavette demain.* "We'll have a nice chat tomorrow." **2.** Informer. *On a trouvé le cadavre de la bavette dans la cour de la taule.* "They found the informer's corpse in the prison yard."

BAVEUSE, *f.* **1.** Gossip. *Ne fréquente pas trop cette baveuse.* "Don't spend too much time with that gossip." **2.** Tongue. *Il a la baveuse bien pendue.* "He talks a blue streak."

BAVEUX, *m.* **1.** Lawyer (more "in" term for BAVARD **2**). **2.** Newspaper. *Ne te cache pas derrière ton baveux; écoute-moi!* "Don't hide behind your newspaper; listen to me." **3.** Tongue kiss. *On a commencé nos ébats par un baveux.* "We began our lovemaking with a wet French kiss."

BAZOU, *m., Que.* = **BAGNOLE.**

BCBG, *adj.* and *m., f., n.* **1.** Acronym for **bon chic, bon genre.** Conservatively chic; belonging to the smart set. *Pour plaire à sa mère il a épousé une BCBG.* "To please his mother he married a social register/junior league/ yuppie type." **2.** Acronym for **beau cul, belle gueule.** A pretty face and a gorgeous bod. *Je bande pour une BCBG.* "I turn on to a nice piece of stuff."

BEAU COMME UN PAF (EN FLEUR)! Beautiful as all get out! (lit. "beautiful as a (flowering) phallus").

BEAU CUL, BELLE GUEULE. See BCBG **2.**

BEAU-DAB, *m.* Father-in-law. *Mon beau-dab était extraordinaire.* "My father-in-law was extraordinary."

BEAU GOSSE, *m.* Handsome man. *Son mec est beau gosse.* "Her guy's good-looking." *Cf.* GOSSEBO.

BEAUF(E), *m.* **1.** Brother-in-law (for **beau-frère**). **2.** Average **petit-bourgeois,** jingoistic Frenchman. *Sa nouvelle pièce de théâtre est raciste et devrait plaire aux beaufs.* "Her new play is racist and will probably appeal to the average prejudiced Frenchman."

BEAUJOLPIF/BEAUJOLPINCE, *m.,* the former is a composite of **Beaujolais** and the *adj.* **olpif.** Beaujolais (wine). *Le mois de novembre est enjolivé par l'arrivée du beaujolpif.* "The month of November is brightened by the arrival of the new Beaujolais wine."

BEAU LINGE, *m.* The smart set. *À l'ouverture du festival il n'y avait que du beau linge.* "Only beautiful people were at the opening of the film festival."

BÉBAR, *youth, invar.* To steal. *Fallait pas la bébar, la bagnole.* "You shouldn't have stolen the car."

BÉBÉ, *m.* Baby. See BUFFET; REFILER LE BÉBÉ.

BÉBÉ ROSE, *m.* Milk with grenadine syrup. *Moi, je prendrai un bébé rose; mon mari un diabolo menthe.* "I'll have a grenadine milkshake; my husband a mint-flavored soda."

BÉBÉ SANS BRAS, *m.* One-liter wine bottle (lit. "armless baby"). *Les ouvriers du port de Brest sont très attachés à leurs bébés sans bras.* "Brest dockworkers are very attached to their bottles of wine."

BÉBÊTE, *f.* **1.** Small insect. *Ça grouille de bébêtes ici.* "This place is alive with creepy-crawlies." **2.** Foolish. *Brigitte est belle, mais bébête; sa sœur déteste ses rires bébêtes.* "Brigitte is beautiful, but childish; her sister detests her silly giggles."

BEC, *m.* Mouth (lit. "beak"). **Avoir une prise de bec avec qn.** To lock horns with s.o. *J'ai eu une prise de bec avec la maitresse de mon mari.* "I crossed swords with my husband's mistress." See CLAQUER DU BEC; CLOUER LE BEC; RESTER LE BEC... TAPER DU BEC. **2.** Obstacle. See TOMBER...BEC.

BÉCANE, *f.* **1.** Bike; motorcycle. *Tu peux aller à pied ou prendre ta bécane.* "You can go on foot or take your bike." **2.** Tool; machine (especially computer). *Je me bats toujours avec ma bécane électronique.* "I'm still struggling with my electronic bike."

BÊCHER. 1. To put on airs. *Avec tes nouvelles fringues, tu bêches!* "You're acting stuck-up in your new clothes." **2.** To snub. *Les dames de la haute m'ont bêchée à l'opéra.* "The high-society ladies snubbed me at the opera."

(SE) BÉCOTER. To bill and coo. *Ils ont passé l'après-midi à se bécoter.* "They spent the afternoon smooching."

BEDAINE, *f.* Potbelly. *Il fait tout pour perdre sa grosse bedaine.* "He's working hard at losing his rubber tire."

BEDONNER. To get/show a paunch. *Pierre bedonne et se compare à une statue du Bouddha.* "Potbellied Pierre compares h.s. to a statue of the Buddha."

BÉGONIA, *m.* **1.** Begonia. **Être dans les bégonias.** To have lost consciousness. *Elle est toujours dans les bégonias.* "She's still unconscious." See CHARRIER DANS… **2.** Female genitalia. *Line réserve son bégonia à Marc.* "Line is saving her pussy for Mark."

BÉGUIN, *m.* **1.** Flirtation (lit. "bonnet"). **Avoir le béguin pour qn.** To have a crush on s.o. *Elle a le béguin pour son prof de musique.* "She has a crush on her music teacher." **2.** Noncommercial love. **Y aller au béguin.** To grant sexual favors without charging. *Elle est sentimentale et y va souvent au béguin.* "She's very sentimental and often does it for nothing."

BÉGUINE, *f.* Rhumba-like dance from the Fr. Antilles. *Le groupe a commencé à jouer la béguine, mais j'ai n'ai pas dansé avec Luc, car je n'ai plus le béguin pour lui.* "The band began the beguine but I didn't dance with Luke because I no longer have a crush on him."

BÉGUINEUSE, *f.* Unreliable prostitute. *Mon maq ne tolère pas les béguineuses.* "My pimp doesn't tolerate those who give it away."

BEIGNE, *f.* Smack. See ALLONGER…BEIGNE; FILER… BEIGNE…; FLANQUER…BEIGNE.

BELLE, *f.* Escape. *Sans la complicité des flics les taulards n'auraient pas pu se faire la belle.* "If the cops hadn't been in on it the jailbirds couldn't have escaped."

BELLE. L'avoir belle. To be on easy street. *Depuis qu'il a hérité gros il l'a belle.* "Ever since he inherited a lot of money he's been on easy street." **En faire voir de belles à qn.** To put s.o. through a ringer. *Son petit voyou de fils lui en faisait voir de belles.* "Her lout of a son made life rough for her." **En faire de belles.** To be up to no good. *Il en a fait de belles avant de se marier.* "He got into a lot of mischief before getting married."

BELLE-DABESSE/BELLE-DOCHE, *joc.,* not *pej.* Mother-in-law. *Ma belle-doche et moi, nous aimons le vin.* "My mother-in-law and I are fond of wine."

BELLE LURETTE. A considerable amount of time (from **heurette,** diminutive of **heure**). *"Il y a belle lurette que j'ai fêté mes vingt piges," dit mon grand-dab.* "'It's been some time since I celebrated my twentieth birthday,' says my grandpa."

BÉNI-OUI-OUI, *m., f.* Sycophant. *Le chef ne s'entoure que de béni-oui-oui.* "The boss keeps only yes-men around him."

BÉNISSEUR, *m.* Sycophant. *Et tu l'as cru, ce bénisseur?* "And you fell for that phony's soft soap?"

BÉNITIER, *m.* **1.** Holy water font. **Se démener comme un diable dans un bénitier.** To make great efforts (lit. "to thrash about like a devil in a holy water font." Demons, vampires and such are said to shun crucifixes and holy water fonts). *Pol s'est démené comme un diable pour se libérer de ses dettes.* "Pol knocked h.s. out to get out of debt." See GRENOUILLE DE BÉNITIER. **2.** Female genitalia. *Ce cureton préfère les bites aux bénitiers et réserve son goupillon aux gars.* "That little priest prefers cocks to cunts and saves his dick for guys." *Cf.* MOUILLER SON GOUPILLON; SIÈGE DU PAPE.

BERGE, *f.* Year (lit. "river bank"). *Elle est toujours vierge malgré ses trente berges.* "She's still a virgin despite her thirty years (of age)."

BERGOUGNAN, *m.* Tough meat. *Gil a fait du bergougnan un succulent bœuf bourguignon.* "Gil transformed the tough meat into a succulent boeuf bourgignon (long-simmered stew)." *Cf.* BARBAQUE.

BERLINGOT, *m.* **1.** Vehicle; any means of transportation, including airplanes (from berline, a coach manufactured in Berlin, Ger.). *Pol fuit tout berlingot et préfère aller à pied.* "Pol avoids all vehicles and prefers to get around on foot." **2.** Clitoris (from a type of hard candy [for sucking] from Carpentras). *J'ai mis son doigt sur mon berlin-got.* "I put his finger on my love button." *Cf.* BONBON 3; BOUTON 3; HARICOT; PÉPITE.

BERLUE, *m.* Illusion. **Avoir la berlue.** To hallucinate. *J'ai cru avoir la berlue en les revoyant ensemble.* "I thought I was seeing things when I saw them together again."

BÉSEF. A lot. *Il n'y en avait pas bésef.* "There wasn't much/many (of it/them)."

BESOGNER. To have sexually (lit. "to work away; drudge") *Le patron les avait toutes besognées.* "The boss had banged them all."

BESOINS, *m., pl.* Nature's needs. See FAIRE SES BESOINS.

BÊTE, *f.* **1.** Beast. See CHERCHER…BÊTE. **2.** Outstanding individual. **C'est la bête!** He or she is brilliant. *Il était la bête de la classe mais il a loupé son exam.* "He was the class star but he failed the exam."

BÊTE COMME CHOU. Easy as pie. *C'est bête comme chou.* "That's a cinch."

BÊTE COMME SES PIEDS. Stupid. *Il est bête comme ses pieds.* "He's as dumb as they come."

BEUR, *m.,* not *pej.,* backslang of **arabe.** Young, French-born, second-generation North African. *Coco a épousé un jeune beur qui la rend très heureuse.* "Coco's married to a young North African who makes her very happy."

BEURGOIS, *pl.* Very assimilated Fr. people of NW African origin. Play on **beur** and **bourgeois.** *Ça fait trois générations qu'on est en France. Nous sommes bien beurgois.* "We've been in France for three generations. We're very mainstream middle-class French."

BEURRE, *m.* **1.** Butter. **Être du beurre; être un (vrai) beurre.** To be a cinch/snap. *C'est du beurre!* It's a piece of cake! **Compter pour du beurre.** To count for nothing. *Nos intérêts ne comptaient que pour du beurre.* "Our interests counted for nothing." See BAIGNER…BEURRE; METTRE…ÉPINARDS; ŒIL…NOIR. **2.** Money. **Faire son**

beurre. To make a bundle, pile. *Ce financier a profité de la crise économique pour faire son beurre.* "That financier took advantage of the economic crisis to make a bundle." See ASSIETTE AU BEURRE.

(SE) BEURRER. 1. To make a bundle. *Il s'est beurré pendant la guerre en faisant du marché noir.* "During the war my brother made a bundle dealing in the black market." **2.** To get soused. *Ils se sont tous bien beurrés.* "They all got dead drunk."

BÉZEF = BÉSEF.

BIBELOT, *m.* Burglar's tool (lit. "ornament"). *Le cambrioleur maugréait contre son bibelot en panne.* "The burglar grumbled about his skeleton key that didn't work."

BIBELOTS, *m., pl.* Male genitalia. *Je préfère les bibelots de mon mari à tous les bijoux du monde.* "I prefer my husband's family jewels to all the jewels in the world."

BIBERONNER. To booze (from **biberon,** "baby's bottle"). *Il ne fout rien depuis qu'il biberonne.* "He hasn't worked at anything ever since he hit the bottle."

BIBINE, *f.* Hooch. *Bush a arrêté la bibine pour Jésus. Pourquoi n'arrêtes-tu pas la bibine pour le Bouddah?* "Bush gave up booze for Jesus. Why don't you get off the bottle for the Buddha?"

BICRAVE. From *Romany.* To deal drugs; to steal. *Qui t'as bicrave ce shit? — Personne. Je l'ai bicrave moi.* "Who sold you that hash?" — "Nobody. I stole it."

BIDE, *m.* **1.** Stomach. *Mon mari a pris du bide.* "My husband's grown paunchy." *Cf.* BIDON 1. **2.** Failure. **Faire** or **ramasser un bide.** To flop. *Son dernier film a ramassé un bide.* "His last movie bombed at the box office." *Cf.* FOUR.

BIDOCHARD, *m.* Pimp, sex trader. *L'autre assassin de Dallas était et bidochard et mouchard.* "The other Dallas assassin was both a flesh-peddler and a police informant."

BIDOCHE, *f.* **1.** Meat. *Ils boudent la bidoche britannique.* "They're leery of British meat." **2.** Flesh. *Le marchand de Venise ne voulait pas se séparer d'une livre de sa bidoche.* "The merchant of Venice didn't want to part with a pound of his flesh." See MARCHAND DE BIDOCHE.

BIDON, *m.* **1.** Belly (lit. "can"; "flask"). *J'en ai plein le bidon.* "My tummy is stuffed." **2.** Bullshit. *C'est du bidon!* "That's a load of crap!"

BIDON, *adj.* Phony. *Il a mis en scène un attentat bidon.* "He staged a phony assassination attempt."

BIDONNER. To cheat. **Bidonner un travail.** To do a half-assed job. *Si on ne le surveille pas, il bidonne son boulot.* "If you don't keep an eye on him, he'll botch the job."

(SE) BIDONNER. To laugh one's head off. *On s'est bidonné en regardant ce comique.* "We laughed our heads off watching that comic."

BIDOUILLEUR, -EUSE, *m., f.* **1.** S.o. who tinkers with gadgets. *Mon mari se croit un parfait bidouilleur.* "My husband thinks he has a way with machines." **2.** Computer hacker/expert. *C'est une bidouilleuse, spécia-liste en pro-grammation.* "She's a computer programming specialist."

BIDULE, *m.* What-do-you-call-it. *J'ai un tiroir plein de bidules que je devrais balancer.* "I've got a draw full of thingamajigs I ought to throw out."

BIEN BALANCÉ, -E. Attractive; well built. *Quelle nana! Pas seulement intello, mais bien balancée.* "What a chick! Not only a brain but a looker too!"

BIENHEUREUX, *m.* Simpleton (lit. "venerable, blessed," pre-saint in the canonization process). *Mon mari est diabolique mais il dort comme un bienheureux.* "My husband is diabolical but he sleeps like a baby."

BIÈRE, *f.* Beer. **Ce n'est pas de la petite bière.** "That's no small potatoes/not to be sneezed at." **Ne pas se prendre pour de la petite bière.** To be conceited; swell-headed. *Il ne se prend pas pour de la petite bière, et à juste titre,* *peut-être.* "He has a high opinion of h.s., and maybe he's right." (A stronger equivalent is **ne pas se prendre pour de la petite merde.** See MERDE.)

BIFTEK, *m.* **1.** Business (lit. "beefsteak"). *C'est pas mon biftek,* ça. "That's not my affair." **2. Biftek roulé.** Penis. *Elle se regale de son biftek roulé, véritable os à moelle juteux.* "She loves feasting on his lovestick, his juicy, marrow-boned lovesteak." *Cf.* OS À MOELLE 2.

BIGLER. To take a look at (lit. "to squint"; "have poor eyesight"). *Viens bigler ce que j'ai trouvé pour toi.* "Take a gander at what I've found for you."

BIGO/BIGOPHONE, *m.* Telephone. **Donner/filer/passer un coup de bigo(phone).** To phone. *N'oublie pas de me passer un coup de bigo demain.* "Don't forget to give me a ring tomorrow."

BILLARD, *m.* Billiards; billiard room, table. *C'est du billard.* "It's a cinch/snap." (Refers to easy-rolling balls, not the game itself). **Monter/passer au billard.** To undergo an operation. *Jean passe demain au billard mais il a le moral.* "John goes under the knife tomorrow, but he's in good spirits."

BIMÉTALLISTE, *m., hum.* Male bisexual (lit. "bimetallist" [advocate of gold and silver coinage]). *Line sait qu'il est ambidextre, bimétalliste mais elle pense que le mariage le changera.* "Line knows he swings both ways but she thinks marriage will change him." *Cf.* VOILE.

BIN'S/BINZ, *m.* **1.** Disorder. *Quel bin's dans son bureau!* "His office is a real mess." **2.** Complicated procedure. *C'est tout un binz pour arriver chez eux.* "It's a real hassle getting to their place."

BIQUE, *f.* Female goat. **Bique et bouc** (lit. "nanny and billy goat"). Active and passive homosexual. *En tôle il a appris à être bique et bouc.* "In jail he learned how to be a flip-flopper."

BIROUTE, *m.* Penis. *"Cette biroute, où avait-elle été avant?",* se demandait-elle. "'Where's this dick been before?' she wondered."

BISBROUILLE *f., Bel.* variant of **bisbille.** Quarrel. *Ils sont à nouveau en bisbrouille.* "They're on the outs again."

BISCOTOS, *m., pl.* Biceps. See ROULER LES BISCOTOS.

BISSER, 1. To repeat as an encore (**un bis**). *Sa nouvelle chanson fut cinq fois bissée.* "Her new song was encored five times." **2.** *Bel., student., sl.* To repeat a course. *Il m'a fallu bisser son cours de merde.* "I had to take his lousy course again."

BISTROUILLE or **BISTOUILLE,** *m.* **1.** Coffee laced with alcohol. **2.** Rotgut alcohol. **3.** (*Bel.* and *NE France*), s.t. valueless. *J'aime le* Irish Coffee *mais pas ce bistrouille.* "I like Irish coffee but not this cheap hooch." *Cf.* BIBINE; GNOLE.

BITE, *m.* = **BITUME.** See RASE-BITE.

BIT(T)E, *f.* Penis. *Raspoutine était archifier de sa maxi bite.* "Rasputin was very proud of his huge cock." See CON À...BITE; PEAU DE BITE; RENTRER... BRAS; SAC À BITES.

BITE À JEAN-PIERRE, *f.* Policeman's billy club (lit. "Jean-Pierre's dick"). *Dans la manif il a reçu un coup de bite à Jean-Pierre.* "He got hit by a policeman's billy club during the demonstration."

BITER. 1. To understand. *Je n'ai rien bité à ton histoire.* "I don't know what you're talking about." **2.** To have carnal knowledge of. *Le philosophe m'a bien bitée et je me sens pleine de sagesse.* "The philosopher gave me a good screwing and I feel full of wisdom." *Cf.* ENTRAVER.

BITONIAU/BITONIO, *m.* Thingamajig. *Il manque un bitonio à cette lampe.* "There's a whatsit missing in this lamp."

BITUME, *m.* Pavement. **Arpenter/faire/polir le bitume.** To be a streetwalker. *Elle a l'habitude d'arpenter le bitume de la rue d'Aboukir.* "She usually works Aboukir Street." See ARRONDISSEMENT À BITUME; RASE-BITE/BITUME.

BITURE, *f.* Bender. **Prendre une biture.** To tie one on. *Il a pris une telle biture qu'il ne pouvait pas conduire.* "He got so loaded he couldn't drive." See (À) TOUTE BARRE/BITURE.

BIZET = BARBEAU.

BIZUT(H), *m.* Freshman. *C'est un bizut et ne connaît pas les règles du bahut.* "He's a frosh and doesn't know the school's rules."

BIZUTAGE, *m.* Hazing. *Le censeur a essayé de supprimer le bizutage.* "The vice principal tried to stop hazing."

BIZUTER. To haze. *Quelques sadiques éprouvaient un plaisir à les bizuter.* "A few sadists took pleasure in hazing them."

BLABLATER. To babble on. *Personne n'écoutait mais il continuait de blablater.* "No one was listening but he kept rattling on."

BLAGUE, *f.* Joke; hoax. *C'est de la (haute) blague!* "That's a bunch of baloney!" See SANS BLAGUE!

BLAGUER. To joke. *Elle ne le prenait pas au sérieux car il aimait blaguer.* "She didn't take him seriously because he liked to kid around."

BLAIRER. To stand. *Elle ne peut pas me blairer, mais moi, je l'adore.* "She can't stand me, but I adore her."

BLANC LIME/BLANC LIMÉ = LIME/LIMÉ.

BLASE or **BLAZE,** *m.* **1.** Name; nickname (from **blason** "coat of arms"). *Au monastère il a pris un nouveau blase.* "He took a new monicker in the monastery." **2.** Nose; face. *Les flics m'ont cassé le blaze.* "The cops broke my schnozz."

BLÉ, *m.* Money; "bread" (lit. "wheat"). See FAUCHÉ (COMME LES BLÉS).

BLED, *m.* from Arabic. **1.** Remote place. *Il habite un bled perdu en Bretagne.* "He lives in the boonies in Brittany." **2.** Hometown. *Mon bled c'est Bordeaux.* "My hometown is Bordeaux."

BLÉDARD, -E *m., f., youth, cités.* Not-yet-assimilated immigrant from rural NW Africa. *Ces blédards essaient quand même d'améliorer leur français.* "All the same, those yokels are trying to improve their Fr."

BLÉDARD, -E, *youth, cités.* Old fashioned, outdated. See RINGARD.

BLÈME, *m.* Problem (from **problème. Blême** is literary for "pallid, wan"). *Y a blème?* "Is there a problem?"

BLINDÉ, -E. 1. Thick-skinned (lit. "armor-plated"). *Assez de baratin; je suis blindé.* "Enough soft talk. I'm impervious to it." **2.** Drunk. *Je chante quand je suis blindée.* "I sing when I'm drunk."

BLING-BLING. Flashy, gaudy. *Il mène une campagne très people, très bling-bling.* "He's waging a very glitzy, media-hyped campaign." (BRILLE-BRILLE is a linguistically "brilliant" alternative created in Que.)

BLOBLOS, *f., pl.* Ample, pendulous breasts. *Il est obnubilé par les nanas à bloblos.* "He's hung up on broads with big boobs." *Cf.* LOLOS.

BLOC, *m.* Station house jail. *Après la bagarre de cette nuit, il a passé la nuit au bloc.* "After the brawl, he spent the night in the jug." **Gonflé à bloc.** To be full of beans. *Elles étaient parties gonflées à bloc au rallye mais n'ont pas gagné.* "They were raring to go when they left for the car rally, but they didn't win."

BLONDE, *f.* **1.** Light (colored) beer. *Tu bois une blonde ou une brune?* "Will you have a light or dark beer?" **2.** *Que.* Girlfriend. *Une seule blonde ne suffit pas à Luc qui aime passer de l'une à l'autre, blonde, brune, ou rouquine.* "One girlfriend isn't enough for Luc, who likes to alternate blondes, brunettes, and redheads."

BLONDASSE, *f. Que, pej.* Dumb broad, nasty girl. *Elle t'a joué un sâle coup, ta blondasse.* "Your little bitch played a dirty trick on you."

BLOUSER. To swindle. *Les promoteurs les ont blousés.* "The property developers took them for a ride."

BOBARD, *m.* Lie; tall story. *Tu ne racontes que des bobards!* "You're talking a load of bull."

BOBÈCHE, *f.*/**BOBÉCHON,** *m.* Head. See (SE) MONTER.

BOBINE, *m.* Face (lit. "reel"; "bobbin"). *Tu en fais une drôle de bobine.* "You've got an odd/sour look about you."

BOBO, *m.* **1.** Superficial wound (children's lang.). *Maman embrassait nos bobos pour les soigner.* "Mother kissed our boo-boos to heal them." **2.** Young, affluent individual with artistic and intellectual interests (from **bourgeois** and **bohèmien**). *Des bobos parisiens ont envahi notre petit village.* "Artsy Parisian yuppies have invaded our little village."

BOBONNE, *f., pej.* Wife. *Ma bobonne ne me comprend pas.* "My wife doesn't understand me."

BOCAL, *m.* Head (lit. "jar"). *Tu n'as rien dans le bocal.* "You've got nothing between the ears." See AGITÉ DU BOCAL.

BOCHE, *m., pej.* German. *Pépé nie avoir été collabo et râle contre les Boches, et les Italboches aussi.* "Grandpa denies having been a collaborator and complains about the krauts, and the wops too."

BŒUF CAROTTES, *pl.* Police Department of Internal Affairs (*Inspection générale des services*). *Les bœuf carottes investiguent les ripoux.* "The Dept. of Internal Affairs is investigating the crooked cops."

BOF! Big deal! So what? Who cares? **La génération bof.** The what-do-I-care generation. *Mon fils cherche à s'engager. Il n'est pas du tout de la bof génération.* "My son is looking for commitment. He's no member of the 'What's it to me?' generation."

BOGE, *m., f.* Bourgeois. *Il était plein de mépris pour les boges.* "He was full of contempt for the bourgeois."

BOIS, *m.* Wood. **Ne pas être de bois.** Not to be made of wood. *Je ne suis pas de bois!* "I have feelings too." **Chèque en bois.** Rubber check. *Bon dieu de bois! Il m'a filé un chèque en bois.* "Jumpin' Jehosophat! His check bounced." See BON…BOIS; FLÛTE; GUEULE DE BOIS; LANGUE DE BOIS.

BOL, *m.* **1.** Bowl. **Prendre un bol d'air.** To get some fresh air. *Il me fallait prendre un bon bol d'air après la réunion politique.* "I needed some good fresh air after the political meeting." **2.** Luck. See COUP DE BOL. **3.** Posterior. **En avoir ras le bol.** To be fed up. *J'en ai ras le bol de toutes tes minauderies.* "I've had it up to here with your affected mannerisms." **4.** Motorcyclist's helmet. *Pour l'épate, il se balade avec son bol sur la tête.* "To impress people he walks around with his helmet on his head."

BONBON, *m.* **1.** Candy. **Coûter bonbon.** To be expensive. *Ta petite fantaisie, ça m'a coûté bonbon!* "Your little whim cost me a pretty penny!" **2.** Hard drugs. *Tu mourras d'une overdose si tu bouffes tant de bonbons.* "You'll OD if you keep consuming all those drugs." **3.** Clitoris. *J'avais le bonbon très excité.* "My clitoris was very excited." See RAS LE BONBON. **4.** Testicles. **Casser les bonbons.** To annoy. *Ils nous cassent les bonbons avec leurs drames familiaux.* "They bug us with their domestic dramas." See CASSE-BONBONS. BON CHIC, BON GENRE. See BCBG **1.**

BONBOUR. Backslang of **Bourbon.** *L'oncle Eugène se fout des beurs et rêve de restaurer les Bonbours.* "Uncle Eugene doesn't care about Ar.-Fr. people and dreams of restoring the Bourbons."

BON DIEU DE BOIS!/BON DIEU DE BOIS DE SAPERLOTTE!/BON SANG DE BOIS!/BON SANG DE BON DIEU DE BOIS! *Euph., hum.* Goodness gracious! Saints alive! God Almighty! *"Bon dieu de bois! Ces maudits enfants de chœur ont à nouveau bu tout le vin de messe," s'écria le curé.* "'Saints alive! Those damned altar boys have drunk all the communion wine again!' the curate cried out." See BOIS; SAPERLIPOPETTE.

BONDIEUSERIE, *f.* **1.** Ostentatious piety. *Ma grand-tante exagère un peu avec sa bondieuserie.* "My great-aunt overdoes it a bit with her show of religiosity." **2.** Kitchy ecclesiastical knickknack. *On a acheté de l'eau bénite du robinet, des assiettes où les yeux s'ouvrent et se ferment,* *et d'autres bondieuseries.* "We bought holy water from the tap, plates with eyes that open and close, and other religious trinkets."

BONHOMME, *m.* **1.** Husband. *Mon bonhomme va bien.* "My husband is well." **2.** Guy. *Qu'est-ce qu'il nous veut, ce bonhomme?* "What does that guy want from us?" **3.** Erect penis. *Il lui courait après, en tenant son bonhomme.* "He ran after her holding his stiff dick." See CHEMIN.

BONICHE, *f., pej.* Servant. *Tu me prends pour ta boniche?* "Do you think I'm your slave?"

BONIMENT, *m.* Sales talk. *Arrête tes boniments!* "Cut the crap!" **Faire du boniment.** To feed someone a line. *Je ne te fais pas de boniment; t'es la femme de ma vie!* "I'm not handing you a line; you're the love of my life."

BONJOUR LES DÉGATS! That means trouble!

BONNE BOURRE! See BOURRE.

BONNE FEMME, *f.* **1.** Wife. *J'arriverai avec ma bonne femme.* "The missus and I will be coming." **2.** Woman, *pej.,* unless accompanied by an *adj.* expressing admiration, such as **une grande bonne femme; une bonne femme charmante.** *Je ne peux pas la blairer, cette bonne femme.* "I can't stand that broad." *Cf.* REMÈDE.

BONNE POIRE = POIRE 3.

BONNES FEMMES, *f., pl.* Females. *Les bonnes femmes sont parties faire les boutiques aujourd'hui.* "The ladies went out shopping today."

BONNET D'ÉVÊQUE, *m.* Rump (fowl); the pope's or parson's nose; part that went over the fence last (lit. "bishop's bonnet"). *Tatie, très croyante et pratiquante, appelle le croupion parfois "le sot l'y laisse," mais jamais "bonnet d'êveque."* "Auntie's a believing churchgoer and sometimes calls it 'the part that went over the fence last,' but never 'the pope's nose.'" *Cf.* AS DE PIQUE **1.**

BONSHOMMES, *m., pl.* Men. *Les bonshommes sont partis à la pêche.* "The men have gone fishing."

BORDEL, *m.* **1.** Brothel. *Lautrec était comme chez lui dans les bordels.* "Toulouse-Lautrec felt right at home in whorehouses." **2.** Disorder. *Sa piaule, c'est un véritable bordel.* "His pad is a real shambles."

BORDEL!/BORDEL DE MERDE! Damn it! Damn it to hell! *Bordel! Tu m'as fait raté mon train.* "Shit! You made me miss my train." See NOM...BORDEL DE MERDE!; PUTAIN...DE BORDEL.

BORDÉLIQUE. Messy. *Fais un effort pour être moins bordélique.* "Try to be less messy."

BORDS, *m., pl.* Edges. **Sur les bords.** Somewhat. *Il est un peu cinglé sur les bords.* "He's a bit cracked (but not over the line)."

BORGNE, *m.* Penis (lit. "one-eyed person"). **Étrangler le borgne.** To masturbate (lit. "to choke the one-eyed man," a reference to the meatus (urinary opening). *J'étrangle souvent le borgne, mais il est increvable.* "I keep strangling (whacking off) the one eyed monster, but he's indestructible."

BOSSE, *f.* **1.** Hump; bump. **Rouler sa bosse.** To knock about; globe-trot. *Nous avons pas mal roulé notre bosse.* "We've done a lot of traveling." **2.** Flair. **Avoir la bosse de qch.** To have a knack for s.t. *Elle a la bosse des maths.* "She has a flair for math."

BOSSER. To work hard. *Il faut que tu bosses si tu veux finir à l'heure.* "You'll have to hustle if you want to finish on time."

BOTTE, *f.* Boot. See CIRER LES BOTTES; LÈCHE-BOTTES; TOMBER EN BOTTE(S).

BOTTER. To get a kick out of (lit. "to kick"). *Le champagne ne le botte pas. Ça le botte—quand sa dominatrice le botte—il est maso.* "He gets no kick from champagne. He gets his kicks when his dominatrix kicks him—he's a masochist."

BOUC. See BIQUE.

BOUCHÉ, -E. Stupid (lit. "blocked"). **Bouché à l'émeri.** Really stupid. *Il reste bouché à l'émeri malgré toutes les explications.* "He's still as thick as ever despite all the explanations."

BOUCHÉE, *f.* Mouthful. **Mettre les bouchées doubles.** To double one's efforts. *Il va falloir mettre les bouchées doubles.* "We're going to have to go all out."

BOUCHER. To cork; stop up. **En boucher un coin à qn.** To astound s.o. *Elle m'en a bouché un coin par sa rapidité d'agir.* "She floored me by acting so rapidly."

BOUCHON, *m.* **1.** Cork. **Mettre un bouchon à qn.** To shut s.o. up. *Mets-toi un bouchon!* "Put a lid on it!" **Pousser le bouchon (un peu/trop loin).** To exaggerate. *Il pousse toujours le bouchon trop loin en parlant de ses amours.* "He always lays it on thick when talking of his love life." See PRENDRE…DU BOUCHON. **2.** Youngest child. *Papa dorlote son petit bouchon.* "Pop pampers the baby of the family."

BOUCHONNEUSE, *f.* Prostitute who encourages men to drink. **Bouchon** means "cork" and her function is less to provide sex than to keep the corks popping. *"Tu me paies un coup, chéri?" me demandait-elle. J'savais pas que c'était un bar à bouchonneuses.* "'Buy me a drink, sweetheart?' she asked. I didn't know it was a B-girl bar."

BOUCLARÈS. Closed; off limits. *Ce bar est bouclarès.* "This bar is off limits."

BOUCLARÈS! "Shut up!" "Put a lid on it!"

BOUCLER. 1. To buckle. **La boucler.** To keep one's mouth shut. *Tu vas la boucler!* "Will you keep your trap shut!" **Boucler la boucle.** To come full circle; loop the loop. *On voulait revenir par Paris pour boucler la boucle.* "We returned via Paris to make it a round trip." *C'est une affaire bouclée.* "It's a done deal." **2.** To imprison. *J'avais trop d'alcool dans le sang; ils m'ont bouclé et retiré mon permis.* "I had too high a blood alcohol level; they locked me up and took away my driving license." **Être bouclé**

chez soi/à la maison. To be cooped up at home. *Mes parents m'ont bouclé toute la semaine.* "My parents grounded me all week."

BOUDIN, *m.* **1.** Blood sausage. **S'en aller/finir/partir/ tourner en eau de boudin.** To flop. *Tous mes efforts sont partis en eau de boudin.* "All my efforts went down the drain." **2.** Sulking (pun on **bouder** [to sulk]). **Faire du/son boudin.** To pout; sulk. *Oui, fais ton boudin, tu n'auras rien de moi.* "Go ahead and sulk—you'll get nothing from me." **3.** Fat girl. *Il préfère un boudin à une maigrichonne.* "He prefers a plump girl to a thin one." **4.** An easy piece/lay. *Yvette n'est pas le boudin que tu crois.* "Yvette isn't the pushover you take her for."

BOUFFER. To eat. **Bouffer du…** To be anti, very hostile to, as in **bouffer du curé/juif.** To be anticlerical/anti-semitic. *Après avoir quitté la prêtrise, il bouffait du curé.* "After leaving the priesthood, he became anticlerical."

BOUFFER DE LA BITE. See CON À…BITE.

(SE) BOUFFER LE NEZ. To quarrel. *On ne peut les laisser ensemble sans qu'il se bouffent le nez.* "You can't leave them alone without their getting into each other's hair/at each other's throats."

BOUFFEUR, -EUSE DE BITE, *m., f.* Fellator, fellatrix. *Gorge-Profonde était une bouffeuse de bites de renommée mondiale.* "Deep-Throat was a world-class cocksucker."

BOUFFI. Puffy. *Tu l'as dit, bouffi!* "You said it, Eddy!" "You can say that again, Henry!" (**Bouffi** serves merely as a rhyming intensifier.)

BOUGNOUL(E), *pej.* Dark-skinned foreigner. *Il est raciste et plein de mépris pour ceux qu'il appelle "bougnoules".* "He's a racist and full of contempt for those he calls 'niggers.'"

BOUGRE, *m.* Individual. *C'est un bon/mauvais/pauvre/ bougre.* "He's a good/rotten/miserable guy/sort/fellow."

BOUGRE! Damn (it)!

BOUGRE D'ÂNE/IMBÉCILE. "You jackass!/idiot!"

BOUGRE DE TEMPS! Rotten weather!

BOUGREMENT. Extremely. *Elle est bougrement sexy.* "She's extremely sexy."

BOUGRESSE, *f.* **1.** Female. *Sa bougresse est hommasse.* "His broad's butchy." **2.** Bitch. *Je ne peux la blairer, la bougresse.* "I can't stand that bitch."

BOUI-BOUI/BOUIBOUIS, *m.* **1.** Low dive. *Pour se changer les idées le millionaire aimait se soûler dans les bouibouis.* "For a change of scenery, the millionaire liked getting drunk in low dives." **2.** Brothel. *Les filles de ce boui-boui ne sont pas très alléchantes.* "The girls in this whorehouse aren't very enticing."

BOUIF, *m.* Shoemaker. *Je cherchais un bouif pour mon talon cassé.* "I looked for a shoemaker for my broken heel."

BOUILLAVE or **BOUYAVE.** *f.* Sex (from *Romany*). *Je suis en mal de bouillave.* "I'm really horny."

BOUILLE, *f.* **1.** Face. **Avoir une bonne bouille.** To have a pleasing face. *Il ne peut pas être dangereux, ce mec; il a une bonne bouille.* "That guy can't be dangerous; he's got a friendly face." **2.** Naïve individual; potential mark for a swindler. *L'arnaqueur savait où trouver les bonnes bouilles.* "The con man knew where to find likely marks." *Cf.* POIRE.

BOUILLON, *m.* **1.** Water (lit. "broth"). **Boire/prendre un bouillon.** To go under. *Il ne savait pas gérer son commerce et a pris un sacré bouillon.* "He didn't know how to manage his business and went flat broke." **2.** Poor restaurant. *Il y a toujours du monde dans ce bouillon.* "This greasy spoon's always crowded." **3.** Criminal's hideout. *La police les a enfin pris dans leur bouillon.* "The police finally captured them in their hideout."

BOUILLONNER. To have many unsold copies (lit. "to bubble"; "boil"). *Ce magazine bouillonne un max.* "That magazine has huge quantities of unsold copies."

BOUL', *m.* from **boulevard**. *On se retrouvait toujours aux restos du Boul' Mich'.* "We always met in restaurants on the Boulevard Saint-Michel."

BOULE, *f.* Head (lit. "bowling ball; billiard ball"). **Avoir les boules. 1.** To be ill at ease/angry. *Ça se voyait qu'il avait les boules.* "It was obvious he was upset." **2.** To be very frightened. *J'avais les boules quand les flics m'ont demandé mes papiers.* "I was scared shitless/witless when the cops asked for my ID." **Avoir la boule à zéro.** To be totally bald. *Il a la boule à zéro et porte une perruque.* "He's completely bald and wears a rug." See PERDRE…BOULE. **3.** *Bel.* Candy. *Emma s'empiffre de boules devant la télé.* "Emma watches TV and stuffs herself with bonbons."

BOULER. To roll. **Envoyer bouler qn.** To tell s.o. to get lost. *Je ne pouvais plus le voir, je l'ai envoyé bouler.* "I couldn't stand the sight of him anymore and sent him packing."

BOULES, *f., pl., Que.* Large breasts. *Il ne cesse de la peloter, boules et plotte comprises!* "He never stops pawing her, boobs and pussy, everything!"

BOULETTE, *f.* Blunder (lit. "pellet"). *J'ai fait une boulette en disant avoir vu son mari avec une fille.* "I made a blunder when I said I'd seen her husband with a girl."

BOULEVARD DES ALLONGÉS = JARDIN DES ALLONGÉS.

BOULONNER. To slave away at a job (lit. "to bolt"). *Je boulonne toute la journée.* "I slave away all day."

BOULOT, *m.* Job. **Au boulot!** "Let's get to work!" **Être boulot-boulot.** To be hard-working. *Il n'est pas baisant le mec; trop boulot-boulot.* "That guy's no fun; too much of a workaholic."

BOULOTTER. 1. To eat. *On n'avait rien à boulotter à la maison.* "We had nothing to eat in the house." **2.** To squander. *Le marin a boulotté sa paye avec les filles du port.* "The sailor blew his wages on the girls in the port."

BOUM, *f.* Young people's party. *On a passé des disques de Trenet à la boum.* "We played Charles Trenet records at the bash." See SURBOUM.

BOUMER. To be in full swing; go well. **Ça boume?** "Everything going OK?"

BOUQUET. Bouquet. **C'est le bouquet!** That's the limit/ last straw; that takes the cake!

BOUQUIN, *m.* Book. *Elle traîne ses bouquins partout.* "She carries her books around with her everywhere."

BOUQUINER. To read. *Elle bouquine dans le métro.* "She reads in the subway."

BOURDE, *f.* Blunder. **Faire une bourde.** To put one's foot in it. *Tu as fait une bourde en parlant de son ancien amant.* "You put your foot in it when you talked about her former lover."

BOURDON, *m.* Bumblebee. **Avoir le bourdon.** To feel depressed. *Toutes les fois qu'il part elle a le bourdon.* "Every time he leaves, she has the blues."

BOURGE, *m., f., pej., abbr. of* **bourgeois.** The middle-class, the affluent. *"À bas les bourges!," criaient les cocos.* "'Down with the privileged,' cried the Commies."

BOURGEOISE, *f.* Wife (lit. "middle-class woman"). *Ma bourgoise ne veut pas aller.* "The missus doesn't want to go." See BAISER À LA BOURGEOISE.

BOURLINGUER. To be a globetrotter. *Il ne s'est jamais marié car il aimait trop bourlinguer.* "He never got married because he was too fond of traveling around."

BOURRATIF, -IVE. Filling. *Je cale; ce pain est trop bourratif.* "I'm not eating any more; this bread is too filling."

BOURRE, *f.* Stuffing (upholstery); wad of hair. **De première bourre.** First rate. *Tout ce qu'il nous a montré était de première bourre.* "Everything he showed us was of excellent quality." **Être à la bourre.** To be pressed for time. *Je ne peux plus attendre; je suis à la bourre.* "I can't wait any longer; I'm in a hurry." **Bonne bourre!**

"Give her a good plugging; have fun!" **Être en pleine bourre.** To be in top shape. *Ce grand tombeur se dit être en pleine bourre mais il me laisse insatisfaite.* "That great ladykiller claims he's in top form but he leaves me unsatisfied." See (SE) TIRER LA BOURRE.

BOURRE, *m.* Policeman. *Ce con de bourre insistait pour me faire souffler dans le ballon.* "That idiot cop insisted on my taking a breath test."

BOURRÉ, -E. Soused. *Il est revenu de la discothèque complètement bourré.* "He came back dead drunk from the discotheque."

BOURRE-MOU, *m.* Hogwash. *Tu ne racontes que du bourre-mou.* "Everything you're saying is a lot of hogwash."

BOURRER. 1. To have sexually (lit. "to stuff"). *Les routiers avaient envie de bourrer la nouvelle serveuse du resto routier.* "The truck drivers wanted to plug the new waitress at the truck stop restaurant." **2.** To beat up. *Les voyous l'avaient bourré de coups.* "The thugs really worked him over." **3.** To accelerate; drive recklessly. *Luc est un chauffard et n'aime que bourrer.* "Luke's a bad driver and just likes to tear up the road."

BOURRER LA GUEULE À QN. To bash s.o.'s face in. *Ferme-la ou je te bourre la gueule.* "Shut your trap or I'll knock your block off."

BOURRER LE CRÂNE/MOU/LA CAISSE À QN. To feed s.o. a bunch of baloney. *Tu veux me faire accroire ça? Va bourrer le mou de qn. d'autre.* "You want me to swallow that? Go try your line on s.o. else."

(SE) BOURRER. 1. To make fat profits. *Il a profité de notre misère pour se bourrer.* "He took advantage of our poverty to make a bundle." **2.** To get plastered. *Si tu me montrais un peu plus de tendresse, je me bourrerais moins.* "If you showed me a little more tenderness, I'd get soused less."

BOURRIQUE, *f.* Pig-headed individual (lit. "donkey"). *Il est têtu comme une bourrique.* "He's as stubborn as a mule."

BOUSEUX, -EUSE, *m., f., pej.* Yokel (from **bouse,** "cow dung"). *Je ne peux plus blairer ce bled, ni ses bouseux.* "I can't stand this hick town or its rubes any more."

BOUSILLAGE, *m.* Tattooing (lit. "screw up"). *Admire mon dernier bousillage!* "Admire my new tattoo!"

BOUSILLE, *f.* = BOUSILLAGE.

BOUSILLER. 1. To botch. *En bricolant ma radio, tu l'as bousillée.* "You screwed up my radio when you tinkered with it." **2.** To kill. *Il a bousillé ses complices.* "He rubbed out his accomplices."

BOUSILLEUR, -EUSE, *m., f.* Tattooer (lit. "bungler"). *Le bousilleur attendait les marins pétés.* "The tattoo artist waited for the drunken sailors."

BOUSOUX = BOUSEUX.

BOUSSOLE, *f.* Compass. *Qu'as-tu fait de ta boussole?* "You're losing it (control, judgement, sense of direction)." See PERDRE LE NORD.

BOUSTIFAILLE, *f.* Food. *Quand est-ce-qu'elle arrive, la boustifaille?* "When's the grub coming?"

BOUSTIFAILLER. To chow down; guzzle. *Arrête de boustifailler et tu seras moins gros.* "Stop eating and drinking so much and you won't be so fat."

BOUSTIFFE, *f.* = BOUSTIFAILLE.

BOUT, *m.* End. **Tenir le bon bout.** To be close to succeeding. *Nous tenons le bon bout.* "We're on the right track." **En connaître un bout.** To be well informed. *Sur le jazz elle en connaît un bout.* "She's knows a thing or two about jazz."

BOUTANCHE, *f.* Bottle. *La boutanche, on va se la faire à nous deux.* "The two of us will split this bottle."

BOUTEROLE, *f.* Church. *La basilique de Montmartre est une sacrée bouterole!* "The basilica of Montmartre is some church!"

BOUTIQUE, *m.* **1.** Shop. **Faire boutique son cul,** *Fr. Caribbean sl.* To prostitute o.s. *Si tu ne me donnes pas le fric je* *ferai boutique mon cul.* "If you don't give me the money, I'll sell my ass." **2.** Male/female genitalia. **Montrer sa boutique.** To expose one's genitals; flash. *Quand ce satyr lui a montré sa boutique, ma grand-tante est tombée dans les pommes.* "When that flasher exposed himself to my great-aunt she passed out."

BOUTON, *m.* **1.** Button. See CIRER. **2.** Pimple. *Elle le trouve beau, malgré ses boutons.* She finds him handsome despite his pimples. **3.** Clitoris. *Il n'a qu'à appuyer sur mon bouton, et je mouille.* "All he has to do is press my love button (stimulate my clit) and I get hot." See ASTIQUER LE BOUTON.

BOUTON D'AMOUR/BOUTON DE ROSE = BOUTON 3. *Cf.* BONBON 3; HARICOT; PÉPITE; TIRE-BOUTON.

BOUTON DE ROSE = BOUTON 3.

BOXON, *m.* = BORDEL.

BOYAU, *m.* Guts. **Avoir le boyau de la rigolade.** To have the giggles/a laughing fit. *Nous avions tous le boyau de la rigolade.* "We all couldn't stop laughing." See TORD-BOYAUX; (SE) TORDRE LES BOYAUX.

BOYAUTANT. Sidesplitting. *C'est boyautant de le voir en trav.* "It's a howl to see him in drag."

(SE) BOYAUTER. To laugh uproariously. *On s'est boyauté pendant son sketch.* "We busted a gut laughing during her sketch."

BRAGUETTE, *f.* **1.** Fly (pants). See ESCALADEUSE DE BRAGUETTE; PÉTER...BRAGUETTE. **2.** Prostitute who works in doorways. *Quand je suis pressé, je m'envoie une braguette, d'ailleurs je ne peux pas me payer une grande horizontale.* "When I'm pressed for time, I get it off with an upright whore; besides, I can't afford a horizontal one."

BRAISE, *f.* Money (lit. "embers"). *Peux-tu me filer de la braise?* "Can you let me have some dough."

BRAISEUX, -EUSE. Wealthy. *Elle n'avait d'yeux que pour les braiseux.* "She was only interested in rich guys."

BRANCHÉ, -E. 1. Up to date; trendy. *Les piercés se croient branchés.* "People who've had piercing (forehead, and so on) think they're very cool." **2.** To be in the know. *Elle est branchée opéra.* "She's a knowledgeable opera buff."

BRANCHER. 1. To connect; plug in. *Le hockey sur glace, ça le branche.* "Ice hockey really turns him on." **2.** To acquaint s.o. with s.t. *Il faut que tu me branches sur ce sujet.* "You'll have to familiarize me with that subject." **3.** To pick up. *Il l'a branchée dans la rue.* "He picked her up on the street."

BRANCHITUDE, *f.* The smart set. *La branchitude a débranché de cette boîte.* "The hip, trendy people gave up on that club."

(SE) BRANCHER. To take up; get interested in. *Mamie s'est branchée sur l'informatique.* "Grandma's gotten interested in computer science."

BRANDON, *m.* Penis (lit. "firebrand"). *Il avait le brandon en l'air.* "His dick was up."

BRANLAGE, *m.* Masturbation. *Il ne pensait qu'au branlage.* "All he thought about was beating the meat."

BRANLÉE, *f.* Severe beating/defeat. *Il a reçu une de ces branlées!* "He got one hell of a beating!"

BRANLER. 1. To do. **Qu'est que tu branles?** "Just what are you doing?" **N'en avoir rien à branler,** *abbr.* **R.A.B.** Not to give a damn. *Tes ébats amoureux, je n'en ai rien à branler.* "I couldn't care less about your love life." **2.** Masturbate. *Je l'ai branlé pour avoir la paix.* "I jerked him off so he'd leave me in peace."

(SE) BRANLER. 1. To masturbate. *Il se branlait en reluquant du porno.* "He whacked off while ogling porn." **2. Se les branler/se branler les couilles.** Not to do a goddamned thing (lit. "to jerk off one's balls"). *Pendant que je bosse, toi, tu te les branles!* "While I slave away, you don't do a fuckin' thing."

(S'EN) BRANLER. Not to care. *De tes sornettes, je m'en branle!* "I don't give a damn about your stupid stories!"

BRANLERIE, *f.* Empty dreams. *Tu t'adonnes trop à la branlerie.* "You indulge in too many idle fancies."

BRANLETTE, *f.* Masturbation. *Plutôt la branlette que le SIDA!* "Better to consult Dr. Jerkoff than to get AIDS!"

BRANLEUR, *m.* **1.** Masturbator. *Les deux branleurs aimaient se masturber de concert.* "The two meat beaters liked to whack off together." **2.** Good-for-nothing boy. *Je refuse que tu sortes avec ce petit branleur.* "I refuse to let you go out with that bum."

BRANLEUSE, *f.* **1.** Very young girl. *Je ne m'intéresse pas aux branleuses.* "I'm not interested in very young girls." **2.** Masturbatrix. *C'est une branleuse extra.* "She gives a great hand job."

BRANLOCHER = BRANLER.

BRANQUE/BRANQUIGNOL/BRANQUIGNOLLE, *m., f.* Crazy person. *Tu me prends pour un branquignol?* "Do you take me for a nut?"

BRAQUEMARD, *m.* Penis. *Je connais des braquemards de toute taille.* "I'm familiar with cocks of every size."

BRAQUER. To commit armed robbery. **1.** *Le supermarché a été braqué.* "The supermarket was held up." **2.** Barge in on; annoy. *Tu aurais pu me bigophoner au lieu de me braquer.* "You could've given me a call instead of dropping in unannounced."

BRAQUOS, *m.* Penis. **Avoir le braquos.** To have an erection. *Il avait le braquos en pensant à elle.* "He had a hard-on thinking of her."

BRAS, *m.* Arm. **Faire le bras d'honneur.** To give someone the finger. *La bagarre a commencé quand il a fait le bras d'honneur à son rival.* "The brawl began when he gave the finger to his rival."

BRASSER DE L'AIR = DÉPLACER DE L'AIR.

BREDOUILLE. Empty-handed. *Il voulait faire fortune mais il est revenu bredouille.* "He wanted to make a fortune but came back with nothing."

BRIC, *m.* Brothel. *C'est un bric classe!* "That's a first-class whorehouse!"

BRICOLEUR, -EUSE, *m., f.* **1.** Handyman; do-it-yourselfer. *Ce bricoleur ne veut pas être déclaré.* "That handyman doesn't want his work to be declared (for taxes)." **2.** Incompetent worker. *Ce n'est qu'une équipe de bricoleurs.* "They're just a bunch of amateurs."

BRICOLO, *m., abbr.* of **bricoleur.**

BRIFFER. To eat. *J'ai très faim; allons briffer!* "I'm very hungry; let's go eat."

BRILLE-BRILLE. See BLING-BLING.

BRILLER. To have an orgasm (lit. "to shine"). *Il est le seul à me faire briller.* "He's the only one who makes me come."

BRINDEZINGUE. Crazy. *Il nous a raconté des histoires brindezingues.* "He told us nutty stories."

BRINGUE, *f.* Binge. *Aux vacances de Pâques on fera la bringue en Floride.* "During Easter vacation we'll have a ball in Florida."

BRIQUE, *f.* Brick. **Bouffer des briques.** To have nothing to eat. *Si tu ne trouves pas de boulot on bouffera des briques.* "If you don't get a job we'll starve." See (NE PAS) CASSER DES BRIQUES.

BRONZE, *m.* Turd. **Couler/mouler un bronze** (lit. "to cast a bronze [statue]"). To defecate. *Il lisait le canard en coulant son bronze.* "He read the newspaper while taking a crap."

BROSSE, *f.* **1.** Drunkeness (lit. "brush"). *T'as pris encore une brosse?—Non, j'suis pas du tout en brosse!* "Are you drunk again?"—"No. I'm definitely not drunk!" **2.** Passive homosexual in prison. *"Si tu ne peux pas être avec celle que tu aimes, aime celui avec tu es,"* disait la *brosse.* " 'If you can't be with the one you love, love the one you're with,' said the jailhouse queen."

BROSSER. 1. To copulate (lit. "to brush"). *Brosse la bien!* "Give her a good fucking!" **2.** To thrash. *La bande l'a brossé.* "The gang beat him up."

BROUTER LE CRESSON/GAZON/LA FRISÉE/PELOUSE/TOUFFE. To practice cunnilingus (lit. "to graze the watercress/grass/curly endive/lawn/tuft"). *Il bande peu mais broute à merveille le cresson.* "He rarely gets it up but he's great at muff diving."

BROUTER LA TIGE. To fellate (lit. "to nibble on the stalk"). *Elle rêvait de brouter tige après tige.* "She dreamed of sucking one cock after another."

BROUTEUSE, *f.* Lesbian. *Les brouteuses aiment se brouter le cresson.* "Dykes like to eat hair pie." *Cf.* PELOUSARDE.

BUBART. Backslang of **BARBU.**

BÛCHE, *f.* Log. See PRENDRE/RAMASSER...BÛCHE.

BÛCHER. To fell trees. **Bûcher un examen.** To cram for an exam. *Elle a réussi son bac sans bûcher.* "She passed her high school exam without having to cram for it."

BUFFET, *m.* Belly (lit. "sideboard"; "buffet"). **Avoir un bébé dans le buffet.** To be pregnant. *J'avais un bébé dans le buffet quand il m'a planquée.* "I had s.t. in the oven when he ditched me." **En avoir dans le buffet.** To have guts/balls. *Il est super, ce mec; il en a dans le buffet.* "That guy's terrific; he's got guts."

BULLE, *f.* Bubble. See COINCER LA BULLE.

BULLER. To loaf. *Il n'aime que buller.* "All he wants to do is hang out."

BURETTE, *f.* **1.** Face (lit. "cruet"). *Quel plaisir revoir ta burette souriante!* "I'm really glad to see your smiling face." **2.** Penis. *Le cureton inspectait la burette de l'enfant de chœur.* "The priest checked out the altar boy's dick."

BURETTES, *f., pl.* Testicles. **Vider les burettes.** To ejaculate (lit. "to empty the cruets"). *Il avait besoin de se vider les burettes.* "He needed to gets his rocks off."

BURNÉ. Large-testicled. *Il était burné et ça se voyait.* "It was obvious that he had big balls."

BURNES, *f., pl.* Testicles. **Casser les burnes à qn.** To be a ball buster. *Tu me casses les burnes!* "You're a real pain in the neck/ass." See CASSE-BURNES.

BUTER. To bump off, do in (lit. "to stumble; score a soccer goal"). *La pègre l'a buté.* "The mob rubbed him out."

BUVABLE. Tolerable (lit. "drinkable"). *Il n'est pas buvable, ce mec.* "That guy's unbearable."

BYZANCE, Byzantium. **Être Byzance!,** youth. To be terrific/the berries (poss. associated with **aisance, plaisance,** and so on, rather than anything Byzantine, such as icons, iconoclasts, corruption, conspiracies, scholars, violence—quite the opposite of "être Byzance!") *Le soleil brillait, les filles m'aimaient. Ah, c'était Byzance!* "The sun was shining, the girls loved me. Ah, that was really living!"

ÇA ARRACHE! See ARRACHER.

ÇA BAIGNE! See BAIGNER.

ÇA CHIE! "What a mess!" See ÇA VA CHIER.

ÇA COINCE! What a stink!

ÇA COLLE, ANATOLE? "How's tricks, Dick?" "Everything OK, Kay?"

ÇA M'INTERPELLE!, See INTERPELLER.

ÇA S'ARROSE! "That calls for a drink!"

ÇA TE LA COUPE! "Top that if you can! That leaves you speechless, doesn't it?"

ÇA VA BARDER = ÇA VA CHAUFFER!

ÇA VA CHAUFFER! Sparks will fly. *Les étudiants sont descendus dans la rue. Ça va chauffer!* "The students are demonstrating in the streets. Things are going to heat up!"

ÇA VA CHERCHER DANS... To add up to approximately.... *Ça va chercher dans les combien, tous ces meubles?* "About how much money is all that furniture going to cost?"

ÇA VA CHIER! "The shit's going to hit the fan!"

ÇA Y EST! "That's it! That's settled! That's done!"

CABANE, *f.* **1.** Ramshackle house; small outbuilding (such as a doghouse). **Faire de la cabane.** To be a burglar.

Faire une cabane. To do a burglary job. *Mon frangin il a fait de la cabane toujours seul, mais fera une prochaine cabane à l'aide de complices.* "He's always done his breaking and entering alone, but he'll do his next job with accomplices." See ATTIGER LA CABANE. **2.** Jail. *Son frangin est toujours en cabane.* "Her brother's still in stir."

CABANE À LAPINS, *f.* Shack. *Je n'aimerais pas habiter leur cabane à lapins.* "I wouldn't like to live in that dump of theirs."

CABANON, *m.* **1.** Provençal cottage. *Le week-end on quitte Marseille pour le cabanon—c'est toute notre vie.* "Week-ends we leave Marseilles for our country cottage—that's our whole life." **2.** Loony bin. *Ton oncle est bon pour le cabanon.* "Your uncle's ready for the nuthouse."

CÂBLÉ, -E. Être câblé. To be hip; trendy (lit. "to have cable TV"). *Nous ne sommes ni branchés, ni câblés: ce ne sont que les valeurs éternelles qui nous intéressent.* "We're neither with it nor up-to-date; we're interested only in eternal values."

CABOCHE, *m.* Head. **Avoir une sacrée/sale caboche.** To be really pigheaded. *Ton dab a une sale caboche.* "Your dad's really pigheaded."

CABOT, *m.* **1.** Corporal. *Ce petit cabot se prend déjà pour Napoléon ou Hitler.* "That little corporal already thinks he's Napoleon or Hitler." **2.** Dog. *Elle a laissé toute sa fortune aux cabots sans foyer.* "She left her fortune to homeless dogs."

CABOTIN, -E, *m., f.* **1.** Ham actor. *Ne traite pas de cabotin ce grand artiste.* "Don't call that great artist a ham." **2.** Show-off. *Arrête de faire le cabotin!* "Quit showing off!"

CABOTINAGE, *m.* Bad acting. *Des critiques trouvaient que la divine Sarah faisait du cabotinage.* "Some critics thought the divine Sarah's (Bernhardt) acting was hammy."

CABOULOT, *m.* Low dive or dump. *"Quel caboulot!" disait Bette.* "'What a dump,' said Bette."

CABOULOTE/CABOULOTIÉRE, *f.* Waitress in a cheap tavern. *La caboulote rêvait de devenir une star de cinéma.* "The waitress in the dive dreamed of becoming a movie star."

CACA, *m.,* children. Poop. *As-tu fait caca?* "Have you done number two?" *C'est du caca.* "That's worthless trash."

CACADE, *f.* Diarrhea (from **caca** and **cascade**). *Il a la cacade et reste à la maison.* "He's got the runs and is staying home."

CACASSE, *f., obs.* for "ass," used only in: **Aller à la cacasse.** To have sex (not necessarily anal). *Mon mec n'a jamais le temps pour la tendresse; il va tout de suite à la cacasse.* "My guy's never got time for tenderness; he just wants nooky right away."

CACHE-FRIFRI, *m.* G-string; skimpy panties. *La strip-teaseuse a pété son cache-frifri.* "The stripper snapped her G-string."

CACTUS, *m.* Problem (lit. "cactus"). *Tout s'est passé sans cactus.* "Everything went off without a hitch." **Avoir un cactus dans la poche/le portefeuille.** To be a miser. *Son oncle a un cactus dans la poche.* "His uncle's a skinflint."

CADAVRE, *m.* Empty bottle/"dead soldier" (lit. "corpse"). *Au nombre de cadavres, on mesurait leur cuite.* "You could tell how drunk they were by the number of empty bottles."

CADEAU, *m.* Gift. **Ne pas être un cadeau.** To be very troublesome. *Son nouvel jules n'est pas un cadeau.* "Her new boyfriend's no bargain." **Ne pas faire de cadeau.** To pull no punches. *La vie ne lui a pas fait de cadeau.* "Life hasn't treated him gently." See PETIT CADEAU.

CADOR, *m.* **1.** Dog. *Mon mari m'exècre mais il adore le cador.* "My husband despises me, but he adores the dog." *Cf.* CLEBARD; CLEBS; MÉDOR. **2.** Boss, top dog (from Ar. *gaddour* "chief"). *Les cadors de la pègre se parlaient en téléconférence, plus sécurisé que les réunions* *au resto.* "The mob bosses communicated by conference call, safer than meetings in restaurants." **3.** *adj.* Skillful; knowledgeable; powerful. *Il est cador en électronique.* "He's a computer whizz."

CAFÉ, *m.* Coffee. **Fort de café.** Strong stuff; exaggerated. *Ton histoire est un peu fort de café.* "Your story is a bit much." See PRENDRE...PAUVRE.

CAFÉ-COUETTE, *m.* Bed and breakfast (lit. "coffee quilt"). *Une bretonne en coiffe tient un chouette de café-couette.* "A Breton woman wearing a traditional head-dress runs a very nice B & B."

CAFEMAR/CAFEMON = CAFETON.

CAFETER, *school.* To inform; tell tales out of school. *C'est toi qui as cafeté.* "You're the one who squealed."

CAFETEUR, -EUSE, *m., f.* School. *Ils ont passé le cafeteur à tabac.* "They beat up the snitch."

CAFETIÈRE, *f.* Head (lit "coffeepot; coffeemaker"). *Il n'a rien dans la cafetière.* "He's got nothing upstairs."

CAFOUILLER. 1. To blunder. *J'ai cafouillé pour venir ici.* "I made one mistake after another in getting here." **2.** To not work right. *Le portable cafouille encore.* "The cell phone's acting up again."

CAFOUILLIS, *m.* Mess. *Quel cafouillis chez eux!* "Their place is a shambles!"

CAGEOT, *m.* Unattractive female (lit. "crate"). *As-tu vu ce cageot?* "Have you seen that dog?"

CAGES À LAPINS. Cheap public housing. *On va démolir les cages à lapins de la banlieue.* "They're going to tear down the public housing in the suburbs."

CAGNA, *f.* Room. *Leur cagna était cracra mais ils étaient heureux.* "Their pad was filthy but they were happy." See CASSER LA CAGNA.

CAGNARD, *m.* Sun. *Je rêve de partir au cagnard.* "I'm dreaming of going off to someplace sunny."

CAÏD, *m.* Top dog (from Ar.). *Il a essayé de se faire passer pour un caïd de l'industrie.* "He tried to pass himself off as a big tycoon."

-CAILLE. Slang suffix, sometimes *pej.* Examples: **mouscaille** (excrement; dire poverty); **Franchecaille** (France).

CAILLER. To be cold (lit. "to curdle"). *Ça caille aujourd'hui.* "It's freezing today."

(SE LES) CAILLER = Se les geler. See (SE) GELER.

(SE) CAILLER LES MICHES. To be extremely cold. *On se caillait les miches dans cet hôtel non chauffé.* "We froze our asses off in that hotel with no heat."

CAILLERA, *f.* Backslang of **racaille.** *La caillera règne dans la ville.* "Criminal elements are in control of the city."

CAILLOU, *m.* Head (lit. "pebble"). *Tu es tombé sur le caillou?* "Have you gone off your rocker?" *La vie est dure comme caillou.* (W. African expression.) "Life is the school of hard knocks (rocks)."

CAISSE, *m.* = **QUÈS,** *m.*

CAISSE, *f.* **1.** Head. See BOURRER…CAISSE; RAS. **2.** Chest. *Tu vas souffrir de la caisse si tu ne t'arrêtes pas de fumer.* "You're going to have lung problems if you don't stop smoking." See ROULER LA CAISSE. **3.** Vehicle. See (À) FOND LA CAISSE. **4.** Fart. See LÂCHER…CAISSE. **5.** Drunkenness. See PRENDRE…CAISSE.

CAISSON, *m.* Head. **(Se) faire sauter le caisson.** To kill (o.s.). *Très déprimé, il s'est fait sauter le caisson.* "He was very depressed and blew his brains out."

CÂLASSE!/CÂLIF!/CALIK!/CALINE!/CALIQUE!/ CALISTIRINE! *Que., euph.* for **calice!** *Calik! Tu me fous la colique avec tes discours bondieusards.* "God damn it! You really piss me off with your pompously pious pronouncements."

CAL(E)CIF, *m.,* slang for **caleçon.** Boxer shorts. See ANDOUILLE…CALCIF; ANGUILLE; FILER…CALCIF.

CALDOCHE, *m., f.* White Caledonian. *Canaques et Caldoches ne s'entendent pas toujours.* "White immigrants and New Caledonian natives don't always get along." See KANAK.

CALE, *f.* Ship's hold. See (À) FOND DE CALE; RAS…CALE.

CALEÇON, *m.* Shorts. See ANGUILLE.

CALENDOS/CALENDOT, *m.* Camembert cheese. *Le calendos de Camembert était le plus dégueu de tous.* "The camembert from Camembert was the yuckiest of all."

(SE) CALER LES AMYGDALES/BADIGOINCES/ JOUES/MOUSTACHES. To eat heartily (lit. "to fill one's tonsils/lips/cheeks/mustache." *Cf.* Eng. "to stuff one's face.") *On pétait la faim et on s'est calé les amygdales.* "We were starving and really put it away."

CALETER = CALTER.

CALIBOIRE! *Que.* Combination of **calice!** and **ciboire!** See SACRE **2.**

CALICE, *m.* Communion Chalice. Used in Que. as an exclamation, **Calice!** Pronounced with a long "a," and often written **câlice** or **câlisse.** Sometimes combined with other rel. expletives: **Calice de crisse de tabarnak d'(h)ostie de ciboire de testament!** "Holy fuckin' Jesus Christ goddamned shit!" See OSTENSOIRE; SACRE **2.**

CÂLINE!/CÂLIQUE!/CÂLISTRINE! *Que., euph.* for **calice.**

CÂLISSE! = **CALICE!** *Que. Câlisse de char de marde!* "Fuckin' goddamned car!" Note: In European Fr. this would be rendered as **Putain de voiture de merde!**

CALOTIN, -E, *m., f.* (From **calotte,** *f.* "skullcap; priest's beret.") **1.** Priest. **2.** Bigoted Catholic. *Les calotins se plaisent à censurer et s'opposent à toute critique.* "The Cathliholies judge and censor everything, but reject all criticism."

CALTER/SE CALTER. To scram. *Je me suis calté directo.* "I hit the road right away."

CALVAIRE, *m.* **1.** Calvary; suffering. *Mon mari, toujours soûl, fait de ma vie un long calvaire.* "My husband's always drunk and makes my life one long martyrdom." **2.** Roadside cross, crucifix. *Les druides bretons prèferent les menhirs aux calvaires.* "Breton druids prefer standing stones to roadside crosses."

CALVAIRE! *Que.* "Damn it!" See SACRE 2. **En calvaire.** Angry. *Il était en beau calvaire!* "He was boiling mad!" See EN CALVAIRE.

CALVANASSE!/CALVASSE!/CALVENUS!/CAL-VETTE!/CALVINCE!/CALVINISSE! *Que., euph.* for **calvaire!**

CAMBRONNE (Pierre). Napoleonic general who, in one version, replied "Merde!" when asked to surrender at Waterloo. *Cf.* General McAuliffe's answer "Nuts! Shit!" to a later surrender demand, also in Belgium. See MOT DE CAMBRONNE; CHAMBRE DE CAMBRONNE; MERDE.

CAMBROUS(S)ARD, -E, *m., f.* Hick. *Je suis heureuse de vivre comme une cambrousarde.* "I'm happy living like a country bumpkin."

CAMBROUS(S)E, *f.* Country. *J'ai quitté la ville pour la cambrousse.* "I left the city for the sticks."

CAMBUSE, *f.* Hovel. *Et si l'on allait à ma cambuse?* "How about going to my pad?"

CAME, *f.* **1.** Merchandise. *Je n'achète que de la bonne came.* "I only buy good stuff." **2.** Drugs. *Elle fait un mémoire sur le rôle de la came dans la religion.* "She's doing a thesis on the role of drugs in religion."

CAMÉ, -E. Stoned; addicted. *Il est camé depuis longtemps mais il s'en sortira.* "He's been a drug addict for a long time but he'll kick the habit."

CAMELOTE, *f.* **1.** Trash. *Ce bidule, c'est de la camelote.* "That thing's a piece of junk." **2.** Goods. *Il a vendu toute sa camelote sur le marché.* "He sold all his stuff at the marketplace." **3.** Sperm. *Il lance trop vite sa camelote.* "He shoots his load too fast."

(SE) CAMER. To take drugs. *Il ne se came plus.* "He's no longer a junkie."

CAMTAR, *m.* Truck. *Les camtars sur la route, c'est l'enfer.* "Trucks on the road mean sheer hell!"

CANARD, *m.* **1.** Lump of sugar in coffee (lit. "duck"). *C'est le canard qui boit mon cafeton.* "It's the sugar that drinks my coffee." See FROID DE CANARD. **2.** Newspaper. See 3 for use in a sentence. **3.** False report; hoax. *Le canard enchaîné est un canard de qualité sans canards.* "*Le canard enchaîné* (The Tied Up Duck) is a quality newspaper without canards." **4.** False note. *Malgré les canards, elle reste une grande diva.* "Despite the wrong notes, she's still a great diva." **5.** Wet kiss, youth. *Ils se sont quittés sur un canard.* "They kissed passionately when they parted."

CANAQUE = KANAK.

CANON, *m.* Glass of wine. *On a bu un canon sur le zinc du caboulot.* "We had a glass of wine at the bar."

CANTINE, *f.* Belly (lit. "cafeteria"; "canteen"). *J'ai la cantine bien remplie.* "I'm stuffed." See BOURRÉ...CANTINE.

CANTINER, *crim.* To buy goods in the prison store. *Si j'avais de l'oseille, je cantinerais des clopes sans avoir à me vendre.* "If I had any bread, I'd buy cigarettes at the store without having to sell m.s."

CANTOCHE, *f.* Canteen. *Et si l'on allait au resto? J'en ai marre de la cantoche.* "How about going to the restaurant? I'm sick of the canteen." See BOURRÉ...CANTOCHE.

CANULE, *f.* **1.** Condom (orig. "cannula," a tube used in medicine for insertion into a body cavity). *Ces canules coûtent chères.* "These rubbers are expensive." **2.** Bastard. *Qu'il me fait chier, cette canule.* "That scumbag really bugs the shit outta me."

CANULER. To annoy. *Arrête de me canuler!* "Quit pushing my buttons."

CAOUA, *m.* Coffee. *Et un petit caoua pour se mettre en route.* "And a cuppa java to help us get started."

CAP, from **capable.** *T'es cap?* "Can you cut the mustard?"

CAPITAL, *m.* Capital. **Petit capital.** Virginity. *Elle sait préserver son petit capital en faisant des fellations époustouflantes.* "She's keeps her virginity by giving mind-blowing blow jobs."

CAPOTE/CAPOTE ANGLAISE, *f.* Condom (lit. "Eng. hooded coat"). (Note: in Brit. slang, "French letter" means "condom.") *Je refuse les michés qui veulent marcher sans capote.* "I reject johns who want to get it on without a rubber."

CARABIN, *m.* Medical student. *Ce carabin ne deviendra jamais toubib.* "That med student will never be a doctor."

CARABINÉ, -E. Very powerful. *J'ai une migraine carabinée.* "I've got one hell of a headache."

CARABISTOUILLE, *f.* Bel. Lying, swindling. *Arrête tes carabistouilles ou je te casse la margouille.* "Stop your scheming or I'll bust your face."

CARAFE, *f.* Head (lit. "carafe"). *Tu n'as rien dans la carafe.* "You're birdbrained." See TOMBER EN CARAFE; RESTER EN CARAFE.

CARAMBOLER. To have sexually. *Ils m'ont carambolée sur la plage.* "They banged me on the beach."

(SE) CARAMBOLER. To crash into. *Les deux motos se sont carambolées superbement.* "The two bikes really smashed into each other."

(SE) CARAPATER. To scram. *L'orage arrive; je me carapate.* "The storm's coming; I'm making tracks."

CARAT, *m.* Year (lit. "carat"). *Il a vingt carats.* "He's twenty." See DERNIER CARAT; PRENDRE DU CARAT.

CARAVELLE. Expensive prostitute, often in a car. (Caravel(le) has been used at various times for types of ships, planes, and cars. *Cf.* **amazone, autobus, montgolfière, wagonnière.**) *Il s'ennuie chez lui et rêve de s'envoyer en l'air avec une caravelle.* "He's bored at home and dreams of getting it off with a high-class hooker."

CARBURANT, *m.* Liquor (lit. "fuel"). *Son carburant c'est le calva.* "Applejack's the drink that keeps him going."

CARBURER À L'ALCOOL = MARCHER À L'ALCOOL.

CARNA. Backslang of **ARNAQUE.**

CARNE, *f.* **1.** Inferior meat. *Ils t'ont refilé de la carne, mais je rejetterais même du tournedos Rossini, car je prépare ma réincarnation.* "They sold you tough meat, but I'd reject even tournedos Rossini because I'm preparing my reincarnation." **2.** *Elle est toute autre qu'une vieille carne.* "She's anything but a nasty old bitch."

CAROLINE, *f.* Passive homosexual. *Il s'est lassé d'être toujours la Caroline.* "He got tired of always being the receiver."

CAROSSÉE = BALANCÉE.

CAROTTE, *f.* Carrot. **1. Les carottes sont cuites!** "It's all over (for him, for us); our goose is cooked." **2.** Theft, swindle. *J'achète plus chez lui. Il me fait carotte.* "I don't buy from him anymore. He rips me off."

CARPETTE, *f.* Spineless person (lit. "rug"). *Ne joue pas la carpette, défends-toi!* "Don't be a wimp; defend y.s."

CARREAU, *m.* Diamonds (cards). See (SE) TENIR À CARREAU.

CARREAUX, *m., pl.* Eyeglasses (lit. "windowpanes"). *J'ai paumé mes carreaux.* "I've lost my glasses."

CARTONNER. To smash up; to be a smash hit. *Son nouvel album va cartonner.* "Her new album will really take off."

CARTOUCHE, *f.* Bullet. **Valoir la cartouche du chasseur.** To be worth having sexually (lit. "worth the hunter's bullet"). *Cette gonzesse vaut bien la cartouche du chasseur.* "That broad's really worth plugging."

CASE, *f.* Cabin; cell; box. See MANQUER UNE CASE.

CASQUE, *m.* **1.** Helmet; hard hat. **Les Casques bleus.** The U.N. peacekeeping force. *Les Casques bleus ont du mal à maintenir la paix.* "The UN peacekeepers are having trouble maintaining the peace." **En avoir plein le casque.**

Que., equivalent of **en avoir ras le BOL. 2.** Glans (penis) in RAYER LE CASQUE.

CASQUER. 1. To put on a condom (lit. "put on a helmet"). *Casque-toi ou casse-toi.* "Either wear a rubber or go to hell." *Cf.* PASSEPORT. **2. Être casqué.** To be wearing a condom. *J'sais pas s'ils étaient tous casqués. J'étais imprudente.* "I don't know if they all used a condom. I was careless." **3.** To pay. *À toi de casquer aujourd'hui.* "It's your turn to shell out today." *Cf.* DOUILLER; RAQUER.

CASSE, *f.* **1.** Damage. *L'ouragan n'a pas fait trop de casse.* "The hurricane didn't do too much damage." **2.** Violent confrontation. *Il risque d'y avoir de la casse pour la manif.* "There'll probably be some rough stuff during the demonstration." **3.** Scrapyard. *Ta bagnole est bonne à foutre à la casse.* "Your jalopy is ready for the scrapyard."

CASSE, *m.* Burglary. *On a fait un casse dans l'imeuble.* "There was a break-in in the building."

CASSE-BONBONS, *m., f., adj.* and *n.* Annoying; annoying person. *Qu'est-ce qu'il peut être casse-bonbons.* "He can be a real ball buster." See BONBON **4.**

CASSE-BURNES = CASSE-BONBONS.

CASSE-COU, *m., f., adj.* and *n.* Daredevil(ish). *C'est une skieuse casse-cou qui descend à une vitesse folle.* "She's a daredevil skier who descends at breakneck speed."

CASSE-COUILLES = CASSE-BONBONS.

CASSE-CUL, *m.* Annoying person. *T'es on ne peut plus casse-cul.* "You couldn't be more of a pain in the ass if you tried."

CASSE-GUEULE, *m., adj.* and *n.* Risky/dangerous place. *Un vrai casse-gueule la route pour monter chez toi.* "The uphill road to your house is full of accidents waiting to happen."

CASSEMENT = CASSE 1.

CASSE-NOISETTES, *m., pl.* Voluntary vaginal contractions during intercourse (lit. "nutcracker"). *Ma moule sait* *faire casse-noisettes et traire un max les mecs.* "My pussy knows how to flex its muscles and milk guys dry."

CASSE-PIEDS, *m., f., adj.* and *n.* Annoying or boring person or situation. *Ce film est d'un casse-pieds fini.* "This film is totally boring."

CASSE-PIPE, *m.* Bloody war. *Il refusait de partir au casse-pipe.* "He refused to go to war (and be cannon fodder)." See CASSER SA PIPE.

CASSER. To break. **À tout casser. 1.** Stupendous. *Ils ont fait un banquet à tout casser.* "They prepared a fantastic banquet." **2.** At the very most. *Ça vaut 20.000 à tout casser.* "That's worth 20,000, tops."

CASSER DU SUCRE SUR LE DOS DE QN. See SUCRE.

CASSER LA BARAQUE. 1. To have a great theatrical success (lit. "to break the cabin"). *La diva a cassé la baraque.* "The diva brought down the house." **2.** To ruin s.o.'s chances/plans. *Méfie-toi de ton associé: il risque de nous casser la baraque.* "Be careful of your partner; he's likely to pull the rug out from under us."

CASSER LA/UNE CROÛTE/GRAINE. To eat. *Et si on cassait la croûte.* "How about a break for a bite to eat?"

CASSER/SE CASSER LA MARGOULETTE/ GUEULE. See MARGOULETTE.

CASSER LA RONDELLE/LE POT/L'ANNEAU/ OIGNON = DÉFONCER....

CASSER LA TÊTE/LES PIEDS. To bore; annoy. *Ça me casse les pieds d'aller à cette réunion.* "Going to that meeting is a real drag."

CASSER LES BONBONS/BURNES/COUILLES/ GLAOUÏS/LES CASSER. See BONBONS; BURNES.

CASSER SA PIPE. To die. *Avant de casser ma pipe, je voudrais me défouler un peu.* "Before kicking the bucket, I'd like to kick up my heels a bit."

CASSER SON ŒUF. To have a miscarriage. *Elle a cassé son œuf la première fois mais s'est rattrapée en faisant* *un doublé.* "She had a miscarriage the first time but made up for it by giving birth to twins."

(NE PAS) CASSER DES BRIQUES/NE RIEN CASSER. To be of little or no interest (lit. "to not break any bricks; to break nothing"). *Ça ne casse pas des briques.* "That's nothing to write home about." *Ton bouquin ne casse rien.* "Your book's hardly earthshaking."

(SE) CASSER. To clear off. *Faut qu'on se casse.* "We've got to split." See CASSOS.

(SE) CASSER LA FIGURE/GUEULE. To fail (lit. "to break one's face"). *Son entreprise est sur le point de se casser la gueule.* "His business is about to go bust."

(SE) CASSER LA TÊTE/NÉNETTE. To rack one's brains. *Je me suis cassé la nénette pour trouver la réponse.* "I racked my brains to find the answer."

(SE) CASSER LE CUL/FION/LES COUILLES. To work one's ass off; bust one's buns/balls. *Il s'est cassé le cul pour élever ses gosses.* "He busted his buns to raise his kids."

CASSEROLE, *f.* Cooking pot. **Chanter comme une casserole.** To sing off-key. *J'adore le chant, mais je chante comme une casserole. "*I adore vocal music, but I sing like a screech owl." **Passer à la casserole. 1.** To get into trouble; to be in for it. *Avec de tels copains tu passeras encore à la casserole.* "With buddies like that you're going to get into hot water again." **2.** To be coerced into sex (Meaning 1. means getting into a "hairy" situation. Meaning 2. refers to a pubic hairy situation). *Les quatre loubards s'approchaient et je savais que j'allais passer à la casserole.* "The four thugs came closer and I knew I was going to get it." *Pour ne pas être virée il fallait que je passe à la casserole.* "I had to put out, so's not to get fired."

CASSEUR, *m.* **1.** Burglar. *La bande de casseurs a été enfin agrafée.* "The gang of second-story men was finally nabbed." **2.** Hoodlum. *Des casseurs ont perturbé la manif.* "Thugs disrupted the demonstration."

(SE) CASSER LE NEZ. To get no answer at the door or on the phone (lit. "to break one's nose"). *On s'est cassé le nez au Musée d'Orsay le jour de fermeture.* "We got no answer at the Orsay Museum on the day it was closed."

CASSE-TÊTE, *m.* Difficult. *Ce problème, c'est un vrai casse-tête.* "That problem's a real headache."

CASSOS in **faire cassos** = **(SE) CASSER.** *Faisons cassos.* "Let's split."

CASTAPIANE, *f.* Gonorrhea. *(Il) y a des castapianes qui résistent aux antibios.* "Antibiotics don't cure all kinds of clap."

CATHO = **CATHOLIQUE.**

CATHODIQUE. Pertaining to TV. See GRAND-MESSE.

CATHOLE, *m., f., pej.* Very devout Catholic. *Notre grand-tante était une cathole folle.* "Our grand-aunt was a religious nut."

CATHOLIQUE. Catholic. **Pas très catholique.** Not on the up-and-up; not "kosher." *Qch. de pas très catholique se passe là.* "S.t. fishy's going on there."

CATIN, *f.* Prostitute. *Il était mordu de cette catin.* "He was nuts about that slut."

CAVALE, *f.* Escape (lit. "mare"). **Être en cavale.** To be a fugitive. *Son fils est en cavale; on ne sait où.* "Her son is on the run; no one knows where he is."

CAVALER. 1. To run, run around; to chase anything in skirts/pants. *Son mari continue à cavaler à droite et à gauche.* "Her husband continues to sleep around." **2.** To annoy. *T'as fini de me cavaler?* "Are you through buggin' me?"

CAVALEUR, -EUSE, *m., f.* Womanizer; man-chaser. *La patronne, grande cavaleuse, m'angoisse.* "The boss is a man-eater and harrasses me (sexually)." *Cf.* COUREUR DE JUPONS; COUREUSE; SAUTE-AU-CRAC; SAUTE-AU-PAF.

CEINTURE, *f.* Belt. **Faire ceinture; se serrer la ceinture.** To do without. *On a fait longtemps ceinture et mainte-*

nant on en profite. "We tightened our belt for some time and now we're reaping the benefits."

(À) CENT SOUS DE L'HEURE. See (S')EMMERDER; (SE) RASER.

CERF, *m.* Stag. **Bander comme un cerf.** To have a very firm erection. *Ce con croit que la corne de rhinocéros le fera bander comme un cerf.* "That idiot thinks that rhino horn is going to make him get it up bone hard."

CERVELLE, *f.* Brain. See (SE) CREUSER.

CÉZIG(UE) = **SÉZIG(UE).**

CHACUN, -E SON TRUC. Whatever turns you on.

CHAGATTE, *f.,* javanais* of **chatte.** Pussy. *Sa petite chagatte est bien étroite.* "She's got a nice tight pussy."

CHAILLE, *f.* Tooth. *À vingt piges il n'avait déjà plus de chailles.* "At twenty he was already toothless."

CHAISE, *f.* Chair. **Avoir le cul entre deux chaises.** See CUL...CHAISES.

CHAMBARD, *m.* Commotion. *Quel chambard chez les voisins.* "What a racket at the neighbors'!"

CHAMBRE DE CAMBRONNE, *f., euph.* Toilet. *Au château hôtel on appelait les chiottes "la chambre de Cambronne".* "In the chateau hotel they called the can 'Cambronne's room.' " See CAMBRONNE.

CHAPEAU, *m.* **1.** Head (lit. "hat"). See (EN) BAVER DES RONDS DE CHAPEAU; PETIT CHAPEAU; TRAVAILLER DU CHA-PEAU. *Cf.* BADA. **2.** Condom. *Tu connais les risques si tu ne portes pas de chapeau.* "You know the risks if you don't wear a rubber." *Cf.* CASQUER. **3.** Foreskin. *T'as vu le film* Le chapeau du p'tit Jésus? "Have you seen the movie *Little Jesus' Foreskin?*" *Cf.* JÉSUS 2.

CHAR, *m., Que.* Car. *Il change de char chaque année.* "He gets a new car every year."

* See explanation of **javanais,** page 200.

CHARCLO, *m.,* backslang of **clochard** ("vagrant"; "bum"). *Ce quartier grouille de charclos.* "This district is full of homeless people."

CHARCUTIER, *m.* Bad surgeon (lit. "pork butcher"; "delicatessen dealer"). *Quel charcutier as-tu vu pour cette jambe cassée?* "Who was the sawbones you went to for that broken leg?"

CHAROGNE, *f.* Bitch; SOB (lit. "carrion"). *Tu fréquentes toujours cette charogne?* "You're still seeing that swine/sow?"

CHARRETTE, *f.* **1.** Car (lit. "cart"). *T'as zyeuté sa nouvelle charrette? C'est classe!* "Have you seen her new set of wheels? Really classy!" **Être/se mettre en charrette.** To be behind. *Notre ville est toujours en charrette pour les illuminations de Noël.* "Our town still lags behind in installing Xmas lights." **Être/faire charrette.** To work hard. *Faut faire charette pour terminer avant la date-limite.* "We've really got to get a move on to finish before the deadline." **2.** Great quantities. *Des amours en poubelle? J'en ai eu des charrettes!* "Busted love affairs? I've had lots of them!"

CHARRIDA, *m.* Crook; con man. *C'était un charrida charmeur et elle lui a fait confiance, hélas.* "He was a winsome con artist and she trusted him, unfortunately."

CHARRIEUR = CHARRIDA.

CHASSE. Slightly drunk. *Un verre suffit pour que je sois chasse.* "One glass is enough to make me tipsy."

CHASSELAS, *m.* Type of grape used for making white wine. **Avoir un coup de chasselas; être de chasselas.** To be drunk. *Il a une sacrée descente pour le Fendant mais prétend qu'il n'a jamais un coup de chasselas.* "He really tanks up on Fendant (Swiss white wine) but says he's never drunk."

CHÂTEAU-LA-POMPE/CHÂTEAU LAPOMPE, *m.* Drinking water (not necessarily pumped from a well). *Après sa crise de foie il ne boit que du Château Lapompe.*

"After problems with his liver he just drinks nature's champagne."

CHATTE, *f.* Pussy (lit. "female cat"). *Ma chatte n'a jamais besoin de lubrifiant.* "My pussy never needs a lubricant."

CHAUD-CHAUD/CHAUDE-CHAUDE = CHAUD, -E.

CHAUD!/CHAUD DEVANT! "Watch out! Coming through!" (as announced by waiters carrying dishes).

CHAUD LAPIN, *m.* Hot number. *Elles étaient trois à se partager ce chaud lapin.* "The three of them shared that hot stud."

CHAUDE-LANCE = CHAUDE PISSE.

CHAUDE LAPINE, *f.* Hot number. *J'ai goûté à sa lamdé; quelle chaude lapine!* "I got a taste of his woman; what a horny broad!"

CHAUDE-PISSE/CHAUDE-PINCE, *f.* Gonorrhea. *Il a couché à droite et à gauche sans capote et a attrapé la chaude-pisse.* "He slept around without rubbers and got the clap."

CHAUFFE, *f.* Swindle (lit. "fire chamber; boiler room"). *Ce resto c'est de la chauffe.* "That restaurant's a ripoff." *Cf.* ARNAQUE.

CHAUFFER. 1. To heat. See ÇA VA CHAUFFER. **2.** To steal. *Le voyou a chauffé mon morlingue.* "The thug stole my wallet."

CHAUSSETTE, *m.* Sock. See JUS…CHAUSSETTE; LAISSER… CHAUSSETTE; RETOURNER…CHAUSSETTE.

CHAUVE À COL ROULÉ = PETIT CHAUVE À COL ROULÉ.

CHÉARA, *youth, cités.* Backslang of **arraché.** See VOL À.

CHÉBRAN, *m.* backslang of **branché.** Hip individual. *Les chébrans ont largué cette boîte.* "The trendy people have deserted that spot."

CHELOU, *youth, cités.* Backslang of **louche.** Weird; suspect. *Ce mec a un air chelou.* "There's something odd about that guy." See LOUCHE.

CHEMISE DE VENUS, *f.* Condom. *Y avait tout un culte autour de la "Sainte Chemise" de Chartres. Plus important distribuer des chemises de Vénus aux pays du Tiers-Monde.* "There was quite a cult around the "Holy Tunic" (allegedly worn by Mary when she birthed Jesus). It's more important to destribute Venus-sheaths to third world countries." See VÉNUS.

CHÈQUE EN BOIS. See BOIS.

CHERCHER. To look for. See ÇA VA CHERCHER.

CHERCHER BASTON. To look for; pick a fight. *Calme-toi; cherche pas toujours baston.* "Calm down; don't be so pugnacious." *Cf.* BASTON.

CHERCHER DES CROSSES À QN./CHERCHER QN. To pick a fight. *Si tu me cherches des crosses, fais gaffe!* "If you're looking for a fight with me, watch out!"

CHERCHER L'HÉMATOME. To look for a fight (lit. "bruise"). *Tu cherches l'hématome?* "You lookin' for a fat lip?"

CHÉROT. Expensive. *Tout est chérot chez cet antiquaire.* "Everything's pricey at that antique dealer's."

CHETRON, *m.,* backslang of **tronche.**

CHEVALIER DE LA ROSETTE. See ROSETTE **2.**

CHEVEU, *m.* **1.** Hair. See COMME...SOUPE. **2.** Problem. *Il y a un cheveu.* "There's a hitch/snag!"

CHEVILLE, *f.* Ankle. **Avoir les chevilles qui enflent.** To be swell-headed. *Depuis qu'il a hérité il a les chevilles qui enflent.* "After coming into that inheritance he's become too big for his britches."

(EN) CHEVILLE. In cahoots with. *Le maire s'est mis en cheville avec la pègre.* "The mayor's in bed with the mob."

CHÈVRE, *m., pej.* Bitch; slut (lit. "nanny goat"). See DEVE-NIR CHÈVRE.

CHIADER. 1. To study hard. *J'ai chiadé mon exam.* "I went all out studying for my exam." **2.** To do s.t. painstakingly. *Ça c'est chiadé!* "That's a thorough job!"

CHIALER. To bawl. *Son gosse n'arrête pas de chialer.* "Her kid never stops crying."

CHIANT, -E. Extremely dull; annoying; shitty. *Ne sois pas chiant!* "Don't be a pain in the ass!"

CHIANTERIE, *f.* Unpleasantness. *Quelle chianterie toute cette paperasse.* "What a crock (of shit) all that paper work." *Cf.* **faire chier** in CHIER 1.

CHIARD, *m., pej.* Brat (orig. one still in diapers). *J'ai fait semblant d'aimer leurs chiards.* "I pretended to like their dirty little brats."

CHIASSE, *f.* **1.** Diarrhea. *La bouffe d'hier m'a foutu la chiasse.* "Yesterday's dinner gave me the runs." See COUPE-CHIASSE. **2.** Unpleasantness. See QUELLE CHIASSE!

CHIATIQUE. Exceedingly annoying. *Tout ce matraquage médiatique est chiatique!* "All that media hype is a real pain in the ass."

CHIB(E) or **CHIBRE,** *m.* Penis. *Garde ton chib dans ton falzar.* "Keep your pecker in your pants." *Cf.* DÉCHIB.

CHIBRER. To copulate. *Mon mari préfere se saouler que chibrer. Il a toujours le chibre mou.* "My husband would rather drink than fuck. His dick's always limp."

CHICHA, *m.* backslang of **haschisch.** See H.

CHICON = CHICHA.

CHICOS. Chic. *Que t'es chicos aujourd'hui!* "My, how elegant you are today!"

CHIÉ, -E. 1. Remarkable; wonderful. *Quel chié prof tu as!* "What an awesome professor you've got." **2.** Rotten. *C'est chié, leur musique.* "Their music's awful." **3.** Brazen. *Elle est chiée de réclamer sans cesse du fric.* "She's got some nerve, constantly asking for money."

CHIÉ!/CHIÉ DE MERDE! Holy shit!

CHIÉE, *m.* Large amount. *Une chiée de courrier arrive chaque jour.* "Everyday a shit pile of mail arrives."

CHIEN, -NE. Mean, rotten. *Qu'est-ce qu'il a été chien avec elle!* "He treated her like a dog!"

CHIEN, *m.* Dog. **Avoir du chien.** To have charm; allure. *Cette fille n'est pas laide; elle a du chien.* "That girl's no dog; she has a certain fascinating s.t." See (SE) DONNER...; GARDER...CHIEN; MAL DE CHIEN; PEAU DE CHIEN.

CHIENLIT, *f.* Disorder (lit. "shit in the bed"). *"La réforme, oui; la chienlit, non" a dit de Gaulle. "La chienlit, c'est lui" scandaient les étudiants.* "'Reform yes, chaos no,' said de Gaulle." "'He's the stinking mess,' chanted the students."

CHIENNE, *f.* Female dog; bitch. **Quelle chienne de vie!** Life's a bitch; a kick in the ass!

CHIER. 1. To defecate. *Son foutu animal a chié partout!* "Her damned animal shit all over the place!" **Faire chier.** To exasperate (lit. "to cause to shit"). *Le maire me fait chier!* "The mayor really pisses me off/makes me want to throw up." See ÇA VA CHIER; ENVOYER CHIER; FAUT...CHIE; GUEULE À CHIER...; NUL À CHIER; TRONCHE À CHIER.... **2. Se faire chier.** To be bored to death. *On s'est fait chier ici depuis trop longtemps. Foutons le camp!* "We've been bored to death here for too long. Let's get the hell out!" To take a great deal of trouble. *On s'est fait chier pour installer la nouvelle maison.* "We busted our buns settling into the new house." **3. Ne pas se faire chier.** To not give a damn; be inconsiderate. *Il ne s'est pas fait chier, celui-là en passant devant tout le monde.* "That guy didn't think twice about pushing in ahead of everybody else."

CHIER DANS LES BOTTES DE QN./FAIRE CHIER QN. To bug s.o. (lit. "to shit in s.o.'s boots"; "make s.o. shit"). *Quand aura-t-il fini de nous faire chier?* "When is he gonna stop pissing us off?"

CHIER DANS SA CULOTTE/SON FROC = FAIRE DANS...CULOTTE.

(EN) CHIER. To go through hell. *Ils en ont chié lors de l'inondation.* "They went through hell during the flood."

CHIERIE, *f.* Unpleasant situation. *Cette grève est une sacrée chierie.* "This strike's a real pain in the ass." See QUELLE CHIERIE!

CHIEUR, -EUSE, *m., f., adj.* and *n.* Lousy person (lit. "shitter"). *Ta gonzesse est une vraie chieuse.* "Your broad's a real stinker."

CHIEUR D'ENCRE. Hack journalist (lit. "ink shitter"). *Ce chieur d'encre a descendu en flammes la diva.* "That ink pisser did a hack job on the diva."

CHIFFE MOLLE, *f.* Wimp (lit. "limp rag"). *Quelle chiffe molle tu fais!* "You really come on like a dishrag." *Cf.* LAVETTE.

CHINE, *f.* Flea market. *Il a vendu tout son Saint-Frusquin à la Chine.* "He sold all his stuff at the flea market."

CHINER AUX PUCES. To go antiquing. *Si on allait chi-ner aus Puces de Clignancourt?* "How about going antique hunting at the Clignancourt flea market?"

CHINETOC/CHINETOQUE, *pej., adj.* and *n.* Chinese/Asian. *Nous sommes partis manger chez les Chinetocs.* "We went out to eat Chinese food."

CHINEUR, -EUSE, *m., f.* **1.** Antique dealer. *Il est chineur de profession.* "He's in the antiques trade." **2.** Practical joker; leg puller. *N'essaie pas de chiner un chineur.* "Don't try to kid a kidder."

CHINMÉ, *youth, cités.* Backslang of **méchant** ("mean, wicked"). Excellent. *Le film était super chinmé!* "The flick was terrific!"

CHINOIS, *m.* **1.** Chinese man. See JAMBE DU CHINOIS. **2.** Penis. See PATINER LE CHINOIS; POLIR LE CHINOIS.

CHIOTTES, *f., pl.* Toilet. *Où sont les chiottes?* "Where's the head?" See BALAI À CHIOTTES.

CHIPER. To swipe. *Qui m'a chipé mes lunettes de soleil?* "Who pinched my sunglasses."

CHIPOLATA, *m.* Penis (lit. "sausage"). *La tantouse avait très faim de chipolata.* "The queen was hungry for meat."

CHIQUE, *f.* Chewing tobacco. See COUPER LA CHIQUE.

CHIQUÉ, *m.* Pretentiousness. *Ne fais pas de chiqué avec moi.* "Don't try to put on airs with me."

(AU) CHIQUÉ. As a bluff. *Il y va toujours au chiqué.* "He always bluffs it out."

CHLAFFE = SCHLAFFE.

CHLINGUER = SCHLINGUER.

CHLOF = SCHLOF.

CHNECK, *f.* Vagina; woman (from Ger. **Schnecke** "snail"). *Elle m'a allumé cette chneck.* "That cunt came on to me."

CHNOQUE = SCHNOQUE.

CHNOUFFE = SCHNOUFFE.

CHNOUFFER = SCHNOUFFER.

CHOCHOTTE, *f.* Affected; fussy person. *Ne fais pas ta chochotte.* "Quit your silly fussing."

CHOCOLAT, *m.* **C'est du chocolat!** "It's a snap!" *Cf.* CRÈME 1; GÂTEAU.

CHOCOTTES, *f., pl.* Teeth. *Cesse de grincer des chocottes.* "Stop gnashing your teeth." **Avoir les chocottes.** To be afraid. *J'ai les chocottes quand il roule à donf.* "My teeth chatter with fear when he drives at top speed."

CHOILLE = CHOUÏA.

CHÔME, *f.,* from **chômage.** *J'en ai ralbol d'être à la chôme.* "I'm sick and tired of being unemployed."

CHÔMDU, *m.* Unemployment. *Ni juilletiste ni aoûtien, toujours en vacances, le chômdu me botte.* "I'm on vacation all the time not just July or August. I dig unemployment."

CHOPER. To catch. *J'ai chopé la grippe cet hiver.* "I got the flu this winter."

CHOPIN, *m.* **1.** Theft. *Des onze ans déjà il en était à son premier chopin.* "He pulled his first job when he was 11." **2.** Lucky break. *Il est temps qu'on fasse un beau chopin.* "We could do with a bit of luck."

CHOPINE, *f.* **1.** Bottle or glass of wine. *Il téte trop la chopine.* "He's too fond of the bottle." **2.** Large penis. *Cuit qu'il était, sa chopine m'a fait une belle jambe.* "Drunk as he was, his big dick was of no use to me."

CHOPOTTE = CHOPINE.

CHOQUOTTES = CHOCOTTES.

CHOSE, *f.* Thing. **Être porté sur la chose.** To be much interested in sex. *Mon grand-dab était très porté sur la chose.* "My granddad was a horny old devil."

CHOU, *m.* **1.** Cabbage. **Dans les choux.** Too late; failed. *C'est dans les choux, hélas, mon petit chou.* "I'm afraid it's gone down the drain, my sweet." **Faire chou blanc.** To fail; draw a blank. *J'ai fait chou blanc à l'exam.* "I drew a complete blank at the exam." **Faire ses choux gras.** To have a field day. *Les journaux ont fait leurs choux gras de ce scandale.* "The newspapers made hay with that scandal." See BÊTE…CHOU; FEUILLE DE CHOU; MON…CHOU. **2.** Head. **En avoir dans le chou.** To be smart. *Son mec en a dans le chou; il ira loin.* "Her guy's got a lot upstairs; he'll go far." See RENTRER…CHOU; FEUILLE… CHOU; TRAVAILLER DU CHOU.

CHOUAYE = CHOUÏA.

CHOUAGA = CHOUCARD, -E.

CHOUCARD, -E. Wonderful (from Romany for "beautiful"). *Ils ont fait un petit mariage choucard.* "They threw a terrific wedding feast."

CHOUCROUTE, *f.* **1.** Sauerkraut. See PÉDALER. **2.** Curly hair. *Tu as vu la choucroute qu'elle se paye, la nana?* "Have you seen that chick's beehive hairdo?" **3.** Hard drug. *C'est un accro de la choucroute.* "He's hooked on the hard stuff."

CHOUETTE, *adj.* Nice. *Elle a dégoté un chouette de boulot.* "She's found a pleasant job."

CHOUETTE, *f.* Nasty woman (lit. "owl"). *Quelle vieille chouette, ta mère.* "Your mother's a nasty old shrew."

CHOUETTE, *m.* Anus. See FILER…CHOUETTE; PRENDRE… CHOUETTE.

CHOUETTE!/CHOUETTE ALORS! That's terrific!

CHOUETTES, *m., pl.* Genuine ID. *Ce jeune sans chouettes vient d'être pincé.* "That minor with a fake ID just got pinched."

CHOUETTOS = CHOUETTE. *C'est chouettos!* That's!/ terrific!/neat!

CHOUÏA, *m.* from Ar. Tiny bit. *Je reprendrais bien un chouïa du gâteau.* "I'd love just another smidgin of the cake."

CHOUQUETTE, *f.* Effeminate homosexual (lit. "sugared cream puff"). *Ne fais pas la chouquette.* "Don't be such a queen."

CHOURAVER. To steal. *C'est pas la première bagnole qu'il a chouravé.* "That's not the first car he's stolen."

CHOURAVEUR, *m.* Thief. *Elle sait qu'il est chouraveur, mais elle l'aime quand même.* "She knows he's a thief but loves him anyway."

CHPROUM = SCHPROUM.

CHRIST! *Que.* Christ! **Un christ de gars!** A real bastard! **Crisse qui pisse!** "Christ's lice! Christ's crabs! Crapping Christ!" (Lit. "Christ who pisses"—intended as a blasphemy, although Catholic dogma asserts that Christ was "true man and true God" who performed human bodily functions during his life on earth.) See OSTENSOIRE! SACRE! **2.**

CHRISTIE!/CHRISTINE!/CHRISTOPHE!/CHRY-SOSTÔME! *Que. euph.* for **CHRIST!**

CHTIBE = SCHTIBE.

CHTILIBEN = SCHTILIBEN.

CHTIMI or **CH'TIMI.** Person from NE France; patois spoken in NE France (from the dialect pron. of **c'est-il moi**). *À Pantruche j'ai perdu mon accent chtimi.* "In Paris I lost my local accent."

CHTOUILLE, *f.* Gonorrhea. *Il avait la trouille que les antibios ne guérissent pas sa chtouille.* "He was afraid the antibiotics wouldn't cure his clap."

CHTUC = SCHTUC.

CHUM, *m., Que.* Intimate friend, steady boyfriend. (From Eng. although the Que. use is less casual.) *Mon nouveau chum me rend heureuse.* "My new boyfriend makes me happy." See FOUFOUNE; TCHOMME.

CIAO = TCHAO.

CIBICHE, *f.* Cigarette. *Ses cibiches puent moins que ses cigares.* "His cigarettes don't stink as much as his stogies."

CIBOGNAQUE!/CIBOLAQUE!/CIBOLE! CIBOULE!/ CIBOULETTE!/CIBOULOT!/CINLIBOIRE! *Que., euph.* for **CIBOIRE!**

CIBOIRE! *Que.* Holy Cow! Damn it! Shit! Lit. "ciborium" (a vessel for consecrated hosts). See CALIBOIRE!; CALICE!; SACRE 2.

CIBOULOT, *m.* Head. *T'as rien dans le ciboulot pour dire une telle connerie.* "You haven't got a brain in your head if you can say a stupid thing like that." See (SE) CREUSER.

CIFELLE, *f.* Thread. *Ça tient avec des bouts de cifelle.* "That's hanging together by a thread."

CIFLARD = SAUCIFLARD.

CIGARE, *m.* **1.** Head. *Il n'a rien dans le cigare.* "He's empty-headed." See COUPE-CIGARE 1. **2.** Penis. **Couper le cigare.** To circumcise (lit. "to cut the cigar"). *Le Zoroastrien Zubin avait peur de se faire couper le cigare.* "Zoroastrian Zubin was afraid to be circumcised." **3.** Turd. *Il a pris le bidet pour un ouatère et a posé un ciga-re dedans.* "He took the bidet for a toilet and crapped in it." See COUPE-CIGARE 2.

CIGARE À MOUSTACHES, *m.* Penis. *Freud disait: "Nous savons tous que le cigare est symbole du cigare à moustaches, mais il restera toujours un cigare."* Freud said: "We all know the cigar's a phallic symbol, but it'll always be a cigar too."

CINÉ, *abbr.* of **cinéma.** Movies; movie theater. *Samedi soir on va au ciné.* "Saturday night we go to the flicks."

CINOCHE = CINÉ.

CINOCHIER, -ÈRE, *m., f.* Movie enthusiast. *C'est une cinochière de première.* "She's an all-out movie buff."

CINOQUE = SINOQUE.

CINTRÉ, -E. Crazy (lit. "curved"). *Ne crois pas que je sois cintrée; je ne déconne pas.* "Don't think I'm bananas; I'm not kidding."

CIRAGE, *m.* Polishing. **Être dans le cirage; être en plein cirage.** To be in a fog (due to fatigue, alcohol, and so on). *Il ne peut pas te répondre; il est dans le cirage.* "He can't answer you; he's groggy."

CIRER. To polish. **N'en avoir rien à cirer.** To not care. *Ton voyou de fils, je n'en ai rien à cirer.* "Your hoodlum son is no concern of mine."

CIRER LES BOTTES/POMPES À QN. To be sycophantic (lit. "to shine s.o.'s boots or shoes"). *Pour avoir le poste, il cire les bottes du patron.* "He's sucking up to the boss to get the job."

CIRER TOUJOURS LE MÊME BOUTON. To put on the same broken record. *Il ne se lasse pas de cirer toujours le même bouton.* "He never tires of harping on the same string."

CIRQUE, *m.* **1.** Hubub; confusion (lit. "circus"). *Avec la grève, la circulation, quel cirque!* "What with the strike, the traffic's some hassle." See EMMENER…CIRQUE; MENER… CIRQUE. **2.** Carrying on. *Arrête ton cirque.* "Cool it! Stop your song and dance!"

CISAILLER. **1.** To fleece (lit. "to shear") *Il s'est fait cisailler.* "He got taken to the cleaners." **2.** To be astounded. *La nouvelle de leur mort m'a cisaillé.* "The news of their death hit me where I live."

CISTRA, *youth, cités.* Backslang of **raciste.** *"Personne n'est cistra ici,"* disait le commissaire. 'Nobody's racist here,' said the police chief."

CITRON, *m.* Head (lit. "lemon"). See (SE) CREUSER.

CLAMSER. To die. *Avant de clamser, le milliardaire veut se faire cloner.* "Before kicking the bucket, the billionaire wants to have h.s. cloned."

CLANDÉ, *abbr.* of **clandestin. 1.** Illegal brothel; gambling den. *Il allait régulièrement dans un clandé.* "He was a regular patron of an illegal cathouse." **2.** Prostitute in an illegal brothel. *L'été j'arpente; l'hiver je suis clandé.* "I walk the streets in the summer; in the winter I work indoors."

CLAOUIS = GLAOUIS.

CLAPET, *m.* Mouth (lit. "valve"). See FERMER SON CLAPET.

CLAPSER = CLAMSER.

CLAQUE, *f.* **1.** Whack. **En avoir sa claque.** To be fed up. *J'en ai ma claque de travailler la nuit.* "I've had it up to here with working nights." See ALLONGER; TÊTE À CLAQUES. **2.** Severe loss. See PRENDRE UNE CLAQUE.

CLAQUE, *m.* Brothel. *La pension de mes darrons ne rapportant rien, j'en ai fait un claque.* "My parents' boardinghouse wasn't making any money so I turned it into a bawdy house." See TÊTE À CLAQUE (*m.*).

CLAQUE-MERDE, *m.* Mouth. See FERMER SON CLAQUE-MERDE.

CLAQUER. 1. To throw money around (lit. "to slam"). *Il claque tout son fric en misant sur les chevaux.* "He blows all his money on the horses." **2.** To exhaust. *Son boulot l'a claquée totalement.* "Her job's really taken it out of her." **3.** To expire. *Il va en claquer de boire comme un trou.* "It'll be the death of him if he keeps on drinking like that."

CLAQUER DANS LES DOIGTS/MAINS/PATTES. To fail; die; go bust. *Ma bagnole m'a claqué dans les mains.* "My car conked out on me."

CLAQUER DU BEC. To be hungry. *Ils ont claqué du bec pendant leur enfance.* "They often went hungry during their childhood."

CLARINETTE, *f.* Penis. See JOUER…CLARINETTE BAVEUSE.

CLASS, *adj.* and *adv.* Finished. *C'est class!* "That's enough, it's all over." **En avoir class de,** *idiom.* To be sick and tired of. *Il en a class de sa nana.* "He's sick and tired of his woman."

CLASSE, *f.* Class. **Avoir (de) la classe; être la classe.** To be classy/wonderful. *C'est la classe!* "That's top-notch."

CLASSE, *adj.* Classy; great. *C'est classe ton bouquin.* "Your book's terrific."

CLAVARDAGE, *m., Que.* Computer chatting (**clavardage** and **clavarder** "to chat," are coined from **clavier** "keyboard" and **bavardage** "chatting"). *La professeure québéquoise a raison de préférer 'clavardage' à "chatting."* "The Que. professor is right in preferring clavardage to "chatting."

CLEB/CLEBS = CLÉBARD.

CLÉBARD, *m.,* sometimes *pej.* Hound. *On ne le voit jamais sans son clébard.* "You never see him without his mutt."

CLENCHE or **CLINCHE,** *f., Bel.* Doorknob. **Être clinche.** To be clumsy, dumb. *Que t'es clinche!* "What an idiot you are!" *Cf.* CLOCHE.

CLÉOPATRE, *proper n.* Cleopatra. *Elle croit avoir le nez de Cléopâtre.* "She thinks she's hot stuff." **Faire Cléopâtre.** To fellate. *Il crache vite son venin quand je lui fais Cléopâtre.* "He comes fast when I suck him off."

CLEPO/CLEUPO, backslang forms of **clope.**

CLICLI, *m.* Clitoris. *Viens me faire guili-guili au clicli.* "Come tickle my clit."

CLIF!/CLISSE!/CLOUSSE! *Que., euph.* for **CHRIST!**

CLITO, *m., abbr.* of clitoris. **Clitoris.** *Mon clito manifestait, mais il s'en foutait.* "My clit was very excited, but he didn't care."

CLITORISER. To stimulate the clitoris. *Viens me clitoriser un peu.* "Come pay some attention to my clit."

CLOCHE, *adj.* Stupid; ridiculous. *Ce que tu peux être cloche!* "Sometimes you're really thick."

CLOCHE, *f.* **1.** Bell. See SONNER. **2.** Stupid person. *Son père, quelle cloche!* "Her father's some dingbat!" **3.** Stomach. See (SE) TAPER LA CLOCHE; (SE) TASSER LA CLOCHE.

CLOCHE, *f.,* from **clochard** (vagrant; bum). Vagrancy. *Il vit à la cloche.* "He's a hobo."

CLODO, from **clochard.** Bum. *La nuit le métro est plein de clodos.* "The subway's full of bums at night."

CLOPE, *f., m.* Cigarette. *File-moi une clope.* "Give me a cigarette."

CLOPE, *m.* Cigarette butt. *Ses mouflets suçaient les clopes perdus dans le sable.* "Her brats sucked on the cigarette butts left in the sand." See DES CLOPES.

CLOPINETTES. See DES CLOPINETTES/DES CLOPINETTES!

CLOPORTE, *f., m.,* play on **clôt porte** (one who locks up). Concierge. *Le cloporte m'apporte chaque jour mon courrier.* "The super brings me my mail every day."

CLOPORTE, *m.* Creep (lit. "woodlouse"). *Je ne peux pas le voir, ce cloporte.* "I can't stand the sight of that creep."

CLOQUE, *f.* Blister. See EN CLOQUE.

CLOU, *m.* Small amount (lit. "nail"). **Ne pas valoir un clou.** To be worthless. *Ta bagnole ne vaut pas un clou.* "Your car's worthless." See DES CLOUX.

CLOUER LE BEC À QN. To shut s.o. up. *Je lui ai cloué le bec en lui disant la vérité.* "I shut him up by telling him the truth."

COALTAR = COLTAR.

COCHON, *m.* Pig. **Copains comme cochons.** Fast friends. *Ils étaient copains comme cochons avant de rencontrer Mimi.* "They were great buddies before meeting Mimi." See TÊTE DE COCHON.

COCHON PAYEUR, *m.* Cash cow (lit. "paying pig"). *"Pour eux on n'est que des cochons payeurs.* "We're just cash cows for them."

COCO, *m., f.* Communist. *C'est un ancien coco.* "He's a former Commie."

COCO, *m.* Fuel (from **carburant**). *Le prix du coco est fou.* "The price of gas is crazy."

COCOLER. *Swiss.* To pamper. *Maman nous a tous cocolés.* "Mom spoiled us all."

COCORICO, *m.* Patriotic cheer alluding to the fighting spirit of **le coq gaulois**. *Papa a poussé des cocoricos quand la France a gagné la coupe mondiale de foot.* "When France won the soccer World Cup, Papa cheered patriotically." See COQ.

COCOTIER, *m.* Coconut palm tree. See DÉCROCHER LE COCOTIER/GRIMPER AU COCOTIER.

COCOTTE, *f.* **1.** Prostitute, *dated* (lit. "hen"). *Elle écrit un mémoire sur cocottes et courtisanes de la Belle Époque.* "She's writing a thesis on tarts and high-class whores of the Belle Époque." **2.** Pressure cooker. See COCOTTE-MINUTE®.

COCOTTE-MINUTE®, *f.* Prostitute who turns many tricks quickly (lit. "pressure cooker"). *Les cocottes-minute encaissaient un fric fou.* "The fast-working hookers made big bucks."

COGNOTER. To stink. *Les chiottes cognotent un max.* "The toilet stinks to high heaven."

COIN, *m.* Corner. See BOUCHER; PETIT COIN.

COINCER. To stink (lit. "to wedge"). See ÇA COINCE.

COINCER LA BULLE. To nap. *Il roule la nuit sans coincer la bulle.* "He drives at night without getting any sleep."

COING, *m.* Quince. **Beurré/bourré comme un coing.** Dead drunk. *Il est rentré beurré comme un coing.* "He came home soused to the gills." See GELÉE DE COING.

COLIBRI, *m.* Disloyal friend (lit. "hummingbird"). *Ne lui fais pas confiance; c'est un colibri.* "Don't trust him; he's a double-crosser."

COLIS, *m.* **1.** Good-looking girl (lit. "package"). *Vise un peu ce beau colis.* "Take a look at that nice chick." **2.** Fart. See LÂCHER UN COLIS.

COLLABO, *m., pej., abbr.* of **collaborateur.** *Ce collabo prétend avoir été résistant.* "That collaborator claims to have been a member of the Resistance in World War II."

COLLE, *f.* Glue. **Être à la colle** = VIVRE À LA COLLE.

COLLER. 1. To glue. *Rien ne colle dans tes arguments.* "Your arguments aren't coherent." See ÇA COLLE, ANATOLE? **2.** To give or put forcefully. See AVOINE; BAFFE; COLLER UN GOSSE.

COLLER AU CUL/TRAIN DE QN. To harass by tagging onto s.o. *J'en ai marre de ce mec qui ne cesse de me coller au cul.* "I'm tired of that guy who follows me around everywhere."

COLLER AUX FESSES = COLLER AU CUL.

COLLER UN GOSSE À UNE FEMME. To get a woman pregnant. *Il lui a collé un gosse mais il dit n'en avoir rien à cirer.* "He got her pregnant but he says it's none of his business."

(SE) COLLER. To shack up with. *Elle l'aime mais ne veut pas encore se coller.* "She loves him but doesn't want to move in with him yet."

(S'EN) COLLER. To not give a damn. *Tes problèmes, je m'en colle!* "What do I care about your problems?"

COLO, *f.* from **colonie de vacances.** *Elle a envoyé ses gosses en colo.* "She sent her kids off to summer camp."

COLONNE, *f.* Penis (lit. "column"). See ASTIQUER LA COLONNE.

COL ROULÉ. See ANDOUILLE...ROULÉ; CHAUVE...ROULÉ; PETIT...ROULÉ.

COLTAR, *m.* Coal tar. **Être dans le coltar; être en plein coltar.** To be in a daze. *Après leur accident de voiture ils étaient en plein coltar.* "After their car accident they were in a stupor."

(SE) COLTINER. 1. To endure. *Non seulement je dois me coltiner un boulot chiant mais aussi le patron et sa sale caboche.* "Not only do I have to put up with that rotten job, I've also got to endure the boss and his lousy temper." **2.** To fight. *Les deux frères se sont coltinés à cause d'une nana.* "The two brothers came to blows over a broad."

COMAC/COMAQUE = COMACO.

COMACO or **COMACOS.** Enormous. *Elle était comaco en attendant ses triplets.* "She was really humongous when expecting her triplets."

COMINGUE = COMMIS.

COMMACE, *youth, cités.* Backslang of **comme ça**. *Je le veux commace.* "I want it this way."

COMME = COMMISS.

COMME PAS DEUX. Like nobody else. *Il a joué aujourd'hui aux échecs comme pas deux.* "Nobody could have played chess today the way he did."

COMME SES PIEDS. See CON…PIEDS.

COMME UN CHEVEU SUR LA SOUPE. At an inopportune time (lit. "like a hair on the soup"). *Cette nouvelle arrive comme un cheveu sur la soupe.* "That news has come at an awkward moment."

COMME UN PIED. Very poorly. *Il chante, danse, et joue comme un pied, mais ça lui fait plaisir.* "His singing, dancing, and playing are lousy, but he enjoys h.s."

COMME UNE FLEUR. 1. Easily. *J'ai fini le boulot comme une fleur.* "I finished the job with no sweat." **2.** Unexpectedly. *Comme une fleur elle m'a annoncé qu'elle me quittait.* "Just like that, she announced she was leaving me."

COMMISS, *f.,* short for **commission.** Accomplice's share of the loot; percentage. *Il travaille à la commiss.* "He works on a commission basis."

COMMISSIONS, *f., pl.* Errands. See FAIRE SES COMMISSIONS.

COMPAS, *m., pl.* Legs (from the "legs" of a compass). See JOUER DES COMPAS.

COMPRENETTE, *f.* Intelligence. *T'as pas la comprenette facile.* "You're slow on the uptake."

COMPRENOIRE = COMPRENETTE.

COMPTER POUR DU BEURRE. See BEURRE 1.

CON, *m.* **1.** External female genitalia. *Elle ferait bien de foutre plus souvent son con sur le bidet.* "She should wash her snatch more often." **2.** Jerk. *Ne fais pas le con!* "Don't be such an asshole." See CONNE; DÉCONNER; DUCON; (SE) RETROUVER…CON.

CON, -NE. Idiotic. *Qu'est-ce qu'il (elle) est con (conne)!* "He's (she's) really foolish." (Note: The *m.* **con** is often used for women also, as in *Qu'est qu'elle est con!*) **Avoir l'air con,** *idiom,* see AIR. See also CON À…; CON COMME….

CON À BOUFFER DE LA BITE/COMME UNE BITE, stronger equivalents of **con comme un balai/panier; con comme ses pieds/la lune.** Absolutely stupid. *Ton pote est con comme une bite.* "Your chum is a dumb dickhead. He doesn't know his ass from his elbow."

CONARD, -E = CONNARD, -E.

CON COMME UN BALAI/PANIER; CON COMME SES PIEDS/LA LUNE. Very stupid (lit. "dumb as a broom or basket; dumb as his feet or the moon"). *Pas la peine de lui parler; il est con comme un balai.* "No point in talking to him; he's a dumb jerk."

(À LA) CON. Worthless; ridiculous. *C'était un film à la con.* "The movie was trash."

CONCHE DE PÉLERIN, *f.* Female genitalia (lit. "pilgrim's conch shell"). *Pendant le voyage à Compostelle* *mon jacques ne rêvait qu'à sa conche de pélerin.* "All through the trip to Compostela, all my dick dreamt of was her pussy."

CONDÉ, *m.* **1.** Policeman. *Ce petit voyou est maintenant condé.* "That little hood's a cop now." **Avoir le condé.** To enjoy police protection for s.t. illicit in return for providing information. *La pègre se méfie de lui, car il a le condé.* "The mob doesn't trust him because he's in cahoots with the cops."

CONDUITE, *f.* Behavior. **S'acheter une conduite.** To turn over a new leaf. *Après la tôle il s'est acheté une conduite.* "After doing time he went straight."

CONDUITE DE GRENOBLE, *f.* Walking papers. *Peu s'en faudrait que je lui fasse la conduite de Grenoble.* "It won't take much more for me to give him the boot."

CONFIT EN DEVOTION. Extremely religious (lit. "pickled/preserved in piety"). *Il a l'air tout confit en devotion mais ce n'est que de la haute tartufferie.* "You'd think butter wouldn't melt in his mouth but it's out and out hypocrisy."

CONNARD. *m.* Jackass; SOB. *Ce connard a embouti ma voiture.* "That dumb bastard smashed into my car."

CONNARDE = CONNASSE.

CONNASSE, *f.* **1.** Contemptible female. *Laisse tomber; c'est une connasse!* "Drop her; she's a dumb bitch." **2.** Cunt. See CON **1.**

CONNE, *f.* Foolish woman. *Quelle conne! Son mec la mène par le bout du nez.* "What a dumb broad; her guy walks all over her."

CONNEAU = CONNARD.

CONNEMENT. Stupidly. *Il a agi connement avec elle.* "He behaved like a real fool with her."

CONNERIE, *f.* Stupid action or speech. *Tout ce que tu dis ou fais, ce ne sont que des conneries.* "Everything you do and say is idiotic."

CONOMÈTRE, *m.* Stupidity gauge (hum. coinage, *Cf.* **pifomètre; trouillomètre**). **Faire péter le conomètre.** To break all records for idiocy. *Une histoire pareille, c'est à faire péter le conomètre.* "S.t. like that is the idiocy to end all idiocy."

CONSTIPÉ, -E. Constipated; strained. **Constipé du morlingue,** see MORLINGUE.

CONTREDANSE, *f.* Parking fine (lit. "quadrille"). *Partons d'ici pour éviter une contredanse.* "Let's get out of here before we get a ticket."

(SE) CONTREFICHE DE QCH. = SE CONTRE-FOUTRE DE QCH.

(SE) CONTREFOUTRE DE QCH., intensifies **se foutre de qch.** To not care at all. *Je me contrefous de ce que tu penses.* "I don't give a good goddamn what you think."

(S'EN) CONTREFOUTRE = (SE) CONTREFOUTRE DE QCH. *Tu vas où tu veux, je m'en contrefous.* "Go wherever you want, I couldn't care less."

CONVERSADE, *f.* Conversation; talk show. *Trop bavarde, Ève ne peut suivre aucune conversade.* "Eve's too much of a chatterbox to listen to anyone else talk."

COPAIN-COPAIN, *adj.* Buddy-buddy. *Luc a toujours été copain-copain avec Marc.* "Luke and Mark have always been great buddies."

COPAINS COMME COCHONS. Thick as thieves. See COCHON.

COQ, *m.* Rooster. **Coq du village.** Local ladykiller, Casanova. *Le coq du village voulait tout de suite me sauter.* "The village Lothario wanted to get into my pants right away." **Être comme un coq en pâte.** To be in clover, be cock of the walk. *Ce maq est un vrai coq en pâte, super bien entretenu par ses poules.* "That pimp's well taken care of by his whores and lives the life of Riley." See COCORICO.

COQUELICOTS, *m., pl.* Menstrual period (lit. "poppies" [a red flower]). *Après son doublé, elle attend le retour de* *ses coquelicots.* "After giving birth to twins, she's waiting for her period to return."

CORMORAN, *m.* Undertaker (lit. "cormorant," a black bird). *Pas baisant, le type avec la gueule d'un cormoran.* "Not very appealing, that guy with his gravedigger face."

CORNARD, *m.* Cuckolded husband (see next entry). *Ce con de cornard ignore qu'elle le trompe avec tous.* "Her chump of a husband doesn't know she's putting horns on him."

CORNOUAILLES. Cornwall (in Brittany). **Aller en Cornouailles** (play on **cornes** [horns], associated with husbands whose wives cheat on them). To be a cuckold. *Ça fait un moment que son mari va en Cornouailles.* "Her husband's been wearing horns for some time."

COT(H)URNE/CO-T(H)URNE, *m.* Roommate. *Quel casse couilles, mon coturne!* "My roommate's a real ball buster." See THURNE.

COTON, *m.* **1.** Cotton. *J'ai les jambes en coton.* "I'm feeling wobbly." **Filer un mauvais coton.** To be in difficult circumstances. *Pol, malade et au chômage, file un mauvais coton.* "Sick and unemployed, Pol's going through a bad patch." **2.** *adj.* Difficult, tricky. *Il a des problèmes coton.* "He has tough problems."

COUCHER AVEC LA FEMME DE L'ADJUDANT. See ADJUDANT.

COUCHERIE, *f., pej.* Casual sex. *Je croyais avoir trouvé l'amour de ma vie mais pour lui ce n'était qu'une coucherie.* "I thought I'd found the love of my life but it was just a one night stand for him."

COUCOUNE, *f., Que.* Naïve girl. *Je fais souvent la coucoune. Les gars aiment ça.* "I often come on as a dumb bunny. Guys like that."

COUDE, *m.* Elbow. See HUILE DE COUDE; LÂCHER...COUDE; LEVER LE COUDE.

COUIC. See (N'Y) PIGER QUE COUIC.

COUILLE, *f.* **1.** Testicle. See COUILLES. **2.** Mistake. *J'ai fait une belle couille.* "I made a beaut of a mistake." **C'est de la couille (en barres, en bâtons).** Worthless. *Tout ce que tu as pris, c'est de la couille en barres.* "Everything you bought is a load of crap." **3.** *m., youth, cités.* Chum. *Il est sorti avec les couilles.* "He's out with his buddies." *Cf.* SAUCE.

COUILLE MOLLE, *f.* Gutless person (lit. "flabby testicle"). *Je refuse de faire quoi que ce soit avec cette couille molle.* "I don't want to do anything at all with that wimp."

COUILLES, *f., pl.* Testicles. **Avoir des couilles (au cul); en avoir.** To be ballsy or gutsy. *Cette gonzesse a des couilles au cul.* "She's a real gutsy lady" (lit. "That broad's got balls on her ass"). **Se faire des couilles en or,** *idiom.* To make a lot of money. *Ils pensaient se faire des couilles en or.* "They thought they were going to make a bundle." **S'en battre les couilles.** To be indifferent (lit. "to flap one's balls"). *Qu'il crève! Je m'en bats les couilles.* "Let him croak! I couldn't care less/I don't give a flying fuck." Note: **Je m'en bats les couilles** and **je m'en branle** are sl. More socially acceptable for "I couldn't care less" is **Je m'en moque.** *Cf.* BALEK!; (S'EN) BRANLER. See (SE) BRANLER **2**; CASSE-COUILLES; CASSER LES COUILLES; (SE) CASSER LES COUILLES; DE MES DEUX; LÂCHER...COUILLES; MES COUILLES!; PARTIR EN COUILLE(S); RAS; TOMBER EN COUILLE(S).

COUILLER = COUILLONNER.

COUILLON, -NE, Really stupid. *Que tu es couillon!* "You're a real idiot." **Avoir l'air couillon,** see AIR.

COUILLON, *m.* Jerk. *Ne fais pas le couillon.* "Don't act like such an idiot."

COUILLONNADE, *f.* Nonsense. *Ça c'est une sacrée couillonnade!* "That's a whole bunch of baloney."

COUILLONNER. To deceive. *On s'est fait tous couillonné par le patron.* "All of us were conned by the boss."

COUILLONNERIE = COUILLONNADE.

COULER UN BRONZE. To defecate (lit. "to cast a bronze statue"). See BRONZE.

(SE LA) COULER DOUCE. To take it easy; live a cushy life. *Lennie rêvait de se la couler douce.* "Lenny dreamed of living off the fat of the land."

COULEUVRE, *f.* Snake. **Avaler des couleuvres.** To face up to hostility (lit. "to swallow snakes"). *Dans mon métier il faut savoir avaler des couleuvres.* "In my profession, you've got to be able to take the heat."

COUP, *m.* **1.** Blow. See ALLONGER; BOURRER 2; ÉCRASER LE COUP; MARQUER LE COUP; TENIR LE COUP; TIRER UN COUP. **2.** Scheme; scam. **Faire un coup,** *idiom. Ils ont fait le coup ensemble.* "They pulled off the operation together." **3.** Drink. **Boire or prendre un coup,** *idiom.* To have a drink. *Allons boire un coup.* "Let's have a drink." **4.** Skill. **Avoir le coup,** *idiom.* To be competent. *Pour diriger son monde, il a le coup.* "He's got what it takes to get people to do what he wants." **5.** Occasional sex partner; sex. *En tant que V.R.P. (voyageur représentant de commerce) je cherche souvent un coup pour la soirée. Parfois je trouve un bon coup, une nana bien baisable.* "As a travelling salesman I often look for s.o. to sleep with and sometimes find a really good lay, a chick really worth fucking." See TIRER UN COUP.

COUP DANS L'AILE. Tipsy condition. *Il a déjà un coup dans l'aile mais il réclame toujours à boire.* "He's already half-loaded but still wants more."

COUP DANS LE NEZ. Drunkenness. *Il a pris un coup dans le nez.* "He got loaded!"

COUP DE BALAI, *m.* Police raid. *Dans ce coup de balai, tous les toxicos des Halles ont été agrafés.* "All the Les Halles area junkies got nabbed during that raid."

COUP DE BARRE/POMPE. See POMPE 2.

COUP DE BOL/VEINE, *m.* Stroke of luck. *C'était un coup de bol de sortir vivant de cet accident.* "Surviving that accident was real luck."

COUP DE FEU, *m.* Period of peak activity. *Impossible de se faire servir au resto; c'était le coup de feu.* "Impossible to get any service; the restaurant was packed."

COUP DE FIL/BIGO/BIGOPHONE, *m.* See BIGO.

COUP DE FILET = COUP DE BALAI.

COUP DE FOUDRE, *m.* Love at first sight (lit. "flash of lightning"). *Ce bracelet, c'était le coup de foudre.* "I saw that bracelet and just had to have it."

COUP DE FOURCHETTE, *m.* Big appetite. *Quel sacré coup de fourchette!* "What a gargantuan appetite!"

COUP DE FUSIL/BAMBOU/BARRE, *m.* Steep bill. *Je ne m'attendais pas à un tel coup de fusil dans ce resto.* "I didn't expect to get fleeced like that in that restaurant."

COUP DE GUEULE, *m.* See POUSSER…GUEULE.

COUP DE JARNAC, *m.* **1.** Unexpected, decisive blow (from a duel fought by Guy de Jarnac). *Ils m'ont filé le coup de Jarnac et c'était la fin des haricots.* "They caught me off guard, thrust home, and it was curtains." **2.** Stab in the back; low blow. *Bourré de cognac, il m'a fait un coup de Jarnac.* "Tanked up on cognac, he pulled a dirty trick on me."

COUP DE PIED DE VÉNUS, *m.* See VÉNUS.

COUP (DE PIED) EN VACHE = COUP DE JARNAC 2.

COUP DE QUEUE/SABRE/GUISOT, *m.* See FILER LE COUP DE GUISOT; SABRE.

COUP DE TÊTE, *m.* Impulse. *Je l'a acheté sur un coup de tête.* "I bought it on impulse."

COUP DE TRAFALGAR, *m.* Violent situation or behavior (from the site of a Fr. naval defeat in 1805). *Mai 1968, c'était le coup de Trafalgar.* "May 1968 was a powder keg."

COUP DE TROP, *m.* Drunkenness. *Il a bu un coup de trop.* "He's had one too many."

COUP DE VIEUX. See PRENDRE…VIEUX.

COUP DU LAPIN, *m.* **1.** Rabbit punch (brutal blow to the neck). *Le truand lui avait fait le coup du lapin.* "The hood rabbit-punched him." **2.** Whiplash. *Il est sorti de l'accident de voiture avec le coup du lapin.* "He suffered a whiplash injury in the car accident."

COUPE-CHIASSE, *m.* Pharmacist (lit. "diarrhea stopper"). *Je pars chez le coupe-chiasse chercher des médicaments.* "I'm going to the drugstore for medicine."

COUPE-CIGARE, *m.* **1.** Guillotine (Lit. "cigar cutter"). *Beaucoup d'aristos ont échappé au coupe-cigare.* "Many aristocrats escaped the guillotine." See CIGARE **1**. **2.** Anus. *Il a des émeraudes au coupe-cigare.* "He's got piles." See CIGARE **3**.

COUPER. To cut. **Couper à qch.** To avoid s.t. *J'ai coupé à l'attente du bus en faisant du stop.* "I avoided having to wait for the bus by hitching a ride." **Ne pas y couper.** To be unavoidable. *Si je rentre tard, l'engueulade, je n'y couperai pas.* "If I get home late, there's no way I'll avoid getting bawled out."

COUPER COMME LES GENOUX D'UNE BONNE SŒUR. To have a dull blade (lit. "to cut like a nun's knees" [blunted by frequent kneeling]). *Je ne peux rien faire avec ce couteau qui coupe comme les genoux d'une bonne sœur.* "I can't do anything with this dull knife."

COUPER LA CHIQUE/LE SIFFLET À QN/LA COUPER À QN. To interrupt. *J'ai perdu le fil; tu m'as coupé la chique.* "I've lost the thread; you cut me off." See ÇA TE LA COUPE!

COUPER LE CIGARE. See CIGARE **2**.

COUPE-TIFS, *m.* Hairdresser. *Mon coupe-tifs est dans le coup.* "My hairdresser's up on the latest styles."

COUP FOURRÉ, *m.* **1.** Sticky situation. *Il a réussi à se sortir de ce coup fourré.* "He managed to get out of a hairy situation." **2.** Dirty trick. *Il avait monté un coup fourré pour divorcer.* "He resorted to underhanded means to get a divorce."

COUPER LE JUS. See JUS **2.**

COUPS DE PIED (AU CUL) QUI SE PERDENT, *m.,* *pl.* Useless disciplining. *Il y a des coups de pied qui se perdent.* "Some people are hopeless cases."

COURAGE ARROSÉ, *m.* Alcohol-inspired courage. *Sans son petit courage arrosé il n'aurait jamais dit ça au chef.* "He never would have said that to the boss without Dutch courage."

COUREUR DE JUPONS, *m.* Skirt chaser. *Elle a eu la malchance d'épouser un coureur de jupons.* "She had the misfortune to marry a womanizer."

COUREUSE, *f.* Promiscuous woman. *Ce coureur de jupons préfère les vierges aux coureuses.* "That philanderer prefers virgins to easy lays."

COURIR LE GUILLEDOU. To look for love (more gallant than **draguer**). *Son dab court toujours le guilledou.* "Her father's still game for a little amorous adventure."

COURIR SUR LE HARICOT/SYSTÈME. To exasperate. *Ce dragueur commence à me courir sur le haricot.* "That guy's coming on to me is getting on my nerves."

COURRIEL, *m.* E-mail. *Je t'enverrai un mail.—Il faut plutôt dire 'un courriel'.* "I'll send you an e-mail.—It's better to say *un courriel.*" (Most speakers still say "*mail,*" sometimes written "*mél.*" But courriel, a Que. coinage from **courrier électronique**, is, happily, gaining ground.) See POURRIEL.

COURT-JUS, *m.* Short circuit. *Il y a un court-jus dans cette prise.* "There's a short circuit in this outlet."

COURT-JUS DANS LA PENSEUSE, *m.* Headache. *Je me suis levé avec un court-jus dans la penseuse.* "I woke up with a headache."

COÛTER BONBON. See BONBON **1.**

COÛTER LES YEUX DE LA TÊTE = COÛTER LA PEAU DES FESSES. See PEAU DES FESSES.

COUVERT TROIS PIÈCES = SERVICE TROIS PIÈCES.

CRABE, *m.* Crab. See FACE DE CRABE; PANIER DE CRABES.

CRAC, *m.* Female genitalia. See CRACK; SAUTE-AU-CRAC.

CRACHER EN L'AIR. To make a wasted effort. *Lui donner des conseils, c'est cracher en l'air.* "Giving him advice is like spitting in the wind."

CRACK, *m.* **1.** Champion, ace. **2.** Vagina. **3.** Crack cocaine. *Ève, non seulement grand crack en informatique est dotée d'un crack mouillé bien tendu, presque la perfection si elle n'était pas accro au crack.* "Eve's not just a computer whiz. She also got a well-lubricated, tight pussy. Her only defect is she's hooked on crack cocaine."

CRACRA. Filthy. *Sa baraque est cracra.* "His place is filthy."

CRADE/CRADINGUE/CRADO = CRACRA.

CRAGNOS or **CRAIGNOS.** Horrible; weird; scary (from **craindre** "to fear"). *C'est craignos chez mes vioques.* "It's really hairy with my parents."

CRAMOUILLE, *f.* Female genitalia. *Sa cramouille mouille bien.* "Her pussy gets excited easily."

CRAMPE, *f.* Cramp. See TIRER SA CRAMPE.

CRAMPETTE = CRAMPE.

CRAMSER/CRAMPSER = CLAMSER.

CRÂNE, *m.* **1.** Head. See BOURRER LE CRÂNE. **2.** Arrest. *Il y a eu un crâne dans le village.* "There was an arrest made in the village."

CRAPOTEUX, -EUSE. Filthy. *Après avoir crapahuté toute la journée, on était crapoteux.* "After hiking over rough terrain all day, we were filthy."

CRAPSER = CLAMSER.

CRAQUANT or **CRAQUOS.** Marvelous; irrestible; hilarious. *On a passé des jours craquos ensemble.* "We spent wonderful days together."

CRAQUER. To go for, fall for (lit. "to crack"). *J'ai craqué pour cette robe. Les mecs me trouveront craquante.* "I couldn't resist that dress. The guys will find me irresistable."

CRAQUETTE, *f.* Female genitalia. *Je voulais lui faire mon numéro de claquettes mais Pol s'interessait plutôt à ma craquette.* "I wanted to do my tap dance routine for him but Pol was more interested in my little crack." *Cf.* CRACK; SAUTE-AU-CRAC.

CRASPEC. Filthy. *Je n'ai jamais vu qch. d'aussi craspec.* "I've never seen anything so grungy."

CRASSOUILLE, *f.* Dirt. *Il est d'une crassouille repoussante.* "He's revoltingly dirty."

CRAVATE, *f.* Necktie. See (S'EN) JETER UN.

CRAYONS, *m., pl.* Legs (lit. "pencils"). See (S') EMMÊLER LES CRAYONS.

CRÈCHE, *f.* **1.** Day-nursery (lit. "crib; creche"). *Après le boulot je vais chercher les enfants à la crèche.* "After work I pick up the kids at the day nursery." **2.** Vagina. **Mettre le bébé Jésus dans la crèche.** To have intercourse. *Mettre le bébé Jésus dans la crèche, ça fait du bien—pas seulement à Noël.* "A good lay is always welcome, not just at Xmas." See JÉSUS **2.**

CRÈCHER. To hang out; to reside; to "crash." *Je voulais crècher chez eux.* "I wanted to crash at their pad."

CRÈME, *f.* **1.** Cream. **C'est de la crème!** It's a cinch/piece of cake. *Cf.* CHOCOLAT; GÂTEAU. **2.** Sweet girl, *youth. Ma crème, c'est toute ma vie.* "My little sweetie pie is everything to me." **3.** Sperm. *Comme Cléopatre elle adore les bains de lait et quand elle fait Cléopatre elle gobe goulument la crème.* "Like Cleopatra she loves milk baths and when she sucks cock she greedily gobbles the cream."

CRÈME!/CRIC!/CRIFFE!/CRIME!/CRIME-POF!/ CRIS!/CRISTAL! *Que., euph. for* **Christ!** *Cris que tu sais me pogner les nerfs.* "Jeez you really know how to get on my nerves."

CRÉMER. To ejaculate. *Il a crémé trop vite.* "He came too fast."

CRESSON, *m.* Female pubic hair (lit. "watercress"). See BROUTER LE CRESSON; IDEM...; RAS...CRESSON.

CRÉTIN, *m.* Moron, cretin (from **chrétien** *"Christian"*). *Ce crétin de curé essaye de nous convertir.* "That idiot priest is trying to convert us."

(SE) CREUSER LE CIBOULOT/CITRON/LA CER-VELLE/TÊTE/ TIRELIRE. To rack one's brains, put one's thinking cap on. *Et si tu te creusais la tirelire un peu?* "Try using your noodle a bit."

CRÈVE-CŒUR, *m.* Heartbreak. *C'était un crève-cœur pour moi quand on s'est séparés.* "It was heartbreaking for me when we separated."

CREVER LA FAIM/DALLE. To be extremely hungry. See DALLE.

CREVER LA GUEULE OUVERTE. To be utterly abandoned (lit. "to croak open-mouthed [with one's tongue hanging out]"). *Elle s'est taillée avec son jules en laissant son mari crever la gueule ouverte.* "She took off with her lover and left her husband to go to hell."

(SE) CREVER LE CUL = (S')ESQUINTER LES TRIPES.

CRIME, *f.,* for **la brigade criminelle,** Fr. equivalent of the FBI. Criminal investigation squad. *La crime a mis la main sur le gangster.* "The Feds caught the gangster."

CRISSE!/CRISSE DE TABERNAK! *Que.* Christ! Jesus Christ! God damn it! *Crisse de tabernak que tu me dégoûtes!* "Christ, how you disgust me!" *Crisse que t'es belle!* "God you're gorgeous!" See SACRE **2.**

CRISSER. *Que.* Verb formed from **chrisse!** Equivalent of *foutre* in **foutre la paix/patience** and **foutre le camp.** *Crisse-moi la paix! Crisse le camp!* "Fer chrissake, lea'me alone an' fuck off!"

CROCS, *m., pl.* Teeth; fangs. **Avoir les crocs.** To be ravenously hungry. *On avait les crocs après cette grande* *balade.* "We wanted to get our teeth into food after that long walk."

CROIX, *f.* Cross. **Faire une croix dessus.** To kiss s.t. goodbye (lit. "*to make a cross over s.t.*). *Il te doit de l'argent? Tu peux faire une croix dessus!* "He owes you money? You can kiss it goodbye!"

CROSSE, *f.* Quarrel (lit. "stick"; "crozier"). See CHERCHER DES CROSSES.

(SE) CROSSER. 1. To fight. *Arretez de vous crosser!* "Stop fighting!" **2.** *Que.* To masturbate. *Quel narcissique! Il n'aime que se crosser et avaler la crème.* "What a narcissist! All he likes to do is whack off and swallow the come."

CROTTE! *euph.* for **merde!** "Damn it! Shoot! Sugar!"

CROTTE VINEUSE, *f.* Excrement that reeks of wine. *Cet engrais sent la crotte vineuse.* "That fertilizer smells of winey shit."

CROUME, *m.* Credit. See À CROUME.

CROÛTE, *f.* Food. See CASSER LA CROÛTE; GAGNER SA CROÛTE.

CUCU(L)/CUCUL LA PRALINE. Silly; nuts. *Qu'est-qu'il est cucul la praline, ton frangin.* "Your brother's really zany."

CUILLER/CUILLÈRE, *f.* **1.** Spoon. **Ne pas y aller avec le dos de la cuiller.** To be unstinting. *Quand tu offres des cadeaux, tu n'y vas pas avec le dos de la cuiller.* "When you give presents, you really go all out." **2.** Hand. See SERRER...CUILLER.

CUISSE, *f.* Thigh. **Avoir la cuisse légère.** To be an easy lay. *Ne croyez pas que j'ai la cuisse légère.* "Don't think it's easy to get into my pants."

CUIT, -E. Drunk (lit. "cooked"). *Il est rentré complètement cuit.* "He came home totally soused."

CUITE, *f.* Drunkenness. See PRENDRE UNE CUITE.

CUL, *adj.* Stupid. **Avoir l'air cul.** See AIR.

CUL, *m.* **1.** Posterior; bottom. **Avoir le cul bordé de nouilles.** To have a cushy job; be very lucky (lit. "to have one's ass in a bed of noodles"). One explanation for this expression is that soft noodles were substituted for the hard religious medals mothers once attached to baby clothes. *Maintenant il a le cul bordé de nouilles.* "Now he's sitting pretty." **L'avoir dans le cul = l'avoir dans le baba.** See BABA. See ASTAP(E); BOUTIQUE 1; (SE) CASSER LE CUL; COLLER AU CUL; COUILLES AU CUL; COUPS DE PIED AU CUL; FEU AU CUL; GROS CUL; LÈCHE-CUL; (SE) MAGNER LE CUL; MON CUL!; PÉTER...CUL; PAPIER-CUL; PISSER AU CUL; RAS; (EN) RESTER...CUL; TAPE-CUL; TIRE-AU-CUL; TORCHE-CUL. **2.** Jackass. *Épouser un cul pareil, quelle conne!* "Marrying an asshole like that, what a dumb broad!" See CASSE-CUL; TROU DU CUL. **3.** Sexual activity. **Aller au cul.** To have sex, a "piece of ass." *Il a la trouille du SIDA et ne va plus du tout au cul.* "He's afraid of AIDS and has stopped having sex." **4.** Pornography. *Le cul, il n'y a que ça qui le branche.* "The only thing that turns him on is porn." See DE CUL. **5.** Luck. *On a eu un sacré cul de trouver cette maison.* "We were incredibly lucky to find this house."

CUL BÉNI, *m.* Holy Joe: prayer sister (lit. "blessed asshole"). *Quel casse-cul, ce cul béni et sa tartuferie; c'est un cul béni sur un cul-de-sac spirituel.* "What a pain in the ass, Mr. Holier-than-thou and his sanctimonious moralizing; he's a Holy Joe on a spiritual dead-end road."

CULBUTER. To have sexually (lit. "to tumble"). *Mussolini, souvent pressé, culbutaient les nanas dans son bureau.* "Mussolini, often in a hurry, used to ball chicks in his office."

CUL ENTRE DEUX CHAISES. In an uncertain state (lit. "ass between two stools"). *T'as encloqué cette loute. Ne reste pas le cul entre deux chaises; épouse-la.* "You knocked up that broad. Don't wait around with a finger up your ass; marry her."

CUL ET CHEMISE. On close terms (lit. "ass and shirt"). *Ma femme est cul et chemise avec les curetons.* "My wife and the priests piss in one pot."

CULOT, *m.* Impudence. *Quel culot il a!* "He's got some nerve!"

CULOTTE, *f.* Underpants. **Baisser sa culotte = baisser son froc.** See FROC. See also CHIER…CULOTTE.

CULOTTÉ, -E. Impudent. *Il fait souvent des remarques culottées.* "He often makes impudent remarks."

CUL SEC! Bottoms up!

CUL-TERREUX, *m., pej.* Rube. *Je suis cul-terreux et fier de l'être.* "I'm a country bumpkin and proud of it."

CURETON, *m., pej. Le cureton défroqué a épousé une ancienne réligieuse.* "The defrocked priest married an ex-nun."

CURETOT/CURETOSSE = CURETON.

CUVER SON VIN. To sleep it off (lit. "to ferment one's wine"). *Va couver ton vin et fous-moi la paix.* "Go sleep it off and leave me alone."

D, *m*. D. See SYSTÈME D.

-DA. Slang suffix. See CHARRIDA; FLAGADA; FLAGDA; MARIDA.

DAAWA, *m., youth, cités.* Disorder, riotous behavior. (From Ar. "mass meeting, assembly"). *C'est quoi ce daawa?* "What's this commotion?" *Cf.* HALA.

DAB/DABE, *m.* **1.** Father. *Son dab faisait tout pour bien l'élever.* "His dad did all he could to bring him up right." **2.** Boss. **Le Grand Dab.** God. *Elle rejette les parrains mafieux et l'idée patriarcale du Grand Dab au ciel.* "She rejects Mafia godfathers and the patriarchal idea of the Big Boss in the sky."

DABE, *f*. Mother. *Elle s'intéresse plutôt à la Déesse-Dabe.* "She's more interested in the Mother-Goddess."

DABES, *m., pl.* Parents. *Mes dabes pètent la forme.* "My parents are in excellent health." *Cf.* DARONS; REMPAS; VIOQUES.

DABESSE = DABE, *f*.

DABUCHE = DABE, *f*.

D'ACHAR/D'ACHAR ET D'AUTOR. See (D')ACHAR.

(À) DACHE. Very far away. *Ils ont envie d'habiter à dache.* "They want to move to the boonies."

DALLE, *f*. Throat (lit. "flagstone"). **Avoir la dalle en pente.** To be forever thirsty. *Nous avons la dalle en pente.* "We need a drink." **Avoir la dalle/crever/péter la dalle.** To be very hungry. *Le boulot fini, je crève la dalle.* "I'm starved after work." See QUE DALLE; (SE) RINCER…DALLE.

DALLEPÉ, backslang of **pédale.**

DAME-PIPI, *f.* Female toilet attendant. *La dame-pipi criait: "N'oubliez pas le service!"* "The toilet attendant cried out: 'Don't forget the service charge!'"

DANS LE CUL LA BALAYETTE!/DANS LE DOS LA BALAYETTE! "It's all over! Curtains! We've been shafted! We've had it up the ass!"

DARD, *m.* Penis (lit. "sting"). See POMPER LE DARD.

DARDILLON, *m., dim.* of **dard.** Penis. **Avoir le dardillon.** To have an erection. *Il avait le dardillon.* "His prick was up."

DARE-DARE. Double quick. *Démarrons dare-dare!* "Let's get going, on the double!" *Cf.* TAF-TAF.

DARGEOT/DARGIF, *m.* Buttocks. *Elle avait un dargeot prometteur.* "She had an inviting derriere."

DARON, *m.* Boss; father; brothel keeper. *Je fais tout pour plaire à mon daron, mais il me bat quand même.* "I do everything to please my boss, but he still beats me."

DARONNE, *f.* Mother; madam (brothel). *Elle était une daronne pour nous toutes.* "She was a mother to all of us."

DARONS, *pl.* Parents. *Parfois mes darons me font chier.* "Sometimes my parents really piss me off." *Cf.* DABES; REMPAS; VIOQUES.

DARRAC/DARRAQUE, *m.* **1.** Hammer. *Heine imaginait Thor et son darrac écraser les cathédrales.* "Heine imagined Thor and his hammer crushing the cathedrals." **2.** Penis. *Son darrac, un vrai derrick, jaillit la sauce qui me fait carburer.* "His dick, a real derrick, gushes the come that keeps me going."

DASS, *m.* Backslang of SIDA (AIDS).

DATTE, *f.* Date. **Ne pas en ficher; foutre une datte.** See DES DATTES.

DDAS. Acronym of **Direction départementale de l'action sociale et sanitaire.** Regional health and social services agency. **Un enfant de la DDAS.** An orphaned or abandoned child sent to foster parents by the agency. *Jean n'a jamais eu de pot. Il était enfant de la DDAS et maintenant il a le dass.* "Jean never had any luck. He was a ward of the state farmed out to foster parents and now he has AIDS."

DÉBALLER. To confess (lit. "to unpack"). *Il m'a enfin déballé toute son histoire.* "He finally revealed the whole story to me."

DÉBALLER LE JAR(S). To talk (thieves') slang. *Ils déballaient le jars pour ne pas être compris.* "They talked slang so as not to be understood."

DÉBANDER. 1. To lose one's erection. *Il débande pour un rien.* "He goes limp at the slightest little thing." **2.** To be afraid. *Ne débande pas devant les flics.* "Don't turn chicken when the cops question you." See SANS DÉBANDER.

DÉBARBOUILLER. To kill (lit. "to give a quick wash [face, car]"). *La pègre l'a vite débarbouillé.* "The mob rubbed him out fast."

DÈBE, from **débile** (mental). Lamebrained. *Cesse de me traiter de dèbe.* "Quit calling me a retard."

DÉBECTANT, -E. Repulsive. *Cette carne pleine de mouches est débectante.* "That meat covered with flies is yucky."

DÉBECTER. To disgust. *Ça me débecte!* "That makes me want to throw up."

DÉBILOS = DÈBE.

DEBS = DÈBE.

DÉBINE, *f.* Extreme poverty. *Elle l'a épousé quand il était en pleine débine.* "She married him when he was at rock bottom."

DÉBINER. To inform on. *Son meilleur copain l'a débiné.* "His best friend ratted on him."

(SE) DÉBINER. To scram. *Ils se sont débinés avant la fin du spectacle.* "They ran off before the end of the show."

DÉBOISÉ, -E. Bald (lit. "deforested"). *Gershwin avait la trouille de se trouver totalement déboisé.* "Gershwin was terrified of winding up totally bald."

(SE) DÉBOISER. To be losing one's hair. *Mon dab ne s'est jamais déboisé.* "My father never lost his hair."

DÉBROUILLE, *f.* Resourcefulness. *Elle s'y connaît dans la débrouille.* "She knows her way around." See SYSTÈME D.

DÈC, backslang of **condé.**

DÉCA, *m.,* from **décaféiné.** Decaffeinated coffee. *Il lui faut son petit déca avant de dormir.* "He needs his little cup of decaf before going to bed."

(SE) DÉCALCIFIER. To take one's underpants off (from **calcif** (shorts); lit. "to lose calcium"). *Il dort sans se décalcifier.* "He sleeps in his briefs."

DÉCALLISSER, *Que.* = **CRISSER.** See CALICE.

DÉCAPANT, *m.* Lousy wine (from the *adj.* **décapant** [abrasive]). *Dans la cave de mon dab il n'y a pas de place pour le décapant.* "In my father's wine cellar, there's no room for any poor-quality wine."

DÈCHE, *f.* Extreme poverty; misfortune. **Être dans la dèche.** To be flat broke. *Tu seras dans la dèche si tu continues à jeter l'argent par les fenêtres.* "You'll be a pauper if you keep wasting money."

DÉCHIB, *m.* Male transsexual. *Il a dejà de gros lolos et pense se faire déchibrer pour devenir un déchib.* "He already has big breasts and is thinking of having his dick cut off to become a transsexual." See CHIBRE.

DÉCONNAGE, *m.* Stupid talk or behavior. *Quel splendide déconnage, le discours du sénateur!* "What a bunch of bull the senator's speech was!"

DÉCONNER. 1. To withdraw from the vagina. *Ma chienne n'a pas été couverte; le grand champion a déconné.*

"My bitch wasn't served; the great champion (dog) pulled out." **2.** To malfunction (said of anything, not just a faltering phallus, as in **1**). *L'allumage de ta bagnole déconne.* "Your car's ignition is on the blink." **3.** To do or say foolish things. *Qu'est-ce qu'il peut déconner ce soir!* "God, he's really full of crap tonight!" See FAUT PAS DÉCONNER! **4.** To enjoy saying or doing foolish things. *On a passé le dimanche à déconner.* "We had fun fooling around on Sunday." See SANS DEC'.

DÉCONNER À PLEINS TUBES. To do or say totally foolish things. *La gniole le fait déconner à pleins tubes.* "Booze makes him a total jerk."

DÉCROCHER. To go off drugs (lit. "to unhook"). *Sa mère s'est battue pour qu'il décroche.* "His mother did all she could to get him to kick the habit."

DÉCROCHER LE COCOTIER/GROS LOT/JACKPOT. To hit the jackpot; make it big. *Il a décroché le cocotier en étant reçu premier au concours.* "He scored a triumph by coming in first in the competition."

DE CUL = DE FESSE.

DEDANS. Inside. See FOUTRE **2**; (SE) FOUTRE DEDANS; RENTRE-DEDANS; RENTRER DEDANS.

DE DERRIÈRE LES FAGOTS. From a special reserve. *Mon grand-dab nous en a sorti une de derrière les fagots.* "My grandpa got out one of his special reserve bottles for us."

DE FESSE. Pornographic. *Pour lui, la vie n'est qu'une histoire de fesse.* "For him, life is only about tits, ass, and pussy."

DÉFONÇARÈS = DÉFONCÉ.

DÉFONCE, *f.* Drug-induced state (high or down). *Ils étaient tous en état de défonce.* "They were all spaced out."

DÉFONCÉ, -E. *m., f., adj.* and *n.* Drugged; drunk. *Il est souvent défoncé à mort.* "He's often totally smashed."

DÉFONCER L'ANNEAU/OIGNON/LE POT/LA RONDELLE. To sodomize (lit. "to break into the anus"). See OIGNON **2**.

(SE) DÉFONCER. 1. To take drugs; get high. *Ils se défoncent en groupe.* "They shoot up together." **2.** To go all out. *Elle s'est défoncée pour élever son môme.* "She did her utmost to bring up her child."

DÉFONCEUSE, *f.* Penis. *Il était heureux que sa défonceuse ne déconnait plus.* "He was glad his tool was in good working order again."

DÉFROMAGER. To remove smegma by having sex (lit. "to de-cheese"). *Le bled manquait d'eau mais la putain défromagait les mecs.* "The village's water supply was short, but the whore kept all the guys' dicks clean."

DÉFROMAGER LE MINARET, dated. To have one's smegmatic penis serviced (said by former Fr. colonials in areas with mosques and minarets). *Le légionnaire cherchait une fatma pour se défromager le minaret.* "The legionnaire looked for a female to clean his pipe." *Cf.* DÉGRAISSER/DÉROUILLER SON PANAIS.

DÉFRUSQUER. To undress. *Défrusque-toi rapidos.* "Take your clothes off, right away!"

DÉG = DÉGUEULASSE.

DÉGAGE! Buzz off!

DÉGAT, *m.* Damage. See BONJOUR LES DÉGATS.

DÉGLINGUER. To break down. *La télé est de nouveau déglinguée.* "The TV's on the fritz again."

(SE) DÉGLINGUER. To deteriorate. *Il se déglingue à force de défonce.* "He's going downhill because of his drug habit."

DÉGOBILLER. To vomit. *Il a dégobillé dans les toilettes de l'avion.* "He barfed in the plane's toilets."

DÉGONFLARD, -E = DÉGONFLÉ.

DÉGONFLÉ, -E. *m., f., adj.* and *n.* Coward; cowardly (lit. "deflated"). *Vous n'êtes qu'une bande de dégonflés.* "You're all chicken."

(SE) DÉGONFLER. To lose one's courage. *Tu ne vas pas te dégonfler au dernier moment?* "You're not going to get cold feet at the last minute, are you?"

DÉGONFLEUR, -EUSE = DÉGONFLÉ.

DÉGOT(T)ER. To find. *J'ai dégoté qch. de super.* "I turned up s.t. marvelous."

DÉGRAISSER SON PANAIS. To have sexually (lit. "to trim the fat off one's parsnip"). See PANAIS.

DÉGROUILLER/SE DÉGROUILLER. To hurry up. *Dégrouille-toi!* "Get a move on."

DÉGUEU = DÉGUEULASSE.

DÉGUEULASSE, *m., f., adj.* and *n.* **1.** Very dirty. *Ce resto est dégueulasse.* "This restaurant is filthy." **2.** Repulsive. *C'est un dégueulasse de lui avoir fait un coup pareil.* "He's a sleaze bag for having done s.t. like that to her." See PAS DÉGUEULASSE.

DÉGUEULASSER. To make a mess. *Ils avaient tout dégueulassé.* "They mucked up everything."

DÉGUEULBIF = DÉGUEULASSE.

DÉGUEULER. **1.** To vomit. *Il a dégueulé sur la moquette.* "He puked on the carpet." **2.** To bad-mouth. *Cesse de dégueuler sur tout le monde.* "Stop running everybody down."

DÉGUEULIS, *m.* Vomit. *Il a fallu nettoyer tout le dégueulis de la nuit.* "Last night's puke had to be cleaned up."

DÉGUEULOIR, *m.* Mouth. *Tu ferais mieux de la fermer, ton dégueuloir.* "You really ought to keep your trap shut."

DÉGUSTER. **1.** To get scolded (ironic use of the lit. "to enjoy"; "taste"). *Qu'est-ce qu'il va déguster quand il rentrera.* "He'll get a real chewing out when he comes back." **2.** To get beat up. *Qu'est-ce qu'ils lui ont fait déguster.* "They gave him a hell of a beating." **3.** To endure. *Avec leur voyou de fils, qu'est-ce qu'ils n'ont pas dégusté!* "They've been through the tortures of the damned with their son."

DÉJ, *abbr.* of **déjeuner.** See PETIT DÉJ.

DE L'AIR! Back off! *De l'air, les mômes; vous faites trop de bruit.* "Beat it, you brats; you're making too much noise."

DÉLOURDER. To open a door. *Elle refuse de délourder quand il arrive bourré.* "She won't open up when he comes home loaded." *Cf.* LOURDE **1.**

(SE) DÉMAQUER. To separate; divorce. *Ils ne parviennent pas à se démaquer malgré leurs querelles.* "They can't bring t.s. to split up in spite of their quarrels."

DÉMENT, -E. Marvelous (lit. "demented"). *La fête était démente.* "The party was mind-blowing."

DÉMERDARD, -E = DÉMERDEUR, -EUSE.

DE MERDE. See PUTAIN DE MERDE.

DÉMERDE = DÉBROUILLE. See SYSTÈME D.

(SE) DÉMERDER. 1. To operate successfully. *Je peux me démerder toute seule.* "I can manage it myself." **2.** To hurry up. *Démerde-toi; l'heure passe.* "Step on it; time's a-wasting."

DÉMERDEUR, -EUSE, *m., f., adj.* and *n.* Resourceful person; shrewd customer. *C'est un sacré démerdeur!* "That guy knows his way around."

DE MES DEUX (COUILLES/FESSES)! Nuts to you! Kiss my ass!

DE MES FESSES. Rotten. *Où as-tu déniché ce bahut de mes fesses?* "Where'd you find this broken-down old heap?"

DEMI-SEL, *m., pej.* Small-time punk or pimp (lit. "lightly salted"). *Ce demi-sel est surveillé par les flics.* "That little shit of a lowlife is being watched by the police."

DE MON CUL = DE MES FESSES.

(SE) DÉMOUSCAILLER = (SE) DÉMERDER.

DEP, backslang of **pédé.**

(SE) DÉPATOUILLER. To get out of trouble. *Tu es assez grand pour te dépatouiller tout seul.* "You're old enough to pick your own chestnuts out of the fire."

DÉPENDEUR D'ANDOUILLES, *m.* Tall, thin man. *Ce dépendeur d'andouille a épousé une naine.* "That beanpole married a dwarf."

(SE) DÉPIEUTER. To get out of bed. *Il s'est dépieuté ce matin du pied gauche.* "He got up on the wrong side of the bed today."

DÉPLACER DE L'AIR. To talk a lot of hot air; waste time. *Son travail n'avance pas car il déplace de l'air.* "His work's getting nowhere because he's chasing his tail."

DÉPOSER LE/SON BILAN. To die. (lit. "to file for bankruptcy; liquidation"). *T'en fais pas; tu es loin de déposer ton bilan.* "Don't get upset; you're hardly at death's door."

DÉPUCELER. To use or open up s.t. (usually a bottle) for the first time; (lit. "to take s.o.'s virginity"). *On a dépucelé une bouteille de derrière les fagots.* "We cracked out a bottle from the special reserve."

DER, *m., f.,* from **dernier. Der des ders,** *m.* **1.** Lowest of the low; last straggler. *Tu ne vas pas épouser ce der des ders?* "You're not going to marry that scum of the earth, are you?" **2.** *f.* The war to end all wars. *Le prof parlait d'une guerre nucléaire et se moquait de Wilson et de sa der des ders.* "The professor talked about a nuclear war and made fun of Wilson and his war to end all wars." **3.** *m.* Last drink before leaving. *On se boit le der des ders et on y va.* "We'll have one for the road and get underway."

DERCHE, *m.* Posterior. *La pauvre bête a reçu un coup de pied dans le derche.* "The poor animal got a kick in the ass."

DERGE = DERCHE.

DÉROUILLADE/DÉROUILLE = DÉROUILLÉE.

DÉROUILLÉE, *f.* Beating. *L'équipe de hockey a pris une dérouillée magistrale.* "Our hockey team was soundly beaten."

DÉROUILLER. 1. To remove the rust from. See PANAIS. **2.** To thrash. *Il a menacé de nous dérouiller.* "He threated to beat us up." **3.** To suffer. *Qu'est-ce que j'ai dérouillé avec cet abcès dentaire!* "What agony I went through with that abcess!" **4.** To have one's first client (prostitute), an extension of meaning **1.** *"Faut dérouiller plus tôt, les filles," dit souvent notre mari.* "'Got to start turning tricks earlier, girls,' our pimp often says."

(SE) DÉROUILLER. To limber up (lit. "to get the rust off"). *Je vais me dérouiller les gambettes un peu avant le petit dej.* "I'm going to stretch my legs a bit before breakfast."

DESCENDRE. To kill. *Les truands l'ont descendu.* "The crooks bumped him off."

DESCENDRE EN FLAMMES. To be attacked verbally. *Faut pas me descendre en flammes tout de suite.* "You don't have to chop my head off right away."

DESCENTE, *f.* Going down; descent. **Avoir une bonne descente.** To be fond of the bottle. *Qu'est-ce qu'il a une bonne descente!* "He can really knock 'em back!"

DESCENTE À LA CAVE/AU BARBU/LAC, *m.* Cunnilingus. *Il commence toujours ses ébats par une descente à la cave.* "He always begins his lovemaking with a muff dive (lit. "going to the cellar." A "cellar" in France is usually a "wine cellar" too)."

DESCENTE DE LIT, *f.* Spineless person (lit. "bedside rug"). *Je ne veux pas sortir avec cette descente de lit.* "I don't want to go out with that doormat."

DES CLOPES/CLOPINETTES. Nothing; practically nothing. *À la mort de son mari elle a hérité des clopinettes.* "At her husband's death she got next to nothing."

DES CLOPINETTES!/CLOUX! = DES DATTES!

DES DATTES! Nothing doing! No way! Not on your life!

DESSALÉ, -E. *adj.* and *m., f., n.* Sexually aware (person). *Elle n'est pas assez dessalée.* "She hasn't been around enough."

DESSALER. To put s.o. wise (sexually); lit. "to desalinate." *Cette nana a besoin d'être dessalée.* "That chick needs to learn a few things."

DEUIL, *m.* Mourning. **Avoir les ongles en deuil.** To have dirty fingernails. *Je ne couche pas avec les mecs qui ont*

125

les ongles en deuil. "I don't sleep with guys who've got dirty fingernails."

DEUX. Two. **Ça fait deux.** To be poles apart. *Le patron et moi, ça fait deux.* "The boss and I don't see eye to eye." See COMME PAS DEUX; DE MES DEUX; EN MOINS DE DEUX.

DEUXIO/DEUZIO. Secondly. *On nous a servi primo l'apéro, deuxio le champagne.* "First they served us the aperitif, then the champagne."

DÉVEINE, *f.* Bad luck. *Les pauvres, ils ont eu la déveine.* "The poor guys, they had bad luck." **Être dans la déveine.** To be down on one's luck. *On est toujours dans la déveine.* "We're still going through a bad patch."

DÉVISSER. 1. To wound; kill (lit. "to unscrew"). *Ils lui ont dévissé la tête.* "They inflicted head wounds on him." **2.** To leave. *Et si on dévissait?* "How about our hitting the road?" **3.** To die. *Il était dévissé depuis huit jours.* "He'd been dead for eight days."

DÉZINGUER. To destroy s.t. or s.o. *Ses complices enragés l'ont dézingué.* "His enraged accomplices bumped him off."

DICO, *m.,* from **dictionnaire.** Dictionary. *Elle a toujours le nez dans les dicos.* "She's always got her nose buried in a dictionary."

DILEUR, *m.,* transcription of Eng. "dealer." Drug dealer. *C'est un dileur de petite envergure.* "He's a small-time dealer."

DINGO, *adj.* and *n.* Crazy. *Complètement dingo, ce mec.* "That guy's completely bonkers."

DINGUE, *adj.* and *n.* **1.** Crazy. *Ce dingue va la faire crever en la frappant ainsi.* "That nutcase'll do her in, beating her like that." **2. Être dingue de qn.** To be nuts about s.o. *Ils sont dingues l'un de l'autre.* "They're crazy about each other." **3.** Incredible. **C'est dingue!** "That's mind-blowing!" See RAIDE DINGUE.

DINGUER. To tumble. See ENVOYER DINGUER.

DIRECTO, from **directement.** Right away. *Dis-le directo.* "Come straight out and say it."

DIRLINGUE = DIRLO.

DIRLO/DIRLOTE, *m., f.,* from **directeur. 1.** Principal. *Le dirlo a mis à la porte deux élèves défoncés.* "The principal expelled two junkie students." **2.** Boss. *Le dirlo a dit non.* "The boss said no."

DISJONCTER. To crack up (lit. "to disconnect"). *Il a complètement disjoncté.* "He totally flipped out."

DJÈSE, *m.* From *nouchi (sl.* from the *Côte d'Ivoire).* Business. *C'est quoi les djèses?* "How's business? What's new?"

DOCHE, *f.* Mother. *La doche et son gone sont partis en vacances.* "The mother and her kid have gone on vacation." *Cf.* BELLE-DOCHE.

DODO, *m., children, hum.* Sleep. **Aller au dodo; faire dodo.** To go to bed. *Je veux faire dodo.* "I want to go beddy-bye."

DODOCHES = DOUDOUNES.

DOIGT, *m.* Finger. See CLAQUER...DOIGTS; OBÉIR AU DOIGT.

DOIGT DANS L'ŒIL. See (SE) FOURRER.

DOIGTER. To finger-fuck. *Pol s'est mis à me doigter et j'ai mouillé, vite fait. Quel doigté il a!* "Pol began to finger-fuck me and I got wet fast. What skillful fingers he has!"

(LES) DOIGTS DANS LE NEZ. Very easily (lit. "with one's fingers in one's nose"). *Je pourrais faire ça les doigts dans le nez.* "I could do that with one hand tied behind my back."

DOIGTS DE PIEDS, *m., pl.* Toes. **Avoir les doigts de pieds en éventail; bouquet de violettes.** To experience orgasm; great pleasure (lit. "have one's toes spread out like a fan; in a bouquet of violets"). *À Toulouse on avait souvent les doigts de pieds en bouquet de violettes.* "In Toulouse we often had great orgasms."

DOLLUCHE, *m.* Dollar. *Cet un Amerluche plein de dol-luches.* "He's a yank with big bucks."

DOMB DOMBI, backslang of **bidon.** *C'est pas du dombi!* "That's no load of bull!"

DOMINO, *m.* Tooth. *Un domino de perdu, réaction en chaîne—les autres ont suivi!* "First I lost one tooth, then the others—the domino effect!"

DONDON, *f.* Hefty lady. See GROSSE DONDON.

DONNER. To inform on. *On ne sait pas qui l'a donné.* "Nobody knows who ratted on him."

DONNER DU CHOUETTE = FILER DU CHOUETTE.

(LE) DONNER EN MILLE. To ask s.o. to guess and guess again. *Qu'est-ce qu'il a bien pu m'offrir? Je te le donne en mille.* "What do you suppose he gave me? You'll never guess!"

DONNER LA GOMME = METTRE LA GOMME.

(SE) DONNER UN MAL DE CHIEN. To take great pains. *Je me suis donné un mal de chien pour préparer la fête.* "I worked like a dog to prepare for the party."

(S'EN) DONNER À CŒUR JOIE. To enjoy o.s. to the hilt. *Qu'est-ce qu'on s'en est donné à cœur joie hier soir!* "Man, did we have a super time last night!"

DONNEUR, -EUSE, *m., f.* Informant (lit. "donor"). *Les flics ont trouvé en lui un bon donneur.* "The cops found a fine fink in him."

DOPE, *f.* Drugs (from Eng.). *Il est toujours en manque de dope.* "He always needs a fix."

DOPER. To stimulate (not necessarily with drugs). *Le gouvernement essaie de doper l'économie.* "The government is trying to prime the economy."

DORER. To gild. **Se faire dorer.** To get sodomized (lit. "to get suntanned"). *Le Duc de Choiseul-Praslin aimait se faire dorer.* "The Duke of Choiseul-Praslin loved being buggered."

DORER LA PILULE. To sweeten the (bitter) pill. *Je le lui dirai, mais je voudrais lui dorer la pilule.* "I'll tell him, but I'd like to cushion the blow."

DOS, *m.* Back. **En avoir plein le dos.** To be fed up with s.t. *J'en ai plein le dos de bosser comme une damnée.* "I'm sick and tired of slaving away." **L'avoir dans le dos,** *idiom.* To lose out. *Pas de chance pour lui, il l'a eu dans le dos.* "He was unlucky and got shafted."

DOUBLÉ, *m.* **1.** Double. **Faire un doublé.** To give birth to twins. *Elle vient d'apprendre qu'elle fera un doublé.* "She's just learned that she's going to have twins." **2.** Second lay (shortly after the first one). (lit. "double"). *Elle se réjouissait toujours du doublé.* "She always enjoyed the second coming."

DOUBLER. To betray. *Il a doublé et son associé et sa femme.* "He double-crossed his partner and two-timed his wife."

DOUCE. *f.* Soft drugs; marijuana. *Il est dingue de la douce.* "He's nuts about grass."

DOUCE, See EN DOUCE; (SE LA) COULER DOUCE.

DOUDOU, *m.,* from *doux* ("sweet"). **1.** Soft, stuffed animal; fetish. *Elle ne peut pas faire dodo sans son doudou.* "She can't sleep without her teddy."

DOUDOU, *f.* Creole, Antilles. Sweetheart; girl. *J'adore ma p'tite doudou.* "I love my little sweetie."

DOUDOUNE, *f.* **1.** Down jacket. *Malgré la doudoune, je me caillais les miches.* "Despite the parka I froze my buns off." **2.** Breast. *Vas-y doucement quand tu me tâtes les doudounes.* "Be gentle when you touch my breasts." **3.** *Que.* Buxom, cuddly woman. *Qu'il fait bon dormir auprès de ma blonde, ma doudoune, ma Rosie rubensienne.* "How good it is to sleep next to my sweetheart, my robust, Rubensian Rosie."

DOUF. *Bel.* Hot, sultry. *Qu'il faisait douf lors des examens!* "Man, it was hot during the exams."

DOUFFE, *f., Bel., student sl.* Drunkeness; hangover. *Après maintes Stella Artois me voilà avec douffe carabinée.* "After lots of Stella Artois here I am with a four-star hangover."

DOUILLER. 1. To pay out or up. *Il s'arrange toujours pour ne pas avoir à douiller.* "He always sees to it that he's not the one who shells out." **2. Ça douille.** That's a gold mine! *Son commerce, ça douille!* "His business is a big money-maker." or: "That costs a fortune." *Élever un môme, ça douille.* "Raising a child means no end of expenses."

DOUL/DOULE, *m.* **1.** Hat. *N'oublie pas ton doul.* "Don't forget your chapeau." **2.** Police informant. *Il avait la gueule d'un doule.* "He looked like a stool pigeon."

DOULOS = DOUL.

DOULOUREUSE, *f.* Hotel bill; restaurant check (lit. "the painful one"). *Aujourd'hui la douloureuse c'est pour moi.* "Today I'll take care of the bad news."

DRACHE, *f., Bel.* Sudden heavy shower. *Si l'on se fait saucer en Belgique, c'est la drache.* "If you get drenched in Belgium it's a *drache.*" *Cf.* FLOTTE.

DRAGUE, *f.* Search for sex; cruising (homosexual) (lit. "dredging"). *On est parti à trois pour la drague.* "The three of us went out hunting/wolfing/cruising together."

DRAGUER. 1. To look for sex (lit. "to dredge"). *Où qu'il aille, il drague.* "Wherever he goes, he's on the make." To cruise (homosexual). *Rorem raconte que lui et Poulenc draguaient souvent ensemble.* "Rorem relates that he and Poulenc often went cruising together." **2.** To pick up (transitive). *Je l'ai draguée au Bois de Boulogne.* "I picked her up in the Bois de Boulogne." Note: **1** is intransitive, used for the sexual impulse in search of an object.

DRAGUEUR, *m.* Skirt chaser; chronic cruiser (homosexual). *Ce café est toujours plein de dragueurs.* "This café is always full of guys on the make."

DRAGUEUSE, *f.* Flirt. *C'est une dragueuse de première.* "She's a first-class flirt."

DRINGUELLE, *f., Bel.*, from Flemish **drinkgeld**. **1.** Tip. *La carte de crédit a presque éliminé les dringuelles.* "The credit card has almost done away with tips." **2.** Pocket money, allowance. *Lors de mon anniversaire papy m'a donné une belle dringuelle.* "Grandpa gave me a nice gift of money for my birthday."

DUCHNOQUE, *m.* Fool. *Ce duchnoque nous a cassé les pieds.* "That jackass bugged us."

DUCON/DUCONNO/DUCONNOSO(F) = DUCHNOQUE.

DUCON-LA-JOIE, *m.* Blissful simpleton; grinning idiot. *Laisse ce ducon-la-joie tranquille.* "Let him live in his fool's paradise."

DUR À CUIRE = DUR DE DUR.

DUR DE DUR, *m.* Masterful tough guy. *Jean Gabin et John Wayne jouaient souvent les durs des durs.* "Jean Gabin and John Wayne often played tough guys."

DUR, -E DE LA FEUILLE. A bit deaf. *Parle plus fort; grand-dab est dur de la feuille.* "Talk louder; gramps is a little hard of hearing."

(À LA) DURE. In a rough way. *Tous ses enfants ont été élevés à la dure.* "All his children were brought up without sparing the rod."

DUSCHNOQUE = DUCHNOQUE.

DYNAMITE, *f.* Cocaine (lit. "dynamite"). *La dynamite a détruit la carrière de la présentatrice.* "Coke destroyed the TV newscaster's career."

(S') ÉCLATER. 1. To have a rip-roaring time. *On s'est éclaté au concert rock.* "We let it all hang it out at the rock concert." **2.** To get high on drugs. *Lui et sa copine s'éclatent chaque soir.* "He and his girlfriend trip every night."

ÉCLUSER. 1. To drink (lit. "to operate sluice gates"). *Le groupe au bar écluse un max.* "That bunch at the bar is really belting them down." **2.** To urinate. *La bière les fait beaucoup écluser.* "Beer makes them piss a lot." See LÂCHER...L'ÉCLUSE.

ÉCOLO, from **écologique.** Ecological. *Un plan écolo a été dressé pour combattre les marées noires.* "An environmental plan has been drawn up to deal with black tides."

ÉCOLO, *m., f.,* from **écologiste.** *Les écolos sont très engagés.* "The greens are very committed."

ÉCRASE-MERDE, *m., f., pl.* Oversize shoes (lit. "shit mincers"). *Essuie tes écrase-merde avant d'entrer.* "Wipe your clodhoppers before coming in."

ÉCRASE! Put a lid on it! Shut up!

ÉCRASER LE COUP. To make peace. *Après deux ans de mésentente, les deux frères ont écrasé le coup.* "After two years of misunderstanding, the two brothers buried the hatchet."

(EN) ÉCRASER. To sleep long or well. *J'attends le dimanche pour en écraser.* "I wait for Sunday to get a good sleep."

ÉCRASER L'AFFAIRE/LE COUP. To keep s.t. quiet. *Enceinte à douze ans, on a essayé d'écraser l'affaire.* "She was pregnant at twelve and they tried to hush it up."

EFFEUILLAGE, *m.* Striptease. *L'effeuilleuse pense faire un effeuillage spirituel pour découvrir l'essentiel.* "The stripper plans to strip down spiritually to discover the essential."

EFFEUILLER LA MARGUERITE. 1. To play "she loves me, loves me not" (lit. "to thin the daisy"). *Elle effeuillait la marguerite en répétant, "(il m'aime) un peu, beaucoup, passionément, à la folie, du tout".* "She plucked the daisy's petals and repeated, "He loves me, loves me not." **2.** To make sexual advances. *Il était trop bourré pour effeuiller la marguerite.* "He was too drunk to come on to anybody." **3.** To strip. *Elle effeuille la marguerite pour son amant.* "She does a striptease for her lover."

EFFEUILLEUSE, *f.* Stripper. *Mencken savait apprécier les effeuilleuses.* "Mencken knew how to appreciate ecdysiasts."

ÉGOÏNER. To copulate (lit. "to saw"). *Othello l'égoïnait chaque nuit.* "Othello gave it to her nightly."

ÉGOUTTER LA/SA SARDINE. To urinate (lit. "to drain the sardine"). *En conduisant il égoutte sa sardine dans une bouteille.* "When driving he takes a leak into a bottle."

EMBALLAGE, *m.* Arrest (lit. "packaging; wrapping up"). *Dans le quartier il y a eu plusieurs emballages.* "Lots of people got busted in the neighborhood."

EMBALLARÈS. Arrested; rounded up. *Je me suis sauvé, mais tous les potes sont emballarès.* "I got away, but all my buddies got busted."

EMBALLER. 1. To arrest (lit. "to wrap up"). *Les flics les ont emballés.* "The cops carted them off." **2.** To please. *Ton projet ne m'emballe pas.* "Your project doesn't do anything for me." **3.** To seduce; have sexually. *Il avait une forte envie de l'emballer.* "He really wanted to make it with her."

(S')EMBALLER. 1. To fly into a rage. *Ce n'est pas grave; ne t'emballe pas.* "It isn't serious; don't fly off the handle." **2.** To be enthusiastic. *La foule s'emballait au match de foot.* "The crowd got carried away at the football game."

EMBARQUER. 1. To arrest. *Cesse la bagarre ou tu seras embarqué par les keufs.* "Stop fighting or the cops will arrest you." **2.** To involve. *Je me suis laissé embarquer dans ses combines.* "I got mixed up in his shady deals." **3.** To take away; swipe. *Mon gamin m'a embarqué tous mes crayons.* "My kid has made off with all my pencils."

EMBISTROUILLER. To pester. *Va embistrouiller qn. d'autre.* "Go bug s.o. else."

EMBRINGUER. To drag into. *J'ai été embringué dans une affaire qui m'a coûté cher.* "I got mixed up in s.t. that cost me dearly."

(S')EMBRINGUER. To get involved. *Pourquoi t'embringuer là-dedans?* "What are you getting mixed up in that for?"

(S')EMBRINGUER MAL. To get off to a bad start. *Leur mariage s'embringue mal.* "Their marriage is getting off to a bad start."

EMBROUILLE, *f.* **1.** Snag; confusion. *Tout s'est passé sans embrouille.* "Everything went off without a hitch." **2.** Shady deal. *Je me tiens à l'écart de ses embrouilles.* "I steer clear of his fishy schemes." **3.** Paris stock exchange. *Les initiés ont fait fortune à l'Embrouille.* "Inside traders made a fortune on the exchange."

ÉMERAUDES, *f., pl.* Hemorrhoids (lit. "emeralds"). *Faire du vélo, c'est rude pour les émeraudes.* "Bicycling is rough on piles."

EMMANCHÉ, *m.* Idiot. *Quel emmanché, celui-là!* "That guy's a real jerk!"

EMMANCHER. To sodomize (lit. "to screw in a handle"). *Il ne pense qu'à se faire emmancher.* "All he thinks about is getting fucked."

(S')EMMANCHER. To have sex. *Les enfants ont surpris leurs parents en train de s'emmancher.* "The children surprised their parents while they were doing it."

(S')EMMÊLER LES CRAYONS/PÉDALES/PIEDS/ PINCEAUX. To get mixed up (lit. "to tangle one's feet"). *Grand-mère, tu t'emmêles les pinceaux.* "Grand-mother, you're getting your wires crossed."

EMMENER LE PETIT/POPAUL AU CIRQUE = MENER...CIRQUE.

EMMERDANT, -E. Very annoying. *Avoir un problème avec le fisc, c'est emmerdant.* "Having a problem with the tax collector is a real bummer."

EMMERDE, *m., f.* **= EMMERDEMENT.**

EMMERDÉ, -E. In difficulty. *Ils sont emmerdés jusqu'au cou.* "They're really in deep shit."

EMMERDEMENT, *m.* Trouble. *Ils ont des emmerdements avec leurs gosses.* "They've got big problems with their kids."

EMMERDER. 1. To bore; annoy. *Cesse de pleurnicher; tu m'emmerdes.* "Quit bawling; you bug me." **2.** To tell to go to hell. *Je t'emmerde! Je vous emmerde!* "Up yours! Fuck off!"

(S')EMMERDER. 1. To be bored to death. *On s'est emmerdé en campant sous la pluie.* "We were bored out of our minds camping in the rain." **2.** To fret. *Pourquoi t'emmerder pour une chose pareille?* "Why worry your head for s.t. like that?"

(S')EMMERDER À CENT SOUS DE L'HEURE = (S') EMMERDER 1.

(NE PAS) S'EMMERDER. 1. To not trouble o.s. about anyone else. *Celle-là, elle ne s'emmerde pas, en se garant sur ma pelouse!* "That broad doesn't give a shit; she parks her car on my lawn." **2.** To have a trouble-free life. *Ils boivent des grands crus à chaque repas; ils ne s'emmerdent pas!*

"They drink great vintage wines with every meal. They're not doing badly for t.s.!"

EMMERDEUR, -EUSE. Troublemaker; nuisance. *Quel emmerdeur!* "What a pain in the ass!"

EMMIELLER, *euph.* for **emmerder.** *Qu'est-ce que je m'emmielle!* "God, what a bore; hassle!"

EMMOUSCAILLER, *euph.* for **emmerder 1.** To annoy. *J'étais emmouscaillé par une foultitude de papiers à remplir.* "I was hassled by heaps of papers that had to be filled out."

EMPAFFÉ, *m.* Dumb bugger. *Espèce d'empaffé!* "You asshole, you!"

EMPAFFER. To sodomize. *Va te faire empaffer!* "Go fuck y.s.! Go get fucked up the ass!"

EMPÊCHEUR DE TOURNER EN ROND. Spoilsport. *N'amène pas à la teuf cet empêcheur de tourner en rond.* "Don't bring that party pooper to the bash."

EMPLÂTRE, *m.* Clod; wimp (lit. "medicated plaster"). *Ne fais pas l'emplâtre.* "Don't be such a jelly doughnut."

EN AVOIR. To be ballsy; tough. See COUILLES.

EN-BOURGEOIS = HAMBOURGEOIS.

ENCADRER. 1. To beat up severely (lit. "to frame [picture]"). *Il l'ont sacrément encadré.* "They really beat him up." **2.** To collide. *Sa voiture a encadré le réverbère.* "Her car wrapped itself around the streetlight." **3.** To endure. *Je ne peux plus l'encadrer.* "I can't put up with him anymore."

ENCAISSER 1. To get hit. *Il a dû encaisser pas mal pour être esquinté à ce point.* "He probably got severely pummeled, judging by the extent of his injuries." **2.** To stand. *Elle ne pouvait plus encaisser sa tyrannie.* "She could no longer bear his tyranny."

ENCALDOSSER. To sodomize. *Max ne fait que m'encaldosser mais me v'là en cloque. Le foutre a dû* *migrer.* "Max just fucks my bum but here I am knocked up. The come must have travelled."

ENCALICE/CIBOIRE/HOSTIE/OSTENSOIRE/SIMO-NAC/ TITI. *Que.* Wonderful; delicious; plentiful. *Tout le repas était en hostie, un délice.* "The whole meal was super, scrumptious." (Note the transition from "supernatural" to "super." According to Catholic doctrine the **hostie** [consecrated host] is supernatural.) *Cf.* (LE) PETIT JÉSUS EN CULOTTE DE VELOURS. See also ÊTRE EN CALICE…TITI.

(S')ENCANAILLER and Swiss variant **S'ENCROUYER.**
1. To go slumming. *Les nantis aiment s'encanailler dans sa boîte.* "The swells like to go slumming in her night-club." **2.** To become vulgar. *Alors, tu crois t'encrouyer en me fréquentant?* "So you think you're degrading y.s. by keeping company with me?"

ENCEINTER/ENCEINTRER. To impregnate. *Elle refusait de dire qui l'avait enceintée.* "She wouldn't say who'd knocked her up."

EN CLOQUE. Pregnant (from **cloque**). **Être en cloque.** To be pregnant. *La lapine est de nouveau en cloque.* "The constant babymaker's pregnant again." **Mettre en cloque.** To impregnate. *Mais on ne sait pas qui l'a mise en cloque.* "But no one knows who got her pregnant."

ENCLOQUER. To impregnate. *C'est pas moi qui l'ai encloquée.* "I didn't knock her up."

ENCROUMÉ, -E. In debt. *Je ne supporte pas être encroumée.* "I can't stand being in debt."

(S')ENCROUMER. To go into debt. *Ils se sont encroumés pour construire leur maison.* "They went into hock to build their house."

ENCULADE = ENCULAGE.

ENCULAGE, *m.* Sodomizing. *Il se lubrifie avant l'enculage.* "He lubricates himself before taking it up the ass."

ENCULÉ, *m.* **1.** Sodomite. *Ils sont tous les deux des enculés.* "They're both asshole buddies." **2.** Rotten person. *Espèce d'enculé, fous-moi la paix!* "You bastard, bugger off!" *Cf.* ENFOIRE.

ENCULER. To sodomize. *Il se met toujours une capote avant de l'enculer.* "He always puts on a rubber before sodomizing her." **Se faire enculer.** To get sodomized. *Espèce d'enfoiré! Va te faire enculer!* "Go fuck yourself faggot ass!/Fuck off, dumb bastard!" *Cf.* ENFOIRER.

ENCULER LES MOUCHES. To quibble (lit. "to sodomize flies"). *Les curetons enculaient les mouches à propos du sexe des anges.* "The priests split hairs concerning the gender of angels."

EN DOUCE. On the quiet; sly. *Elle s'arrange toujours pour sortir en douce.* "She always manages to sneak out discreetly."

EN ÊTRE/EN ÊTRE COMME UN PHOQUE. To be one of them (esp. homosexuals). *Ça crève les yeux qu'il en est.* "It's obvious he's one of them."

ENFANT, *m., f.* Child. **Faire un enfant dans le dos à qn.** To betray s.o. *Ce n'est pas la première fois que tu me fais un enfant dans le dos.* "It's not the first time you've stabbed me in the back."

ENFANT DE CHŒUR, *m.* Choirboy. *Le petit copain de ta fille n'est pas un enfant de chœur.* "Your daughter's little friend is no angel."

ENFANT DE SALOPE! "You bastard! SOB" (lit. "trollop's son").

ENFER, *m.* Hell. *J'ai vécu un enfer avec lui.* "Living with him was hell." **D'enfer.** Fantastic; impressive. *Ce joueur de tennis a un service d'enfer.* "That tennis player has a wicked serve."

ENFILER. To have sexually. *Il avait juste le temps de l'enfiler.* "He had just enough time to throw her one."

(S')ENFILER. 1. To copulate. *Ils cherchaient un coin tranquille pour s'enfiler.* "They looked for a quiet nook to make love in." **2.** To guzzle; devour. *J'ai pris le temps de* *m'enfiler un sandwich.* "I took the time to gobble down a sandwich." **3.** To take on s.t. difficult. *C'est toujours moi qui m'enfile les corvées.* "It's always me who gets stuck with the tough jobs."

ENFOIRÉ, -E. *m., f., adj.* and *n.* Stupid bastard. *Bande d'enfoirés—foutez le camp!* "You bunch of shitheads—get the hell out."

ENFOIRÉ, *m.* Homosexual. *Il croyait à tort qu'il était le seul enfoiré du bled.* "He believed, mistakenly, that he was the only queer in town."

ENFOIRER. To sodomize. *La tantouse rêvait de se faire enfoirer par toute l'équipe.* "The queen dreamed of being had by the whole team." *Cf.* ENCULER.

EN GAMIN. Female superior position. *Tous les deux aimaient mieux biter en gamin.* "Both of them preferred screwing with her on top."

ENGIN, *m.* Large penis (lit. "device"). *J'ai pris peur quand il a sorti son engin.* "I got frightened when he took out his weapon."

ENGRAISSER LES ASTICOTS. To be dead and buried (lit. "to fatten the maggots"). *Ça fait belle lurette qu'elle engraisse les asticots.* "She's been pushing up daisies for some time now."

ENGUEULADE, *f.* **1.** Severe reprimand. *Il aura une engueulade maison pour avoir découché.* "He'll get one hell of a bawling out for not having come home last night." **2.** Big argument. *Ils se sont quittés sur une engueulade.* "They parted after a stinking row."

ENGUIRLANDER. To reprimand (ironic use of "to garland"). *Je suis en retard; qu'est-ce que je vais me faire enguirlander par mes vioques.* "I'm late; my parents are going to read me the riot act."

ÉNIÈME. Umpteenth. *Je te demande pour la énième fois d'être polie avec mon nouveau mari.* "I'm asking you for the umpteenth time to be polite to my new husband."

ENJAMBER. To have sexually (lit. "to step over"). *Tu veux te l'enjamber, celle-là? Elle ne mouille que pour moi.* "You want to get it on with her? She just goes for me."

ENJAMBEUR, *m.* Womanizer; sexually potent male. *Max, grand enjambeur, les embourbe toutes, les encaldosse tous.* "Max, great cocksman/studhorse, fucks all the broads and buggers all the boys."

EN LOUCÉDÉ/LOUCÉDOC/LOUSDÉ/LOUSDOC, largonji* forms of **en douce.**

EN MOINS DE DEUX. On the double. *En moins de deux j'ai fait mes valises.* "I packed my bags in two shakes of a lamb's tail."

ENSUQUER. To exhaust. *La balade à ski et la Williamine nous avaient ensuqués.* "We were really knocked out by the ski outing and the pear brandy."

ENTARTAGE, *f.* Pieing, caking (the act of throwing a *tarte à la crème,* a cream pie or cake at s.o.). *Cf.* ALLONGER UNE…TARTE.

ENTARTER. To throw a pie/cake at s.o. *Dans beaucoup de films muets les prétentieux se retrouvent bien entartés.* "In many silent movies the pretentious wind up with a pie in the face."

ENTERRER. To bury. **Enterrer sa vie de garçon.** To have a bachelor party before getting married. *Il a enterré sa vie de garçon mais pense garder sa garçonnière.* "He's had his bachelor party with the boys but still plans to keep his bachelor's pad."

ENTIFLE = ANTIFLE.

ENTORTILLER. To cajole (lit. "to wind"). *Je l'ai entortillée un max pour qu'elle sorte avec moi.* "I sweet-talked her a lot so she'd go out with me."

ENTOURLOUPE/ENTOURLOUPETTE, *f.* Swindle. *N'essaie plus de me faire des entourloupettes.* "Don't try to pull any more dirty tricks on me."

* See explanation of **largonji,** page 215.

ENTRAVER. To understand (lit. "to hinder"). *Je n'ai entravé que pouic dans tout ça.* "I didn't understand diddly in all that." *Cf.* BITER **1**, PIGER QUE COUIC.

ENTRÉE DES ARTISTES/DE SERVICE, *f.* Anus (lit. "stage/service entrance"). *Pour ne pas l'engrosser, je la baise par l'entrée de service.* "So as not to knock her up, I bugger her."

ENTREFESSON = ENTREMICHON.

ENTREJOUFFLU = ENTREMICHON.

ENTREMICHON, *m.* Cleft separating the buttocks. *Elle portait un string pour qu'on admire son entremichon.* "She wore a G-string so people could admire her anal cleavage."

ENTUBER. 1. To sodomize. *Elle n'était pas d'accord pour se faire entuber.* "She didn't agree to take it up the ass." **2.** To swindle. *Je ne me laisserai plus entuber par ce vendeur.* "I won't get taken in again by that salesman."

ENVAPÉ, -E. Drunk; stoned. *Ils étaient tous envapés par cette gniole.* "They were all soused on that hooch." *Cf.* VAPÉ.

ENVIANDER. To sodomize. *Avec son gros os à moelle il les a enviandées toutes les deux.* "He buggered both of them with his big, thick lovesteak."

ENVOYÉ, -E. Sent. **(Bien) envoyé!** Well said! Well done! *Ça c'est bien envoyé!* "Right on! You said it!"

ENVOYER CHIER QN. To tell s.o. to go to hell. *Il me baratinait mais je l'ai envoyé chier.* "He fed me a line but I told him to piss off."

ENVOYER DINGUER/VALDINGUER QN. See VALDINGUER.

ENVOYER PAÎTRE QN. = ENVOYER BALADER QN.

ENVOYER PROMENER QN. = ENVOYER BALADER QN.

ENVOYER QN. SE FAIRE FOUTRE. To tell s.o. to fuck off. *Je les ai envoyés se faire foutre.* "I told them to fuck off."

ENVOYER SUR LES FRAISES = ENVOYER SUR LES ROSES.

ENVOYER SUR LES ROSES. See ROSE.

(S')ENVOYER. 1. To consume rapidly. *Il s'est envoyé un whisky et un sandwich.* "He belted down a whisky and gobbled a sandwich." **2.** To take on a difficult job. *Qui s'envoie la corvée du nettoyage?* "Who's going to tackle the cleaning up?" **3.** To have sexually. *Cette gonzesse, je me l'enverrais bien.* "I'd sure like to get into that broad's pants."

(S')ENVOYER DES FLEURS. 1. To trade compliments (lit. "to send one another flowers"). *Ils s'envoient des fleurs.* "They're a mutual admiration society." **2.** To trade insults, ironic. *Vous n'avez pas fini de vous envoyer des fleurs?* "Are you through throwing brickbats at each other?"

(S')ENVOYER EN L'AIR. To have sex. *Ils se sont retirés pour s'envoyer en l'air.* "They went off to make love."

ÉPATE, *f.* Ostentation. **Y aller à l'épate.** To show off. *Il y va toujours à l'épate.* "He's always trying to put on the dog."

ÉPATER LA GALERIE. To impress people. *C'est pour épater la galerie que tu t'es fringuée de la sorte?* "Have you gotten y.s. up like that to get people to notice you?"

ÉPINARDS, *m., pl.* Spinach. See METTRE…ÉPINARDS.

ÉPINGLER. To arrest (lit. "to pin"). *On a rapidement épinglé les casseurs.* "The burglars got nabbed fast."

ÉPONGE, *f.* Drunk (lit. "sponge"). *C'est une éponge finie.* "He's a confirmed alcoholic."

ÉPONGES, *f., pl.* Lungs. *Je suis partie au bord de la mer pour mes éponges.* "I went to the seashore for my lungs."

ESCALADEUSE DE BRAGUETTE, *f.* **1.** Prostitute (lit. "zipper climber"). *Le Sentier grouille d'escaladeuses de braguette.* "The Paris garment district is crawling with hookers." **2.** Nymphomaniac. *Il y avait plusieurs* *escaladeuses de braguette dans notre classe.* "There were several girls with hot pants in our class."

ESCALOPE, *f.* Tongue (lit. "cutlet [meat]"). See ROULER... ESCALOPE.

ESCALOPES, *f., pl.* **1.** Ears. *Ouvre bien tes escalopes.* "Open your ears now." **2.** The labia majora. *J'avais les escalopes en flammes.* "My lips were hot."

ESCOFFIER. 1. To steal. *Il a escoffié la formule de mon élixir d'amour.* "He stole the formula for my love potion." **2.** To kill. *Qui voulait escoffier les grands cuisiniers?* "Who wanted to kill the great chefs?"

ESGOURDER. To listen; hear. *Esgourdez, Edith va goualer.* "Listen up! Edith's going to sing."

ESGOURDES, *f., pl.* Ears. *Ouvre tes esgourdes; j'ai qch. d'important à te dire.* "Open your ears; I've got s.t. important to tell you."

ESPADOCHES/ESPAGAS, *f., pl.* Sandals. *Porter des espagas dans la neige? T'es barjo!* "Wearing sandals in the snow? You're nuts!"

ESPINGO, *m. adj.* and *n., pej.* Spaniard. *Goya et d'autres espingos vivaient en exil à Bordeaux.* "Goya and other Spaniards lived in exile in Bordeaux."

ESPINGOUIN = ESPINGO.

(S')ESQUINTER LES TRIPES. To knock o.s. out to do s.t. (lit. "to ruin one's guts"). *Je me suis esquinté les tripes pour toi, et tu t'en fous!* "I busted my buns for you and you don't give a damn!"

ESSENCERIE, *f., Senegal.* Gas station. *Les essenceries sont en penurie d'essence.* "The gas stations are running out of gas."

ESSOREUSE, *f.* Noisy motorbike (lit. "spindryer"). *Les essoreuses m'agressent les esgourdes.* "Noisy bikes bother my ears."

ESTAMPER. To fleece. *Si on va dans ce resto, on se fera estamper.* "If we go to that restaurant, we'll get taken."

ESTANCO, *m.* Small café (from Sp. "tobacco shop"). *On va s'arrêter au petit estanco du bled pour boire un pot.* "We'll stop at the town's little café to have a drink."

ESTI!, *Que., euph. for* **hostie!**

ESTOGOME OR ESTOME, *m.* Stomach. *J'ai l'estome fragile.* "I've got a sensitive tummy."

ET DES POUSSIÈRES. A bit more. *Elle a dix ans et des poussières.* "She's just a little over ten."

ET TA SŒUR! Mind your own business!

ÉTENDRE. 1. To floor (lit. "to spread out"). *Il a été étendu d'un crochet de gauche.* "He was knocked out by a left hook." **2.** To fail an exam. *Je bosse dure pour ne pas me faire étendre en maths.* "I work hard so as not to get shot down in math."

ÉTOILE FILANTE, *f.* Occasional prostitute (lit. "shooting star"). *Je défends mon coin et chasse les étoiles filantes.* "I defend my turf and chase away the amateurs."

ÉTOUFFER LE COUP = ÉCRASER LE COUP.

ÉTRANGLER LE BORGNE/POPAUL. See BORGNE.

ÊTRE. To be. See EN ÊTRE; Y ÊTRE; Y ÊTRE POUR QCH.

ÊTRE EN BAPTÊME/CALICE/CALVAIRE/CIBOIRE/ (H)OSTIE/MAUDIT/SACRE/SIMONAC/TABER- NAC/TITI. To be angry (i.e. disposed to use *calice,* etc., as exclamations of disapproval, rage). *Pourquoi t'es tout le temps en titi?* "Why are you on edge all the time?" See JOUAL VERT; SACRE **2.**

EUCHARESSE! *Que., euph. for* **eucharistie!** "Damn it to hell!" (The "eucharist" is consecrated bread and wine used for Communion.) *Cf.* CIBOIRE!; HOSTIE!; SACRE **2.**

EUZIG(UE)S = LEUR(S)ZIGUE(S).

ÉVENTAIL, *m.* Fan. **Avoir les doigts de pieds; avoir les orteils en éventail** (lit. "to have one's toes spread out like a fan"). **1.** To laze around. *Ce week-end j'aimerais bien* *avoir les orteils en éventail.* "I'd like to put my feet up this weekend." **2.** To have an orgasm. See DOIGTS DE PIED.

(S')EXPLIQUER. 1. To quarrel. *"Allez vous expliquer ailleurs," a dit le barman.* "'Go fight/have it out someplace else,' said the bartender." **2.** To practice prostitution. *Celles qui s'expliquent dans le 8ème sont bien fringuées et vous offrent le champagne.* "Those who work the 8th arrondissement are well dressed and offer you champagne."

EXTRA, from **extraordinaire.** Marvelous. *La soirée était extra.* "It was a wonderful evening."

EXTRA, *m.* Special treat. **Se faire/s'offrir un extra.** To splurge. *Si l'on se faisait un extra chez Bocuse?* "How about splurging and going to Bocuse?"

FACHO, *adj.* and *m. n., pej.* Fascist. *Les fachos et les cocos se sont bagarrés.* "The Fascists and the Commies slugged it out."

FAÇON, *f.* Way, manner. **Sans façon(s).** Unpretentious; casual. **Façon façon,** *W.African.* Strange; complicated. *J'peux pas accepter sans façon. La situation est trop façon façon.* "I can't accept just like that. The situation's too odd."

FAF = FACHO.

FAFFES, *m., pl.* Identity paper. *On m'a piqué mes faffes.* "S.o. swiped my ID."

FAGOT, *m.* **1.** Firewood. **Sentir le fagot** (lit. "to smell of kindling wood"). To be a burning offense. "*Les opinions de ce cureton sentent le fagot,*" *pensait le cardinal.* "'That little priest's opinions smell of heresy,' thought the cardinal." See DE DERRIÈRE LES FAGOTS. **2.** Ex-convict. *On ignorait qu'il était un fagot.* "We didn't know he was an ex-con."

FAGOTÉ, -E. Dressed. *Elle était ahurie de se trouver sur la liste des plus mal fagotées de l'année.* "She was shocked to find h.s. on the list of the year's worst-dressed women." See AS DE PIQUE.

FAIBLE. Weak. See TOMBER FAIBLE.

FAIRE. To do. **La faire à qn.** To fool s.o. *On ne me la fera pas!* "They won't pull the wool over my eyes!" **Être fait (comme un rat).** To get arrested. *Après des mois de* *planque il a été fait.* "After hiding out for months they finally busted/cornered him." See FAUT LE FAIRE; SAVOIR Y FAIRE; (ÇA) COMMENCE À BIEN FAIRE.

FAIRE DANS SON FROC/SA CULOTTE. To be very afraid. *Il fait dans son froc pour rien.* "He shits/pisses in his pants for the slightest little thing."

FAIRE DES PATTES D'ARAIGNÉE. To gently caress erogenous zones (lit. "to make spider legs"). *Il aimait lui faire des pattes d'araignée tout autour de son angora.* "He enjoyed making love taps around her pussy."

FAIRE LES POCHES À QN. To go through s.o's pockets; to pick a pocket. *Son gosse lui fait les poches.* "His kid pilfers from his pockets."

FAIRE NI UNE NI DEUX. To do s.t. unhesitatingly. *Il est parti sans faire ni une ni deux.* "He left just like that."

FAIRE SES BESOINS/COMMISSIONS, *euph.,* children. To eliminate waste. *Je sors le chien pour qu'il fasse ses besoins.* "I take the dog out so he can do his business." *As-tu fait toutes tes commissions, la petite et la grande.* "Did you do number 1 and number 2?"

FAIRE SON AFFAIRE À QN. To rub out. *Malgré ses gardes du corps, la flingueuse lui a fait son affaire.* "Despite his bodyguards, the contract killer bumped him off."

FAIRE UN FROMAGE DE QCH. To dramatize (lit. "to make a cheese of s.t."). *C'est pas la peine d'en faire un fromage.* "It's not worth making a big thing out of it."

FAIRE UN MONDE/SAC/UNE HISTOIRE DE QCH. = FAIRE UN FROMAGE.

FAIRE UN TABAC. See TABAC **2.**

(SE) FAIRE DU FRIC/POGNON = (SE) FAIRE.

(SE) FAIRE QN. 1. To put up with s.o. *Je ne peux plus me les faire, ses mômes.* "I can't stand her brats anymore." **2.** To have sex with s.o. *Nous nous la sommes faite!* "We banged her."

(SE) FAIRE ROULER. To get swindled. *Je me suis vraiment fait rouler par ce garagiste.* "That mechanic really took me for a ride."

(S'EN) FAIRE. To worry. *"Dans la vie faut pas s'en faire; moi, j'ne m'en fais pas,"* chantait Maurice Chevalier. "'Life's not for fretting; I don't sweat it,' sang Maurice Chevalier."

FAISAN, *m.* Crook (lit. "pheasant"). *Tu crois à ce faisan de promoteur?* "You believe that con artist real estate developer?"

FAISANDÉ, -E, *adj.* and *m. n.* (S.t.) fishy (lit. "gamey"). *L'officier trouvait qu'il y avait qch. de faisandé au Danemark.* "The officer thought there was s.t. rotten in Denmark."

FAISEUR, -EUSE D'ANGES, *m., f.* Illegal abortionist. *Les faiseurs d'anges râlaient quand on a légalisé l'avortement.* "The back alley abortionists complained when abortion was legalized."

FAISANDIER = FAISAN.

FAIT, -E. Drunk. *Cette fois-ci il est bien fait.* "This time he's really soused."

FALZAR, *m.* Pants. *Il voulait des falzars rouges, comme ceux des pêcheurs.* "He wanted red pants, like the fishermen's."

FANTAISIE, *f.* Fellatio (lit. "imagination"; "whim"). *Elle aimait commencer par une fantaisie.* "She liked to start things off with a little blow job."

FARCIR. 1. To riddle with bullets (lit. "to stuff"). *Après le braquage, la devanture de la banque était farcie de balles.* "After the holdup, the front of the bank was all shot up."

(SE) FARCIR. 1. To have sexually. *Je me la farcirais bien.* "I'd sure like to plug her." **2.** To endure. *Je me suis farci une longue attente chez le dentiste.* "I had to put up with a long wait at the dentist's."

FASTAGA or **FASTOCHE.** Easy. *Ton problème est fastoche.* "Your problem's easy."

FATMA/FATMUCHE, *f., pej.* Ar. woman; woman (from Fatima, Mohammed's daughter, a popular Ar. first name). *Dans ta cape tu ressembles à une fatma.* "Your cape makes you look like an Arab woman."

FAUCHE, *f.* Petty theft. *Cet accro vit de la fauche.* "That junky lives by shoplifting."

FAUCHÉ, -E (COMME LES BLÉS). Penniless (lit. "cut down like stalks of wheat"). *Pas de vacs cette année; nous sommes fauchés comme les blés.* "No vacation this year; we're flat broke."

FAUCHER. To steal (lit. "to mow"; "reap"). *On a fauché mon pépin.* "Somebody swiped my umbrella."

FAUCHMAN = FAUCHÉ.

FAUT LE FAIRE! That's really s.t.! *Débarquer avec sa smala sans prévenir—faut le faire!* "Descending unannounced on us with her tribe—what do you think of that!"

FAUT PAS DÉCONNER! Cut the crap!

FAUT QUE ÇA CHIE!, (lit. "it's got to shit!"). "No more dawdling. Let's get this show on the road!"

FAUX COMME UN JETON = FAUX JETON.

FAUX CUL/DERCHE, *m.* Hypocrite (lit. "fake ass"). *Je ne veux plus voir ce faux cul.* "I don't want to see that two-faced bastard again."

FAUX JETON, *m.,* Phony. *C'est un faux jeton.* "He's as phony as a three-dollar bill."

FAVEUR, *f.* Fellatio (lit. "favor"). *Par courtoisie elle lui fait souvent une faveur.* "As a courtesy, she often gives him head."

FAVOUILLE, javanais of **fouille.**

FAYOT, *m.* Toady (lit. "bean"). *Je l'insupporte, ce fayot.* "I can't stand that ass-kisser."

FÉBOU, *f.,* backslang of **bouffe.** Food. *Qui fait la fébou ce soir.* "Who's cooking dinner tonight?"

FÉCA, *m.,* backslang of **café.** *Ton féca, c'est de la pisse d'âne.* "Your coffee's dishwater."

FÉE BLANCHE, *f.* Cocaine (lit. "white fairy"). *La fée blanche le faisait dialoguer avec Freud et Sherlock Holmes.* "Under the spell of cocaine, he talked with Freud and Sherlock Holmes."

FÉE BRUNE, *f.* Opium (lit. "dark fairy"). *Elle n'achetait que des ivoires jaunis dans les fumeries de la fée brune.* "She bought only ivory carvings yellowed in opium dens."

FÉE DU LOGIS, *f.* Perfect housewife (lit. "the home's fairy"). *Sa femme est une occase et la fée du logis.* "His wife's an occasional prostitute and a perfect homemaker."

FÉE VERTE, *f.* **1.** Hashish. *Il ne pouvait pas vivre sans la magie de la fée verte, magie qui s'est transformée en fée Carabosse.* "He couldn't live without the magic of hash, magic that turned bad." **2.** Absinthe. *La fée verte célèbre son retour.* "Absinthe is making a comeback."

FEMMELETTE, *f.* **1.** Weak woman. *Elle aimait jouer à la femmelette.* "She liked playing the clinging vine." **2.** Wimp. *Le critique traitait Hamlet de femmelette.* "The critic called Hamlet a wimp."

FENDANT, -E. Hilarious (lit. "splitting"). *Quelle histoire fendante!* "What a side-splitting story!"

FENDANT, *m.* Pants. *Il vient d'acheter un nouveau fendant.* "He just bought a new pair of pants."

FENDARD = FENDANT.

FENDASSE, *f.* Female genitalia; female, *pej. Cette fendasse se gratte toujours la fendasse.* "That cunt's always scratching her cunt."

(SE) FENDRE LA GUEULE/PÊCHE/PIPE. To laugh one's head off. *Il n'y a pas de quoi se fendre la gueule.* "That's anything but a laughing matter."

FENDUE = FENDASSE.

FENÊTRIÈRE, *f.* Prostitute who solicits from her window; prostitute on display in a brothel window. *Elle a* *été fenêtrière et à Amsterdam et à Hambourg.* "She was showcased in both Amsterdam and Hamburg."

FERME-LA!/LA FERME!/FERME TA GUEULE! "Shut your face/trap! Put a lid on it!"

FERMER SON CLAPET/SA GUEULE. To shut up. *Il pourrait bien fermer son clapet!* "I wish that guy would keep his trap shut!"

FERMER SON CLAQUE-MERDE, stronger version of previous entry. *Ferme ton claque-merde.* "Shut your fucking mouth!"

FERRAILLE, *f.* Small change (lit. "scrap metal"). *Je n'avais que de la ferraille.* "All I had were a few measly coins." See TAS DE FERRAILLE.

FESSE, *f.* **1.** Buttock. *Les cannibales ont coupé une fesse à la servante de Cunégonde.* "The cannibals cut one buttock off Cunegonde's servant's butt." **2.** Woman as sex object. *Si tu cherches de la fesse, va dans ce troquet.* "If you're looking for a piece of ass, go to that bar." See DE FESSE; (N')Y ALLER QUE D'UNE FESSE. *Cf.* CUL **3.**

FESSES, *f., pl.* Buttocks. **Mes fesses!** "My ass!" See COLLER AUX FESSES; DE MES DEUX; DE MES FESSES; (SE) MAGNER LES FESSES; OCCUPE...FESSES; PEAU DES FESSES; SERRER LES FESSES; TIRE-FESSES.

FESTOUILLE, *f.* Party. *Une petite festouille de temps en temps ça fait du bien.* "A nice little bash or shindig now and then is just the thing."

FÊTE, *f.* Party. **Faire sa fête à qn.** To beat s.o. up. *On lui a fait sa fête à la sortie du bar.* "They beat him up when he left the bar." **Ça va être ta fête!** ironic. "You're going to get what's coming to you!"

FEU, *m.* Fire. **(Il n') y a pas le feu!** "Where's the fire? What's the rush?" See COUP DE FEU; PÉTER LE FEU.

(AVOIR LE) FEU AU CUL/AUX FESSES/QQ. PART. 1. To be in a great hurry. *Tu pars déjà? Tu as le feu qq. part?* "You're leaving already? Do you have to catch a
151

train/put out a fire somewhere?" **2.** To be horny. *Déjà à quatorze ans elle avait le feu aux fesses.* "Already at fourteen, she was a sexpot."

FEUILLE, *f.* **1.** Leaf. **Regarder/voir la feuille à l'envers.** To have sex in the country or under a tree (lit. "to see the underside of the leaf"). *Après le déj sur l'herbe ils ont regardé la feuille à l'envers.* "After eating on the grass they had a roll in the hay." **2.** Ear. See DUR… FEUILLE.

FEUILLE DE CHOU, *f.* Newspaper. *Ne te cache pas derrière ta feuille de chou.* "Don't hide behind your newspaper." **Avoir les oreilles en feuilles de chou.** To have cauliflower ears. *Le boxeur a les oreilles en feuilles de chou.* "The boxer has cauliflower ears."

FEUILLE DE ROSE, *f.* Anilinctus. *Même quand c'est lavé, elle refuse de faire feuille de rose.* "She won't ream/ do a rim job even on a washed rosebud."

FEUJ, *adj.* and *m. n.,* backslang of **juif.** Jew; Jewish. *Nous aimons la cuisine feuj.* "We like Jewish cooking."

FIASC/FIASQUE, *m.* from **fiasco.** Failure. *C'était le fiasc total.* "It was a total flop."

FICELLE, *f.* String. See TIRER SUR LA FICELLE; TIRER LES FICELLES; CONNAÎTRE…FICELLES.

FICELLÉ, -E. Dressed up. *Regarde comme tu es mal ficelée.* "Look at how badly you've gotten y.s. up." See AS DE PIQUE.

FICHAISE = FOUTAISE.

FICHER, dated, less vigorous synonym of FOUTRE.

(SE) FICHER = (SE) FOUTRE.

(S'EN) FICHER = (S'EN) FOUTRE.

FICHTREMENT = FOUTREMENT.

FICHU, -E = FOUTU, -E. See AS DE PIQUE.

FICHUMENT = FOUTUMENT.

FIEFFÉ, -E. Out-and-out. *"Je ne suis ni phallo ni facho." "Tu es un menteur fieffé."* "I'm neither a sexist nor a fascist." "You're a damned liar."

FIÉROT, *adj.* and *m. noun.* Swell-headed. *Il n'y pas de quoi faire le fiérot.* "You've got little reason to be so stuck-up."

FIFILLE, *f.* Sweet little girl. *C'est bien la fifille à sa maman.* "She's her mother's little darling."

FIFINE, *f.* Sanitary napkin. *Ne jette pas ta fifine dans le pot.* "Don't throw your rag down the toilet bowl."

FIGNARD/FIGNARÈS = FIGNE.

FIGNE, *m.* Anus. **Donner/lâcher du figne.** To practice passive homosexuality. *Jean Genet a commencé très jeune à lâcher du figne.* "Jean Genet began putting out when he was very young."

FIGNEDÉ/FIGNOLET/FIGNON = FIGNE.

FIGUE, *f.* Female genitalia (lit. "fig"). *Sa figue ne se détendait pas.* "Her snatch didn't relax."

FIGUES, *f., pl.* Testicles. **Avoir les figues molles.** To have low sexual desire. *Je sais faire bander même ceux qui ont les figues molles.* "I know how to get even the limpest dicks up."

FILER. 1. To spin. See FILER…AMOUR. **2.** To give. *File-moi des ronds.* "Give me some money." **3.** To follow. *Il ne savait pas que les flics le filaient.* "He didn't know the cops were tailing him."

FILER À L'ANGLAISE. To take French leave; slip off. *Nous avons filé avant la fin du concert.* "We left discreetly before the end of the concert."

FILER DU CHOUETTE/EN FILER. To be homosexually passive. *Des fois il aime filer du chouette, mais pas toujours.* "Sometimes he likes playing the female role, but not always."

FILER LE COUP DE GUIZOT. To have sex. *Cet historien godant a toujours envie de filer le coup de guizot.* "That horny historian always wants to get his end in."

FILER LE PARFAIT AMOUR. To live together bliss-fully with the love of one's life (lit. "to spin out [weave a web of] perfect love"). *Malgré ses cinq divorces, il rêve toujours de filer le parfait amour.* "Despite his five divorces, he's still dreaming of romantic love."

FILER UN COUP/UNE BEIGNE/JAVA/PÊCHE/ RACLÉE/TREMPE À QN. To smack s.o. *Si tu continues ton cirque, je vais te filer une raclée.* "If you keep acting up like that, I'll give you a whack."

FILER UN COUP DANS LE CALCIF = FILER… GUIZOT.

FILLE, *f.* Prostitute (lit. "girl"). *Il aime se payer une fille de temps en temps.* "He likes an occasional encounter with a working girl."

FILLE D'AMOUR, *f.* Full-time prostitute working for a pimp or madam. *Malheureuse enfant, elle était heureuse de devenir une fille d'amour.* "After a troubled child-hood, she was happy to become a full-fledged, totally pledged whore."

FILLE DE JOIE, *f.,* dated for **fille.**

FILLE DE L'AIR. See JOUER…AIR.

FILOCHE, *f.* Shadowing. **Prendre qn. en filoche.** To have s.o. followed. *Ce dileur a été pris en filoche.* "They put a tail on that dealer."

FILS À PAPA, *f.* Son whose father makes things easy for him. *Ne fais pas de ton fils un fils à papa.* "Don't turn your boy into a daddy's boy without initiative."

FILS DE PUTE/PUTAIN. SOB (lit. "whore's son"). *Fous le camp, fils de pute.* "Fuck off, dickhead."

FIN DES HARICOTS, *f.* Curtains; all done for. *Ce sera la fin des haricots si la star tombe malade.* "It'll be all over if the star gets sick."

FINE GUEULE, *f.* Gourmet. *On invitera cette fine gueule chez maman.* "We'll invite that connoisseur of fine food to Mom's house."

FINI, -E. 1. Done for. *Je ne suis pas encore finie, malgré mon grand âge.* "It's not over and done with for me, despite my advanced age." **2.** Complete. *Ce gosse est un paresseux fini.* "That kid's as lazy as they come."

FION, *m.* **1.** Anus. See (SE) MAGNER LE FION; (SE) CASSER… FION. **2.** Luck. **Avoir du fion.** To be lucky. *Il a eu du fion, tomber sur une femme pareille.* "He was lucky, finding a woman like that."

FIOTTE, *f., pej.* (Contraction of regional ***filotte*** [little girl]). Passive homosexual; S.O.B. *Fous le camp sale fiotte!* "Piss off, fuckin' faggot/ damn bastard."

FISSA, *youth, cités.* Fast (from Ar.). *Faisons fissa!* "Let's hurry it up!"

FISTULE, *f.* Fistula. **Avoir de la fistule,** *idiom.* To be lucky. *Malgré tout, il a eu de la fistule.* "Despite everything, he was lucky."

SE FIXER. To shoot up drugs. *Il se fixe toujours avec une seringue à jeter.* "He always shoots up with a disposable needle."

FLAG, from **in flagrante delicto. Être pris en flag.** To be caught red-handed. *Sa femme l'a pris en flag avec sa maîtresse.* "His wife caught him and his mistress in the act."

FLAGADA. Exhausted. *Surexcité hier, flagada aujourd'hui.* "Frenetic yesterday, pooped out today."

FLAGDA, *m.,* argot for **flageolet.** Bean. *J'aime bien le gigot, mais sans flagdas.* "I like leg of lamb, but without beans." Note: In America, mint often accompanies leg of lamb; in France, leg of lamb is usually served with little lima beans.

FLAMBER. To be a big gambler or spender; to squander. *Il a flambé toute ses économies avec sa nana.* "He blew all his savings on his girlfriend."

FLAMBEUR, -EUSE. Professional/chronic gambler. *Dostoyevski était un grand flambeur.* "Dostoyevski was a chronic gambler."

FLAN, *m.* Nonsense (lit. "custard"). **C'est du flan.** "That's horse manure." See (EN) RESTER...FLAN.

FLANC, *m.* Side. **Être sur le flanc.** To be exhausted. *Après ce travail j'étais sur le flanc.* "I was all done in after that job." See TIRER AU FLANC.

FLANQUER UNE BAFFE/BEIGNE/RACLÉE À QN. To slap s.o. *Le prof avait envie de lui flanquer une beigne.* "The teacher felt like whacking him."

FLAPI, -E. Exhausted. *Dieu merci, c'est vendredi; je suis flapie.* "Thank God it's Friday; I'm bushed."

FLASHER SUR QN./QCH. To feel a sudden rush for s.o./s.t. *J'ai flashé sur les deux, la nana et sa bagnole.* "I really went for both of them, the chick and her car."

FLÉMINGITE, *f.* Lazy. *Pour ce qui est de faire le ménage, j'ai la flémingite aiguë.* "When it comes to doing the housework, I'm the laziest guy in the world."

FLEMME, *f.* Laziness. *J'ai la flemme d'y aller.* "I'm too lazy to go there." See TIRER SA FLEMME.

FLEUR, *f.* Favor (lit. "flower"). *Il m'a fait une fleur en me remplaçant au boulot.* "He did me a favor by taking my place at work." See COMME UNE FLEUR; (S')ENVOYER DES FLEURS; MARCHAND DE FLEURS; PERDRE SA FLEUR.

FLEUR BLEUE, *f.* Incurably romantic. *J'aime son côté fleur bleue.* "I like his sentimental side."

FLIBUSTIER, *m.* Swindler. *Cet antiquaire est un flibustier.* "That antique dealer's a crook."

FLIC, *m.* Policeman from *Ger.* **fliege** ("fly"). *Il est devenu flic comme son dab.* "He became a cop like his dad."

FLICAILLE, *f.* The police. *La flicaille est partout à cause de la manif.* "The fuzz are everywhere because of the demonstration."

FLINGUE, *m.* Pistol. *Son flingue est toujours à portée de main.* "His piece is always within reach."

FLINGUER. To shoot. *Les truands l'ont flingué pour se sauver.* "The crooks blew him away so they could escape."

(SE) FLINGUER. To be very depressed (lit. "to commit suicide"). *Ne te flingue pas pour une amourette perdue.* "Don't worry y.s. sick over a broken love affair."

FLINGUEUR, -EUSE, *m., f.* Trigger-happy killer; contract killer. *La flicaille se méfiait de ce flingueur de première.* "The cops were on their guard around the notorious killer."

FLIP, *m.* Drug-induced depression; depression. *Ce livre est le flip fini.* "That book's a total downer."

FLIPPANT, -E. Depressing; creepy. *C'est flippant de voir tant de sans abris.* "It's depressing to see so many homeless people."

FLIPPER. 1. To be or get depressed (orig. as a result of taking drugs). *Tous ces mendigots dans le métro, ça me fait flipper.* "All those beggars in the subway get me down." **2.** To be stressed. *Je flippais avant de passer à l'exam.* "I was keyed up before the exam."

FLIQUER. To place under police surveillance. *C'est le quartier le plus fliqué mais toute cette flicaille ne sert à rien.* "That district's crawling with cops, thick as flies, but all that fuzz gets nowhere."

FLOP(P)ÉE, *m.* A large amount. *On a acheté une flopée de réserves.* "We stocked up on a whole bunch of stuff."

FLOTTE, *f.* Water; rain; drink. *J'ai reçu toute la flotte.* "I got soaked to the skin."

FLOTTER. To rain. *Il a flotté toute la journée.* "It poured all day."

FLOTTEURS, *m., pl.* Big breasts. *Avec des flotteurs pareils elle ne risque pas de se noyer!* "With bazooms like that, she's in no danger of drowning!"

FLOUSE/FLOUZE, *m.* Money. *Il se balade toujours avec du flouse plein les poches.* "He always walks around with plenty of dough on him."

FLOUSER. To fart. *Les fayots nous ont fait flouser toute la nuit.* "The beans made us fart all night."

FLÛTE, *f.* 1. Flute. See JOUER…FLÛTE; 2. Leg. See JOUER DES FLÛTES.

FLÛTE!, *euph.* for **foutre!** Gosh darn! Gosh damn!

FOFOLLE, *f. adj.* and *n.* Scatterbrained. *Ne fais pas attention; elle fait sa fofolle.* "Don't bother about her; she's acting crazy." *Cf.* FOUFOU.

FOIN, *m.* 1. Hay. **Faire du foin.** To make noise; create scandal. *Quand les flics ont fouillé leur appart, ça a fait du foin.* "There was quite a rumpus when the fuzz searched their apartment." 2. Poor-grade tobacco; marijuana. *Il plantait du foin dans le jardin de sa grand-mère.* "He planted 'grass' in his grandmother's garden."

FOIRADE, *f.* 1. Diarrhea. *Nous avons terminé notre gueuleton avec une bonne foirade.* "Our fine feast ended up with everyone having the runs." 2. Fear. *Il avait la foirade en voyant les gangsters.* "He was scared shitless when he saw the gangsters." 3. Failure. *Je ne m'attendais pas à une telle foirade.* "I wasn't expecting everything to go down the toilet/to be a total washout like that."

FOIRARD, -E = FOIREUX, -EUSE.

FOIRE, *f.* Fair. **C'est la foire ici!** "This place is a madhouse!" **Faire la foire.** To celebrate. *Les bonshommes sont partis faire la foire.* "The guys have gone out on a binge."

FOIRE D'EMPOIGNE. Free-for-all; rat race. *Lors des soldes, c'est la foire d'empoigne dans les grands magasins.* "When it's sale time in the department stores, it's everyone for h.s."

FOIRER. 1. To defecate. *Le chien a foiré sur la moquette.* "The dog crapped on the carpet." 2. To go wrong; fail. *J'ai foiré complètement à l'exam.* "I really screwed up on the exam."

FOIREUX, -EUSE. Unlikely to succeed. *La plupart de ses projets sont foireux.* "Most of his projects are of doubtful value."

FOIRIDON/FOIRIDONDAINE = FOIRE.

FOLDINGUE. Crazy. *Il conduit à une vitesse foldingue.* "He speeds like a madman."

FOLICHON, -ONNE. Pleasant. See PAS FOLICHON.

FOL(L)INGUE = FOLDINGUE.

FOLKEUX, -EUSE, *m., f.* Folk music player or enthusiast. *On ira au festival des folkeux.* "We'll go to the folk musicians' festival."

FOLKLO *m.,* from **folklorique.** Old-fashioned; weird. *Toute la famille est folklo.* "The whole family are eccentrics."

FOLLE, *f.* Effeminate homosexual (lit. "madwoman"). *Les grandes folles éclataient de rire.* "The mad queens burst out laughing."

FOLLE PERDUE/FOLLE TORDUE, more emphatic for FOLLE.

(À) FOND DE CALE. Flat broke (lit. "at the bottom of the ship's hold"). *Le chômage l'a mis à fond de cale.* "He's unemployed and at rock bottom."

(À) FOND LA CAISSE. 1. At top speed (car or motorcyle). *Il roule toujours à fond la caisse.* "He always drives at top speed." **2.** All out. *Il marche toujours à fond la caisse.* "He always gives it everything he's got."

FORMIDABLE, *m.* Large glass of beer (one liter in northeast Fr.; a half-liter (pint) elsewhere). *Il buvait formidable sur formidable.* "He drank one mug of beer after another."

FORTICHE, *m., f.* Brainy. *Tu es fortiche.* "You've got smarts."

FOUDRE, *m.* Lightning. See COUP DE FOUDRE.

FOUFOU. Crazy. *Il est un peu foufou ce jeunot.* "That kid's a bit cracked."

FOUFOUNE/FOUFOUNETTE, *f.* Female genitalia. *Elle portait une jolie robe à froufrous mais je ne pensais qu'à dévoiler sa foufoune.* "She was wearing a nice frilly dress, but all I could think about was getting at her snatch."

FOUFOUNE, *f., Que.* **1.** Buttock. M*a femme s'est fait refaire les foufounes. Je l'amais mieux avant.* "My wife had her butt redone. I liked her better before." *Cf.* FESSE. **2.** Sexual activity. *Pas de foufoune avec moi. Ton chum de foufoune m'a tout raconté.* "No sex with me. The guy you're sleeping with told me everything." *Cf.* CUL **3.** and Eng. "piece of ass," "sell one's ass."

FOUILLE, *f.* Pocket (lit. "search"; "archaeological dig"). **C'est dans la fouille!** "It's in the bag." **En avoir plein les fouilles.** To be very rich. *Tes vioques en ont plein les fouilles.* "Your parents are loaded."

FOUILLE-MERDE, *m., f.* Muckraking journalist; scandalmonger. *La vie sans histoires du prince faisait le désespoir des fouille-merde.* "The prince's uneventful life made the muckrakers very unhappy."

FOUILLE PERCÉE, *f.* Person with holes in his or her pocket. *Pas possible d'économiser avec ma fouille percée de mari.* "Impossible to save anything with a spendthrift husband like mine."

FOUILLER. To have sexually (lit. "to rummage"). *Il avait une envie folle de la fouiller.* "He really wanted to plug her."

(SE) FOUILLER. To go through one's pockets. **Tu peux te fouiller.** "No way! Go to hell!"

FOUILLETTE = FOUILLE.

FOUILLOUSE = FOUILLE.

FOUINARD, -E, *m., f.* Busybody. *Je ne suis pas fouinarde, mais je fais les poches de mon mari.* "I'm not a snoop but I go through my husband's pockets."

FOULARD, *m.* Scarf. See BANDER FOULARD.

FOULEPINE, *Que., from Eng.* "full pin." All-out, at top speed. *Il roulait foulepine.* "He drove at top speed."

(SE) FOULER. To work hard. See RATE.

FOULTITUDE, *f.* Crowd; large amount. *La prêtresse énonce une foultitude de béatitudes pour nous aider à vaincre nos* *mauvaises attitudes.* "The priestess expounds heaps of beatitudes to help us overcome our bad attitudes."

FOUNETTE = FOUFOUNE.

FOUR, *m.* Flop (lit. "oven"). *Les dernières pièces de Tennessee Williams, descendues en flammes par la critique, ont été des fours.* "Tennessee Williams' last plays, roasted by the critics, were flops."

FOURBI, *m.* Stuff. *Il avait tout un fourbi dans le grenier des vioques.* "He had a pile of junk in his parents' attic."

FOURCHETTE, *f.* Fork. See COUP DE FOURCHETTE.

FOURCHETTES, *f., pl.* Legs. See JOUER…FOURCHETTES.

FOURMI, *f.* Small-time drug dealer (lit. "ant"). *Cette fourmi a été écrasée par les grands dileurs.* "That pissant dealer got crushed by the big guys."

FOURRÉ. See COUP FOURRÉ.

FOURRER. To have sexually (lit. "to stuff"). *Ma grand-tante, vieille fille, n'a jamais voulu être fourrée.* "My old-maid great-aunt never wanted to get laid."

(SE) FOURRER. To make a mistake. **Se fourrer le doigt dans l'œil (jusqu'au coude).** To make a whale of a mistake (lit. "to stuff one's finger into one's eye [as far as one's elbow]"). *Je me suis fourré le doigt dans l'œil en imaginant qu'il avait une maîtresse.* "I was very much mistaken when I thought he had a mistress."

FOUTAISE, *m.* Nonsense. *Tes arguments, c'est de la foutaise.* "Your arguments are a bunch of baloney."

FOUTEUR, -EUSE DE MERDE, *m., f.* Troublemaker. *Méfie-toi de cette fouteuse de merde.* "Watch out for that shitmixer."

FOUTOIR, *m.* Messy place; dump. *Je ne retrouve rien dans ce foutoir.* "I can't find anything in this mess."

FOUTRAQUE. Wild; whacky; wonderful. *Son nouvel album est total foutraque!* "Her new album's totally awesome."

FOUTRE, *m.* Sperm. *Ce gosse se branle sans arrêt et sent toujours le foutre.* "That kid never stops jerking off and always smells of sperm."

FOUTRE. 1. To have sex. *Il aimait la foutre sous le cerisier.* "He liked to lay her under the cherry tree." *Va te faire foutre!* "Go fuck y.s./go to hell!" See ENVOYER…FOUTRE. **2.** To put; fling, sling ("slang" derives from "sling" and **foutre** is a popular sl. verb). *Le prof nous a dit de ne pas foutre le verbe "foutre" partout.* "Teach told us not to put (use) the verb *foutre* everywhere." **Le/la foutre qq part./où je pense/au cul.** To shove it. See QUELQUE PART; OÙ JE PENSE. **Foutre la merde.** See MERDE. **3.** To do. *Il n'a jamais rien foutu à l'école.* "He never did any work at school." **Ne pas en foutre une datte/rame/ramée.** Not to do a goddamned thing. See RAME. **N'en avoir rien à foutre.** To be totally indifferent to s.t. *Tes emmerdes, je n'en ai rien à foutre!* "Your problems are no skin off my nose." **4.** To give. **Foutre les jetons/le trac/la trouille.** To frighten. *Le film d'épouvante nous a foutu la trouille.* "The horror film gave us the willies." **Foutre un coup/une baffe/beigne/ raclée/trempe à qn.** To give s.o. a whack. See FILER UN COUP … À QN.

FOUTRE! Fuck it! Damn it to hell!

(SE) FOUTRE À. To begin. *Quand vas-tu te foutre au boulot?* "When are you going to get to work?"

FOUTRE À LA PORTE, FOUTRE DEHORS. To throw out. *Je l'ai foutu à la porte.* "I threw him out."

(S'EN) FOUTRE COMME DE L'AN QUARANTE/ S'EN FOUTRE PAS MAL/COMME DE SA DERNIÈRE CHEMISE/COMPLÈTEMENT. To not give a damn. *De tes conseils, je m'en fous pas mal.* "I couldn't care less about your advice."

FOUTRE DEDANS. To mislead. *Il m'a foutu dedans avec ses explications à la gomme.* "He really put me up shit's creek with his lousy explanations." See MERDE; MERDIER.

(SE) FOUTRE DEDANS. To make a mistake. *Je me suis foutu dedans, pour mes calculs.* "I screwed up in my calculations."

(SE) FOUTRE DE QCH. = S'EN FOUTRE.

(SE) FOUTRE DE QN./DE LA GUEULE DE QN. To pull s.o.'s leg. *Ne te fous pas de ma gueule.* "Don't put me on."

(SE) FOUTRE DU MONDE. To not care about anyone or anything and behave outrageously. *Tu nous redemandes du fric? Tu te fous du monde?* "You're asking us for money again? Who the hell do you think you think you are?"

FOUTRE EN L'AIR. To ruin. *L'ordinateur a foiré et tout son travail a été foutu en l'air.* "The computer screwed up and all his work is in the electricity."

(SE) FOUTRE EN L'AIR. To commit suicide. *Hedda voulait qu'il se foute en l'air de façon élégante.* "Hedda wanted him to do h.s. in elegantly."

FOUTRE EN POUBELLE. To junk. *Toutes ses peintures sont à foutre en poubelle.* "All his paintings should be trashed."

(SE) FOUTRE EN ROGNE. See ROGNE.

FOUTRE LA PAIX. See PAIX.

FOUTRE L'ARGENT PAR LES FENÊTRES. To waste money. *Je n'ai pas d'argent à foutre par les fenê-tres.* "I haven't got money to throw down the drain."

FOUTRE LE CAMP. To clear out. *Fous-moi le camp!* "Get the hell out! Fuck off! Piss off!"

FOUTREMENT. Extremely. *C'était foutrement bon ton frichti!* "Your meal was damned good!"

FOUTRE PAR TERRE. To chuck it all. *Parfois j'ai envie de tout foutre par terre.* "Sometimes I feel like saying to hell with it all."

FOUTRE RIEN. Not a goddamned thing. *Je n'en sais foutre rien.* "I don't know a fucking thing about it."

FOUTU, -E. 1. Done for. *C'est foutu d'avance!* "It's doomed before starting!" **2.** No good; useless; lousy. *Quelle foutue maison!* "What a dump!" **3.** Broken; *Ton magnétoscope est foutu.* "Your VCR's busted." **4.** Built. *C'est appareil* *est mal foutu.* "This appliance is poorly constructed." *Cette nana est bien foutue.* "That broad's stacked."

FOUTU, -E COMME L'AS DE PIQUE/COMME QUATRE SOUS. Badly dressed. See AS DE PIQUE.

FOUTU DE. Capable of; likely to. *Il n'est pas foutu d'arriver à l'heure.* "He's incapable of arriving on time."

FOUTUMENT = FOUTREMENT.

FOYI, *youth, cités,* from Bambara, a lang. spoken in Mali, Burkina Faso, and Côte d'Ivoire. Nothing. *Y a foyi à bouffer ici.* "There's nothing to eat here."

FRAGO, *m., photographers jargon.* Perfect photo (from Fragonard, painter of highly polished canvases). *C'est pas un frago mais quand même une bonne photo.* "It's not perfection, but it's still a fine photo."

FRAÎCHE, *f.* Cash. *Au marché ils exigent de la fraîche.* "At the market, they want to be paid in cash."

FRAIS, *m., pl.* Expenses. **Arrêter les frais.** To call it quits. *C'est fini! J'arrête les frais.* "That's it. I've had enough." See PRINCESSE.

FRAISE, *f.* **1.** Strawberry. See ENVOYER…FRAISES; SUCRER LES FRAISES. **2.** Face; individual. **Ma/ta/sa/fraise/nos fraises,** and so on. *Vos fraises, qu'est-ce que vous en pensez?* "You guys, what do you think of that?" See RAMENER SA FRAISE.

FRAMBOISE, *f.* Clitoris (lit. "raspberry"). *J'avais la framboise très excitée.* "My clit was very excited."

FRANCFORT, *m.* Finger (lit. "Frankfurt" from **saucisse de Francfort** "frankfurter"). Fingers. *Mimi avait les francforts gelés.* "Mimi's fingers were cold." *Cf.* MERGUEZ **2;** OSSELETS.

FRANCHECAILLE, *f.* France. *Churchill trouvait la Franchecaille archifromagère ingouvernable.* "Churchill thought cheese-producing France impossible to govern."

FRANCHOUILLARD, -E. French; chauvinistically Fr. *Mon beau-dab n'achète que franchouillard.* "My father-in-law only buys French."

FRANCHOUILLARD, *m.* French. *L'Académie franchouillarde défend le franchouillard.* "The French Academy defends the French language."

FRANCO. Right away. *Vas-y franco. Épouse-la!* "Get cracking! Marry her!"

FRANGIN, *m.* Brother; buddy. *Son frangin l'accompagne partout.* "Her brother accompanies her everywhere."

FRANGINE, *f.* Sister. *Il fait passer sa petite amie pour sa frangine.* "He passes off his girlfriend as his sister."

FRANGINS, *m., pl.* Freemasons. *Tolstoy décrit les rites secrets des frangins.* "Tolstoy describes the secret rites of the Masons."

FRAPPADINGUE. Completely crazy. *Il est frappadingue, mais heureux.* "He's totally bananas, but happy."

FRAPPE, *f.* Hoodlum (lit. "punch; kick"). *Ton frangin n'est qu'une petite frappe.* "Your brother's just a little punk."

(SE) FRAPPER. To hit or tap o.s. **Ne pas se frapper.** Not to worry. *Ne te frappe pas!* "Don't sweat it!"

FRENCHER. *Que.* To tongue-kiss (from Eng. "French kiss"). *Tu ne sais pas bien frencher.* "You don't how to French-kiss." *Cf.* GUÉLAN; ROULER UN PALOT.

FRÉROT, *m.* Younger brother. *Son frérot l'a surpris avec sa nana.* "His kid brother caught him and his girlfriend by surprise."

FRIC, *m.* Money. *Il est plein de fric.* "He's got lots of bread." See SAINT-FRIC.

FRIC-FRAC, *m.* Burglary. *Ils ont subi plusieurs fric-frac.* "They've been burgled frequently."

FRICHTI, *m.* Meal. *Ça sent le bon frichti.* "That smells like good cooking."

FRICOT = FRICHTI.

FRICOTER. 1. To cook. *Tout ce qu'il fricote est drôlement bon.* "Everything he cooks is super." **2.** To plot. *Qu'est-ce qu'ils peuvent bien fricoter ensemble?* "I wonder what

165

they're cooking up together." **3.** To have sex. *Ils ont longtemps fricoté avant de se marier.* "They were shacking up long before they got married."

FRI-FRI. Female genitalia. See CACHE-FRI-FRI.

FRIGO. Cold. *Il fait frigo aujourd'hui.* "It's cold today."

FRIGO, *m.,* from **frigorifique.** Refrigerator. *Les nouveaux frigos respectent l'environnement.* "New fridges are environmentally friendly."

FRIME, *f.* Face; sham. *C'est de la frime, tout ce qu'il dit.* "That's all phony, everything he says."

(SE) FRINGUER. To get dressed; buy clothes. *Il se fringue aux puces.* "He gets his clothes at the flea market."

FRINGUES, *f., pl.* Clothes. *Les fringues, c'est son dada.* "Clothes are her hobby."

FRIPES, *f., pl.* Clothes. *Ils vendent des fripes sur le marché.* "They sell clothes in the market."

FRISÉE, *f.* Female pubic hair (lit. "curly endive"). See BROUTER LA FRISÉE.

FRITE, *f.* French fry. **Avoir la frite.** To be in great shape. *Je n'ai pas la frite aujourd'hui.* "I'm not feeling so hot today."

FROC, *m.* Pants. **Baisser son froc.** To eat humble pie. *Il avait tort mais refusait de baisser son froc.* "He was wrong but wouldn't get off his high horse." See FAIRE... FROC; CHIER...FROC.

FROLO, *m., youth, cités,* from a character (not the hunchback) in the movie *Le Bossu de Notre Dame,* based on the V. Hugo novel). *C'est pas un frolo pour toi.* "He's not the boy for you."

FROLOTINE or **FROLLOTTE,** *f., youth, cités.* Girl. *Tu l'as vue ma frolotte?* "Have you seen my girl?" *Cf.* GO; MEUF; RACLI; RATE; CHNECK.

FROM = FROMEGI.

FROMAGE, *m.* Cheese. See FAIRE UN FROMAGE.

FROMAGES, *m., pl.* Feet. *Ses fromages tapent un max.* "His feet really stink."

FROMEGI, from **fromage.** *De Gaulle était fier des fromegis de la Franchecaille.* "De Gaulle was proud of France's cheeses."

FROMETEGOM/FROMETON/FROMGOM = FROMEGI.

FROUCHELER, *Bel.* To bill and coo; engage in heavy petting. *Au cinoche Gil nous a frouchelées toutes les deux, ma sœur et moi. Il avait la langue et les mains très baladeuses.* "At the movies Gil kissed and pawed us both, my sister and me. His hands and tongue were busy."

FRUSQUES, *f., pl.* Clothes. *D'où viennent ces frusques?* "Where do those clothes come from?"

FRUSQUIN = SAINT FRUSQUIN.

FUGUE, *f.* Escapade; fugue (music). **Faire une fugue.** To run away. *Quand Bach a vu Mlle Buxtehude il a vite fait une fugue.* "When Bach saw Miss Buxtehude he ran off fast."

FULL PIN = FOULEPINE.

FUMACE/FUMASSE. Furious. *Je suis fumace d'avoir loupé mon rendève.* "I am really ticked off at having missed my appointment."

FUMANT, -E. Marvelous. *Quelle histoire fumante!* "What a wonderful story!"

FUMER. To be angry (lit. "to smoke"). *J'ai attendu deux heures. Je fumais.* "I waited two hours. I was furious."

FUMIER, *m.* SOB (lit. "fertilizer"). *Je ne parle plus à ce fumier.* "I don't talk to that bastard anymore."

FURAX, -E. Furious. *J'étais furaxe d'avoir crevé.* "I was boiling mad at having had a flat tire."

FURIBARD, -E. Angry. *Les dabs était furibards qu'elle parte avec ce flambeur.* "Her parents were enraged at her going off with that professional gambler."

FUSEAUX, *m., pl.* Legs. See JOUER DES FUSEAUX.

167

FUSIL, *m.* Stomach (lit. "rifle"). *Depuis ce matin je ne me suis rien mis dans le fusil.* "I haven't had anything to eat since this morning." See COUP DE FUSIL.

FUSIL À TROIS COUPS/TROUS, *m.* Prostitute practicing oral, vaginal, and anal sex (lit. "triple-barreled shotgun"). *Line, vrai fusil à trois coups, est très recherchée.* "Line, a versatile working girl, is much in demand."

FUSILLER. To fleece (lit. "to shoot"). *Il s'est fait fusiller par son avocat.* "His lawyer took him to the cleaners."

GABELOU, *m., pej.* Customs officer; tax collector (from **gabelle** "salt tax"). *Dans ce film les gabelous harcelaient Sophia Loren à cause d'une mortadelle.* "In that movie customs officers hassled Sophia Loren because of a mortadella sausage."

GÂCHE, *f.* Job (lit. "trowel"). *J'ai une gâche qui me permet d'élever mes mômes.* "I've got a job that allows me to bring up my kids."

GÂCHER. 1. To work. *Gâcher ne m'a jamais fait peur.* "I was never afraid of work." **2.** To spoil. **Gâcher le métier.** To work or sell for less than the standard rate. *Les travailleurs au noir nous gâchent le métier.* "The undeclared workers are spoiling it for us."

GADANG-GADANG. *Que.* Pretentious, la-dee-da. *Tu te donnes toujours des airs gadang-gadang.* "You always put on fancy airs."

GADIN, *m.* **1.** Head. *J'ai mal au gadin.* "I have a headache." **2.** Fall. See PRENDRE UN GADIN; RAMASSER UN GADIN.

GADJO or **GADJI,** *m.* Average Joe; naïve, nondescript person; guy (orig. a Gypsy term for a non-Gypsy). *Danse pas avec ce gadjo.* "Don't dance with that guy."

GADOUE, *f.* **1.** Mud; muck; slush. *La neige fond; il y a de la gadoue partout.* "The snow's melting and there's slush everywhere." **2.** Mess. *Ils ne savent que foutre de la gadoue partout.* "All they can do is mess up everything."

GADOUILLE = GADOUE.

GAFFE, *m.* Prison guard. *Les gaffes participaient aux partouses.* "The prison guards took part in the orgies/daisy chains."

GAFFE, *f.* **1.** Blunder. *J'ai fait une gaffe en lui parlant de la visite de son mari.* "I made a mistake telling her about her husband's visit." **2.** Guard duty; sentinel. **Faire gaffe.** To be on one's guard. *Fais gaffe ou la flicaille t'agrafera.* "Watch out or the cops will get you."

GAGA. Gaga. *À 82 ans elle est loin d'être gaga.* "She's far from senile at 82." **Être gaga de qn.** To be gone on s.o. *Il est complètement gaga de son chien.* "He dotes on his dog."

GALÈRE, *f.* Hard work. *Mon travail de nuit, c'est la galère!* "My night job's a real grind!"

GALÉRER. To work hard; have a rough time. *J'ai galéré pour réussir mes exams et galéré deux ans au chômage.* "I worked like a dog to pass my exams and I spent two rough years on unemployment."

GALERIE, *f.* Crowd (lit. "gallery"). **Amuser la galerie.** To be the life of the party. *Il n'est bon que pour amuser la galerie.* "All he's good for is clowning around."

GALÉRIEN, *m.* Galley slave. **Mener une vie de galérien.** To lead a dog's life. *J'ai mené une vie de galérien pour construire ma maison.* "I worked like a slave to build my house."

GALÉRIENNE, *f.* Shopping center prostitute. *La galérienne racolait en regardant les vitrines.* "The prostitute solicited as she looked at the shop windows."

GALETTE, *f.* Money (lit. "crêpe"). *Les voisins ont de la galette.* "The neighbors are rolling in dough."

GALIPETTE, *f.* Somersault. **Faire des galipettes.** To fool around; fool around sexually. *Ce n'est ni l'endroit ni le moment pour faire des galipettes.* "This is neither the time nor the place for a roll in the hay."

GALOCHE, *f.* Clog. See ROULER…GALOCHE.

GALOCHER = ROULER UNE GALOCHE.

GALON, *m.* Stripe (military). See PRENDRE DU GALLON.

GALOPIN, *m.* Small glass of beer. *Juste le temps pour un galopin.* "Just enough time for a short one."

GALUCHE, *f.* Gauloise® cigarette. *Mon dab ne fumait que des galuches bleues.* "My pop smoked only Gauloises in the blue pack."

GALURE or **GALURIN,** *m.* Hat. *J'ai déjà porté ce galurin à Ascot mais il m'en faudra un neuf pour Auteuil.* "I wore this hat at Ascot but for Auteuil I'll need a new one."

GAMAHUCHE, *f.* Oral sex (fellatio and cunnilingus). *Ils prenaient un grand plaisir à la gamahuche.* "They really enjoyed 69."

GAMAHUCHER. To have oral sex. *Gamahucher, c'est pas son genre.* "Oral sex isn't her thing."

GAMBERGE, *f.* Deep thought. *Après mûre gamberge, j'ai fini par dire oui.* "After careful consideration, I finally said yes."

GAMBERGER. To think hard; worry. *Tu gamberges trop à ce problème.* "You worry your head/give too much thought to that issue."

GAMBETTE, *f.* Leg. *Mistinguette et Marlene Dietrich étaient très fières de leurs gambettes.* "Mistinguette and Marlene Dietrich were very proud of their gams."

GAMELLE, *f.* Dish. See PRENDRE…GAMELLE; RAMASSER… GAMELLE.

GARDER UN CHIEN DE SA CHIENNE À QN. To bear a grudge against s.o. *Elle lui garde toujours un chien de sa chienne pour avoir été trompée.* "She still has it in for him because he cheated on her."

GARGUE, *f.* Throat. *Le tenor a toujours mal à la gargue.* "The tenor's still got a sore throat."

171

GÂTEAU, *m.* **C'est du gâteau!** "That's a piece of cake, a cinch."

GÂTERIE, *f.* Oral sex (lit. "little treat"). *J'adore lui faire une gâterie.* "I love giving him a present down there."

GAUCHE, *f.* The left wing. **La gauche caviar,** *usually pej.* Affluent Socialists or Communists who profess to love the proletariat. *La gauche caviar est parfois aussi hypocrite que les bourgeois guindés et bien-pensants.* "Parlor pinks are often as hypocritcal as self-righteous, uptight upper-class people."

GAUCHO, *adj.* and *n.* Left wing; left-winger. *Le prof est gaucho mais pas bolcho.* "The professor's a leftist but not a Commie."

GAUFRE, *f.* See MOULE À GAUFRES; PRENDRE...GAUFRE; RAMASSER...GAUFRE.

GAULDO/GOLDO = GALUCHE.

GAULE, *f.* Penis (lit. "long pole/rod"). See ASTIQUER LA GAULE.

GAULER. To copulate. **Être bien gaulé.** To be well-hung. *Pol est assez bien gaulé mais il ne sait pas bien gauler.* "Pol's got pretty good equipment but he doesn't know how to use it."

GAULUCHE = GALUCHE.

GAVOUSSE, javanais of **gousse.**

GAY, *adj.* and *n.* Male homosexual. *Ce sont des gays et des gousses qui fréquentent cette disco.* "Gay guys and lesbos go to that disco."

GAZER. To go (fast/well/bad, and so on) [lit. "to gas"]). *"Ça gaze avec ton mec?" "Pour l'instant ça ne gaze pas fort."* "Everything going OK with you and your guy?" "Right now things aren't too hot."

G.D.B. = GUEULE DE BOIS.

GÉANT, -E. Terrific (lit. "gigantic"). *La teuf était géante!* "The party was fantastic!"

(SE) GELER. To freeze. **Se geler les couilles; glaouis; Se les geler.** To be very cold; to freeze one's balls off. *On se les gèle. Rentrons vite!* "It's cold enough to freeze the balls off a brass monkey. Let's go back fast."

GERBE, *f.* Vomit (lit. "bouquet"). *Pendant la tempête il y avait de la gerbe partout sur le bateau.* "During the storm there was puke all over the boat."

GERBER. To vomit. *Ta lèche, c'est à gerber.* "Your ass-kissing makes me want to throw up."

GERBOISE, *f.* = **GITON.**

GI! = **GY!**

GICLÉE, *f.* Spurt; squirt. See LÂCHER…GICLÉE.

GICLER. To scram. *Ralbol de tes magouilles; tu vas gicler, vite fait.* "I've had it with your conniving; get out of here fast."

GIFLE, *f.* Slap. See TÊTE À GIFLES.

GIGI = **GIGOLETTE.**

GIGO! = **GY!**

GIGOLETTE, *f.* Young girl; floozy (lit. "turkey leg"). *Une gigolette m'a dragué au bar.* "A tart tried to pick me up at the bar."

GIGOLO, *m.* **1.** Gigolo. *Elle est généreuse avec ses gigolos.* "She's generous with her gigolos." **2.** Jack (cards). *Sa dame a pris son gigolo.* "Her queen took his jack."

GIGOLPINCE, *m.* Gigolo. *Son gigolpince guinche bien.* "Her gigolo's a good dancer."

GIGOT, *m.,* Leg; thigh; buttock (lit. "leg of lamb"). *Ses gigots étaient serrés un max dans son jean.* "Her ample legs were squeezed into her tight jeans."

GIGOT! = **GY!**

GIGOTER. To dance (lit. "to fidget; wriggle"). *Allons gigoter ce soir!* "Let's shake our dancing legs tonight."

GIGOTEUR, *m.* Dancer. *C'est un beau couple de gigoteurs.* "They're an attractive dancing couple."

GINGIN = JINJIN 2.

GIRAFE, *m.* Giraffe. See PEIGNER LA GIRAFE.

GITON, *m.* Young passive homosexual. *Le richard choyait son giton.* "The old moneybags pampered his darling boy."

GIROFLÉE (À CINQ FEUILLES), *f.* Slap (lit. "five-leaved gillyflower"). *Il avait mérité cette belle giroflée à cinq feuilles.* "He deserved the good whack he got."

GIVRÉ, -E. Crazy; drunk (lit. "frosted over"). *Lui il est né givré et elle est givrée dès le matin.* "He was born crazy, and she's drunk all day."

GLAND, -E. Stupid. *Je ne te croyais pas aussi glande.* "I didn't think you were that much of a dope."

GLAND, *m.* Penis (lit. "acorn"; "glans penis"). See POMPER LE GLAND.

GLANDER. To waste time. *J'aime glander le week-end.* "I like to loaf on weekends." **N'avoir rien à glander.** To not give a damn. *Nous n'avons rien à glander de toutes tes histoires.* "We couldn't care less about your actions."

GLANDES, *f., pl.* Glands. **1. Avoir les glandes.** To be angry. *J'ai les glandes dès que je la vois.* "Just the sight of her infuriates me." **2. Foutre les glandes à qn.** To irritate s.o. *Fous le camp, tu me fous les glandes!* "Fuck off. You piss me off!"

GLANDEUR, -EUSE, *m., f.* Loafer. *Je ne veux pas embaucher ce glandeur.* "I don't want to hire that lazy bum."

GLANDILLEUX, -EUSE. Difficult; tricky. *Il s'est lancé dans des investissements glandilleux.* "He took a chance on risky investments."

GLANDOUILLER = GLANDER.

GLANDOUILLEUR, -EUSE = GLANDEUR, -EUSE.

GLANDOUILLEUX, -EUSE = GLANDILLEUX, -EUSE.

GLANDU, *m.* Fool. *Quel glandu!* "What a jerk!"

GLAOUIS, *m., pl.* Testicles. See CASSER; (SE) GELER.

GLAVIOT, *m.* Gob of spit. *Quelle infection, ces glaviots sur le trottoir!* "How revolting, all those gobs of spit on the sidewalk."

GLAVIOT(T)ER. To spit. **Glavioter sur qn.** To treat s.o. like dirt. *Il glaviote sur tous à la mairie.* "He's full of contempt for everybody at city hall."

GLINGLIN, *m.,* children. Ringing. *Ça fait glinglin.* "It's going ding-dong." See SAINT-GLINGLIN.

GLISSER UN FIL = LÂCHER UN FIL.

GNAF, *m.* Shoemaker (from "Gnafron," character in traditional Lyon puppet theater). *J'ai porté mes godasses chez le gnaf.* "I took my shoes to the shoemaker."

GNANGNAN. Silly; trashy; spineless. *L'actrice est gnagnan est le film aussi.* "The actress is silly and the film too."

GNARD, -E = GNIARD, -E.

GNAULE = GNÔLE.

GNIARD, -E, *m.* **1.** Child. *Ce week-end, pas de gniards avec nous.* "Let's spend the weekend without the kids." **2.** Individual. *Comment s'appelle-t-il (elle) ce gniard (cette gniarde)?* "What's that guy's/broad's name?"

GNIAULE/GNIÔLE = GNÔLE.

GNIOUF = GNOUF.

GNOGNO(T)TE, *f.* Trifle. *Le travail qu'il te reste, c'est de la gnognotte.* "The work you've still got to do doesn't amount to a hill of beans."

GNÔLE, *f.* Hard liquor. *Son dab fabrique une sacrée gnôle.* "Her dad makes terrific hooch."

GNON, *m.* Punch; dent. *Ma voiture a pris deux gnons dans le parking.* "My car got dented in two places in the parking lot."

GNOUF, *m.* Prison. *Il vient de sortir du gnouf.* "He just got out of the slammer."

GO, *f., W. African, youth, cités.* Girl. *Elle se croit une go qualifiée mais c'est une go périmée.* "That chick thinks she's great in bed but she's past it." *Cf.* IGO.

GO. See TOUT DE GO.

GOBER. 1. To swallow. *Son mec l'embobine et elle gobe tout.* "Her guy's feeding her a line and she falls for it all." **2.** To stand. *Je ne peux plus le gober, ce type.* "I can't stomach that guy anymore."

GOBER LES MOUCHES. To stand by idly (lit. "to gulp down flies"). *Au lieu de gober les mouches, agis donc!* "Instead of just twiddling your thumbs, do s.t!"

GODANT = GODEUR.

GODASSE, *f.* Shoe. *La mer a emmené mes godasses que j'avais laissées sur le sable.* "The sea claimed the shoes I left on the sand."

GODE = GODEMICHÉ; GODET.

GODEMICHÉ, *m.* Codpiece. *Elle a toute une collection de godemichés.* "She has quite a collection of codpieces."

GODER. To be sexually excited; to have an erection (lit. "to bulge"). *Par sa démarche ondulante elle fait goder tous les mecs.* "Her sexy walk gets all the guys horny."

GODET, *m.* Glass. **Avoir le godet.** To be lucky. *Dans sa vie il a eu le godet.* "He's been lucky in life."

GODEUR, -EUSE. Horny. *Elle n'est pas du tout guindée, plutôt godeuse.* "She's not at all stuffy; she's randy."

GODILLER = GODER.

GODILLEUR, -EUSE, *m., f.* Highly sexed person. *Les partouzards cherchaient des godilleurs.* "Those into group sex looked for strongly sexed people."

GODILLOT, *m.* Boot. *Je me suis payé une paire de godillots pour la montagne.* "I bought a pair of boots for mountain climbing."

GODILLOT, *adj.* and *m. n.* Party hack; party regular. *Ils ont triomphé grâce aux godillots.* "Thanks to the regulars, they won."

(À) GOGO. Galore. *On servait du champagne à gogo.* "They served champagne in abundance."

GOGO, *m.* Sucker. *C'est qch. pour les gogos.* "That's s.t. for chumps."

GOGOL = GOL.

GOGUENOTS; GOGUES, *m., pl.* Toilet. *Vise la propreté des goguenots.* "See whether the john's clean."

(EN) GOGUETTE. Tipsy. *Les marins en goguette faisaient les guinguettes.* "The drunken sailors toured the waterfront bars."

(SE) GOINFRER. To make a bundle (lit. "to stuff o.s."). *Ce maq se goinfre sur le dos de ses filles.* "That pimp is making a pile by exploiting his girls."

GOL, *adj.* and *m. n.* Fool; foolish. *Je serais vraiment gol de marcher dans les combines de ce gol.* "I'd have to be a real moron to fall for that jerk's schemes."

GOLDO = GAULDO.

GOMME, *f.* Gum. See METTRE LA GOMME.

(À LA) GOMME. Useless. *Qu'est-ce, ce truc à la gomme?* "What is this piece of junk?"

GONCE = GONZE.

GONCESSE = GONZESSE.

GONDOLANT, -E. Hilarious. *Ce film est vraiment gondolant.* "That film's a real scream."

(SE) GONDOLER. To laugh uproariously (lit. "to buckle"). *On s'est gondolé toute la soirée.* "We laughed our heads off all night."

GONE, *m.* Child (popular in Lyon, but used elsewhere too). *Les gones lui ont foutu une raclée.* "The kids beat him up."

GONESSE, *f.* Child. *La gonesse a déjà trop de poupées.* "That brat's already got too many dolls."

GONFLAGA = GONFLÉ.

GONFLANT, -E. Irritating. *Qu'est qu'elle est gonflante!* "God, is she a pain!"

GONFLE, *f.* Lie (lit. "swelling"). *La gonfle c'est son fort.* "He's good at making up tall stories."

GONFLÉ, -E. 1. Brave (lit. "swollen"). *Elle est gonflée de partir seule.* "She's got guts, leaving on her own." **2.** Impudent. *Il est vraiment gonflé de me demander une chose pareille.* "He's got some nerve asking me for s.t. like that."

GONFLÉ, -E À BLOC. See BLOC.

GONFLER. To exasperate (lit. "to inflate"). **Gonfler qn.; les gonfler à qn.** *Qu'est-ce qu'il me les gonfle!* "My God, does he get on my nerves!"

GONFLETTE, *f.* Bodybuilding. *Ce titi s'est mis à la gonflette.* "That little kid has taken to pumping iron."

GONSE = GONZE.

GONSESSE = GONZESSE.

GONZE, *m.* Fellow. *C'est un brave gonze.* "He's a swell guy."

GONZESSE, *f.* Female; wife; girlfriend. *Sa gonzesse est bien balancée.* "His babe's really stacked."

GONZIER = GONZE.

GORGEON, *m.* Glass; drink. *Et si l'on se tapait un gorgeon?* "How about our having a drink?"

(SE) GORGEONNER. To get drunk. *Il aime se gorgeonner au pastis.* "He likes to get soused on pastis."

GORILLE, *m.* Bodyguard. *Le ministre ne sort jamais sans ses gorilles.* "The minister never goes out without his bodyguards."

GOSSE, *m., f.* Child. *Elle est venue avec sa flopée de gosses.* "She came with her pack of kids." See BEAU GOSSE; TIRE-GOSSE.

GOSSEBO, backslang of **beau gosse.**

GOTHA, *m.* Elite (from the registry of royals formerly published in *Gotha*, Ger.). *Son dab appartient au gotha de la pub.* "Her father's an advertising bigwig."

GOUALANTE, *m.* Popular song. *Vas y de ta petite goualante.* "Go ahead and sing your little song now."

GOUALER. To sing (loud). *Edith Piaf et Ethel Merman savaient les goualer.* "Edith Piaf and Ethel Merman knew how to belt them out."

GOUDOU, *f.* Lesbian. *J'ai horreur des mecs; je n'aime que les goudous.* "I can't stand men; I only like lesbos."

GOUGNE = GOUGNOT(T)E.

GOUGNOTTAGE, *m.* Lesbianism. *Elle est mariée, mais très tentée par le gougnottage.* "She's married, but very tempted by Sapphic love."

GOUGNOT(T)E = GOUINE.

GOUGNOT(T)ER. To be a lesbian. *Elle gougnotte depuis de nombreuses années.* "She's been a dyke for many years."

(SE) GOUGNOTTER = SE GOUINER.

GOUGOUNE, *f., Que.* Plastic sandal. *Ces gougounes vont t'esquinter les pieds.* "Those flip-flops'll ruin your feet."

GOUGOUNE, *adj., Que.* = **NIAISEUX.**

GOUINE, *f.* Lesbian. *Les gouines au bar sont superbes.* "The dykes at the bar are beauties."

(SE) GOUINER. To practice lesbianism. *Sa patronne et elle se gouinent.* "She and her female boss are getting it on together."

GOULAFRE. *Bel., NE France.* Gluttonous. *Jean est aussi goulafre que son père.* "John is as gluttonous as his father."

(SE) GOUPILLER. To turn out. *Tout s'est bien goupillé.* "Everything went off without a hitch."

GOUPILLON, *m.* Penis (lit. "holy water sprinkler"). See MOUILLER LE GOUPILLON.

GOUPILLONER = MOUILLER LE GOUPILLON.

GOURBI, *m.* Hovel. *Ils devraient nettoyer leur gourbi.* "They ought to clean up their pad."

GOURDE. Stupid. *Pour prendre une initiative, qu'est-ce qu'elle est gourde!* "When it comes to showing some initiative she's really dim-witted!"

(SE) GOURER. To make a mistake. *Je me suis gouré de date.* "I got the dates mixed up."

GOURMANDISE, *f.* Fellatio (lit. "gluttony"). *La gourmandise, est un des sept péchés capitaux, mais lui faire une gourmandise, c'est mon péché mignon.* "Gluttony is one of the seven deadly sins, but eating him is my delicious little indulgence."

GOUSSE/GOUSSE D'AIL, *f. Elle est gousse et il est gay et c'est un couple heureux.* "She's a dyke and he's gay and they're a happy couple."

(SE) GOUSSER = (SE) GOUINER.

GOUZI-GOUZI, *m.* Tickle-tickle. **Faire des gouzi-gouzis; faire gouzi-gouzi.** To tickle. *Je ne ris pas quand tu me fais gouzi-gouzi car je sais me concentrer.* "I don't laugh when you tickle me because I know how to concentrate."

GRAF, *m., abbr.* of **graffito, -i.** *Ce gone se balade avec sa bombe à graf.* "That guy walks around with his can of graffiti spray."

GRAILLANCE or **GRAILLE,** *f.* Food. *À la graille!* "Come and get it! Soup's on!"

GRAILLER. To eat. *Filons au resto; (il n')y a rien à grailler à la maison.* "Let's go to the restaurant; there's nothing to eat in the house."

GRAIN, *m.* **Avoir un (petit) grain.** To be crazy. *Il n'aurait pas un grain, par hasard?* "Isn't he a bit touched?"

GRAIN DE CAFÉ, *m.* Clitoris (lit. "coffeebean"). *Mâchouiller mon grain de café l'excite.* "Munching on my clit excites him."

GRAINE, *f.* Seed. **Bonne/mauvaise graine.** The right/ wrong stuff. *Lui c'est de la mauvaise graine, sa frangine de la bonne (graine).* "He's a bad egg/bad news, but his sister's got the right stuff." **Graine de…** Potential. *C'est une graine d'artiste.* "She's a budding artist." See CASSER LA GRAINE; (EN) PRENDRE…GRAINE.

GRAINER = GRAILLER.

GRAISSE D'OIE/GRAISSE DE CHEVAUX DE BOIS. Snake oil. *Tout le laïus de ce camelot est à la graisse d'oie.* "That peddler's line is phony."

GRAISSER LA PATTE. To bribe. *On obtient tout de lui en lui graissant la patte.* "If you cross his palm with silver you can get anything you want."

GRAND-DAB(E), *m.* Grandfather. *Grand-dab aime guincher.* "Gramps likes to dance."

GRAND-DABE, *f. Il ne sort pas toujours avec grand-dabe.* "He doesn't always go out with Grandma."

GRANDS-DAB(E)S, *m. pl.* Grandparents. *Mes grands-dabs sont très chouettes.* "My grandparents are super."

GRAND-DUC, *m.* Grand Duke. See TOURNÉE.

GRAND-MÈRE, *f.* Double bass (musical instrument). *Il prenait grand soin de sa grand-mère en la transportant.* "He was very careful of his double bass when traveling." See PELOTEUR DE GRAND-MÈRE.

GRAND-MESSE CATHODIQUE/GRAND-MESSE MÉDIATIQUE or simply **GRAND-MESSE,** *f.* Ritual watching of the 8 P.M. TV news in France; any major prime time media event (media version of "High Mass"). *Lors de sa grand-messe le président a encore jacté d'une guerre possible.* "During his TV appearance the president again talked about a possible war." Note: **Cathodique**, here a pun on **catholique**, refers to a TV cathode-ray tube. Fewer and fewer people go to High Mass (**grand-messe**), or any mass, but many are faithful TV watchers. They practice **la religion cathodique** not **la religion catholique.** The TV screen has been compared to a "sacred altar." See MESSE.

GRANDIVEUX, *m. Bel.* Pretentious person. *Ce grandiveux con me tape sur le système.* "That pretentious jerk gets on my nerves."

GRAPPE, *f.* Male genitalia (lit. "bunch/cluster [grapes, for example"]). See LÂCHER LA GRAPPE.

GRATIN, *m.* The elite. *Elle fréquente le gratin.* "She hangs out with the upper crust."

GRATINÉ, -E. Excessive. *Sa gaffe était bien gratinée.* "He made a whale of a blooper."

GRATTE, *f.* **1.** Guitar (**gratter** = "to scratch"). See JOUER… GRATTE. **2.** Money on the side. *Cet avocat s'est enrichi en faisant des grattes.* "That lawyer got rich by a taking his cut (of transactions)."

GRATTICHE, *f.* Scabies. *Son môme avait la grattiche.* "Her kid had scabies."

GRAT(T)OS, from **gratis.** Free of charge. *Le vin était gratos au resto.* "The wine was free at the restaurant."

(SE) GRATTER LA HURE. To shave (lit. "to scratch one's hairy face." **Hure de sanglier** means "boar's head"). *Je me suis coupé en me grattant la hure.* "I cut m.s. shaving."

GRAT(T)OUILLER. To scratch; itch. *Ses papillons d'amour le gratouillent.* "His crabs make him itchy."

GRATTOUSE = GRATTICHE.

GRAVOS/GRAVOSSE, *adj.* and *m., f.* nouns; *javanais* of **gros/grosse.** *Tu es trop gravos pour entrer dans ce blouson.* "You're too fat to get into that jacket."

GRELOTS, *m., pl.* Testicles (lit. "little bells"). *Elle sait bien me jouer de la flute et faire sonner mes grelots.* "She sure knows how to blow me and ring my chimes."

GRELUCHE, *f.* Woman. *La greluche d'à côté passe la tondeuse.* "The broad next door's mowing the lawn."

GRENOBLE. See CONDUITE DE GRENOBLE.

GRENOUILLAGE, *m.* Wheeling and dealing (business). *C'est un spécialiste du grenouillage.* "He's good at wheeling and dealing."

GRENOUILLE DE BÉNITIER, *f.* Holy Joe (lit. "frog in the holy water font"). *La grenouille de bénitier, devenue panthéiste, est partie vivre près d'un étang aux grenouilles.* "The church lady, turned pantheist, has gone to live by a frog pond."

GRENOUILLES DE BIDET, police. Semen stains. *Après le viol, les flics recherchaient des grenouilles de bidet.* "After the rape, the cops looked for traces of semen."

GRENOUILLEUR, -EUSE. Wheeler and dealer. *Quel fameux grenouilleur!* "What a sleazy operator!"

(SE) GRIFFER (LA TRONCHE). To put on one's makeup (lit. "to scratch [one's face]"). *J'attendais qu'elle ait fini de se griffer.* "I waited for her to finish putting on her war paint."

(SE) GRIFFER LE MACARONI. To masturbate. *Il s'est griffé le macaroni en buvant du chianti.* "He jerked off while drinking chianti."

GRILLER. To grill. **C'est grillé!** "That's all over." **Être grillé.** To be found out. *Le double agent a été grillé.* "The double agent's cover was exposed."

GRILLER UNE CIBICHE/CLOPE/TIGE. To light up a cigarette. *Je grille une clope vite fait avant le boulot.* "I have a quick smoke before work."

GRILLER UN FEU (ROUGE). To go through a (red) traffic light. *Il a une suspension de permis pour avoir grillé un feu.* "His driver's license has been suspended because he went through a red light."

(EN) GRILLER UNE = GRILLER UNE CIBICHE.

GRIMACE, *f.* Grimace. See SOUPE À LA GRIMACE.

GRIMPER. To have sexually (lit. "to climb"). *Il m'a grimpée dans la grange.* "He had me in the barn."

GRIMPER À L'ARBRE/AU COCOTIER. To hit the ceiling. *Ne grimpe pas au cocotier quand j'aborde ce sujet.* "Don't fly off the handle every time I bring up that subject."

GRIMPER AUX ARBRES. legal. To exaggerate. *Le témoin a grimpé aux arbres.* "The witness laid it on thick."

GRINGUE, *m.* **Faire du gringue à qn.** To make advances to s.o. *Il me fait du gringue pour me grimper.* "He comes on to me because he wants to get into my pants."

GRINGUER. To flirt with. *Il m'a gringuée au bal.* "He made a pass at me at the dance."

GRISBI, *m.* Money. *Gary, lourd de grisbi, engageait un orchestre gitan.* "Gary, rolling in dough, hired a gypsy orchestra."

GRISETTE, *historical.* Shop girl of easy virtue. *Elle chante le rôle d'une des grisettes de* La veuve joyeuse. "She's singing the role of one of the grisettes in *The Merry Widow.*"

GROGNASSE, *f. pej.* Unattractive, elderly female; floozy. *Quelle grognasse, la concierge!* "What an old bag/hag, the concierge!"

GROLLE, *f.* Shoe. See TRAÎNER SES GROLLES.

GROLLES, *f., pl.* Fear. **Avoir les grolles.** To be afraid. *On avait les grolles dans la maison hantée.* "We had the willies in the haunted house."

GROS, *m.* Fat cat. *Tu vas avoir à faire à un gros; sois prudent.* "You'll be dealing with a big shot; be careful."

GROS, GROSSE. Excessive (lit. "fat"). *Ta gonfle est un peu grosse.* "Your tall story's a bit much."

GROS BONNET, *m.* Bigwig.

GROS COMME UNE MAISON. As plain as the nose on your face. *C'était gros comme une maison mais tu n'as rien vu.* "It was plain as day but you didn't see anything."

GROS-CUL, *m.* Big truck (lit. "fat ass"). *Impossible de doubler ce gros-cul.* "Impossible to pass that juggernaut."

GROS LARD/GROS PLEIN DE SOUPE, *m.* Fat guy. *Ce gros lard se la coule douce.* "That fatso takes things easy."

GROS ROUGE (QUI TACHE). Cheap, hearty red wine (that makes stains). *Un pique-nique sans gros rouge n'est* *pas un pique-nique.* "A picnic without good old red wine isn't a picnic."

GROSSE DONDON, *f.* Very fat woman. *Il n'aime que les grosses dondons.* "He likes only fat broads."

GROSSE LÉGUME, *f.* Prominent person. *Des grosses légumes assistaient au marriage.* "VIPs attended the wedding." *Cf.* HUILE **2.**

GROSSE MICHE, *f.* Broad-bottomed woman. *J'aimerais la plaquer, cette grosse miche, mais elle s'accroche.* "I'd like to dump that fat-assed broad but she keeps hanging on." See MICHES.

GROSSIUM = GROS, *m.*

(SE) GROUILLER. To hurry up. *Il faut se grouiller avant l'orage.* "We better get cracking before the storm."

GRUE, *f.* Prostitute (lit. "crane"). *Les grues veulent se syndicaliser.* "The whores want to form a union." See PIED DE GRUE.

GUÉDRO, backslang of **drogué.** Drug addict. *C'est un guédro de longue date.* "He's been a junkie for some time."

GUÉLAN, *youth, cités.* To tongue-kiss (backslang of **languer**). *Guélan-moi profond.* "Give me a deep Fr. kiss."

GUENON, *f.* Ugly woman (lit. "female monkey"). *C'est une guenon, mais il l'adore.* "She's ugly, but he adores her." **Avoir la guenon.** Drugs. To have a monkey on one's back. *Quand il a la guenon, il est hystéro un max.* "When he needs a fix, he's wired."

GUÊPE, *f.* Wasp. **Avoir la guêpe = avoir la guenon.** See PAS...GUÊPE.

GUETTE-AU-TROU, *m., f.* Midwife (lit. "watcher at the hole"). *La guette-au-trou a beaucoup de boulot les nuits de pleine lune.* "The midwife is very busy on nights when the moon is full."

GUEULANTE, *f.* Yell. See POUSSER...GUEULANTE.

GUELARD, -E. Flashy. *Quelle couleur gueularde!* "What a loud color!"

185

GUEULE, *f.* **1.** Face. **Faire la gueule; faire/tirer une de ces gueules; faire une gueule longue comme ça.** To sulk; pull a long face. *Il me fait la gueule; je ne sais pas pourquoi.* "He gives me dirty looks; I don't know why." **Avoir de la gueule.** To look great. *Qu'est-ce que tu as de la gueule avec ce chapeau.* "You look terrific in that hat." **2. Ma/ta/sa gueule.** Individual. See POMME **2.** See also: BOURRER LA GUEULE; CASSE GUEULE; (SE) CASSER LA GUEULE; COUP DE GUEULE; CREVER LA GUEULE OUVERTE; (S'EN) METTRE…GUEULE; (EN) PRENDRE… GUEULE; (SE) FENDRE LA GUEULE; FERME…; FERMER…; FINE GUEULE; (SE) PAYER LA GUEULE; (SE) PÉTER LA GUEULE; POUSSER…GUEULE; SALE GUEULE.

(TA) GUEULE! VOS GUEULES! Shut your trap!

GUEULE À CHIER DESSUS. Disgusting face (lit. "face you want to shit on," vulgar equivalent of SALE GUEULE).

GUEULE À COUCHER DEHORS (AVEC UN BILLET DE LOGEMENT DANS SA POCHE) = SÂLE GUEULE.

GUEULE D'AMOUR, *f.* Don Juan; Lothario. *Quelle gueule d'amour cet acteur!* "What a Casanova, that actor!"

GUEULE DE BOIS, *f.* Hangover. *Trop de champagne et c'est la gueule de bois.* "Drink too much champagne and you'll have a hangover."

GUEULE DE CON = SÂLE GUEULE.

GUEULE D'ENTERREMENT, *f.* To look like one is at a funeral. *Il est arrivé avec une gueule d'enterrement car elle avait bousillé sa voiture.* "He arrived looking depressed because she had banged up his car."

GUEULE DE L'EMPLOI, *f.* To look the part. *Ce croque-mort a vraiment la gueule de l'emploi.* "That undertaker really looks the part."

GUEULE D'EMPEIGNE = SÂLE GUEULE.

GUEULE DE RAIE = SÂLE GUEULE.

GUEULE DE TRAVERS = SÂLE GUEULE.

GUEULER. 1. To yell. *Il ne peut s'empêcher de gueuler sur tous et sur tout.* "He can't help sounding off at everything and everybody." **2.** To have a loud, garish color. *Ils ont choisi un mobilier qui gueule.* "They selected gaudy furnishings." *Cf.* GUEULARD.

GUEULER COMME UN SOURD. To yell one's head off. *J'ai beau gueuler comme un sourd; ce môme n'en fait qu'à sa tête.* "Fat lot of good it does for me to yell my head off; that kid just does what he wants."

GUEULER COMME UN VEAU. To weep profusely. *Le gosse gueulait comme un veau après une raclée bien méritée.* "The brat bawled his eyes out after a well-deserved beating."

GUEULETON, *m.* Feast. *Leur gueuleton était super.* "Their big feed was terrific."

GUEULETONNER. To feast. *Ils gueuletonnent chaque samedi soir.* "They like to have a hearty meal every Saturday night."

GUÉZER, *by apheresis from* MERGUEZ **3,** *youth, cités.* To copulate. *Nous l'avons guézée toute la nuit.* "We fucked her all night."

GUGUS = GUS(SE).

GUIBOLLES, *f., pl.* Legs. *J'en ai plein les guibolles après une journée de boulot.* "My legs really feel it after a day at work."

GUICHET. See PETIT GUICHET.

GUIDOUNE, *f., Que.* Flashy tart, prostitute. *Catherine est foldingue des gars mais elle n'est pas une guidoune.* "Catherine is man-crazy, but she's not a whore."

GUIGNE, *f.* Bad luck. **Avoir la guigne.** To have hard luck. *J'ai vraiment la guigne depuis quelque temps.* "I've really been down on my luck for some time."

GUIGNOL, *m.* Eccentric. *C'est un guignol; il ne passera pas aux élections!* "He's a crackpot; he won't be reelected."

GUIGNON = GUIGNE.

GUILI-GUILI = GOUZI-GOUZI.

GUILLEDOU. See COURIR LE GUILLEDOU.

GUIMAUVE, *f.* **1.** Slushy sentiment (lit. "marshmallow"). *Tes poèmes, c'ést de la guimauve.* "Your poems are treacly/ shmaltzy." See BANDER GUIMAUVE. **2.** Guitar. *Je me suis payé une nouvelle guimauve.* "I bought a new guitar."

GUIMBARDE, *f.* Old car. *Comment peux-tu rouler avec cette guimbarde?* "How can you drive that old heap?"

GUINCHE, *f.* **1.** Dance. *On y va pour cette guinche?* "Shall we dance?" **2.** Dance hall. *La guinche est pleine à craquer ce soir.* "The dance hall's bursting at the seams tonight."

GUINCHER. To dance. *Tous veulent guincher avec moi.* "Everybody wants to dance with me."

GUINCHEUR, -EUSE, *m., f.* Dancer. *C'est un bon guincheur de tango.* "He's a good tango dancer."

GUINDAILLER. *Bel.* To celebrate. *Mon fils ne pense qu'à guindailler.* "All my son thinks about is partying."

GUINDE = GUIMBARDE.

GUISE = GUISOT.

GUISOT/GUIZOT. 1. Leg. *Mes guizots lâchent.* "My legs are giving out." **2.** Penis. See FILER LE COUP DE GUIZOT.

GUS(SE), *m.* Guy. *Tu connais ce gus?* "Do you know that dude?"

GWADADA or **GWADA.** Guadeloupian. See MANDININA.

GWAYANA. Guyanese. See MANDININA.

GY! OK! Affirmative! Roger!

H, *m.,* from **hachisch.** Hashish; heroin; narcotics. *Il dit qu'il fume du H pour sa santé.* "He says he smokes hash for his health."

HABILLÉ, *m.* Uniformed policeman. *Les habillés défilaient pour la Saint Patrick.* "The boys in blue paraded on St. Patrick's Day."

HACHÈS/HACHESSE, *pron.* of *abbr.* HS **(hors service).** Exhausted (lit. "out of order"). *J'arrête pour aujourd'hui; je suis hachès.* "I'm calling it a day; I'm knocked out."

HAFNAF = AFANAF.

HALLUCINÉ, -E, *m., f.* Crazy person. *C'est un halluciné, mais fascinant dans ses intervalles lucides.* "He's a crackpot, but fascinating in his lucid intervals."

HAMBOURGEOIS, *m.,* from **en-bourgeois.** Plainclothes policeman (lit. "hamburger"). *Des hambourgeois se sont mêlés à la foule.* "Plainclothes policemen took positions in the crowd."

HANNETON, *m.* Cockchafer; May/June bug. See (PAS) PIQUÉ.

HARD, *m.* Hard-core porn; hard rock. *Il n'aime que le hard mais il bande de moins en moins.* "All he likes is hard-core porn and hard rock but he doesn't get hard much any more."

HARICOT, *m.* **1.** Clitoris (lit. "bean"). *J'ai mis son doigt sur mon haricot.* "I put his finger on my clit." **2.** Foot; toe. See COURIR SUR…; (LA) FIN.

(DES) HARICOTS! Practically nothing! *Je refuse de turbiner pour des haricots.* "I won't work my ass off for peanuts."

(SE) HARNACHER. To dress (lit. "to harness up"). *Juste le temps de m'harnacher et j'arrive.* "I'll get into my gear and be right over."

HARNAIS, *m., pl.* Clothes; fashion accessories (lit. "harnesses"). *Pour le concert je me ferai belle en mettant tous mes harnais.* "I'll get all dolled up for the concert."

HARPION = ARPION.

HARPONNER. To buttonhole (lit. "to harpoon"). *J'évite de me faire harponner par des chronophages.* "I avoid getting buttonholed by time-wasters."

HASCH = H.

HASTIE! *Que., euph. for* **Hostie!**

HAUTE, *f.,* short for **haute societé.** High society. *Notre boniche est obnubilée par les gens de la haute.* "Our maid's obsessed with the upper crust."

HEBDO, *m., abbr.* of **hebdomadaire.** Weekly periodical. *Je suis rédactrice-en-chef d'un hebdo pour clodos.* "I'm editor-in-chief of a weekly news magazine for hobos."

HÉLICO, *m., abbr.* of **hélicoptère.** Helicopter. *Qui a perfectioné l'hélico, Sikorsky ou Seversky?* "Was it Sikorsky or Seversky who perfected the chopper?"

HÉNAURME. Enormous. *Elle fait d'hénaurmes fautes d'orthographe.* "She makes humongous spelling errors."

HÉRISSON, *m.,* police. Problem suspect (lit. "porcupine"). *Le psychiatre a indiqué aux flics comment s'y prendre avec ce hérisson.* "The psychiatrist told the cops how they should handle that hard nut to crack."

HIBISCUS, *m.* Female genitalia. *Elle se caressait l'hibiscus sous le bananier.* "She fondled herself under the banana tree."

HIC, *m.* Snag. *C'est là le hic!* "That's where the trouble is."

HIRONDELLE, *f.* Uninvited guest (lit. "swallow"). *À la teuf il y avait plus d'hirondelles que d'invités.* "There were more gate-crashers than invited guests at the bash."

HISTOIRE DE BELGES, *f.* Joke ridiculing Belgians. *Ce mufle aime raconter des histoires de Belges, telles que: "Pourquoi les Belges vont-ils au WC avec un fusil?" — "Pour chasser les mauvaises odeurs."* "That oaf likes to tell dumbbell-Belgian jokes like: "'Why do Belgians go to the toilet with a rifle?' — 'To chase (hunt) the foul odors.'""

HISTOIRES, *f., pl.* Menstruation. *Quand la dame aux camélias avait ses histoires elle portait un camélia rouge.* "When the lady of the camellias had her period she wore a red camellia."

HIVIAU/HIVIO, *m.* Winter. *On se les caille en hivio chez toi.* "Your house is freezing in winter."

HOLKIF/HOLPÈTE = OLPICHE/OLPIF.

HOMMELETTE, *f.,* (play on **homme** *and* **omelette**). Wimp. *Quelle hommelette tu fais!* "You're a real Caspar Milquetoast."

HORLOGE, *f.* Clock. *L'horloge; la petite horloge.* Heart. *Son horloge battait normalement durant la montée du Mont Blanc.* "His ticker beat normally when climbing Mont Blanc."

HOSTIE! *Que.* "Holy Shit! Fuck it! *Hostie! T'as bousillé mon ordinateur!* "God damn it to hell! You've screwed up my computer!" **Hostie au lard!/Hostie au paparmane!** "Jesus fuckin' Christ!" (Lit. "sacred host made of lard [bacon]/peppermint." According to Catholic dogma only wheat can be transubstantiated into the communion host. "Lard" and "peppermint" [**menthe poivrée** in standard Fr.] are meant to intensify the blasphemy.)

191

Frequently shortened to **ostie!** Sometimes combined with other **sacres** to intensify: **Hostie câlisse de tabernac' de crisse!** See EN CALICE!…HOSTIE!…; OSTENSOIR; SACRE **2.**

HOSTIE, *f., prostitution jargon.* Turd consumed by a coprophiliac client (lit. "consecrated host"). *Certains kiffent la douche dorée, d'autres michetons barjots adorent s'agenouiller pour recevoir l'hostie, pour eux le sacrement de l'excrement, la vraie transsubtantiation.* "Some turn on to golden showers (urination), other crazy johns love to kneel to receive the host, the sacrament of excrement, real transubstantiation for them."

HOSTINATION!/HOSTIQUE! *Que., euph. for* **hostie!**

HOSTO, *m.,* from **hôpital.** Hospital. *Elle est pique-fesse à l'hosto.* "She's a nurse at the hospital."

HÔTEL DE PASSE = MAISON DE PASSE.

HOURI(E), *f.* Girl; broad (orig. "paradise maiden" in the Koran). *Le mollah n'aimait pas qu'on appelle une fille non-céleste "houri".* "The mullah didn't like noncelestial girls being called 'houris'."

HOUST(E)! = OUST(E)!

HS = HACHÈS.

HUBLOTS, *m., pl.* Eyes; eyeglasses (lit. "portholes"). *Sans ses hublots il ne voit que dalle.* "He's as blind as a bat without his glasses."

HUILE, *f.* **1.** Oil. See BAIGNER DANS L'HUILE. **2.** Big shot. *Toutes les huiles assistaient à la première.* "All the VIPs were present at the premiere." *Cf.* GROSSES LÉGUMES.

HUILE DE BRAS/COUDE, *f.* (lit. "elbow grease"). *Ce boulot, je l'ai fait à l'huile de coude.* "I used elbow grease to do that job."

HUIT, *m.* Fr. kiss in which the tongue traces a figure 8, a sign of infinity, like the circle, because there is no break. *"Mimis à 8"* can be used in letters the way "love and kisses" or "xxxx" are used in Eng. *Cf.* QUATRE-VINGT-HUIT.

(S')HUMECTER LE GOSIER/LES AMYGDALES. To have a drink (lit. "to moisten one's gullet/tonsils"). *Pendant le prèche il avait envie de s'humecter le gosier.* "During the sermon he felt like wetting his whistle."

HUPPÉ, -E. Upper crust (lit. "crested [bird]"). *Il respirait mal dans ce milieu huppé.* "He felt ill at ease in those upper-class surroundings."

HURE, *f.* Head; hairy face. See (SE) GRATTER.

HURLUBERLU, -E, *adj.* and *m., f. n.* Oddball; kook. *Il est un peu hurluberlu et je n'écoute que la moitié de ce qu'il raconte.* "He's a bit scatterbrained and I only listen to half of what he says."

HYPER/HYPRA. Very. *Elle est hypra calée en maths.* "She's super-smart in math."

HYSTÉRIQUE, *f.* Nymphomaniac. *Son fiancé ne savait pas qu'elle était une hystérique.* "Her fiancé didn't know she was a nympho."

HYSTÉRO, *abbr.* of **hystérique.** Hysterical. *Tous ça l'a rendu hystéro.* "All that made him hysterical."

HYSTÉRO, *m., f.* Bundle of nerves. *C'est un hystéro de premiére.* "He's a nervous wreck."

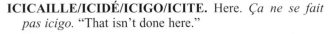

ICICAILLE/ICIDÉ/ICIGO/ICITE. Here. *Ça ne se fait pas icigo.* "That isn't done here."

IDEM. Ditto. *Il sera baisé et toi idem.* "He'll be screwed and so will you."

IDEM AU CRESSON. All the same. *Avec ou sans, c'est idem au cresson.* "With or without, it doesn't matter."

IÈCHE, backslang of **chier.** To be extremely bored. *Qu'est-ce qu'on s'est fait ièche ce week-end!* "God what a shitty, boring weekend!"

IGO, *m., W. African, youth, cités.* Guy. *Des igos, elle en a à gogo, cette go.* "That chick's got guys galore." *Cf.* GO; KHO.

ILLICO (PRESTO). Right away. *L'hélico va décoller illico.* "The chopper's taking off right away."

IMBITABLE. Incomprehensible. *Son laïus m'était imbitable.* "His spiel was all Greek to me." *Cf.* BITER.

IMBLAIRABLE. Unbearable. *Il est imblairable quand il est soûl.* "He's impossible when he's drunk." *Cf.* BLAIRER.

IMBUVABLE. Insufferable (lit. "undrinkable"). *Ne l'invite plus; il est imbuvable.* "Don't invite him again; he's too much to take."

IMPAIR, *m.,* criminal. Sell-out (lit. "uneven number"; "social indiscretion"). *"Tu sais ce qui t'attend après ton* *impair," lui dit le parrain.* " 'You know what's in store for you after your little song to the cops,' said the godfather.''

IMPASSE, *f.* Dead end. **Faire l'impasse/une impasse sur qch.,** school. To skip over part of the syllabus when studying for an exam. *J'ai fait une impasse sur Victor Hugo; hélas, je l'ai payée!* "I didn't bother to review Victor Hugo, and boy did I regret it!"

IMPAYABLE. Hilarious (lit. "unpayable"). *Tonton est impayable quand il mime Charlot.* "Uncle's a scream when he imitates Charlie Chaplin."

IMPEC, *abbr.* of **impeccable.** Marvelous. *On descend au Ritz! C'est impec!* "We'll stay at the Ritz! That's terrific!"

IMPEC! Exactly right! You said it!

IMPER, *m., abbr.* of **imperméable.** Raincoat. *Je préfère mon pébroc à mon imper.* "I'd rather take my umbrella instead of my raincoat."

IMPER À POPAUL/POPOL. Condom (lit. "Popaul's [dick's] raincoat"). *N'oublie pas las impers à Popaul.* "Don't forget the rubbers." *Cf.* K-WAY.

INCENDIAIRE, *f.* Car-based prostitute who specializes in fellatio (lit. "arsonist"). *Il cherchait une incendiaire ardente pour lui faire un pompier.* "He was looking for an ardent head-job specialist to put out his phallic fire."

INCENDIER. To reprimand (lit. "to set fire to"). *Le prof a incendié l'élève inco.* "The teacher read the riot act to the incorrigible pupil."

INCOLLABLE. Unbeatable (lit. "nonstick"). *Aux jeux de la télé il est incollable sur les questions de musique.* "He can't be caught on music questions in TV game shows."

INCONNU AU BATALLION. S.o. the speaker has never heard of. *C'est un inconnu au batallion qui a renseigné la police.* "A total stranger informed the police."

(S') INCRUSTER. To wear out one's welcome (lit. "to become imbedded"). *Je ne m'incruste jamais car, comme dit Franklin, "les poissons et les invités puent au bout de* *trois jours.''* "I never overstay my welcome, because 'fish and guests begin to stink after three days,' as Franklin said."

INCRUSTEUR, -EUSE, *m., f.* Gate-crasher. *C'est un incrusteur de première.* "He's an accomplished gate-crasher."

INDÉCROTTABLE. Incorrigible (lit. "s.o/s.t. you can't get the crud off"). *(Ne) perds plus de temps avec lui; il est indécrottable.* "Don't waste any more time on him; he's hopeless."

INDIC, *m., abbr.* of **indicateur.** Police informer. *C'est connu de tous qu'il est un indic.* "Everybody knows he's a fink."

INFECT, -E. Revolting. *Ton copain est infect.* "Your buddy's a scuzzball."

INFECTADOS, *m.* Cheap cigar. *On ne voit jamais ce vieux schnoque sans son infectados.* "That old fogey's never without his stogie."

INFECTION, *f.* S.t. revolting. *Quand les égouts refoulent, c'est une infection.* "It's disgusting when the sewers overflow."

INFICHU, -E. Incompetent. *Elle est infichue de s'occuper du ménage.* "She can't keep up with running the house."

INFO, *f., abbr.* of **information.** Tip. *Le turfiste m'a filé une info pourrie.* "The racetrack tout gave me a bum steer."

INFOS, *f., pl.* News. *J'écoute les infos sur plusieurs canaux.* "I listen to the news on several stations."

INSTALLER/EN INSTALLER. To show off. *Cesse d'installer; tu nous fatigues.* "Quit hamming it up; you bore us."

INSTIT, *m., f., abbr.* of **instituteur,-trice.** Elementary school teacher. *Mon fils aime bien sa nouvelle instit.* "My son likes his new elementary school teacher."

INSTRUMENT, *m.* Penis. *La plupart des mecs ne savent pas bien jouer de leur instrument.* "Most guys don't know how to use their equipment right."

INTELLO, from **intellectuel.** High-brow. *La pièce était trop intello pour nous.* "The play was too cerebral for us."

INTELLO, *m., f.* Intellectual. *Mao et Fidel exigeaient que les intellos soient aussi des manuels.* "Mao and Fidel required eggheads to be manual laborers too."

INTERDIT, -E DE SÉJOUR. Banned from. *Ce soulard est interdit de séjour dans cette boîte.* "This place is off-limits to that drunk."

INTERPELLER. To stir (lit. "call out to"). **Ça m'interpelle!** "That really gets to me." **Ça m'interpelle quelque part!,** ironic. *Ta kyrielle de plaintes, ça m'interpelle qq. part.* "Your endless litany of complaints has touched my heart!"

INTOX(E), *f.,* from **intoxication.** Disinformation. *L'intox sévit dans les médias.* "The media are loaded with propaganda."

INTOXIQUO = TOXICO.

IROQUOIS, *m., f.* Individual (punk, for instance) with a Mohawk haircut. *Une bande d'iroquois avait terrifié ma grand-tante.* "My great-aunt was terrified by a gang of Mohawk-headed punks."

IROQUOISE, *f.* Mohawk haircut. *Pépé veut se coiffer à l'iroquoise.* "Grandpa wants to get a Mohawk."

ISOLOIR, *f.* Urinal (lit. "voting booth"). *L'isoloir était une infection.* "The urinal was filthy."

ITALBOCHE/ITALGO/ITALO, *m., pej.,* dated. Italian. *Allons à ce nouveau resto italo.* "Let's go to that new guinea/dago restaurant."

ITOU. Also. **Et moi itou!** And me too!

IVOIRE, *m.* Ivory. **Écraser/taquiner l'ivoire.** To play the piano. *Si tu taquinais un peu l'ivoire, on pourrait danser.* "If you tickled the ivories a bit, we could dance."

IVRE-DÉZINGUÉ, -E. Dead drunk. *Ils étaient tous ivre-dézingués.* "They were all smashed out of their minds."

197

JACQUES. Fool. **Battre/faire le Jacques.** To act the clown. *Paul se plaît à faire le Jacques.* "Paul enjoys playing the fool."

JACQUOT/JACQUES, *m.* **1.** Jimmy (orig. staff carried by pilgrims to St. James of Compostella). **2.** Safe-deposit box. *Le jacquot du casseur a forcé tous les jacquots de la banque.* "The burglar's crowbar jimmied every safe-deposit box in the bank." **3.** Penis; dildo. *Mon garagiste est bien monté, mais je préfère mon jacquot.* "My car mechanic's well hung, but I prefer my vibrator." **4.** Parrot. *As-tu déjeuné Jacquot?* "Polly want a cracker?"

JACTANCE, *f.* Smooth fast talk (lit. "haughtiness"). **Avoir de la jactance,** *idiom.* To have the gift of gab. *Il bégayait mais maintenant il a de la jactance.* "He used to stutter but now he's got the gift of gab."

JACTER. To talk. See ARGOMUCHE. **Jacter sur.** To bad-mouth. *Pour jacter, tu te poses là, mais évite de jacter sur les autres.* "You're a master gabber, but try not to bad-mouth others."

JAFFE, *f.* Food. **À la jaffe!** "Soup's on! Come and get it!"

JAFFER. To eat. *Tu ne penses qu'à jaffer.* "All you think about is eating."

JAFFLE = JAFFE.

JAJA, *m.* Wine. *Il ne peut jaffer sans jaja.* "He can't eat without wine."

JALIANCE = JALMINCE/JALMINCERIE.

JALMINCE. Jealous. *Tu ne serais pas jalmince, par hasard?* "Is it possible you're jealous?"

JALMINCE/JALMINCERIE, *f.* Jealousy. *La jalmincerie de mon mari est insupportable.* "My husband's jealousy is unbearable."

JAMBE, *f.* Leg. **Faire une belle jambe.** To be useless. *Ça nous fera une belle jambe!* "Fat lot of good that'll do us!" **Faire qch. par-dessous la jambe.** To do sloppy work. *Ce bricolo ne fait son boulot que par-dessous la jambe.* "That cowboy always does a bum job." See also LEVER LA JAMBE; PARTIE DE JAMBES; ROND DE JAMBE; TENIR LA JAMBE; TIRER…JAMBES; TRAITER…LA JAMBE.

JAMBE DU MILIEU, *f.* Penis. *Il marche avec une canne, mais sa jambe du milieu est toujours vaillante.* "He walks with a cane but his middle leg's still sturdy."

JAQUETTE, *f.* Male homosexual (lit. "woman's jacket"). **Être/filer/refiler de la jaquette (flottante).** To be one of them. *Elle sait que son fils est de la jaquette.* "She knows her son's gay."

JAR, *m.,* from **jargon.** Criminals' slang. *Les gangsters avaient un jar à eux.* "The gangsters had their own brand of slang." See DÉBALLER LE JAR.

JARDIN DES ALLONGÉS, *m.* Cemetery. *La plupart de mes vieux amis sont déjà au jardin des allongés.* "Most of my old friends are already in the boneyard."

JARNAC. See COUP DE JARNAC.

JARRETELLE, *f.,* police. Tapped telephone conversation (lit. "garter"). *Le tribunal a refusé d'écouter les jarretelles.* "The court refused to listen to the bugged phone conversations."

JASPIN/JASPINAGE, *m.* Gossip. *Tout cela n'est qu'du jaspinage.* "All that's just idle chatter."

JASPINER. To talk. *Il jaspine un anglais-lavabo.* "He speaks broken English." See ARGOMUCHE.

JASPINEUR, *m.* Lawyer. *Son jaspineur l'a vendue.* "Her mouthpiece sold her out."

JAVA, *f.* Wild party. *On va faire une java de toutes les javas.* "We're going to have a blast to end all blasts." See PARTIR EN JAVA; FILER UNE…JAVA.

JAVANAIS, *m.* Slang words created by inserting **-av-, -va-,** and **-ag-.** Examples: **chagatte = chatte; javardavin = jardin; javeudavi = jeudi; pavute = pute.** Lit. **Javanese,** also influenced by **j'avais.** Note: The computer language Java is unrelated.

JAVARDAVIN, *m.,* javanais of **jardin**. *Cultive ton javardavin.* "Cultivate your garden!"

JAVELLISÉ, *m.* Squeaky clean homosexual (lit. "chlorine bleached"). *Il ne couche qu'avec son javellisé, qui n'oublie jamais le préso.* "He only sleeps with his Mr. Clean, who never forgets rubbers."

JAVEUDAVI, *m.* javanais of **jeudi**. *Le javeudavi, je suis d'humeur joviale, j'honore Jupiter en ne travaillant pas.* "Thursdays I'm jolly; I honor Jove and don't work."

JEAN-FESSE, *m.* Useless person. *Espèce de Jean-Fesse, tu ne fous rien!* "You lazybones, you do nothing!"

JEAN-FOUTRE, *m.* Worthless individual. *Je l'ai traité de grand Jean-Foutre.* "I told him he was a no-good bum."

JEAN-NU-TÊTE. Penis (lit. "baldy-bean Johnny"). *J'ai pris mon jean-nu-tête dans la fermeture éclair.* "My dick got caught in the zipper."

(LE) JEAN ROSSET, *m., Swiss.* Sun. *Même si le soleil n'est pas au rendez-vous les Vaudois aiment saluer le Jean Rosset.* "Even if the sun isn't shining the people of the Vaud (canton) like to salute the sun."

JE-M'EN-FICHISME = JE-M'EN-FOUTISME.

JE-M'EN-FICHISTE = JE-M'EN-FOUTISTE.

JE-M'EN-FOUTISME, *m.* Indifference. *Le client n'est plus roi; c'est le je-m'en-foutisme qui règne.* "The customer is no longer king; what do I care?/what's it to me? is the prevailing attitude."

JÈSE, *m.* Jesuit. *Il a étudié chez les jèses.* "He studied with the Jesuits."

JÉSOME! *Que. euph.* for Jésus!

JÉSUS, *m.* **1.** Teen-age homosexual. *Il est mort à Venise en contemplant son Jésus.* "He died in Venice contemplating his teenage darling." **2.** Erect penis. *Elle s'agenouillait devant son Jésus adoré.* "She knelt in adoration before his erect cock." See CRÈCHE. *Cf.* CHAPEAU **2.**

JÉSUS DE LYON, *m.* Pork salami. *Ce Jésus de Lyon est bien tendre, car Yvette s'en sert comme godemichet.* "This salami's nice and tender because Yvette uses it as a dildo."

JETÉ, -E. Crazy. *Je fais tout pour l'éviter; il est jeté un max.* "I go out of my way to avoid him; he's totally bananas."

JETER. To throw. **En jeter.** To be impressive. *Sa julie et sa moto, elles en jettent!* "His broad and his bike are really hot stuff!" See CRAVATE.

JETER DU JUS/JETER SON JUS. To make a big impression. *Les fringues du trav jettent toujours du jus.* "The drag queen's clothes are always a knockout."

(S'EN) JETER UN/S'EN JETER UN DERRIÈRE LA CRAVATE. To belt down a drink. *Et si on s'en jetait un avant le boulot?* "How about a shot before getting to work?"

JETON, *m.* Hit; punch (lit. "token"). *En réparant la lampe j'ai pris un jeton.* "I got a shock when repairing the lamp." See FAUX JETON; FAUX COMME UN JETON.

JETONS, *m., pl.* Jitters. *J'ai eu les jetons quand je l'ai vue évanouie par terre.* "I got the willies when I saw her passed out on the floor." See FOUTRE LES JETONS.

JEU. Game. **Faire/jouer/sortir le grand jeu.** To go all out. *On a eu le contrat mais il fallait jouer le grand jeu.* "We got the contract but we had to give it everything we had."

JINJIN, *m.* Brains. *Tu n'as rien dans le jinjin.* "You haven't got a brain in your head."

JINJIN = JAJA.

JOBARD, -E. 1. Gullible (from the biblical Job). *Je ne te croyais pas aussi jobard.* "I didn't think you were that naïve." **2.** Crazy. *Il est jobard de t'avoir embrinqué dans une histoire pareille.* "He's nuts, getting you mixed up in s.t. like that."

JOBARD,-E. *m., f.* **1.** Dupe. *Ce combinard sait trouver les jobards.* "That slick operator has no trouble finding suckers." **2.** Crazy person. *Quelle bande de jobards!* "What a bunch of loonies!"

JOISSE = JOICE.

JO, *m., Que.* (Pronounced "djo." Perhaps from Eng. "jugs," sl. for "breasts.") Breast. *Frotte-moi le clito avec ton jo. C'est sensass!* "Rub my clit with your tit. It's sensational!"

JOJO. Attractive; great. *Tu n'es pas jojo dans ta robe et tout ce que tu me racontes n'est pas très jojo non plus.* "You're not very attractive in that dress and everything you're telling me isn't very appealing either."

JOJO, *m.,* from biblical Joseph who resisted Potiphar's wife's advances. **Faire son jojo.** To behave prudishly. *Il est assez lubrique mais aime faire son jojo.* "He's quite lecherous but enjoys playing the Puritan."

JO-LA-BRICOLE. Petty criminal. *Le parrain se riait de ce Jo-la-bricole.* "The godfather laughed at the small-time hood."

JONC, *m.* **1.** Gold (lit. "rush; rattan"). *Le jonc est en baisse.* "(The price of) gold is going down." **2.** Money. **Avoir du jonc.** To be rich. *Il a du jonc et pourrait être moins près de ses sous.* "He's got plenty of money and could be less tightfisted."

JONCAILLE, *f.* Gold jewelry. *Elle ne portait pas du toc, mais de la joncaille.* "She wore gold jewelry, not junk."

JOSEPH. Se faire appeler Joseph. See ARTHUR.

JOUAL, *m.* Strongly accented, provincial Fr. with large admixtures of Eng., and some borrowings from native languages such as Tamarac, Cree, and Mi'kmaq spoken by some, but by no means all, Fr. Canadians. From the pronunciation of **cheval.** *Beaucoup de Français ont du mal à piger le joual.* "Many French people have trouble understanding 'joual'."

JOUAL VERT, *Que.* **Être en joual vert.** To be angry (and likely to use swear words such as those found in the entry SACRE **2**). *Crisse-moi la paix, j'suis en plein joual vert.* "Fer chrissakes quit buggin' me, I'm all worked up." Also exclamation **Joualvert**! "Good Goddammit!"

JOUER (À) LA FILLE DE L'AIR. To beat it; run away. *Incapable de supporter l'internat, il a joué la fille de l'air.* "He couldn't take boarding school and cleared out."

JOUER À TOUCHE-PIPI. 1. To play doctor. *Les gosses jouaient à touche-pipi.* "The kids played doctor." **2.** To engage in heavy petting. *Ils jouaient à touche-pipi dans la bagnole.* "They fooled around in the car."

JOUER DE LA FLÛTE. To fellate (lit. "to play the flute"). *Elle aimait jouer de la flûte en écoutant* La flûte enchantée *et en pensant à Pan, Krichna, et Kokopelli.* "She liked to play the skin flute while listening to *The Magic Flute* and thinking of Pan, Krishna, and Kokopelli." *Cf.* TURLUTER.

JOUER DE LA GRATTE. To play the guitar. *Des étudiants jouaient de la gratte dans le métro.* "Students were playing the guitar in the subway."

JOUER DES COMPAS/FOURCHETTES/FUSEAUX/ GUIBOLLES. To run off; to scram. *Dès qu'il a vu les flics il a joué des fuseaux.* "As soon as he saw the cops he ran off."

JOUER DES FLÛTES/UN AIR DE FLÛTE. To beat it. *Tu ne penses qu'à jouer un air de flûte, mais écoute-moi d'abord.* "All you want to do is hit the road, but listen to me first."

JOUER LA VEUVE DE PROVINCE/D'ALENÇON/DE CARPENTRAS/VIERZON, and so on, *finance.* To get scared and sell securities at a loss. *Pris de panique, il a joué la veuve de Vierzon.* "He got panicky and took a loss."

JOUER LE FILS DE LA REPASSEUSE. To hesitate before engaging a prostitute (lit. "to act the ironer's son." **Repasser** means "to walk past or back and forth; to iron clothes"). *Tu vas cesser de jouer le fils de la repasseuse, oui ou merde?* "You gonna quit jerkin' my strings? Are we gonna get it on or not?" *Cf.* KANGOUROU.

JOUER UN AIR DE CLARINETTE BAVEUSE. To fellate (lit. "to play a tune on the drooling clarinet"). *Après avoir joué un air de clarinette baveuse, elle a senti jouer tout un orchestre en soi.* "After going down on him, she heard a whole orchestra playing in her." *Cf.* JOUER DE LA FLÛTE.

JOUIR. 1. To have great pleasure/an orgasm. *"Il est jeune et beau et me fait jouir,"* a dit Arletty au tribunal. " 'He's young and handsome and makes me come,' said Arletty to the court." **2.** To experience pain, *ironic. Mon mal de dent me fait jouir.* "I've got a toothache that's driving me up the wall."

JOUISSIF, -IVE. Intensely pleasurable. *Jouissives nos amours au bord de l'eau, mais moins juissif la visite chez le toubib.* "Our lovemaking on the beach was ecstasy, but the visit to the doctor was less of a thrill."

JOURDÉ, *m.* Day. *Mes jourdés ne sont plus tristes à cause de toi.* "My days are no longer sad, because of you."

JOURNAILLE, *f.* = **JOURDÉ.**

JOURNALEUX, -EUSE, *m., f., pej.* Hack writer. *La critique de ce journaleux est déplorable.* "That hack's review is disgraceful."

JOURNANCHE, *f.* = **JOURDÉ.**

JOURNE, *m., f.* = **JOURDÉ.**

JOYEUSES, *f., pl.* Testicles. *Mes joyeuses soufrent sur la selle de bicyclette.* "My nuts ache on the bicycle seat."

JULES. Jules/Julius. **Se faire appeler Jules,** see ARTHUR.

JULES, *m.* **1.** Male. *Vous ne pouvez entrer dans cette boîte qu'accompagnée par un jules.* "You can't get into this place unless you're with a guy." **2.** Steady boyfriend; husband. *À ma connaissance, elle vit sans jules, ni amant ni mari.* "So far as I know, she doesn't have a lover or a husband." **3.** Pimp. *Ces filles travaillent pour le même jules.* "Those girls work for the same pimp."

JULIE, *f.* **1.** Female. *Il n'a pas encore trouvé la julie de ses rêves.* "He hasn't yet found the girl of his dreams." **2.** Steady girlfriend/mistress; wife. *Il n'a été fidèle à aucune de ses julies, maîtresses ou épouse.* "He wasn't faithful to any of the women in his life, the mistresses or the Mrs."

JULIE DU BRÉSIL, *f.* Cocaine. *C'est la Julie du Brésil qui a ruiné sa carrière.* "Nose candy ruined her career."

JULOT = JULES 1, 2.

JUMELLES, *f., pl.* Buttocks (lit. "twin sisters"). *Ne pose pas tes jumelles sur ce banc fraîchement peint.* "Don't park your fanny on this freshly painted bench."

JUPÉ, -E. Drunk. *Son mari n'est supportable que jupé.* "Her husband is unbearable except when he's drunk."

JUPETTE, *f.* Drunkenness (lit. "short skirt"). *Elle a pris une jupette au champagne.* "She got drunk on champagne."

JUPON, *m.* Skirt. See COUREUR DE JUPONS.

JUPONNÉ = JUPÉ.

JUS, *m.* **1.** Water; liquid (lit. "juice"). See TIRE-JUS. **2.** Sperm. See LÂCHER LE JUS. **3.** Electricity. **Avoir du jus.** To be strikingly elegant. *Quoiqu'elle porte, elle a du jus.* "Whatever she wears, she's a classy lady." **Couper/ mettre le jus.** To switch off or on. *L'orage a coupé le jus.* "The storm cut the electric current."

JUS DE CHAPEAU/CHAUSSETTE/CHIQUE, *m.* Weak coffee (lit. "hat/sock/tobacco juice"). *Ce jus de chaussette ne m'ennervera pas.* "This dishwater isn't going to make me jumpy."

JUTANT, *m.* Pimple. *Ça lui était jouissif de presser ses jutants.* "He really got off on squeezing his zits."

JUTE, *m.* Sperm. *La bouffeuse de bite se demandait si le jute était calorifique.* "The cocksucker wondered whether cum was calorific."

JUTER. 1. To ejaculate. *J'aime quand il met du temps avant de juter.* "I like it when he takes his time before coming." **2.** To be impressive = JETER; JETER...JUS. **3.** To be lucrative. *Leur commerce jute bien.* "Their business is making fat profits."

JUTEUX, -EUSE. Very profitable (lit. "juicy"). *Sa maison close est juteuse.* "Her brothel's a real money-maker."

KAINF, *youth, cités.* African (modified backslang of **africain**). *Y'avait plus de babtous que de kainfs à la teuf.* "There were more whites than blacks at the party."

KAKARNAK! *Que., euph. for* **tabernak!,** although *kaka (caca)* "poop" isn't a particularly euphonious euph. See OSTENSOIRE; SACRE **2.**

KANAK, (from Polynesian *kanak* "human"). Native inhabitant of New Caledonia. *Il y a des Kanaks qui veulent l'indépendance.* "Some indigenous inhabitants of New Caledonia want independence." See CALDOCHE; CANAQUE.

KANGOUROU, *m.* Potential prostitute's client who doesn't hire her right away (lit. "kangaroo," when the potential client "hops" around before deciding). *Ce kangourou m'a fait perdre beaucoup de temps.* "That john made me lose a lot of time." *Cf.* JOUER…REPASSEUSE.

KANGOUROUS, *m., pl.* Menstruation. **Avoir ses kangourous.** To have one's period. *J'ai des kangourous très réguliers.* "My periods come on regularly."

KARLOUCH, *m., youth, cités.* Black African (from Ar.). *Elle préfère coucher avec des karlouchs.* "She prefers to sleep with blacks."

KARNA, *f.,* backslang of **arnaque.**

KASBA(H), *f.* House; place. *On a été danser dans une de ces kasbahs!* "That was some joint we danced in!"

KAWA, *m.* (Cup of) coffee. *Je prépare le kawa.* "I'll prepare the java."

KEBLA, *adj.* and *n.,* backslang of "black." Black. *Des keblas vendaient leurs marchandises devant la basilique de Montmartre.* "Blacks were selling their wares in front of the Basilica of Montmartre."

KÉBRA, backslang of **braquer.** To stick up. *Ils ont été kébra dans leur voiture.* "They were robbed in their car."

KEN, backslang of **niquer.**

KÉPA, *m.,* backslang of **paquet.** Dose of cocaine. *File-moi un képa.* "Pass me a coke fix."

(DU) KÈS = (DU) QUÈS.

KÉTAINE. *Que.* Kitschy, corny; ridiculous. *Toujours habillée comme la chienne de Jacques tu fais kétaine.* "You always dress badly and you look ridiculous, like something the dogs dragged in." *Cf.* RINGARD.

KEUD! = QUEUDE!

KEUF, *m.,* backslang of **flic.** Policeman. *Les keufs les ont toutes interrogées.* "The cops questioned them all."

KEUM, *m.,* backslang of **mec.** Guy. *Comment ça va, le keum?* "How you doin', fellah?"

KEUPON, *m.,* backslang of **punk.** Punk; punk rocker. *Je ne danse pas avec ces keupons.* "I'm not dancing with those punks."

KEUT, backslang of **ticket.** Ticket. *Prends un keut pour moi.* "Buy a ticket for me."

KEZACO? = QU'ES-ACO?

KHO, *m., youth, cités.* Guy; chum (from Ar. for "brother"). *Wesh kho, viens avec nous.* "Ho bro, come with us." *Cf.* COUILLE; POTO.

KIF, *m.* **1.** Hashish; mixture of tobacco and hashish. *Ce kif est dégueu.* "This junk is revolting." **2.** *m. C'est du kif!* "That's six of one, half dozen of the other."

KIF(F)ER. To get high or off on. *Ta gonze, je la kiffe.* "Your girl turns me on."

KIFKIF/KIF-KIF/KIF. The same. *Que j'aille en bus ou en métro, c'est kif-kif.* "It makes no difference whether I go by bus or subway."

KIF-KIF BOURRICOT/KIF-KIF LE MÊME SAC. Intensifiers of **KIFKIF/KIF-KIF/KIF.**

KIKI, *m.* **1.** Neck; Adam's apple. See SERRER LE KIKI. **2.** Child's penis. *Elle prenait bien soin de retracter le prépuce du kiki de son fils.* "She took care to retract her son's prepuce." **3.** Short-haired, casually dressed homosexual. *Des kikis arrivaient en moto.* "Clean-cut-looking gays arrived on motorbikes."

KISDÉ, *m.,* backslang of **déguisé.** (Plainclothes) police-man. *Fais gaffe, c'est un kisdé.* "Watch out, he's a cop."

KLEB/KLEBS/KLÉBARD = CLEB/CLEBS/CLÉBARD.

KOKÉ, *Fr. Caribbean.* To have sex. *Allons koké sous les palmiers.* "Let's get it on under the palm trees."

KRO, *f.,* abbr. of **Kronenbourg**®, a brand of beer. Can of beer. *Il balançait les kros vides par la vitre de sa bagnole.* "He threw the empty beer bottles out of the car window."

(À) KROUM(E) = À CROUM(E).

KROUMIR, *m.* Old fogey. *C'est un club plein de vieux kroumirs.* "The club members are all old fossils."

KROUTCHOU, *f.* Hard drugs. *Sa kroutchou lui revient cher.* "His drug habit is costly."

KROUTCHOU, *m.,* backslang of **choucroute** (*sauer-kraut*). Theft. *Il est accro et fait kroutchou souvent.* "He's a junkie and often steals."

K-WAY®, *m.* Condom (lit. "windbreaker"). *Le K-way a crevé, si puissant était son zob.* "His penis was so strong, the bag broke."

KYRIELLE, *f.* (From the repeated liturgical chanting of *kyrie eleison* "Lord have mercy.") A string or series of s.t. *Elle est toujours entourée d'une kyrielle de gosses.* "She's always surrounded by a gang of kids."

LÀ. There; here. **Avoir qn. là.** To have had it with s.o. *Je l'ai là.* "I'm fed up with him."

(OH) LÀ! LÀ! (LA! LA!) My oh my (oh my)!; Isn't that s.t.! Just look at that!

LA BARBE! "Damn it, that's enough!"

LABATEM, louchébem* of **tabac.**

LAC, *m.* **1.** Lake. See TOMBER…LAC. **2.** Female genitalia (lit. "lake"). *Mon lac mouille toujours pour lui.* "My snatch always gets wet for him." See DESCENTE…LAC.

LÂCHER. To release. **Les lâcher.** To fork over money. *Mémé ne veut pas les lâcher.* "Granny won't come up with the dough."

LÂCHER DU FIGNE. See FIGNE.

LÂCHER L'AFFAIRE/LE COUDE/LES BASKETS À QN. To leave s.o. in peace (lit. "to release s.o.'s case/elbow/ sneakers"). *Lâche-moi les baskets!* "Get off my case/back, will you!"

LÂCHER LA GRAPPE À QN. To leave s.o. in peace (stronger version of previous entry (lit. "to get off s.o. genitals [male]"). *Veux-tu me lâcher la grappe.* "Will ya quit bustin' my balls!"

LÂCHER LE JUS/LA CRÈME/UNE GICLÉE. To ejaculate (lit. "to release the juice/cream/a spurt"). *Il aime*

*See explanation of **louchébem,** page 220.

limer avant de lâcher la crème. "He likes to take his time before dropping his load."

LÂCHER LE MORCEAU/PAQUET. To confess. (Lit. "to drop the piece/package.") *Il a mis du temps avant de lâcher le morceau.* "It took some time before he spilled the beans; dropped the cookies."

LÂCHER LES COUILLES À QN. = **LÂCHER LA GRAPPE.**

LÂCHER MÉDOR. To fart. See MÉDOR.

LÂCHER SON VENIN. See VENIN.

LÂCHER UN COLIS/UNE CAISSE/LOUF(F)E/ LOU-ISE/PERLE. To fart. *Qui vient de lâcher une louise ici?* "Who's been farting here?"

LÂCHER UN FIL/L'ÉCLUSE. To urinate (lit. "to release a thread; sluice gate"). *Il s'est précipité pour lâcher l'écluse.* "He ran out to take a leak."

LÂCHEUR, -EUSE, *m., f.* Unreliable person. *Quelle bande de lâcheurs; ils nous ont laissé tout le boulot.* "What a bunch of deadbeats; they left us all the work."

LACRYMO, *f.* short for **(bombe/grenade) lacrymogène.** Tear gas (bomb). *Dans la manif, fais gaffe aux lacrymos.* "Be on the lookout for tear gas during the demonstration."

LADÉ. Here; there. *Mets-toi ladé pour la photo.* "Stand over there for the photo."

LAFÉQUÉ/LAFÉQUÈS, *m.,* largonji of **café.** Coffee. *C'est l'heure du laféqué.* "It's time for a cup of coffee."

LA FERME! See FERME-LA!

LAGA/LAGO/LAGUCHE = **LADÉ.**

LAISS'BET'/LAISSE BÉTON, backslang of **laisse tomber!** Let it drop/ride!

LAISSE COURIR/PISSER/TOMBER! Let it go/drop! Forget it!

LAISSE PISSER LE MÉRINOS! Lit. "let the sheep piss." "Wait for the right moment! Bide your time! Let things take their course!"

211

LAIT, *m.* Milk. **Boire du petit lait,** *idiom.* To savor praise of o.s. *Je bois du petit lait quand il admire mes fringues.* "I just love it when he admires my clothes." See SOUPE AU LAIT.

LAIT DE CHAMEAU/PANTHÈRE/TIGRE, *m.* Pastis (lit. "camel/panther/tiger milk". *On a bu de l'ouzo, espèce de lait de tigre grec.* "We drank ouzo, a kind of Greek pastis."

LAÏUS, *m.* Speech (often long-winded). *Tout ça, ce n'est que du laïus!* "That's all a lot of hot air!"

LAÏUSSER. To speechify. *On s'endort quand il laïusse.* "We fall asleep when he drones on."

LAMEDÉ/LAMDÉ, *f.,* largonji of **dame.** Woman; wife. *Il a plaqué sa lamdé.* "He got rid of his wife." See LARGONJI.

LAMFÉ, *f.,* largonji of **femme.** Woman. *Sa lamfé a le popotin opulent.* "His broad's got a really fat ass." See LARGONJI.

LAMPE, *f.* Stomach. See (SE) METTRE QCH., ... LAMPE.

LANCE-FLAMMES, *m.* Cigarette lighter (lit. "flame launcher"). *J'ai paumé mon lance-flammes.* "I've lost my cigarette lighter."

LANCELOT, *m.* Fireman (play on **lancer l'eau** and **Lancelot** [Jack of clubs, as well as the figure from Arthurian legend]). *Les lancelots ont éteint l'incendie avec l'eau du lac.* "The firefighters put out the fire with water from the lake."

LANCE-PARFUM, *m.* Machine gun (lit. "perfume launcher"). *Les gangsters sortaient leurs lances-parfum.* "The gangsters took out their tommy guns."

LANCE-PIERRES, *m.* Catapult. See MANGER AU LANCE-PIERRES.

LANCEQUINE, *f.* **1.** Water; rain. *La lancequine a enfin cessé.* "It's finally stopped raining." **2.** Urine. *Il y a de la lancequine partout dans les chiottes.* "The toilet's covered with piss."

LANCEQUINER. To weep; rain; urinate. *L'argotnaute a traduit Verlaine par: "Il lancequine dans mon palpitant* *comme il lancequine sur le bled."* "The slang scholar translated Verlaine as: 'It's blubbering in my old pump, just as it's pissing rain on the city.' "

LANGOUSE = LANGUE.

LANGOUSTE/LANGOUSTINE, *f.* **1.** Prostitute (lit. "spiny lobster"). *Il cherchait une langoustine pour calmer son chagrin.* "He looked for a working girl to soothe his sorrow." **2.** Mistress. *Il y a eu plusieurs langoustes dans sa vie.* "He had several mistresses in his life."

LANGUE, *f.* Tongue. **Donner sa langue au chat.** To stop trying to guess (lit. "to give one's tongue to the cat." Cf. Eng. "cat got your tongue?"). *Aucune idée! Je donne ma langue au chat.* "No idea. I give up." **Avoir la langue bien pendue; ne pas avoir la/sa langue dans sa poche.** To be a fast or clever talker (lit. "to have a well-hung tongue; not to have one's tongue in one's pocket"). *Les représantants n'ont jamais la langue dans leur poche.* "Salesmen are never at a loss for words." **Avoir la langue qui fourche.** To make a slip of the tongue. *La fourche m'a langué.* "I made a tip of the slung." See SOUPE DE LANGUES; TIRER LA LANGUE.

LANGUE DE BOIS, *f.* Wooly/waffly talk (lit. "wooden tongue"). *Je ne pige rien à sa langue de bois.* "I make nothing out of his gibberish."

LANGUE FOURRÉE, *f.* Wet kiss. *Il m'a fait une langue fourrée, inoubliable!* "He French kissed me; it was unforgettable!" *Cf.* FRENCHER; GUÉLAN; HUIT; ROULER UN PALOT.

LANGUETOUSE = LANGUE.

LANGUE VERTE, *f.* Slang. *Pépé, toujours très vert, se plaît à parler la langue verte.* "Grandpa, still spry, enjoys talking slang."

LANTERNE, *f.* **1.** Lantern. **Éclairer sa lanterne.** To elucidate one's ideas. *Éclaire un peu ta lanterne.* "Try to shed some light on what you're getting at." See VESSIE. **2.** Stomach. See (SE) METTRE QCH.; (SE) TAPER SUR LA LANTERNE.

LANTERNES, *f., pl.* Eyes. *Allume tes lanternes!* "Open your eyes!"

LAPEUSE, *f.* Lap dancer, nude stripper who wiggles lasciviously and bumps and grinds on a client's lap (from Eng. "lap"). *Pas même la lapeuse n'arrivait à le faire bander.* "Not even the lap dancer could get him up."

LAPIN, *m.* Guy (lit. "rabbit"). **Un sacré lapin.** A swell fellow. *C'est un sacré lapin, ton pote.* "He's one hell of a guy, your buddy." See CHAUD LAPIN; COUP DU LAPIN.

LAPINE, *f.* Woman who gives birth to many children. *Marie-Thérèse et d'autres Habsbourgeoises étaient de vraies lapines.* "Maria Theresa and other Hapsburg ladies were real baby manufacturers."

LAPINER. To breed like rabbits. *Elle voulait bien se marier mais ne pas lapiner.* "She did want to get married but she didn't want to produce brat after brat."

LARBIN, -E, *m., f.* Waiter or waitress; servile person. *Il était larbin de métier et le larbin de sa langoustine.* "He worked as a waiter and was his mistress' doormat."

LARBINOS = LARBIN.

LARD, *m.* Pork fat. **Ne pas savoir** OR **se demander si c'est du lard ou du cochon.** Not to know what to make of s.t. *Sa proposition, je ne savais pas si c'était du lard ou du cochon.* "I couldn't make head or tail of his proposal." **Faire son lard; (se) faire du lard.** To put on the pounds. *Je me suis fait du lard pendant les vacances.* "I gained weight during my vacation." See RENTRER…LARD; TÊTE DE LARD. *Cf.* LÉZARDER.

LARDON, *m.* Small child. **(Avoir) un lardon dans le tiroir.** To be pregnant. *Je suis revenue de vacances avec un lardon dans le tiroir.* "I came back pregnant from my vacation."

LARGE, *m.* Open sea. **Être au large.** To be rich. *On est au large; on peut se payer des vacs.* "We're rolling in it; we can afford to go on vacation."

LARGEAU/LARGEO(T)LARGEOS. By far. *J'ai gagné, largeau!* "I won by a wide margin."

LARGONJI, from **jargon.** Slang system, possibly from former Fr. Indochina, in which "l" replaces the first letter; the original first letter is shifted to the final syllable that can end in **-é, -ès, em, ic, iche, oque, -uche.** Example: **café** becomes **laféké** or **laféquès.**

LARGUER. To dump; ditch (lit. "to release"). *Son jules l'a larguée.* "Her boyfriend dumped her."

LARGUER LES AMARRES. To go away (lit. "to cast off"). *On était content de larguer les amarres de ce bled maudit.* "We were glad to get the hell out of that damned town."

LARIGOT. See (À) TIRE-LARIGOT.

LARME/LARMICHETTE, *f.* Small quantity of liquid (lit. "tear"). *Je voudrais une larmichette de cognac.* "I'd like just a wee drop of cognac."

LASCAR, *m.* **1.** Shrewd dude; great guy. *Quel sacré lascar, ton pote.* "Your buddy's one hell of a guy." **2.** No-good bum. *Ce drôle de lascar ne m'inspire pas confiance.* "I don't trust that good-for-nothing."

LATTES, *f., pl.* Walking shoes. *Ma grand-tante ne porte que des lattes.* "My great-aunt wears only walking shoes."

LAUCHEM, largonji of **chaud.**

LAVABO, *m.* Confirmed alcoholic (lit. "washbasin." Lots of liquid goes down both the alcoholic and the sink). *Ce lavabo a bu toute la bouteille.* "That lush drank the whole bottle."

LAVASSE, *f.* Watery, poor tasting coffee, soup, and the like. *Ton potage c'est de la lavasse.* "Your soup's dishwater."

LAVETTE, *f.* **1.** Wimp (lit. "dishrag"). *Quelle vraie lavette tu fais!* "You come across as a real wimp!" *Cf.* CHIFFE MOLLE; FEMELETTE. **2.** Tongue. *Je me suis brûlé la lavette.* "I burned my tongue."

LÈCHE, *f.* Apple-polishing. **Faire de la lèche.** To bootlick. *Il fait de la lèche au prof.* "He brown-noses the teacher."

LÉCHÉ, -E. Well done (lit. "licked." Cf. Eng. "spit and polish"). *Son topo était bien léché.* "Her presentation was first-rate."

LÈCHE-BOTTES, *m., f.* Servile flatterer (lit. "bootlicker"). *C'est un lèche-bottes du PDG.* "He's one of the managing director's ass-kissers."

LÈCHE-COUILLES/LÈCHE-CUL, *m., f.* Ass-kisser (lit. "balls- or ass-licker"). *Cherche qn. d'autre pour faire le lèche-cul.* "Find somebody else to be your ass-kisser."

LÈCHE-POMPES = LÈCHE-BOTTES.

LECTURE, *f.* Reading. **Être en lecture.** (Prostitution.) To be with a client. *Il a dû attendre Mimi qui était en lecture.* "He had to wait for Mimi who was busy with a client."

LÉGER. Easy. **Faire du léger/dans le léger.** To take the line of least resistance. *Aux autres les risques; moi je ne fais que dans le léger.* "I let others take risks; I just go for a sure thing."

LÉGITIME, *f.* Wife. *Sa légitime était jalouse de sa langoustine.* "His wife was jealous of his mistress."

LÉGUME, *f.* See GROSSE LÉGUME.

LÉGUMISER. To lounge or bum around (from **légume** [vegetable]). *J'ai légumisé tout le week-end.* "I loafed all weekend." *Cf. faire du* LARD; LÉZARDER.

LERCHE, largonji of **cher.** Expensive. *Rien n'est jamais trop lerche pour toi.* "Nothing's ever too pricey for you."

LEULEUR/LEUR, from **contrôleur.** Subway conductor. *J'ai voyagé à l'œil aujourd'hui; les leurs sont en grève.* "I rode free today; the conductors are on strike."

LEUR(S) ZIGUE(S). Them/themselves. *Méfie-toi de leurs zigues.* "Watch out for them."

LEVER LA JAMBE. To be a promiscuous woman (lit. "to lift the leg"). *On raconte qu'elle lève facilement la jambe.* "They say she's an easy lay."

LEVER LE COUDE. To drink heavily (lit. "to raise [bend] one's elbow"). *Depuis son divorce il lève le coude.* "He's been hitting the bottle since his divorce."

LEVRETTE, *f.* Greyhound bitch. **En levrette.** Doggy style. *Il aime tirer son coup en levrette.* "He likes to mount her from behind." See PRENDRE...LEVRETTE.

LEZ, *m.* Problem. *L'enregistrement s'est fait sans lez.* "The recording session came off without a hitch."

LÉZARD, *m.* Problem (lit. "lizard"). *(Il n') y a pas de lézard!* No problem!

LÉZARDER. To laze around (often in the sun). *J'aime lézarder sur le sable.* "I like to bask in the sun."

LÉZOUILLE = LEZ.

L.H.O.O.Q. Marcel Duchamp painted a mustachioed Mona Lisa (*La Gioconde*) titled **L.H.O.O.Q.** When said quickly this yields: *Elle a chaud au cul.* "She's got hot pants (lit. "her ass is hot"). See CUL **1.**

LICAILLE = LIQUETTE.

LICHAILLER = LICHER.

LICHER. To tipple. *Assez liché! Au boulot!* "Enough boozing! Get to work!"

LICHETTE, *f.* Tiny bit. *J'en veux bien une lichette.* "I'd like a nibble."

LIEUVE, *m., f.,* largonji of **vieux.** Old person. *"Faites l'amour avec une lieuve; elle te sera si reconaissante,"* conseillait Franklin.* " 'Make love to an old woman; she'll be so grateful to you,' advised Ben Franklin." See LARGONJI.

LIMER. To copulate with slow concentration ("to file"). *J'aurais aimé la limer, mais il fallait faire vite.* "I would have liked a long, lengthy screw, but we had to hurry."

(SE) LIMER. To masturbate. *Les taulards se limaient dans leurs cellules.* "The jailbirds jerked off in their cells."

217

LIMITE DE L'ÉPURE, *f.* Edge of a drawing. **Dépasser/ franchir/sortir des limites de l'épure.** To go beyond the pale or limits of a subject or situation. *Ses blagues grivoises sortaient des limites de l'épure.* "He went too far with his spicy stories."

LIMOGER. To dismiss high officials. *Après le scandale, le président a limogé des généraux et des ministres.* "After the scandal, the president sent generals and ministers to Coventry (put them out to pasture)."

LIMOGES, *m., f.* Provincial person (not necessarily from Limoges, famous for porcelain). *À la disco ce soir, que des Limoges.* "Nothing but squares from the sticks in the disco tonight."

(SE) LINGER. To get dressed up; to buy clothes. *Elle se linge chez les grands couturiers.* "She gets her duds from the great dress designers."

LION, *m.* Lion. **Avoir bouffé/mangé du lion.** To be raring to go. *À son dernier match il avait bouffé du lion.* "He was full of beans at his last match."

LIQUEMOUZE = LIQUETTE.

LIQUETTE, *f.* Shirt. *Je lui ai payé une nouvelle liquette Lacoste.* "I bought him a new Lacoste shirt."

LISBROQUE, *f.* Need to urinate. *Il a été pris soudain d'une lisbroque.* "He suddenly felt a strong urge to pee."

LISBROQUER/LISSEBROQUER, largonji of **pisser.** To urinate. *Il lisbroquait toutes les dix minutes.* "He took a leak every ten minutes."

LISBROQUEUSE, *f.* Men's room. *Cette tapette passe tout son temps à draguer dans les lisbroqueuses.* "That fag spends all his time cruising in men's rooms."

LISPOQUER = LISBROQUER.

LISSÉPEM = LISSEBROQUER.

LOFFE = LOUFOQUE.

(À) LOILPÉ/À LOILPUCHE, largonji of **à poil.**

LOLITA, *f.* Underage prostitute; older prostitute trying to pass h.s. off as a teeny-bopper (influenced by the Nabokov novel). *Il n'aime que les lolitas, les mineures ou les plus âgées.* "All he likes is nymphets, or those pretending to be jailbait."

LOLO, *m.,* children. Milk. *Ça c'est du lolo!* "That's nice stuff!"

LOLOCHES/LOLOS, *m., pl.* Breasts. *Ses lolos dansaient quand elle courait.* "Her tits shimmied and shook when she ran." See SOUTIEN-LOLOCHES.

LONBEM, louchébem of **bon.** *Lonbem, ton frichti!* "Your grub's great!"

LONGUET. Rather long. *Ce film est un peu longuet sur les bords.* "This movie is a bit on the long side."

LOPAILLE/LOPAIL-LEKEM = LOPE.

LOPE, *f., pej.* **1.** Homosexual. *On ne savait pas qu'il était lope.* "We didn't know he was queer." **2.** Coward; informer. *Ce salaud de lope a dénoncé ses copains.* "That rotten coward informed on his buddies."

LOPER. To sodomize. *On t'a lopé en taule?* "Did you get corn-holed in the slammer?"

LOPESSE/LOPETTE = LOPE.

(SE) LOQUER. To dress. *Elle n'est pas belle, mais sait se loquer.* "She's not beautiful but knows how to dress."

LOQUES, *f., pl.* Clothing (lit. "rags"). *Elle crée et vend des loques.* "She's in the rag trade."

LOQUEUR, *m.* Tailor. *Les loqueurs de Saville Row à Londres sont réputés.* "London's Savile Row tailors are well known."

LOUB(S)/LOUBARD, *m.* Young thug. *Une bande de loubards terrorise la cité.* "A gang of hoodlums is terrorizing the housing development."

LOUBARDE = LOUPIOTE.

LOUCHE, *f.* **1.** Ladle. **À la louche.** Approximately. *C'est un bouquin de 300 pages, à la louche.* "The book comprises roughly 300 pages." **2.** Hand. *J'ai refusé de lui serrer la louche.* "I refused to shake his hand." **3.** Head. See (SE) PRENDRE LA LOUCHE.

LOUCHÉBEM/LOUCHERBEM, *m.* Variation of LARGONJI, created by Lyon and Paris butchers. The most common suffix is **-em,** often preceded by **b,** although other consonants are also found. Examples: **labatem = tabac; lonbem = bon; lounèmes = nous; louivème = oui; luctrème = truc.**

LOUCHERBEM, *m.* louchébem of **boucher.** Butcher. *Notre loucherbem est devenu végétarien!* "Our butcher has become a vegetarian!"

LOUF/LOUFTINGUE, largonji of **fou.** Crazy. *Tu es louftingue de te mêler de ça.* "You're nuts to get mixed up in that." See LARGONJI.

LOUFERIE, *f.* Madness. *J'en ai marre de tes louferies.* "I'm fed up with your nuttiness."

LOUF(F)E, *f.* See LÂCHER UN COLIS…LOUF(F)E.

LOUF(F)ER. To fart. *Sa femme avait loufé, mais par galanterie il s'est déclaré coupable.* "His wife cut the cheese, but he gallantly took the blame."

LOUFOQUE = LOUF/LOUFTINGUE.

LOUFOQUERIE = LOUFERIE.

LOUISE. See LÂCHER UN COLIS.

LOUIVÈME, louchébem of **oui.** Yes. *Quand est-ce que tu me diras "Louivème!"?* "When will you say 'Yes!' to me?"

LOULOU, *m.* **1.** Hood. See LOUBARD. **2.** Darling. *Embrasse-moi, mon loulou.* "Kiss me, my sweet."

LOULOUTE, *f.* **1.** Flighty young girl. *C'est une drôle de louloute.* "She's a hard-to-figure, snippety thing." **2.** Darling. *On y va, les louloutes!* "Let's be on our way, my chickadees."

LOUNÈMES, louchébem of **nous.** We; us. *On y va, lounèmes aussi!* "Let's go, us too."

LOUP, *m.* Wolf. **Avoir connu/vu le loup.** To have had sex for the first time with a man (lit. "to have known or seen the wolf." Said of a young girl). *Ça fait longtemps que j'ai connu et apprivoisé le loup.* "It's been some time since I met and mastered the sexual animal, man."

LOUPER. To miss; fail. *Ça n'a pas loupé!* "That's just what I expected!"

LOUPER LE COCHE. To miss an opportunity (lit. "the coach"). *J'ai loupé le coche en tardant à me décider.* "I missed the boat by making up my mind too late."

LOUPIOT, -IOTTE, *m., f.* Child; kid. *Mon loupiot, tâche d'être sage.* "Try to behave y.s., my child."

LOUPIOTE, *f.* Small lamp. *Je te laisse une loupiote allumée.* "I'll leave a small light on for you."

LOURD, -E. 1. Heavy. **La faire lourde.** To drone on. *Tu la fais lourde et tu m'emmerdes.* "You're going on and on and bugging me." **2.** Rich. *Ton tonton est lourd de sous.* "Your uncle's loaded."

LOURDE, *f.* **1.** Door. *Elle est partie en claquant la lourde.* "She slammed the door when she left." **2.** Hard drug. *C'est une lourde dangereuse.* "That's a dangerous hard drug."

LOURDER. 1. To close up. *Les magazes sont déjà lourdés.* "The stores are already closed." **2.** To kick out; get rid of s.o./s.t. *Je me suis fai lourdé de tous les bars du bled.* "I've been thrown out of all the bars in town."

LOURDINGUE. Ham-handed; lame-brained. *Je ne te croyais pas aussi lourdingue.* "I didn't think you were that thick."

LOUSTIC, *m.* Joker (from Ger. **lustig** [jolly]). *C'est un drôle de loustic!* "He's an oddball." **Faire le loustic.** To play the fool. *Quand finiras-tu de faire le loustic?* "When are you going to stop acting like a jerk?"

LOUTE, *f.* **1.** Woman; girl. *Ma nouvelle loute est de Bordeaux.* "My new girlfriend is from Bordeaux." **2.** Darling. *Ma loute, je t'adore!* "My little honey, I adore you!"

LOVÉ, *m.* Money. *Va te lover avec ton lové, tu l'aimes tant.* "Go cuddle up with your money, you love it so much." Note: This **lové** is from Romany for "coin" and is not related to **se lover** (to coil).

LSD, *f.,* letters standing for *"elle suce debout"* (she sucks standing up). Tiny woman. *Il est un géant mais sa nana est une LSD.* "He's a giant but she's practically a dwarf."

LUC, *m.,* inversion of **cul.** *Assez de tes histoires de luc.* "Enough of your smutty stories."

LUCARNE, *f.* **1.** Dormer window; skylight. **Voir de sa lucarne.** To see s.t. from one's own point of view. *Vous voyez ça de votre lucarne.* "You see that from your own perspective." **2.** Posterior. *Ta lucarne va aimer ce lubrifiant à base de fleurs de lotus.* "Your ass is going to like this lotus-blossom lubricant."

LUCIOLE, *f.* Flamboyant homosexual (lit. "firefly"). *Luc, pédoque rentré, cache ses talents et fuit les lucioles.* "Closet queen Luke hides his light under a bushel and flees flaming faggots."

LUCTRÈME, *m.,* louchébem of **truc.**

LUISARD or **LUISANT,** *m.* Sun. *Oui, vénérez le luisant, qu'on l'appelle Apollon, Amida, Amaterasu, Lugh, ou Mazda, mais soyez prudents.* "Yes, worship the sun, whether you call it Apollo, Amida, Amaterasu, Lugh or Mazda, but be prudent." *Cf.* (LE) JEAN ROSSET; MAHOMET; MOULANA.

LUNDI. See SAINT-LUNDI.

LUNE, *f.* Buttocks (lit. "moon"). *L'étudiant s'amusait à montrer sa lune.* "The student got off on mooning (displaying buttocks)." See CON...LUNE; TAPER...LUNE.

LUNÉ, -E. Être bien/mal luné. To be in a good/bad mood. *À cette heure-ci je ne suis jamais bien lunée.* "At this time of day I'm never in a good mood."

LUNES, *f., pl.* Menstruation. **Avoir ses lunes.** To have one's period. *Je l'évite quand elle a ses lunes.* "I stay away from her during her period."

LUSTUCRU? from **l'eusses-tu cru?** (would you have believed that?). "Well what do you know! Isn't that the living end!"

LUSTUCRU, *m.* Chump. *Ce combinard me prenait pour un lustucru.* "That slick operator thought I was a dope."

LUZERNE, *f.* Hashish (lit. "alfalfa"). *Des nuages de luzerne tourbillonaient dans la boîte.* "Clouds of hash swirled in the night club."

MABOUL. Crazy. *Tu es maboul si tu te jettes dans cette eau glacée.* "You're nuts if you dive into that cold water."

MAC = MAQUEREAU.

MACAB = MACCHABÉE.

MACACHE!/MACACHE BONO!/MACACHE BON-BON!/MACACHE ET MIDI SONNÉ. "Nothing doing! No way! No go!"

MACARONI, *m.* **1.** Italian, *pej. Elle ne sort qu'avec des macaronis.* "She only goes out with spaghetti-benders." **2.** Penis. *Le macaroni de mon marin est plein de sauce.* "My sailor's dick has plenty of spunk." See (SE) GRIFFER.

MACC(H)ABÉE/MACC(H)AB, *m.* Corpse. *La marée ammenait sur le sable les maccabées du naufrage.* "The tide deposited the corpses from the shipwreck on the sand."

MACDO, *m., abbr.* of McDonald's. **Se faire un macdo,** *idiom.* To go for a burger. *Le Ritz ce soir ou on se fait un macdo?* "The Ritz tonight, or shall we go for a burger?"

MACHIN, *m.* Whatsit. *Ça sert à quoi, ce machin?* "What's this gizmo good for?"

MACHIN(CHOSE)/MACHINCHOUETTE/MACHIN-TRUC = TARTEMPION.

MAGNE-TOI!/MAGNEZ-VOUS! "Get moving!"

(SE) MAGNER LE CUL/FION/POPOTIN/TRAIN/LA RONDELLE/LES FESSES. To move one's butt; hurry it up. See TRAIN.

MAGOUILLARD = MAGOUILLEUR.

MAGOUILLE, *f.* Wheeling and dealing. *J'ai horreur des magouilles des politicards.* "I'm turned off by the politicians' horse trading."

MAGOUILLEUR, -EUSE. *m., f.* Sharp operator. *Ta copine est une sacrée magouilleuse.* "Your friend's a real wheeler and dealer."

MAHOMET, *m.* Sun (lit. Mohammed. *Cf.* MOULANA). *Je rêve de mahomet et de vacances.* "I'm dreaming of sunshine and vacation time."

MAHOUSSE = MAOUSSE.

MAILLE, *f.* Money. *J'suis en mal de maille.* "I really need some bread."

MAIN, *f.* Hand. **Avoir un poil dans la main.** To be very lazy. *Qu'est-ce qu'on va faire avec ce gosse? Il a un poil dans la main.* "What are we going to do with that kid? He's chronically lazy." See BALADEUR; CLAQUER...MAINS.

MAISON. Excellent; immense. *On m'a promis une récompense maison.* "They promised me a huge reward."

MAISON J'T'ARQUEPINCE = MAISON POULAGA.

MAISON CLOSE/MAISON DE PASSE, *f.* Brothel. *Les hôtels complets, je n'avais le choix qu'entre une maison de passe ou dormir à la belle étoile.* "The hotels were full and my only choice was between a whorehouse and sleeping outside."

MAISON DE TOLÉRANCE, *f., euph.* for **bordel** (not a place where multi-cultural values are respected but one where sex is tolerated). *Je tiens ce lit baldaquin d'une vieille maison de tolérance.* "I got this canopied bed from an old bordello."

MAISON POULAGA/POULMAN/PARAPLUIE, *f.* Police. *La maison poulaga est arrivée tard sur la scène du crime.* "The fuzz arrived late at the scene of the crime."

MAÎTRE-FRUITIER, *m.* Swiss for **maître-fromagier.** Cheese merchant. *Le maître-fruitier veille sur la maturité de ses fromages.* "The cheese merchant monitors the ripeness of his cheeses."

MALABAR, *m.* Well-built man. *Son gosse est devenu un sacré malabar.* "Her kid's become quite a muscle man."

MAL-BAISÉ, -E, *m., f.* Sexually uptight person; difficult individual (lit. "ill-fucked"). *Ça se voit, c'est une mal-baisée.* "It's obvious she's all screwed up (because she's not getting laid)."

MALBAR, *m.* Bouncer. *Aussi malabar qu'il était, le malbar avait la trouille de se mêler à la bagarre.* "As brawny as he was, the bouncer was afraid of getting mixed up in the brawl."

MAL DE CHIEN, *m.* Great difficulty. *J'ai eu un mal de chien à obtenir ces places de théâtre.* "I had a hell of a time getting these theater tickets." See (SE) DONNER.

(IL Y A) MALDONNE. There's a mistake. *(Il) y a maldonne avec ce rencart.* "There's a mix-up concerning the appointment."

(DE) MALHEUR. Damned. *Débranche ce bigo de malheur!* "Disconnect that (god)damned telephone."

MALLE, *f.* Trunk. **Se faire la malle** (lit. "to pack one's trunk"). To pick up and go. *Ralbol de notre appart; on se fait la malle!* "We've had it up to here with our apartment; we're getting out."

MALPT!, *abbr.* of **Merde à la puissance treize!** (Shit to the thirteenth power). "All the luck in the world!" See MERDE **2.**

MAMOURS, *m., pl.* Hugs and kisses. **Faire des mamours.** To spoon. *Après l'école on se faisait des mamours dans la bagnole.* "After school we used to neck in the jalopy."

MANCHE, *f.* Sleeve. **Faire/taper la manche.** To beg. *C'est triste de voir toute cette jeunesse faire la manche dans le métro.* "It's sad to see all those young people begging in the subway."

MANCHE, *m.* Handle (broom). **Avoir le manche.** To have an erection. *Coincé contre une nana dans le métro, il avait le manche.* "Pressed against a girl in the subway, he had a boner."

MANCHE À BALAI, *m.* **1.** Skinny person (lit. "broomstick"). *Ce mannequin n'est qu'un manche à balai.* "That model's just skin and bones." **2.** Penis. *On finit de balayer et ensuite je te montrerai comment je me sers de mon manche à balai à moi.* "We'll finish sweeping up and then I'll show you how I use my rod."

MANCHE À COUILLES, (lit. "handle with balls") = **MANCHE À BALAI 2.**

MANDININA, *invar.* Inhabitant of Martinique. *Les Mandina, les Gwada, et les Gwayana ont tous la nationalité française.* "The people of Martinique, Guadalupe, and Guyana are all Fr. nationals." Note: Standard Fr. is **les Martiniquais, Gaudaloupéens, Guyanais.**

MANDOLINE, *f.* Mandolin. **Jouer de la mandoline.** To masturbate (female). *Elle était aux anges en jouant de la mandoline.* "She was in ecstasy playing with herself."

MANETTE, *f.* Lever. **À fond les manettes!** "At full speed/ throttle!"

MANGER À TOUS LES RÂTELIERS. To play the field to one's advantage (lit. "to eat at every trough"). *Il se démerde pour manger à tous les râteliers.* "He sees to it that he gets his gravy no matter where it comes from."

MANGER AU LANCE-PIERRES. To grab a quick bite to eat. *J'en ai marre de manger au lance-pierres; fais-moi un bon gueuleton.* "I'm sick of eating on the run; make me a big meal."

(SE) MANGER/SE MANGER LES DENTS/LA FACE/ FIGURE. To fall; fall flat. *Il s'est mangé la face en VTT.* "He took a fall on his mountain bike."

MANGEUSE D'HOMMES/DE MECS, *f.* Strongly sexed woman. *C'est une mangeuse d'hommes, laide, mais populaire.* "She's an unattractive but popular nymphomaniac."

227

(SE) MANIER = SE MAGNER.

MANIF, *f., abbr.* of **manifestation.** Demonstration. *Elle participe à toutes les manifs de gauche, et aussi, parfois de droite.* "She takes part in all the left- and some right-wing demonstrations too."

MANITOU, *m.* Big wheel; boss. *J'ai essayé de voir le grand manitou, sans succès.* "I tried, unsuccessfully, to see the big cheese." *Cf.* GROSSE LÉGUME; HUILE; PONTE; PONTIFE.

MANOUCHE, *m.* Gypsy; gypsy language. *Beaucoup de mots d'argot proviennent du manouche.* "Many slang words come from gypsy talk."

MANQUE DE BOL!/MANQUE DE POT! Tough luck!

MANQUER UNE CASE. Not to have all one's marbles. *Il lui manque une case.* "He's not playing with a full deck."

(NE PAS) MANQUER D'AIR. To have some nerve. *Il ne manque pas d'air, le mec, de me faire du rentre-dedans.* "That guy's got some nerve, making advances to me."

MAOUS, -SE. Humongous. *Il s'est payé une maousse de voiture.* "He bought a huge car."

MAQ = MAQUEREAU.

MAQUAGE, *m.* Cohabitation. *Ils vivent en maquage.* "They're shacking up together." Note: The legal term for cohabitation is **concubinage.**

(SE) MAQUER. To cohabit. *Ils ont décidé enfin de se maquer.* "They finally decided to live together."

MAQUEREAU, *m.* Pimp. *Ce réalisateur emploie deux maquereaux.* "That movie director has two pimps working for him."

MAQUERELLE, *f.* **1.** Procuress; brothel madam. *Lola a l'allure d'une maquerelle.* "Lola looks like a madam." **2.** *cités.* Old lady; gossip. See WESHKEN.

MARAVE, *f.* From Romany for "to beat." Fisticuffs. **Chercher marave,** *idiom.* To be out for a fight. *Fais gaffe, c'est un type à chercher marave pour un rien.* "Watch out, that guy is quick to let go with his fists."

228

MARAVER. 1. To beat up. *Ce soulard voulait tous nous maraver.* "That drunk wanted to beat us all up." **2.** To be excessive. *Ça marave dur dans resto.* "They really hit you hard in this restaurant (the bill is steep)."

MARCHAND DE BARBAQUE/BIDOCHE/FLEURS, *m.* Pimp; white slaver (lit. "meat or flower seller"). *Il est repoussant, ce marchand de barbaque.* "That flesh peddler is revolting."

MARCHAND DE MORT SUBITE, *m.* Bad doctor (lit. "dealer in sudden death"). *N'appelle surtout pas ce marchand de mort subite.* "By no means call that quack sawbones."

MARCHANDE D'AIL, *f.* Lesbian. *C'est un couple de marchandes d'ail.* "They're a lesbian couple."

MARCHANDE D'AMOUR, *f.* Prostitute. *C'est une marchande d'amour qui ne vend pas cher son amour!* "She's a hooker who doesn't charge much for her favors."

MARCHANDE DE CHAIR HUMAINE, *f.* Brothel keeper; madam. *La marchande de chair humaine règnait en abbesse sur une collection de belles filles.* "The madam reigned like an abbess over a group of beautiful girls."

MARCHE À L'OMBRE! "You'd better lay low (lit. "walk in the shade")."

MARCHE OU CRÈVE! "Keep on going or croak!" "Do or die!"

MARCHER. 1. To participate (lit. "to walk"). *Je comprends ce que vous voulez, mais je ne marche pas.* "I know what you want, but count me out." **2.** To fall for s.t. *Tu essaies de me faire marcher?* "Are you putting me on?"

MARCHER À CÔTÉ DE SES POMPES. See POMPE.

MARCHER À L'ALCOOL/À LA DYNAMITE/AU CAFÉ/AUX DROGUES. To function by means of alcohol, cocaine, coffee, or drugs. *Il marche au beaujolpif; sa femme marche au café.* "He's never without his Beaujolais; his wife can't live without coffee."

MARCHER À L'OUBLI. To pretend not to know; function by means of repressing. *Il nie ses crimes et marche à l'oubli.* "He denies his crimes and goes about his business in seeming ignorance of them."

MARDE, *f., Que.* variant of **merde.** *Baptême! T'as de nouveau marché dans la marde.* "Shit! You've walked in shit again."

MARGOULETTE, *f.* Face. *Il voulait lui casser la margoulette.* "He wanted to smash his face in." **Se casser la margoulette.** To fall flat on one's face. *Il voulait montrer son astuce, mais il s'est casse la margoulette.* "He wanted to show how smart he was but he fell flat on his face."

MARGOULIN, *m.* Sharp business operator. *Tu n'auras pas d'aubaine chez ces margoulins.* "You won't get any bargains from those sharks."

MARGUERITE, *f.* Condom (lit. "daisy"). *Ça l'émoustillait d'exposer ses marguerites de toutes couleurs et tous parfums.* "It turned him on to display all his rubbers in many colors and scents."

MARI, *m.* Pimp with several girls working for him (lit. "husband"). *Ce mari ne prend pas bien soin de ses femmes.* "That pimp doesn't take good care of his women."

MARIE-COUCHE-TOI-LÀ, *f.* Floozie (lit. "Marie, lie down here"). *Elle a une gueule de Marie-couche-toi-là.* "She looks like an easy piece."

MARIDA. To marry. *Ma fille est à marida.* "My daughter is of marrigeable age."

(SE) MARIDA. To get married. *Elle voulait tout de suite qu'on se marida.* "She wanted us to get married right away."

MARIÉE, *f.* Glass or mug of beer with a big head (lit. "bride" [dressed in white]). *Il buvait mariée sur mariée.* "He drank one foaming mug after another."

MARIE-LOUISE = LOUISE.

MARIE-PISSE-TROIS-GOUTTES. *f.* Very young girl (lit. "Marie-piss-three-drops"). *Il veut une bandeuse, pas* *une Marie-pisse-trois-gouttes.* "He wants a sexpot, not a dry little slip of a girl."

MARIE-POPO(T)TE, *f.* Woman who spends all her time cooking. *Il cherche une Marie-popote comme épouse.* "He's looking for a homebody/good cook to be his wife."

MARIE-SALOPE, *f.* **1.** Slovenly woman. **2.** Bloody Mary (vodka and tomato juice). *Cette Marie-salope se soûle à la Marie-salope.* "That sloppy cow gets drunk on Bloody Marys."

MARIOLE, -OLLE, *m., f.* Clown. *Cesse de faire le mariole!* "Quit fooling around."

MARRANT, -E. Very funny. *Zape; le film n'est pas marrant.* "Change channels; the movie isn't very funny."

MARRE. Enough. **En avoir marre.** To be fed up with. *J'en ai marre de toutes vos disputes.* "I'm sick and tired of your quarrels." *(Il) y en a marre!* "That's enough, damn it!"

MARRER. To laugh. *Tu me fais marrer!* "You crack me up!"

(SE) MARRER. To enjoy o.s. *Qu'est-ce qu'on s'est marré à la teuf!* "What a blast we had at the party!"

MARTEAU. Crazy. *Tu es marteau de sortir ton bateau par cette tempête.* "You're nuts to take your boat out in this storm." *Cf.* MASSE **3.**

MASO, *abbr.* of **masochiste,** *adj.* and *n. Il faut être maso pour t'aimer.* "Loving you means having to be a masochist."

MASSE, *f.* **1.** Mass. *T'as aimé son roman?—Pas des masses.* "Did you like his novel?"—"Not much." **2.** Earth (electrician's jargon). *Il faut que tous ces fils soient mis à la masse.* "All these wires have to be grounded." **3.** Sledgehammer, mace. **Être à la masse.** To be crazy/drunk/spaced out. *T'es complètement à la masse!* "You're off your rocker!" *Cf.* TAPÉ; MARTEAU. The idea is that s.o. has been hit on the head (**tapé sur la tête**) with a **coup de marteau/coup de masse** (hammerblow).

MASTOC. Huge; oversized. *Je n'aime pas cette architecture mastoc.* "I don't like that megalomaniac architecture."

231

(SE) MASTURBER LES MÉNINGES, stronger variant of **se creuser... méninges.** See MÉNINGES.

MATER. 1. To subdue. *Ils ont maté l'incendie.* "They got the fire under control." **2.** To look; watch; peep; spy. *Mate bien si la patrouille passe.* "Keep an eye out if the patrol passes."

MAT'/MATE, *m., abbr.* of **matin.** *Il part au boulot à trois heures du mat'.* "He leaves for work at three in the morning."

MATHEUX, -EUSE, *m., f.* Mathematician; eager math student. *Aucun n'est matheux dans la famille.* "Nobody in the family's any good at math."

MATHS, *m., pl.* Mathematics. *Ma frangine a la bosse des maths.* "My sister has a flair for math."

MATON, *m.* **1.** Prison guard. *Les matons n'ont rien vu.* "The guards didn't see anything." **2.** Father; parents (in pl.). *Un taulard a plus de droits que moi chez les matons.* "A jailbird's got more rights than me with my parents."

MATOU, *m.* Male; lover (lit. "tomcat"). *Ma minette est en mal de matou.* "My pussy really needs a man."

MAUDIT! *Que.* Damn it!; Hell! *Maudit que t'es bebête!* "Hell, you're some dumbbell!" Can also be used to intensify swear words (see SACRE **2** as in **Maudit calvaire!** "God damn it to hell!").

MAX, *abbr.* of **maximum. Un max.** The greatest; mostest. **Assurer un max.** To be stunning. *Dans sa robe fendue elle assure un max.* "She's a knockout in her dress, open at the side."

MEC, *m.* Guy; dude; boyfriend. *Il y avaient de beaux mecs sur la plage, mais elle n'avait d'yeux que pour son mec.* "There were handsome guys on the beach, but she had eyes only for her boyfriend."

MECA, backslang of **came.**

MÉCA, backslang of **camé.**

MEC À MEC/MEC POUR LES MECS, *m.* A man among men but not among women. *Elle a failli épouser* *un mec pour les mecs.* "She almost married a guy who goes for guys."

MEC À PASSIONS, *m.* Male in search of prostitutes for kinky sex. *Les filles redoutaient le Marquis de Sade, un sacré mec à passions.* "Whores feared the Marquis de Sade who was out for kinky sex."

MÉCANIQUES, *f., pl.* Shoulders. See ROULER LES MÉCANIQUES.

MÉCHANT, -E. Powerful (lit. "mean"). *Mary a un méchant service au tennis.* "Mary has a wicked tennis serve."

MÈCHE, *f.* Wick. **Être de mèche.** To be in cahoots/partnership with. *Pour mon anniversaire-surprise ma femme et ma fille étaient de mèche.* "For my surprise birthday party my wife and daughter teamed up."

MÉDOR, *m.* **1.** Familiar dog name, comparable to "Fido." *Bas les pattes, Médor!* "Keep your paws (hands) off that, you dog!" **Lâcher Médor.** To cut a fart. *Le chien l'aurait fait? C'est bien toi qui as encore lâché Médor.* "The dog did it? You're the one who's let loose a fart again." *Cf.* LÂCHER UN COLIS. **2.** Racehorse (dated). *Sa famille est dans la mouise mais il ne se passionne que pour les médors.* "His family's starving but all he's interested in is the ponies."

MEFFE = MEUF.

MÉFU. To smoke. Backslang of **fumer.** *Ici méfu est interdit. Allons dehors.* "There's no smoking here. Let's go outside."

MEG, *variant* of **meg,** *abbr.* of **méga** (huge). **Le Meg des Megs/le grand Meg/Mec.** God. *C'est une mangeuse de mecs qui croit très fort au Meg des Megs!* "She's a nympho who believes strongly in the Big Guy in the Sky."

MÉGALO, *m., f., adj.* and *n., abbr.* of **mégalomane.** Megalomaniac. *Ce sont tous les deux des mégalos de première.* "Both of them are total ego trippers."

MÉGOTER. To skimp. *Il n'a pas mégoté pour marier sa fille.* "He spared no expense for his daughter's wedding."

(LA) MEILLEURE. The best one yet. **Ça, c'est la meilleure!** "That takes the cake! That's unbelievable!"

MEK À MEK = MEC À MEC.

MÉLASSE, *f.* Molasses. **Être dans la mélasse.** To be in the soup. *Depuis qu'il chôme il est dans la mélasse.* "He's been in a pickle ever since he lost his job."

(SE) MÊLER. To interfere. **De quoi je me mêle?** "What business is that of yours?"

MÊLÉ-CASS, *m.* Cassis with brandy (or vermouth). **Voix de mêlé-cass.** Raspy voice (orig. due to alcohol abuse). *Cesse de chanter; ta voix de mêlé-cass me casse les oreilles.* "Stop singing; your screechy voice is busting my ears."

MÉLO, *m., abbr.* of **mélodrame.** Tearjerker. *Tes amours sont de véritables mélos!* "Your love affairs are real soap operas."

MELON, *m.* **1.** Head. *Pour couvrir son melon déplumé il porte un chapeau melon.* "He wears a derby to cover his bald head." **2.** Arab, *pej. Il est raciste et pour lui ils ne sont que des "bougnoules" ou des "melons".* "He's a racist and for him they're just 'gooks' or 'Ay-rabs.' "

MEMBRÉ. Limbed. **Bien/mal membré.** With a large/small penis (lit. "strong- or weak-limbed"). *Mon nouveau mec est foutrement bien membré.* "My new boyfriend is wonderfully well hung."

MÉMÉ, *f.* Granny; Grandma. *Mémé et pépé fêtent leurs noces d'or.* "Grandma and Grandpa are celebrating their golden wedding anniversary."

MÉMÈRE, *f., adj* and *n.* Granny; old lady. *Ce chapeau fait mémère.* "That hat makes you look dowdy."

MÉNAGÈRE, *f.* Prostitute posing as a housewife (lit. "housewife"). *La ménagère racolait au marché.* "The whore, posing as a housewife, solicited at the market."

MENDIGOT, -E. Beggar; vagrant. *Ma grand-tante donne des bonbons aux mendigots.* "My great-aunt gives candies to beggars."

MENER LE PETIT/POPAUL AU CIRQUE. To get one's end in; have sex (lit. "to take the little lad to the circus"). *Ce soir j'espère mener le petit au cirque.* "I'm hoping to get laid tonight."

MENER UNE VIE DE BÂTON DE CHAISE. To live riotously. *Après avoir mené une vie de bâton de chaise, elle est partie en quête d'un gourou dans l'Himalaya.* "After a wild life, she left to look for a guru in the Himalayas."

MÉNINGES, *f., pl.* Brains (lit. "meninges"). **Se creuser/fatiguer/fouler/remuer les méninges.** To rack one's brains. *Je vais me creuser les méninges pour préparer ce topo.* "I'm going to put my thinking cap on to prepare that report." **Faire marcher ses méninges.** To use one's head. *Si tu faisais marcher tes méninges, tu trouverais la réponse.* "With a little mental effort, you'd find the answer." See also stronger MASTURBER.

MERDAILLON, *m.* Nasty kid or individual. *Fout le camp, espèce de petit merdaillon.* "Beat it, you little shit."

MERDE, *f.* Excrement; trash; shit. **C'est de la merde! C'est une merde!** "That's junk/crap!" **C'est la merde! C'est une de ces merdes!** "That's a real/damned mess!" **Être dans la merde.** To be up shit's creek. *Depuis qu'il chôme ils sont dans la merde.* "Since he's been unemployed they've been in a bad way." **Foutre/semer la merde.** To create disorder. *Tu adores semer la merde là où tu passes.* "You love to screw things up wherever you go." **Ne pas se prendre pour de la/pour une (petite) merde.** To have an inflated opinion of o.s. *Le sénateur ne se prend pas pour une petite merde.* "The senator thinks his shit doesn't stink/thinks he's hot shit." See EMMERDER; FOUILLE MERDE; MOT DE CAMBRONNE; PUTAIN DE MERDE.

MERDE!/MERDE ALORS! Goddamnit! Holy shit!

MERDE! Good luck! *Avant d'entrer en scène tous lui ont dit "merde!"* "Before she went out on stage everybody said " 'break a leg!' " *Cf.* MALPT!

(OUI OU) MERDE? Yes or no? *"Je serai ton vice-président? Oui ou merde?," a dit Nixon à Eisenhower.* " 'Am

235

I going to be your vice president? Shit or get off the pot!' said Nixon to Eisenhower."

MERDER. To fail to function; fuck up. *Juste au moment de partir la voiture a merdé.* "The car conked out just as I was going to leave."

MERDEUX, -EUSE, *m., f.* Pretentious kid; nasty individual. *Cette merdeuse se gare toujours devant ma porte de garage.* "That fucking bitch always parks in front of my garage door."

MERDIER, *m.* Terrible mess. *Dans quel merdier je me suis mis?* "What kind of a damned mess have I gotten myself into?" **Foutre le merdier** = **foutre la merde,** see MERDE.

MERDIQUE. Rotten. *Cet hôtel est vraiment merdique.* "This hotel's a real dump."

MERDOUILLE, *f.* Crap; bad scene. *"Quelle merdouille! Cette machine est toujours en panne.* "What a crock of shit! That machine is always going on the blink."

MERDOUILLER/MERDOYER. To screw up. *À mon exam j'ai merdouillé.* "I screwed up on my exam."

MERGUEZ, *f.* **1.** Small, spicy sausage (from Ar.) *Un couscous sans merguez? Mais non!* "A couscous without merguez? No way!" **2.** Finger. *Je suis d'origine maghrébine mais je me sens français jusqu'au bout des merguez.* "I'm of NW African descent, but I consider myself Fr. down to my fingertips." *Cf.* FRANCFORT; OSSELET. **3.** Penis. *Ma chagatte affamée a besoin de se régaler de ta merguez.* "My hungry cunt needs to feast on your penis meat." *Cf.* CHIPOLATA; GUÉZER.

MERLAN, *m.* **1.** Whiting (fish). See REGARDER…MERLAN. **2.** Pimp. *J'aimerais changer de merlan.* "I'd like a new main man."

MERLICH! It's no big deal (from Ar.). *T'as perdu aux cartes, merlich! Demain tu gagneras.* "You lost at cards. No sweat. Tomorrow you'll win."

MES COUILLES! "You're full of it!" "Nuts to you!"

MESSE, *f.* Mass. **La messe est dite.** It's all over (lit. "mass has been said"). *Inutile d'en discuter. La messe est dite.* "No point discussing it. It's over and done with." **Folle à la messe et molle à la fesse.** Pious, passionate woman (a classical male ideal increasingly rare in reality because piety, not passion, has gone out of fashion). **Messe basse.** Low mass (said *sotto voce,* without singing). *Pas de messes basses!* "No whispering/conspiring!" See GRAND-MESSE.

METTRE. To beat (lit. "to put"). *Qu'est-ce que les flics lui ont mis!* "The cops really worked him over!"

METTRE DU BEURRE DANS LES ÉPINARDS. To improve one's lot (lit. "to put butter in the spinach"). *Elle chante dans les églises pour mettre du beurre dans les épinards.* "She sings in churches to pick up a nice bit of extra money."

METTRE EN PERCE. To tap a barrel. **Mettre une fille en perce.** To take a girl's virginity. *Ça n'a pas été, facile mais je l'ai enfin mise en perce.* "It wasn't easy, but I finally popped her cherry."

METTRE LA GOMME. To accelerate; go all out. *Pour en finir j'ai mis toute la gomme.* "To get it done, I gave it the gun."

METTRE LE GRAPPIN SUR. To get one's hooks into. *Sa grand-dabe voulait qu'elle mette le grappin sur le comte.* "Her grandmother wanted her to get her hooks into the count."

METTRE LE JUS. See JUS 2.

METTRE LE PAQUET/LA SAUCE. See PAQUET; SAUCE 1.

METTRE LE POISSON DANS LE BOCAL. To copulate (lit. "to put the fish into the bowl"). *Mon mec n'a que ça dans la tête, mettre le poisson dans le bocal.* "All my boyfriend thinks about is screwing."

METTRE LES ADJAS. See ADJA.

METTRE LES PIEDS DANS LE PLAT. To put one's foot in it. *Pour mettre les pieds dans le plat, tu t'y connais.* "When it comes to making goofs, you're in your element."

(SE) METTRE QCH./S'EN METTRE JUSQUE-LÀ/ S'EN METTRE PLEIN LA GUEULE/LAMPE/ LANTERNE/PANSE. To indulge in gluttony (lit. "to put it away; put it in to the limit; stuff one's face or belly"). *Les vins et les desserts étaient à volonté et on s'en est mis plein la lampe.* "Wines and desserts were unlimited with the meal so we really stuffed our faces."

MEUF, backslang of **femme,** used also for *"girl." Elle est sympa cette meuf!* "She's a nice chick!"

MEUMEU. Outstanding. *Ce qu'il est meumeu, ton blouson.* "What a neat jacket!"

MÉZIG(UE)/MÉZIGO,*pron.* Me; myself; yours truly. *Quant à mézig, je dis non.* "As for me, I say no." *Cf.* TÉZIG(UE); SÉZIG(UE); NO(S)ZIGUE(S); VOZIGUE; LEUR(S) ZIGUE(S).

MÉZIG(UE), *m.,* police slang. Self-important person. *Le lieute Colombo triomphe toujours des mézigues criminels qui le toisent.* "Lt. Colombo always gets the better of the smart-ass criminals who look down on him."

MICHÉ/MICHET/MICHETON, *m.* Prostitute's client. *Pour restreindre la prostitution, les flics agrafent aussi les michés.* "To discourage prostitution, the cops are arresting johns too."

MICHES, *f., pl.* **1.** Buttocks (lit. "loaves; buns"). **Avoir les miches (à zéro/à glagla)/avoir les miches qui font bravo,** *idioms.* To be very afraid. *À la vue des extraterrestres, on avait les miches à glagla.* "When we sighted the aliens from outer space, we were scared shitless." See (SE) CAILLER LES MICHES; GROSSE MICHE. **2.** Breasts. *On reluquait ses petites miches dans son corsage et ses grosses miches dans sa jupe.* "We ogled her titties in her blouse and her ass in her skirt."

MICHTO or **MICHMICH.** From Romany (Gypsy). **1.** Good; interesting; pleasant. *Le prof a jacté du vrai, du bon et du beau—bref, tout ce qui est michto.* "The prof talked about the true, the good, and the beautiful. In short, everything nice." **2.** Beautiful, handsome. *J'suis pas assez michto pour* *toi?—Si, au contraire. Mais je ne couche pas avec mes étudiants.* "You don't find me attractive enough?"—"Yes I do. But I don't sleep with my students."

MIEL!/MIETTE! *Euph. for* **merde!** (Lit. "Honey!/ Crumb!"). Shoot! Sugar!

MIFA, *f., youth, cités.* Family. Backslang of **famille.** *Il viendra avec toute la mifa—reum, reup, reus, reuf—toute la smala.* "He'll come with his whole family—mom, pop, sis, bro—the whole tribe."

MILLEFEUILLE, *m.* **1.** Layered, creamy pastry. *C'est du millefeuille!* "That's a piece of cake." **2.** Female genitalia. *Quel délice, son millefeuille!* "How delicious, her box!"

MIMI. Cutesy. *C'est pas mimi, ça?* "Isn't that precious?"

MIMINE, *f.* Darling. *Viens avec moi, mimine!* "Come with me, sweetheart!"

MIMINES, *f. pl.* Hands. *Mimi avait les mimines froides.* "Mimi's hands were cold."

MINA-MINA, *m.* Successful compromise. *Ce mina-mina sera avantageux pour nous deux.* "That trade-off will be good for both of us."

MINARET, *m.* Penis (lit. "minaret"). See DÉFROMAGER LE MINARET.

MINCE (ALORS)! *euph. for* **merde (alors)!** "Gosh darn!" "Holy cow!"

MINE, *f.* Look. **Avoir bonne mine,** ironic. To look foolish (lit. "to be looking good"). *Si tu loupes cette occasion tu auras bonne mine.* "You'll look like an idiot if you let that opportunity pass you by."

MINE DE RIEN! Unprepossessing; casually; just like that. *Mine de rien, tu as réussi à obtenir ce que tu voulais.* "No one would have thought it, but you succeeded in getting what you want."

MINET, *m.* **1.** Female genitalia (lit. "pussycat"). *Ton minet me fait de l'œil sous ton bikini.* "Your pussy is winking at me from your bikini." **2.** Effeminate fop. *Il est minet mais pas travelo.* "He's a dandy but not a transvestite."

MINETTE, *f.* **1.** Young girl (lit. "pussycat"). *Chaque samedi soir on draguait les minettes.* "Every Saturday night we tried to pick up broads." **2.** Pussy ("cat" and "female genitalia"). **Faire minette.** To perform cunnilingus. *D'abord je lui ai fait minette, ensuite je l'ai prise en levrette.* "First I ate pussy, then I took her doggy style."

MINOU = MINET 1.

MINOUNE, *f., Que.* **1.** Old car. *Pol adore sa minoune.* "Po really loves his old car." **2.** Pussy (both senses: "feline" and "female genitalia"). *Mais il adore davantage ma minoune à moi.* "But he loves my cunt even more."

MINUS, *m.* Insignificant person. *Tu t'intéresses à ce minus?* "You're interested in that nobody?"

MINUTE, PAPILLON! Hold on a minute there! Hold your horses!

MIOCHE, *m., f.* Little kid. *Les mioches ont bousillé le jardin avec leurs ballons.* "The kids have messed up the garden with their balloons."

MIRAUD = MIRO.

MIRETTES, *f., pl.* Eyes. *Il rêvait souvent des mirettes d'Arletty.* "He often dreamed of Arletty's eyes."

MIRO. With poor vision. *T'as rien trouvé? T'es miro?* "You didn't find anything? Do you need glasses?"

MISER. To fuck; sodomize (lit. "to place a bet"). *Le croupier m'a souvent misée, mais je n'ai jamais gagné à la roulette.* "The croupier often screwed me, but I never won at roulette."

MISO, *m. abbr.* of **misogyne.** Misogynist. *Après son quatrième divorce il est devenu miso.* "After his fourth divorce he became a woman hater."

MISTIGRI, *m.* = **MINET 1; MINETTE 2.**

MITA-MITA = MINA-MINA.

MOB, *f., abbr.* of **mobylette** *(nom déposé).* Mobylette®. *J'ai eu ma mob d'occase.* "I bought a used pedal bike."

MOELLE, *f.* Marrow. See OS À MOELLE; TIRE-MOELLE.

MŒURS, *f.* Morals. **Les Mœurs,** short for **la brigade de la police des mœurs.** The Vice Squad. *La "Ligue Pour La Suppression des Vices" voulait que les Mœurs soient plus vigilants.* "The 'League for the Suppression of Vice' wanted the Vice Squad to be more watchful."

(C'ÉTAIT) MOINS UNE! That was a close shave/call!

MOIS, *m.* Month. See TOUS...MOIS.

MOLASSE/MOLASSON, -ONNE. *Adj.* Slow as molasses. *Merde, que tu es molasse!* "Damn it, you're some slowpoke!"

MOLASSON, -ONNE, *m., f.* Lazy or flabby person. *Quelle bande de molassons!* "What a bunch of spineless louts!"

MÔME, *f.* Young girl. *"Jolie Môme" est une belle chanson de Léo Ferré.* " 'Pretty Girl' is a nice song by Leo Ferré."

MÔME, *m., f.* Kid. **Pisser un môme.** To give birth. *Chaque année elle pissait un môme.* "She shit out a brat every year." (Note that Fr. slang is more on the mark, anatomically, than the equivalent Eng. expression.) See TIRE-MÔME.

MONACOS, *m., pl.* Money. *J'étais sans monacos à Monte Carlo.* "I had no bread in Monte Carlo."

MON CUL! "My ass!" "You're full of it!"

MON (PETIT) CHAT/CHOU/LAPIN. My (little) honey/ sweetie/dearie/darling.

(LA) MONDAINE = LES MŒURS.

MONDE, *m.* World. **Il y a du monde!** That packs a punch. That's really s.t. (in standard Fr. "it's crowded"). *Ta nouvelle moto, il y a du monde!* "That's one mountain of power, your new bike!" See FAIRE UN MONDE.

(IL Y A DU) MONDE AU BALCON. See BALCON.

MON DOU!, *Que., euph.* for **Mon Dieu** but probably from **mon doux Seigneur** (my sweet Lord). *Mon Dou, tu vas* *rater le train!* "Good Lord, you're going to miss the train."

MONNAIE, *f.* Coin; currency. **Monnaie courante.** Widespread. *Beaucoup de mots d'argot sont devenus monnaie courante.* "Many slang words are in common use." See COMMENCER...MONNAIE.

MONNAIE DE SINGE. See PAYER EN MONNAIE DE SINGE.

MONORGUE = MÉZIGUE.

(BIEN/MAL) MONTÉ. See MEMBRÉ.

MONTÉ COMME UN ÂNE/BOURRICOT/CHEVAL/TAUREAU. To be hung like a mule/horse/bull. *Il se croit monté comme un taureau; quel con!* "He thinks he's hung like a bull; what a fool!"

MONTÉ COMME UN SERIN. To be hung like a canary; have minimal sexual equipment. *Il était complexé d'être monté comme un serin.* "He was self-conscious about his tiny pecker."

(SE) MONTER LA BOBÈCHE/LE BOBÉCHON/LA TÊTE. To get excited. *Arrête de te monter le bobéchon. Du calme!* "Don't get y.s. all worked up. Cool it!"

MONTGOLFIÈRE, *f.* Prostitute more interested in sex than money; nymphomaniac (lit. "hot air balloon"). *La montgolfière le transporte toujours au septième ciel.* "The nympho always takes him to seventh heaven."

MONTGOLFIÈRES, *f., pl.* **1.** Testicles. *Ses montgolfières sortaient de son slip étroit.* "His balls popped out of his tight briefs." **2.** Breasts. *Ses montgolfières prenaient l'air au dessus de son soutien gorge.* "Her lovely bunch of coconuts were out in the air above her bra."

MORCEAU, *m.* Piece. **Bouffer/cracher/lâcher le morceau.** To confess. *Il a enfin craché le morceau à la mondaine.* "He finally sang to the Vice Squad."

MORDRE. To understand (lit. "to bite"). *Tu mords?* "(Do) you get it?"

MORDU, -E. Taken with s.o./by s.t. *Son mec, elle en est mordue, mais lui il est plus mordu des courses de chevaux.* "She's nuts about her guy but he's more hung up on the ponies/horse racing."

MORFAL(E), *m.* Glutton. *Cessez de manger comme des morfales!* "Stop eating like pigs."

MORFALER/SE MORFALER. To eat gluttonously. *En taule je rêvais de me morfaler.* "I dreamed of pigging out when I was in stir."

MORFALOU = MORFALE.

MORLINGUE, *m.* Wallet. **Constipé du morlingue.** Stingy. *Pas drôle de sortir avec ce constipé du morlingue!* "No fun going out with that tightwad!" *Cf.* CACTUS; OURSIN.

MORPION, *m.* Pubic louse. *Elle ne savait pas qui lui avait collé ses morpions.* "She didn't know who'd given her crabs." *Cf.* PUNAISE.

(À) MORT. Totally; all out (lit. "to death"). *N'oublie pas de chauffer à mort la salle de bains.* "Don't forget to put the heat up high in the bathroom."

MORT. See RAIDE DEF; RAIDE MORT.

MORT AUX VACHES! "Down with the cops/fuzz/pigs! (lit. "death to the cows")."

MORTEL!, *youth.* Fantastic! (lit. "deadly"). *Mortel le week-end!* "The weekend was awesome!"

MORTIBUS. Dead as a doornail. *Plus d'espoir; il est mortibus.* "No hope; he's stone-cold dead."

MORUE, *f.* **1.** Slut (lit. "cod [fish]"). *Une bande de morues arpentait les couloirs de l'hôtel.* "A bunch of hookers made the rounds of the hotel corridors." **2.** Nasty woman. *Vieille morue!* "Old bag/hag/bitch!"

MORVE, *m.* Nasal mucus; snot. See TIRE-MORVE.

MORVEUX, -EUSE, *m., f.* Jerk (lit. "snotty-nosed brat/individual"). *Espèce de petit morveux!* "You dumb little nerd!"

MOSES! or **MOSUS!** *Que.* (From Eng. In Fr. "Moses" is *"Moïse."* Note Eng. "Holy Moses!") Damn it! Shit! *Mosus! Tu te prends pour qui?* "Jesus, who the hell do you think you are?" See SACRE **2.**

MOT DE CAMBRONNE, *m.* The "S" word (*euph.* for **merde,** esp. in the sense "Good luck!") *Avant mon concours ma grand-tante m'a chuchoté, "le mot de Cambronne!"* "Before my exam my great-aunt whispered the S word to me." See CAMBRONNE.

MOT DE CINQ LETTRES = MOT DE CAMBRONNE.

MOTTE, *f.* Vagina; mons veneris (lit. "mound"). *La motte de beurre sur la table, et ta motte à côté de moi au plumard—quelle vie heureuse!* "A block of butter on the table and your box next to me in bed—life is wonderful!"

MOTUS (ET BOUCHE COUSUE)! "Mum's the word!" "Keep it quiet!" "Button your lip." (Note: **Motus** is pseudo Latin for **mot** [word]. **Bouche cousue** is "mouth stitched up.") *Cf.* MUTCHELL!

MOU, *m.* Stomach. See BOURRER...MOU; RENTRER...MOU.

MOU, MOLLE. Flabby. See BANDER MOU.

MOUCHACHA, *f.,* from Sp. **muchacha.** Girl. *Il est mordu de cette mouchacha.* "He's nuts about that chick."

MOUCHACHO, *m.,* from Sp. **muchacho.** Boy. *On a envoyé le mouchacho en colo.* "We sent the kid off to camp."

MOUCHARDER. To inform. *Quel salaud, il nous a tous mouchardés!* "That SOB, he finked on all of us!"

MOUCHE, *f.* Fly. See ENCULER LES MOUCHES.

MOUCHER. To reprimand (lit. "to blow" [nose]"). **Les morveux veulent moucher les autres,** *proverb.* "That's like the pot calling the kettle black."

MOUFLET, -ETTE, *m., f.* Kid. *On ne la voit jamais sans ses mouflets.* "You never see her without her kids."

MOUFTER/MOUF(F)ETER. To protest; grumble. **Sans moufter; ne pas moufter.** Not to bat an eyelid. *Quand* *les flics lui ont demandé ses paps, il n'a pas moufté.* "When the cops asked for his ID, he didn't turn a hair."

MOUILLE, *f.* Mouth. *Donne-moi un baiser sur la mouille.* "Give me a wet one."

MOUILLER. To experience vaginal/clitoral orgasm (lit. "to wet"). *Elle mouille un max avec moi.* "The earth really moves for her when she's with me." **(En) mouiller pour qn.** To be sexually excited by s.o. (of either sex). *Il en mouille pour elle.* "He's got the hots for her."

MOUILLER LA BARBE/LAITUE. To urinate (said of women). Lit. "to wet the beard/lettuce." *La bière me donne envie de mouiller la barbe.* "Beer makes me want to pee."

MOUILLER LE GOUPILLON. To get one's end in (lit. "to moisten the holy water sprinkler"). *Il avait toujours rêvé de mouiller le goupillon avec une bonne sœur.* "He'd always dreamed of dipping his wick into a nun."

MOUILLER SA CHEMISE/LIQUETTE. To work very hard (lit. "to wet one's shirt", as in "to sweat"). *Il n'a pas peur de mouiller sa chemise pour aider sa famille.* "He's not afraid of knuckling down and doing work to help his family."

MOUILLER/MOUILLER SA CULOTTE ET SON FROC. To be afraid (lit. "to wet one's underpants and pants"). *Il mouille pour un rien.* "He pisses in his pants over the slightest little thing."

MOUILLER UNE ARDOISE. To urinate (lit. "to wet a slate"). *Verse-moi encore une chope; je vais mouiller une ardoise.* "Pour me another mug (of beer); I'm going to take a leak."

MOUILLES, *f., pl.* Buttocks. *Elle est molle aux mouilles.* "She's got a tender ass."

MOUILLES = MICHES 1.

(SE) MOUILLER. To take a risk. *Il n'a pas voulu se mouiller par peur des représailles.* "He didn't want to stick his neck out because of possible reprisals."

MOUISE, *f.* Poverty; hard luck. **Être dans la mouise.** To be hard up financially. *Elle a été dans la mouise un an avant de retrouver un boulot.* "She had a year of rough going before she found a job again."

MOUKÈRE, *f., pej.* North African woman; woman; prostitute (from Sp. **mujer**). *Ce maq bat ses moukères.* "That pimp beats his women."

MOULANA, *m.* Scorching sun (from Ar. for "Our Master," a title of Allah [God]. *Cf.* MAHOMET). *On a visité les temples des dieux solaires sous un moulana brûlant.* "We visited the temples of the solar deities under a blazing sun." *Cf.* LUISARD.

MOULE, *f.* **1.** Female genitalia (lit. "mussel"). *Sa moule bien musclée s'accrochait à ma colonne.* "Her well-muscled snatch clutched my column (cock)." Note: Mussels cling to **bouchots** (posts) placed in coastal waters. **2.** Luck. **Avoir de la moule.** To be very lucky. *Elle a eu de la moule à la loterie.* "She hit it big in the lottery." **3.** Fool. *Quelle moule!* "What a dumb jerk!"

MOULE À GAUFRE(S), *m.* Real idiot (lit. "waffle iron"). *Cesse de me prendre pour un moule à gaufres.* "Stop treating me like a lamebrain."

MOULE-BOULES/MOULE-BURNES, *m.* Tight-fitting jeans (lit. "balls' molder"). *Je l'avais trouvé sexy dans son moule-boules, mais quel minus au lit!* "I thought him sexy in his tight jeans but what a loser in bed!"

MOULÉ. Molded. **Bien moulée.** Very shapely. *Sacrément bien moulée, la strip-teaseuse!* "The stripper's got curves in all the right places."

MOULER UN BRONZE. To defecate (lit. "to cast a bronze statue"). See BRONZE.

MOUMOUNE, *f., Que.* **1.** Fearful person. *Sois pas moumoune!* "Don't be chicken!" **2.** Male homosexual. *Quand ma femme est enceinte ou indisposée je vais voir les moumounes.* "When my wife's pregnant or unwilling I go see the fags."

MOUMOUTE, *f.,* Wig; toupee. *Ça se voit que le présentateur de télé porte une moumoute.* "It's obvious the TV announcer is wearing a rug."

MOURON, *m.* Pimpernel (herb of the primrose family whose flowers close at the approach of bad weather). **Se faire du mouron.** To worry o.s. sick. *Ne vous faites pas de mouron; les prisonniers seront libérés.* "Don't be upset; the prisoners will be rescued."

MOUSCAILLE, *m.* Excrement; trouble. *Ils sont dans une mouscaille pas possible.* "They're really in deep doo-doo."

MOUSMÉ, *f.* Girl; woman. *Il a épousé une mousmé japonaise.* "He married a Japanese girl."

MOUSSE, *f.* **1.** Froth. **Se faire de la mousse.** To get all worked up. *Tu te fais de la mousse pour rien.* "You're getting in a lather for nothing." **2.** Beer. *On se tape une bonne mousse?* "Shall we go for a nice beer?"

MOUSSER. To foam. **Se faire mousser.** To praise o.s. *Il ne loupe jamais une occasion de se faire mousser.* "He never misses an opportunity to blow his own horn." **Se faire mousser le créateur.** To jerk off; cream one's jeans (lit. "to get the creator all frothy/lathered up"). *Il ne pouvait plus prier et s'est fait moussé le créateur.* "He couldn't pray anymore and jerked off."

MOUSTACHUE, *f.* Butch homosexual. *Cette tantouze ne veut coucher qu'avec des moustachues.* "That old queen just wants to get it on with he-man gays."

MOUSTAGACHE, *f.* javanais of moustache. *Le kaiser et Clemenceau avait des moustagaches impressionantes.* "The kaiser and Clemenceau had impressive mustaches."

MOUTARD, *m.* Young boy; apprentice. *C'est un moutard sympa.* "He's a nice lad."

MOUTON À CINQ PATTES, *m.* **1.** Rarity (lit. "sheep with five feet"). *Les manuscrits de Descartes, Racine, sont des moutons à cinq pattes, réclamés par mes clients.* "Manuscripts by Descartes and Racine are great rarities sought after by my customers." **2.** Strange bird or duck. *Il se méfie* *de Dolly, qu'il trouve un mouton à cinq pattes.* "He doesn't trust Dolly, whom he takes to be a real weirdo."

MOUTRAVE. To urinate (from Romany). *Moutrave au jardin, ça fait pousser les orties.* "Pissing in the garden makes the nettles grow."

-MUCHE. *Sl. suffix. Not pej.* From an old adj. for "excellent." Paris district **Ménilmontant** became world-famous as **Ménilmuche** in songs by Maurice Chevalier. See ARGOMUCHE; FATMUCHE; TRUCMUCHE.

MULE, *f.* Mule. See TÊTE DE MULE.

MULE AVEUGLE, *m.* Unwitting drug carrier (lit. "blind mule"). *Les stups de l'aéroport ont agrafé la mule aveugle.* "The airport narcs nabbed the unsuspecting mule."

MULTIPRISE, *m.* Female/passive male homosexual, open to all comers (lit. "electrical adaptor"). *Es-tu prêt à t'envoyer la multiprise assise au bar?* "Are you ready to get it on with that slut at the bar?"

MÛR, -E. Drunk (lit. "ripe"). *Après tous ces cocktails elle était bien mûre.* "After all those cocktails she was well pickled."

MURGE, *f.,* Drunkenness. *Ils avaient tous une sacrée murge.* "They were all dead drunk."

(SE) MURGER. To get drunk. *On s'est foutrement murgé hier soir au Quartier Latin.* "We really tied one on last night in the Latin Quarter."

MUSEAU, *m.* Face (lit. "muzzle"). See (SE) SUCER LE MU-SEAU.

MUSICO/MUSICOS, *m.* Musician. *Le musicos se démerdait pour créer de l'ambiance.* "The musician did his best to liven things up."

MUSIQUER. To complain. *Tu vas encore longtemps musiquer?* "Will you be playing your violin much longer?"

MUTCHELL! Silence! From Romany, but probable influence of **muet** and **mutisme.** See MOTUS!

MYTHO, *m., abbr.* of **mythomane. 1.** Pathological liar. *Je n'en crois rien; c'est un mytho de première.* "I don't believe any of it; he's an out-and-out liar." **2.** Lie. *Ton laïus est pétri de mythos.* "Your long-winded speech is full of lies."

MYTHO, *adj.* Lying. *Il est incroyablement mytho.* "You wouldn't believe how full of crap he is."

NANA, *f.* Girl. *Les nanas sont de sortie ce soir.* "The girls are out tonight."

NANAR(D), *m.* Low budget '30s and '40s movies. *Je ne regarde que les nanars.* "All I watch are trashy '30s and '40s movies."

NARPI, backslang of **pinard.**

NARVALO, *m.* from Romany. Zany good-for-nothing. *C'est un narvalo mais rigolo!* "He's a no-good nut, but he's amusing."

NARZO, backslang of **zonard.**

NASE or NAZE, *m., f.* **1.** Yokel; fool. *Tu ressembles à un nase fringué comme ça.* "You look like a rube/jerk dressed like that." **2.** *adj.* Broken down (orig. "syphillitic"). *L'ordinateur est naze.* "The computer's crashed." **3.** Exhausted. *J'suis total nase fait de me battre avec l'electronique.* "I'm all worn out from struggling with technology." **4.** Drunk; crazy. *Pas surprenant que j'suis complètement naze.* "Not surprising, I'm completely out of my head."

NATCHAV!, from Romany. "Let's blow this hole!" *Cf.* TCHAVE.

NAVET, *m.***1.** Turnip. See SANG DE NAVET. **2.** Trashy book or movie. *Et le livre et le film sont des navets.* "Both the book and the movie are trash."

NÉNÉS, *m., pl.* Breasts. *Elle n'a que douze ans mais trouve ses nénés trop petits.* "She's only twelve but thinks her titties are too small."

NÉNETTE, *f.* **1.** Girl. *Quelle sacrée nénette!* "She's one hell of a chick!" **2.** Head. See (SE) CASSER LA NÉNETTE.

NÉNUPHAR, *m.* Female genitalia (lit. "waterlily"). *Courbet, Monet, et tous les grands auraient adoré peindre son nénuphar.* "Courbet, Monet, and all the great ones would have loved to paint her bush."

NET, *abbr.* of Internet. *Est-ce que l'on peut te trouver sur le net?* "Can I find you on the Web?" *Cf.* TOILE **2.**

NEUILLE = NOILLE.

NEUNEU. Foolish. *Ce qu'elle peut être neuneu, ta frangine!* "Your sister is sometimes really birdbrained!"

NEUNŒIL = NŒIL.

NEZ, *m.* Nose. **Avoir qn. dans le nez.** To be hostile to s.o. *Après cette vacherie, je l'aurai à vie dans le nez.* "After that dirty trick I'll hate him forever." See (SE) BOUFFER LE NEZ; (SE) CASSER LE NEZ; COUP...NEZ; DOIGTS...NEZ; PIQUER DU NEZ; SENTIR...NEZ; VERRE.

NIAFFE = GNAF.

NIAISER, *Que.* To play the fool; to play s.o. for a fool. *Arrête de me niaiser.* "Quit putting me on."

NIAISEUX, *Que.* for standard Fr. **niais.** Stupid; foolish. *Quel film niaiseux!* "What an idiotic movie!" *Cf.* NEUNEU.

NIAULE = GNÔLE.

NIBARDS/NIBS = NICHONS.

NICHE, *f.* **1.** Doghouse (lit. "niche"). **À la niche!** "To your doghouse" (to a dog). "Beat it"; "hit the road!" (to a human). **2.** Practical joke; dirty trick. **Faire une niche à qn.** *Il passe son temps à me faire des niches.* "He spends his time playing jokes on me."

NICHONS, *m., pl.* Breasts. *Très jeune, elle avait déjà d'énormes nichons.* "She already had big knockers when she was very young."

NIÔLE = GNÔLE.

NIOUZES, *f., pl.,* phonetic Fr. rendering of "news". News (TV and Internet). *Mémé ne loupe jamais l'heure des niouzes.* "Granny never misses the news on TV."

(SE) NIPPER. To dress. *Elle n'a jamais su se nipper.* "She never knew how to dress."

NIQUER. 1. To copulate. **Va te faire niquer!** "Fuck off!" **Nique ta mère.** "Go fuck your mother. **2.** *youth,* To destroy. *Les casseurs lui ont niqué sa bagnole.* "The hoodlums smashed up his car."

NITOUCHE, from **n'y touche (pas).** See SAINTE NITOUCHE.

NŒIL, *m.* Eye. *Le froid me fait pleurer les nœils.* "The cold makes my eyes tear."

NŒUD, 1. Knot. **Un sac ou paquet de nœuds.** A tangle of problems. *Laissons tomber ce sac de nœuds.* "Let's not get into that can of worms." **2.** Penis; glans. *Mors-moi le nœud!* (Lit. "Bite my dick's head.") "Kiss my ass!/Suck the knotty end of my fuckstick!" See POMPER...NŒUD; TÊTE DE NŒUD.

NOICH, *youth, cités.* Chinese; Asiatic (backslang of **chinois**). *J'habite le quartier noich.* "I live in Chinatown."

NOILLE/NOÏE, *f.* Night. *Le comte ne sort que la noille.* "The count only goes out at night."

(AU) NOIR. See AU BLACK/NOIR/SCHWARZ.

NOISETTE, *f.* Testicle (lit. "hazelnut") See CASSE-NOISETTES.

NOIX, *f.* Jerk (lit. "walnut"). *Quelle vielle noix!* "What an old fool!"

(À LA) NOIX/À LA NOIX DE COCO. Crummy (lit. "coconut"). *C'est un roman à la noix.* "That's a trashy novel."

NOM DE DIEU DE BORDEL DE MERDE! "Goddamn' fuckin' shit almighty!"

NOM DE NOM! For God's sake!

NOM D'UN CHIEN/NOM D'UNE PIPE! "For heaven's sake!" "Ye Gods!"

NO(S)ZIGUE(S). Us. *C'est pas pour noszigues, ça.* "That's not for us."

NOUBA, *f.* Party. **Faire la nouba.** To party. *Ils ont fait la nouba trois jours durant.* "They partied for three days straight."

NOUILLE, *f.* Idiot (lit. "noodle"). **Quelle nouille!** "What a jackass!"

NOUILLE DE MER, *f.* Condom floating on water (lit. "sea noodle"). *La marée descendante déposait les nouilles de mer sur le sable mouillé.* "The ebbing tide left the aquatic rubbers on the wet sand."

NOUNE, *f.* Female genitalia. *Dès le matin de mon adolescence ma noune s'ouvrait à la lumière de l'amour.* "In early adolescence my pussy opened to the light of love."

NOUNOUNE, *f., Que.* Foolish girl. *Line n'est pas du tout nounoune.* "Line is certainly no silly goose."

NOYE = NOILLE.

NUL À CHIER/NULACHE. Really rotten. *Ces rappeurs sont nulaches!* "Those rappers are shitty!"

NUL DE CHEZ NUL. Rock-bottom rotten; totally worthless. *Tu me traites comme ça, c'est nul de chez nul!* "You treat me like that? That's the pits."

NUMÉROTER. To number. See ABATTIS.

NUNU/NUNUCHE. Gullible; goofy (from **ingénu**). *J'annule l'abonnement de cette revue trop nunuche.* "That review is too idiotic and I'm canceling my subscription."

NUTS = backslang of thunes.

-O. Frequently found slang suffix, as in **alcoolo** = **alcoolique; apéro** = **apéritif; intello** = **intellectuel; préso** = **préservatif; proxo** = **proxénète; réglo** = **réglementaire.**

OBÉIR AU DOIGT ET À L'ŒIL. To be absolutely obedient. *J'insupporte qu'on ne m'obéisse pas au doigt et à l'œil.* "I won't put up with not being obeyed to the letter."

OBLIGADO/OBLIGEMAN. Required. **Faire qch. obligado.** To be pressured into doing s.t. *J'ai sorti la poubelle obligado.* "I was strong-armed into taking out the garbage."

OCCASE, *f.* **1.** Opportunity (from **occasion**). *Faut pas louper cette occase!* "Mustn't miss that opportunity." **2.** Occasional prostitute. *Ça change d'aller au radada avec une occase.* "Getting it on with an occasional hooker makes for a change."

(D')OCCASE, from **d'occasion.** Secondhand. *Je l'ai eu d'occase.* "I got it secondhand."

OCCUPE-TOI DE TES FESSES!/T'OCCUPE! "Mind your own damned business! Keep your own nose clean."

-OCHE. Suffix that can make a word humorous, casual, or pej. Examples: **cinoche** = **cinéma; fastoche** = **facile; téloche** = **télévision.**

OD, *f., pron.* as in Fr. **(odé),** from Eng. "to OD." **Faire une OD.** To die of a drug overdose. *Vas-y mollo, sinon tu feras une OD!* "Go easy or you'll OD!"

ŒIL, *m.* Eye. **Avoir qch. à l'œil.** To get s.t. free. *On a eu nos places à l'œil.* "Our tickets were complimentary." **Avoir qn. à l'œil.** To keep an eye on s.o. *L'État omniprésent vous a à l'œil.* "Big Brother is watching you." See (SE) FOURRER; OBÉIR; (SE) RINCER; TAPE-À-L'ŒIL; TAPER DANS L'ŒIL.

ŒIL AU BEURRE NOIR, *m.* Black eye. *À part un œil au beurre noir, il s'en est bien sorti.* "Apart from a black eye, he came through pretty well."

ŒUF, *m.* Egg. **Aller se faire cuire un œuf.** To go fly a kite. *Si tu crois que je marche dans ta combine, va te faire cuire un œuf!* "If you think I'm part of your scam, you can go jump in the lake!" See CASSER SON ŒUF; FACE.

ŒUFS SUR LE PLAT. Tiny titties (lit. "(two) fried (sunny-side up) eggs"). *Avec ses œufs sur le plat elle n'a aucune chance de devenir la Reine des Vendanges.* "Flat-chested as she is, she has no chance of becoming Harvest Queen."

OIGNON, *m.* **1.** Luck. **Avoir de l'oignon; avoir l'oignon qui décalotte.** *À la roulette de Monte Carlo nous avons eu de l'oignon!* "We were lucky at roulette in Monte Carlo." **2.** Anus. **Défoncer l'oignon** or **foutre/taper dans l'oignon.** To sodomize. *Il le lui a foutu dans l'oignon.* "He gave it to him up the ass." **Passer/taper sous l'oignon.** To penetrate vaginally from behind. *Elle préfère que je lui passe sous l'oignon pour une meilleure pénétration.* "She likes me to go in from behind for better penetration."

OIGNONS, *m., pl.* Onions. **Mes/tes/ses/nos/vos/leurs oignons.** My (and so on) own business. *Laisse tomber; ce sont ses oignons et pas les tiens!* "Let it drop; it's her business, not yours."

(À) OILP/OILPÉ, backslash of **à poil.** See POIL.

OINJ, backslash of **joint.**

OISEAU, *m.* Bird. **Être aux oiseaux,** *Que.* To be very happy. *Bien sûr il est toujours aux oiseaux avec sa cervelle d'oiseau.* "Of course he's always blissful because he's birdbrained." *Cf. être aux* ANGES.

OLKIF = OLPICHE/OLPIF.

OLPÈTE/OLPETTE = OLPICHE/OLPIF.

OLPICHE/OLPIF. Excellent. *Tout à la teuf était olpiche.* "Everything was peachy at the party."

OR, *m.* Gold. **C'est de l'or en barre.** "That's rock solid; as good as gold!" See ROULER SUR L'OR.

(EN) OR, *m.* **En or.** Wonderful. *J'ai un dab en or!* "My father's just wonderful."

ORCHESTRE, *m.* Orchestra. **Femme/homme orchestre.** Person of many talents. *Line fait la femme-orchestre au bal du samedi soir.* "Line's the one woman band at the Saturday night dance." *Mon mari est un vrai homme-orchestre.* "My husband wears many hats."

OREILLE, *f.* Ear. See SORTIR PAR…OREILLE.

OREILLES EN FEUILLES DE CHOU. See FEUILLES… CHOU.

ORPHELINES, *f., pl.* Testicles (lit. "orphans"). *Les eunuques de la cité interdite ont récuperé leurs orphelines.* "The eunuchs of the forbidden city got their balls back."

ORTEILS = DOIGTS DE PIEDS.

OS, *m.* Bone. **Jusqu'à l'os.** Thoroughly; utterly. *Son maq l'a possédée jusqu'à l'os.* "Her pimp owned her totally." See TOMBER…OS.

-OS. Suffix much used by youth from the 1960s to the 1980s. Now more generally used. Examples: **braquos = braquemard; cassetos = cassette; musicos = musicien; rapidos = rapide; zygos = zygomatique.**

OS À MOELLE, *m.* **1.** Nose (lit. "marrow bone"). *Quelle renommée, l'os à moelle de Jimmy Durante et celui de Cyrano.* "How famous were Jimmy Durante's and Cyrano's schnozzes!" **2.** Penis. *Son os à moelle fait du bon bouillon en moi.* "His cock makes good stock (spermal soup) in me."

OSEILLE, *m.* Money (lit. "sorrel"). *As-tu vu* Prends l'oseille et tire-toi *de Woody Allen?* "Have you seen Woody Allen's *Take the Money and Run?*"

OSSELETS, *m., pl.* Fingers (lit. "little [ear] bones; knuckle-bones [game]"). *"On va lui couper les osselets, un par un," menaçaient les ravisseurs.* "'We're going to cut his fingers off, one by one,' threatened the kidnappers."

OSTENSOIRE! *Que.* God damn it! Shit! (From **ostensoire,** "monstrance" [a vessel for showing the consecrated host].) *Ostensoire! Cesse de sacrer de manière si ostentatoire. Les sacres se disent à bon escient, en famille, entre amis.* "Damn it! Quit cussing so ostentatiously. Quebec cuss words are to be used with discretion, with family and friends." *Cf.* CÂLISSE!; CIBOIRE!; (H)OSTIE!; SACRAMENT!; SACRE **2.**

OSTI!/OSTIE!, *Que.* = **HOSTIE!**

OSTINATION! *Que.* = **HOSTINATION!**

OUAH! "Wow! Ooh!"

OUAIS. "Yup; yeah."

OUALLOU! "No way! Nothing doing!"

OUA-OUA, *m., pl.,* children. Toilet. *Jusqu'à dix ans elle refusait d'aller aux oua-oua toute seule.* "Till she was ten, she wouldn't go to the toilet alone."

OUATÈRES = **WATERS.**

OUBLI, *m.* Forgetting; omission. See MARCHER À L'OUBLI.

OUF, *m., backslang of* **fou.** Lunatic. *Ton pote, c'est un ouf!* "Your buddy's a nut."

OUILLE! "Ouch!"

-OUILLE. Ending on slang words, often *pej.* Examples: **magouille; merdouille; papouille; petzouille.**

OUIOUINE, *f.* Sanitary napkin. *Je n'utilise plus les ouiouines.* "I don't use sanitary napkins anymore."

OUI OU MERDE? See (OUI OU) MERDE?

OÙ JE PENSE! The place I'm thinking of; where the sun don't shine. *Votre critique, vous pouvez vous la foutre, où je pense!* "You can stuff your review you know where!"

OURS, *m., pl.* Bears. **Avoir ses ours.** To have one's menstrual period. *J'avais mes ours et une méchante migraine.* "I was having my period and a nasty headache."

OURSIN, *m.* Sea urchin. **Avoir des oursins dans la fouille/poche/le morlingue.** To be stingy (lit. "to have spiny sea urchins in one's pocket/wallet"). *Mes vioques ont des oursins dans la fouille.* "My parents are really tightfisted."

-OUNE. Sl. suffix popular in Que. See COUCOUNE; DOUDOUNE **3**; FOUFOUNE **2**; GUIDOUNE; GOUGOUNE; MINOUNE; MOUMOUNE; NOUNOUNE; PITOUNE; TOUTOUNE.

-OUSE/OUZE. Sl. suffix, sometimes *pej.* Examples: **partouse = party; picouse/piquouse = piqûre; pinouze = pinard; planquouse = planque; sidouze = SIDA; tantouze = tante.**

OUST(E)!/ALLEZ OUST(E)! "Get going! Get a move on!"

OUTIL, *m.* Tool. See REMBALLER SES OUTILS.

OUTILLÉ. Equipped with tools. **Être bien outillé.** To have a large tool (penis). *Ce bas-duc est bien outillé.* "That runt's well hung."

OUVRIR LES GRANDES EAUX DE VERSAILLES. To start crying. *Je cède dès qu'elle ouvre les grandes eaux de Versailles.* "Once she turns on the tears, I give in." Note: The palace of Versailles was famous for its waterworks and fireworks.

OVERDOSE = OD.

PACHAVE, *youth, invar.* To sleep (from Romany). *Faut que je pachave.* "Got to get some z's."

PACSIF/PACSON. Package. **Gagner/toucher le pacson.** To make a bundle. *Mémé a touché le pacson.* "Granny struck it rich."

PAF. Drunk. *Le cocktail m'a rendue complètement paf.* "The cocktail totally plastered me."

PAF, *m.* Penis. *Il était trop paf pour trouver son paf pour pisser.* "He was too pissed to find his dick and take a piss." See BEAU...PAF; SAUTE-AU-PAF.

PAIN. 1. Bread. **Avoir du pain sur la planche** (lit. "to have bread on the board"). To have a lot of work. *Avec le déménagement, j'ai du pain sur la planche.* "What with moving, I've got a lot on my plate." **2.** Whack. *Sa joue a gonflé après le pain qu'elle lui a fiché.* "His check swelled up after the smack she gave him." **3.** Wrong note. *Malgré tous les pains, ses accros étaient ravis.* "Despite all the wrong notes, her fans were delighted."

PAIX, *f.* Peace. **La paix!** "Shut up, that's enough now!" **Ficher/foutre la paix à qn.** To leave s.o. in peace. *Fiche-moi la paix!* "Quit bugging me!"

PALPER. To make a bundle (lit. "to feel"). *L'avocat a dû palper au passage.* "The lawyer probably lined his pockets along the way (in the course of a transaction)."

PALPITANT, *m.* Heart. *Son palpitant a lâché.* "His ticker gave out."

PALOT/PALOT BAVEUX, *m.* French kiss. See ROULER UN PALLOT.

PALUCHE, *f.* Hand. *Liszt avait des paluches impressionantes.* "Liszt had impressive hands."

(SE) PALUCHER. To masturbate. *Après avoir joué du Rachmaninoff, il s'est paluché.* "After playing Rachmaninoff, he saw Dr. Jerkoff."

PANAIS, *m.* Penis (lit. "parsnip"). **Dégraisser/dérouiller/planter/tremper son panais.** To have sexually; dip one's wick. *Il ne laisse jamais passer l'occasion de tremper son panais.* "He never misses an opportunity to get his."

PANAM(E), dated. Paris. *Elle était venue à Paname pour gagner des ronds.* "She had come to Paris to make money."

PANARD, *m.* Foot. *Elle lui écrasait toujours les panards en dansant.* "She always stepped on his feet when dancing." See PRENDRE SON PANARD.

PANET = PANAIS.

PANIER, *m.* Basket. **Mettre dans le même panier.** To lump together. *Elle est lui sont à mettre dans le même panier.* "The two of them are of the same ilk." **Mettre la main au panier.** To pinch or grope s.o.'s behind. *S'il essaie de me mettre la main au panier il aura un pain.* "If he tries to goose me, I'll slap him." See CON…PANIER.

PANIER À SALADE, *m.* Police van (lit. "salad shaker"). *La flicaille les a tous embarqués dans le panier à salade.* "The fuzz took them all away in the paddy wagon."

PANIER D'AMOUR, *m.* Vagina. *Catherine la Grande les aimait bien montés pour bien remplir son panier d'amour impérial.* "Catherine the Great liked men who were well endowed to fill up her imperial love box."

PANIER DE CRABES, *m.* Place full of tension and hostility (lit. "crab cage"). *Je suis heureuse d'être sortie de ce panier de crabes.* "I'm glad to be out of that vipers' nest."

PANSE, *f.* Belly. See (SE) METTRE QCH. DANS…PANSE.

PANTOUFLARD, -E, *m., f.* Stay-at-home (from **pantoufle,** "slipper"). *Mes vioques sont des pantouflards.* "My parents are old sticks-in-the-mud."

PANTRUCHE = PANAM.

PAPA GÂTEAU, *m.* **1.** Overindulgent father. *Elle a eu de la chance d'avoir eu un papa gâteau.* "She was lucky to have had a generous dad." **2.** Sugar daddy. *Je n'ai jamais eu de boulot, grâce à mon papa gâteau.* "I've never had a job, thanks to my sugar daddy." See BAISER À LA PAPA.

PAPE, *m.* **1.** Pope. **Sérieux comme un pape.** Solemn-faced; serious. *La gosse triste était sérieuse comme un pape.* "The sad little girl was solemn-faced." See TÉLÉPHONER AU PAPE. **2.** Penis. See SIÈGE; TÉLÉPHONER AU PAPE. *Cf.* PONTIFE 2.

PAPELARDS, *m., pl.* Identity papers. *Les flics m'ont demandé mes papelards.* "The cops asked for my ID."

PAPIER, *m.* Paper. **Être dans les petits papiers de qn.** To be in s.o.'s good books. *Il fait tout pour être dans les petits papiers de la patronne.* "He's trying hard to be on the good side of the boss."

PAPIER-CUL/PAPIER Q, *m.* Toilet paper. *Elle achète du papier Q parfumé.* "She buys scented toilet paper."

PAPILLON, *m.* Parking ticket (lit. "butterfly"). *J'ai une collection de papillons non payés.* "I have a collection of unpaid parking tickets."

PAPILLON D'AMOUR, *m.* Pubic louse (lit. "love butterfly"). *T'inquiète; il ne t'a refilé que des papillons d'amour!* "Take it easy; all he gave you was crabs!"

PAPILLON DU SÉNÉGAL, *m.* Penis. *Elle s'était essayée à toute une collection de papillons du Sénégal.* "She tried out a whole gamut of cocks."

PAPOUILLE, *f.* Tickle. **Faire des papouilles.** To feel up. *Il m'a fait des papouilles en dansant.* "He pawed me when we were dancing."

PAP'S = PAPELARDS.

PÂQUERETTE, *f.,* **1.** Daisy. **Au ras des pâquerettes.** At base level. *Je ne suis pas pimbèche, plutôt au ras des pâquerettes.* "I'm not stuck up, rather, down to earth." **2.** Vagina. *Il aime baiser en levrette sa paquerette.* "He likes to hump her doggie-style."

PAQUET, *m.* Package. *Mettre le paquet.* To go all out; shoot the wad. *Pour en finir ce soir, j'ai mis le paquet.* "I went whole hog to finish tonight."

PARANO, *adj., abbr.* of **paranoïaque.** Paranoid. *Qu'est-ce qu'il est parano!* "God, is he uptight!"

PARANO, *m., f., abbr.* of **paranoïaque.** Paranoiac. *Même les paranos ont des ennemis.* "Even paranoiacs have enemies."

PARANO, *f., abbr.* of **paranoïa.** Paranoia. *Te voilà repartie en complète parano!* "There you go off the deep end again."

PARE-BRISE, *m.* Eyeglasses (lit. "windshield). *Il a paumé son pare-brise.* "He lost his glasses."

PARE-CHOCS, *m., pl.* Breasts (lit. "bumpers"). *Ses pare-chocs étaient irrésistibles.* "Her front bumpers were overpowering."

PAREIL. Similar. **C'est du pareil au même.** "It's six of one, half a dozen of the other."

PARFUM, *m.* Perfume. **Mettre qn. au parfum.** To put s.o. in the picture. *Pourrais-tu me mettre au parfum à propos des nouveaux réglements?* "Can you fill me in on the new regulations?"

PARIGOT, -E, *adj.* Parisian. *Elle a perdu son accent parigot.* "She lost her Parisian accent."

PARIGOT, -E, *m., f. Cette provinciale est devenue on ne peut plus Parigote.* "That girl from the provinces has become ultra-Parisian."

PARLOT(T)E, *f.* Idle talk. *C'est de la parlote pour ne rien dire.* "That's just hot air."

PAR TERRE. On the ground. See (SE) ROULER PAR TERRE.

PARTI, -E. Slightly drunk; stoned. *À la Saint Sylvestre ses vioques étaient bien partis, mais lui, il était complètement parti.* "On New Year's Eve his parents were tipsy but he was spaced out."

PARTIE CARRÉE, *f.* Orgy with two couples. *Elle n'aime que les parties carrées.* "All she goes for are foursomes."

PARTIE DE JAMBES EN L'AIR, *m.* Lovemaking. *Le pique-nique s'est terminé par une partie de jambes en l'air.* "The picnic ended up with a roll in the hay."

PARTIES/PARTIES HONTEUSES, *f. pl.* Genitals. *Ce moraliste a honte de ses parties honteuses.* "That moralist is ashamed of his private parts."

(C'EST) PARTI MON KIKI! Off you go! Away we go!

PARTIR EN COUILLE(S). To go down the drain. *Mon exam loupé; c'est une année de travail partie en couille.* "I failed my exam; there's a year's work in the garbage."

PARTIR EN JAVA. To have a ball. *On est parti en java sur la plage.* "We had a blast on the beach."

PARTOUSARD, -E, *m., f.* Participator in group sex. *Ce bled est un nid de partousards.* "This town is a nest of wife-swappers."

PARTOUSE, *f.* Group sex. *Leurs réunions ne sont que des partouses.* "Their get-togethers are just orgies."

PARTOUSER. To participate in group sex. *Je ne voulais plus partouser et mon mari m'a quittée.* "I didn't want any more group sex and my husband left me."

PARTOUZARD = PARTOUSARD.

PARTOUZE = PARTOUSE.

PAS DÉGUEULASSE! Not half-bad (lit. "not disgusting"). *Pas dégueulasse ton petit vin de derrière les fagots.* "Not bad at all, your special reserve wine."

PAS FOLICHON! Not very agreeable. *Nos repas de famille ne sont pas très folichons.* "Our family dinners aren't much fun."

PAS FOLLE LA GUÊPE! Not as dumb as s.o. looks; not as foolish as s.t. seems (lit. "the wasp's not crazy"). *Elle a fait sa valise sans oublier le fric—pas folle la guêpe!* "She packed her bags without forgetting the money— she's no fool!"

PASSADE, *f.* Brief affair. *Je lui ai pardonné ses passades, mais je n'accepte pas sa nouvelle liaison.* "I've pardoned his little flings but I can't accept his new relationship."

PASSE, *f.* Pass. **En passe de.** On the point of. *Elle est en passe de devenir une grande star.* "She's about to become a big star." **Faire une passe.** To turn a trick. *Pour plaire à son maq elle fait le plus possible de passes.* "To please her pimp she turns as many tricks as possible."

PASSE BOURGEOISE, *f.* Paid sex with a married woman. *Son mari savait qu'elle faisait des passes bourgeoises pour arrondir leurs fins de mois.* "Her husband knew she did a little screwing on the side to help with the monthly bills."

PASSEPORT, *m.* **1.** 100-euro bill (lit. "passport"). *Le detective privé a les poches pleines de passeports pour graisser les pattes et ouvrir les portes.* "The private detective has pockets full of 100-euro notes to grease palms and open doors." **2.** Condom. *Mes michetons savent que sans passeport ils n'entrent pas.* "My johns know that I won't let them in without a rubber."

PASSE RAIDE, *f.* Basic price for a session with a prostitute. *Ma passe raide est très raisonnable.* "My price for a quickie is very reasonable."

PASSER À TABAC. To beat up. See TABAC.

PASSE SÈCHE/SIMPLE = PASSE RAIDE.

(QUEL) PATAQUÈS! What a fuss/scandal!

PATATE. Head (lit. "potato"). **En avoir gros sur la patate.** To have a lot on one's mind; be distressed. *Elle en avait gros sur la patate quand il l'a laissée tomber.* "She was distraught when he dropped her." See RAS…PATATE.

(ET) PATATI ET PATATA. And so on and on.

PATAUGER DANS LA SEMOULE = **PÉDALER.**

PATIN, *m.* Tongue kiss (lit. "skate"). **Filer/rouler un patin.** *Il m'a filé un des ces patins.* "He gave me a real wet one."

PATRAQUE. Slightly sick. *Aujourd'hui je me sens patraque.* "I'm feeling a bit under the weather today."

PATTE, *f.* Leg. (lit. "animal leg; paw"). **Aller à pattes.** To go on foot. **En avoir plein les pattes.** To be fed up. *J'en avais plein les pattes de toujours aller à pattes au boulot.* "I was sick and tired of always hoofing it to work." See CLAQUER...PATTES; TIRER...PATTES.

PAUMÉ, -E, *adj.* Bewildered. *On était tous les deux paumés.* "We were both all mixed up."

PAUMÉ, -E, *m., f.* Misfit. *C'est un enfant de paumés.* "The child's parents are dropouts."

PAUMER. To lose. *Je paume sans cesse mes clefs.* "I keep losing my keys."

(SE) PAUMER. To be all mixed up. *Je me paume sur la carte routière à toutes les sorties d'autoroute.* "I'm completely lost with the road map every time I get off the highway."

PAUVRE. Poor. *Pauv' type!* "What a jerk/washout/loser!" See PIANO DU PAUVRE; PRENDRE...PAUVRE. PAUVRE CON/TARÉ/TYPE!

PAVUTE, javanais of **pute.**

PAXON = **PACSON.**

PAYE, *f.* Long time (lit. "pay"; "payroll"). *Ça fait une paye qu'on ne s'est pas pris de vacs!* "It's been ages since we've had a vacation."

(ÇA) PAYE! What a scream/howl/gas!

PAYER. To treat (lit. "to pay"). *Tu me paies un pot?* "Will you buy me a drink?"

PAYER EN MONNAIE DE SINGE. (lit. "to pay in monkey money"). To fob off; welch. *Cet escroc de promoteur a payé ses ouvriers en monnaie de singe.* "That crooked real estate developer let his workers whistle for their money."

(SE) PAYER. To have to endure (ironic use of the lit. meaning "to treat o.s. to"). *Le même mois je me suis payé un accident de voiture et une jambe cassée au ski.* "The same month I had the luck to smash up my car and break my leg skiing."

(SE) PAYER LA FIOLE/GUEULE/POIRE/TÊTE DE QN. To make fun of s.o. *Tu te paies ma tête?* "Are you putting me on?"

(SE) PAYER UN JETON (DE MATE) = PRENDRE UN JETON (DE MATE).

(S'EN) PAYER/S'EN PAYER UNE TRANCHE. To have a good time. *Ce dernier weekend on s'en est payé.* "Last weekend we had a blast."

PD = PÉDÉ.

PEAU, *f.* Skin. **Avoir qn. dans la peau.** To be madly in love with. *Son gangster de jules, elle l'a vraiment dans la peau.* "She's really gone on her gangster boyfriend." **Avoir la peau de qn./faire la peau à qn.** To kill s.o. *Les truands ont fait la peau de deux otages.* "The gangsters knocked off two hostages." **Bien/mal dans sa peau.** To feel comfortable/uncomfortable. *Entourée d'aristos au resto rup je me sentais mal dans ma peau.* "I felt ill at ease in the ritzy restaurant surrounded by aristocrats." See RAS...PEAU.

PEAU DE BALLE/PEAU DE BITE/ZÉBI/ZOB, *f.* Nothing (lit. "dick skin"). *Ce boulot te rapportera peau de balle.* "You'll get zilch from that job."

PEAU DE CHIEN, *f.* Old whore (lit. "dog skin"). *Comme dit la chanson: "À la Bastille on aimait bien Nini peau de chien."* "As the song says: in the Bastille district, everyone loved Nini, the dear old whore."

PEAU DE SAUSS/SAUCISSON, *f.* Shoddy merchandise (lit. "sausage skin"). *Ça ne vaut rien; c'est de la peau de saucisson!* "That's worth nothing; it's junk!"

PEAU DES FESSES, *f.* Very expensive (lit. "skin of the buttocks"). *Ça m'a coûté la peau des fesses.* "That cost me an arm and a leg."

PEAU DE VACHE, *f.* Bitch; SOB. *Son prof est une vraie peau de vache.* "Her teacher's a real bastard."

PÉBROC/PÉBROQUE, *m.* Umbrella. *Ma grand-tante se servait de son pébroc pour se défendre.* "My great-aunt used her umbrella to defend h.s."

PÊCHE, *f.* **1.** Peach. **Poser sa pêche.** To defecate. *Le chien a posé sa pêche devant ma porte.* "The dog pooped in front of my door." **2.** Head. **Avoir la pêche.** To look great; be in great shape. *En ce moment j'ai la pêche.* "Right now, I'm feeling great." See (SE) FENDRE…PÊCHE. **3.** Blow. *Il a pris une pêche en pleine gueule.* "He got whacked right in the kisser." See FILER UNE PÊCHE.

PÉCHO, backslang of **choper.**

PECLO, backslang of **clope.**

PÉCORE = **PEDZOUILLE.**

PÉCU = **PAPIER-CUL.**

PEDALE, *f.* **1.** Pedal. **Mettre la pédale douce.** To go easy, behave tactfully (lit. "to use the soft pedal"). *Si tu penses la plaquer, mets la pédale douce.* "If you're thinking of ditching her, try to break it to her gently." See PERDRE LES PEDALES. **2.** Male homosexual. *Être de la pédale.* To be a homosexual. *Luc ne veut pas que tous sachent qu'il est de la pédale.* "Luke doesn't want everybody to know that he's gay." *Cf. être du* BATIMENT; JAQUETTE. **Pédale douce.** Discrete homosexual (opposite of PÉDÉ *comme un phoque;* LUCIOLE; TAPETTE). *Luc, pédale douce, a adoré le film* Pédale Douce. "Luke, a low-key queen, loved the movie *Pédale Douce* ("Good-Natured Gay"). *Cf.* PÉDÉ.

PÉDALER DANS LA CHOUCROUTE/SEMOULE/LE YAOURT. To be getting nowhere fast (lit. "to be pedaling in sauerkraut/semolina/yogurt"). *Les négociations pédalent dans la semoule.* "The negotiations are bogged down."

PÉDÉ, *abbr.* of **pédéraste.** *m.* Homosexual. **Pédé comme un phoque.** Really queer. *Marc est fier d'être pédé comme un phoque.* "Mark is proud of being a flaming faggot."

PÉDOQUE = PÉDÉ.

PEDZOUILLE, *m.* Yokel. *Des pédés parigots draguaient les pedzouilles.* "Parisian queens were cruising country bumpkins."

PÈGRE, *f.* The underworld. *Le maire a été acheté par la pègre.* "The mayor was in the mob's pocket."

PEIGNE-CUL/PEIGNE-DERCHE, *m.* Lazy good-for nothing (lit. "ass comb"). *Moi, je turbine pendant que ce peigne-cul se la coule douce.* "I slave away while that lazy bum takes it easy."

PEIGNÉE, *f.* Beating. *Tu vas voir la peignée que je vais te flanquer.* "Just wait until you get the beating I'm going to give you."

PEIGNER LA GIRAFE. To waste time in idle pursuits (lit. "to comb the giraffe"). *Dans ma vie j'ai peigné des troupeaux de girafes.* "I've spent my life in no end of useless projects."

PEIGNE-ZIZI = PEIGNE-CUL.

PEINARD, *adv.* With no problems. *Je fais mon jogging chaque jour peinard.* "I do my daily jogging in peace and quiet."

PELLE, *f.* **1.** Shovel. **À la pelle.** In quantity. *Les couples désunis, il y en a à la pelle.* "The world is full of people who've fallen out of love." **2.** Fall; flop. See PRENDRE...PELLE; RAMASSER...PELLE. **3.** Tongue kiss. See ROULER UNE PELLE.

PELLETER DES NUAGES. *Que.* To build castles in Spain (lit. "to shovel clouds"). *Arrête de pelleter des nuages! Au boulot!* "Enough stargazing. Get to work!"

PELOTAGE, *m.* Petting. *Papa ne permet pas le pelotage à table.* "Dad doesn't permit smooching at the table."

PELOTE, *f.* **1.** Fortune (lit. "ball of yarn"). **Faire sa pelote.** To make a mint. *Ils se sont fait une petite pelote en travaillant au noir.* "They made a small fortune moonlighting." **2.** *Que.* See PLOTTE.

PELOTER. To feel up. *Il ne peut pas m'approcher sans me peloter.* "He can't come near me without pawing me."

PELOTES, *f., pl.* Testicles. *Dédé ne pouvait plus rentrer ses pelotes dans son jean rétréci.* "Andy could no longer get his balls into his tight (shrunk) jeans."

PELOTEUR, *m.* Groper. *Les peloteurs du métro attendent les rames bondées.* "Subway mashers wait for crowded trains."

PELOTEUR DE GRAND-MÈRE, *m.* Street or subway musician slang. Double bass player. *Notre peloteur de grand-mère s'accompagnait en chantant.* "Our double bass player accompanied h.s. in a song."

PELOUSARDE, *f.* Lesbian. *On dit qu'elle et sa sœur seraient des pelousardes.* "They say she and her sister are lezzies."

PELOUSE, *f.* Lawn. See BROUTER…PELOUSE/TOUFFE.

PENDRE AU CUL/NEZ. To be hanging over one's head (lit. one's "ass or nose"). *La grève, ça nous pend au nez.* "We're faced with the strike that's looming."

PENDU, *m.* Hanged man. **Avoir une veine de pendu.** To be very lucky. *Il a une veine de pendu; son roman sera édité.* "He's a lucky devil; his novel's going to be published."

PENSEUSE, *f.* Head. See COURT-JUS…PENSEUSE.

PENTE, *f.* Slope. **Avoir la dalle en pente.** To drink a lot (lit. "to have a slating slope," as in one for liquor to slide down easily). *Mon dab a la dalle en pente.* "My dad's a lush."

PÉPÉ, *m.* Grandpa. *Pépé voulait se remarier à 95 ans.* "Gramps wanted to get married again at 95."

PÉPÉE, *f.* = **NANA.**

PÉPÈRE, *m.* and *adj.* Comfy; easy. *Casse-cou à vingt ans, mais à quarante il mène une vie pépère.* "At twenty he was a daredevil but at forty he's living a soft life."

PÉPIN = PÉBROC.

PÉPIN, *m.* Problem (lit. "pip"). *Il a eu un gros pépin avec sa voiture.* "He had a major problem with his car."

PÉPITE, *f.* Clitoris (lit. "gold nugget"). *Elle s'en branle de ma bite mais ça l'exite quand je lui lèche la pépite.* "She's indifferent to my dick, but it excites her when I lick her clit." *Cf.* BONBON 3; BOUTON; HARICOT; PRALINE.

PÉQUENOT = PEDZOUILLE.

PERDRE LE NORD/LA BOUSSOLE/BOULE. To lose control, direction; go crazy (lit. "lose the north/compass/one's head"). *Je croyais notre couple au beau fixe mais tout d'un coup Luc a perdu le nord.* "I thought all was smooth sailing for the two of us but suddenly Luc lost it."

PERDRE LES PÉDALES. To lose one's head. *Je m'inquiète de perdre les pédales pour un rien.* "It upsets me when I go nuts over trifles."

PERDRE SA FLEUR (D'ORANGER). To lose one's virginity. *Il n'a pas su que j'avais perdu ma fleur d'oranger sur la plage.* "He didn't find out that I had lost my cherry on the beach."

PÉRIF/PÉRIPH, *m., abbr.* of **périphérique.** Beltway. *Prenons la départementale; le périf bouchonne.* "Let's take the secondary road; the main road is bumper to bumper."

PERLE, *f.* Fart. See LÂCHER UN COLIS…PERLE.

PERPÈTE/PERPETTE, *f., abbr.* of **perpétuité.** Life sentence. *Il avait pensé éviter la perpette mais on l'a condamné à perpette.* "He thought he wouldn't get life, but he did."

(À) PERPETTE (LES ALOUETTES/BAINS/OIES). In the back of the beyond. *Ils ont quitté Paris pour s'installer à Perpette-les-Bains!* "They left Paris to live in the boonies."

PERVENCHE, *f.* Female traffic cop (lit. "periwinkle"). *J'ai évité le papillon en faisant du charme à la pervenche.* "I didn't get a ticket because I turned on the charm to the meter maid."

PET, *m.* Fart. **Ne pas valoir un pet (de lapin).** To be worthless. *Tes pets-de-nonne ne valent pas un pet de lapin.* "Your fritters (lit. "nun's farts") aren't worth a rabbit's fart."

PÉTARD, *m.* **1.** Noise (from firecrackers, backfiring, and the like). **Faire du pétard.** To create an uproar/scandal. *Quand ils apprendront la nouvelle ça fera du pétard.* "When they find out about that, it's going to make waves." **2.** Revolver. *Il a tout de suite sorti son pétard.* "He took out his revolver right away." **3.** Posterior. *Lili a un pétard aguichant.* "Lily has an attractive ass." See RAS…PÉTARD. **4.** Cannabis cigarette. *Il fume un pétard aux WC; son pétard le fait planer.* "He's smoking a joint in the john; he gets high on his own petard."

PÉTASSE, *f.* Slut. *Vise cette pétasse à vélo!* "Look at that broad on the bike!" **Avoir la pétasse** = **avoir la pétoche.** See PÉTOCHE.

PÈTE = PÉTARD 3, 4.

PÉTÉ, -E. Drunk; stoned. *Il est rigolo quand il est un peu pété, mais moins drôle quand il l'est à donf.* "He's a riot when he's a little high, but less funny when he's completely pissed."

PÈTE-DANS-LE-SABLE, *m., f.* Short person (lit. "ass in the sand"). *C'est ce pète-dans-le-sable qui veut jouer au basket?* "Is that the little runt who wants to play basketball?"

PÉTER DANS LA SOIE. See SOIE.

PÉTER LA FAIM/DALLE = CREVER LA FAIM/ DALLE.

PÉTER PLUS HAUT QUE SON CUL/DERRIÈRE. To be pretentious (lit. "to fart higher than one's ass"). *Depuis qu'elle a épousé le duc elle pète plus haut que son cul.* "Since marrying the duke she's swell-headed."

(SE) PÉTER LA GUEULE. To get smashed. *Après s'être pété la gueule au whisky et au shit il s'est pété la gueule en voiture.* "After getting smashed on whisky and hash he smashed up his car."

271

(SE) PÉTER LA PANSE/SOUVENTRIÈRE. To overeat. *Au gueuleton on s'est bien pété la panse.* "We really stuffed our bellies at the feast."

(SE) PÉTER LA RUCHE. See RUCHE.

PÈTE-SEC, *m.* Authoritarian, sharp-tongued person (lit. "dry-ass"). *Pas drôle de jacter avec ce pète-sec.* "No fun talking to that martinet."

PÉTEUX, *m.* = **PÉTARD.**

PÉTEUX, -EUSE, *m., f.* Pretentious person. *Toutes des péteuses, ces nanas du 16ème (arrondissement)!* "Those girls from the 16th **(arrondissement)** are all stuck-up!"

PETIT CADEAU, *m.* Prostitute's fee. *Quand un miché oublie mon petit cadeau, mon maq le lui rappelle.* "When a john forgets my little consideration, my pimp reminds him."

PETIT CHAPEAU, *m.* Condom (lit. "little hat"). *Il se balade avec plein de petits chapeaux dans la poche.* "He walks around with plenty of rubbers in his pocket."

PETIT CHAUVE À COL ROULÉ, *m.* Penis (lit. "little baldie in a turtleneck"). *Son petit chauve à col roulé était immense.* "His pecker was huge."

PETIT COIN, *m.* Toilet. *Le bigo sonnait pendant que j'étais au petit coin.* "The phone rang while I was in the can."

PETIT CREVÉ, *m.* Cheap little punk/mobster. *Ce petit crevé s'est fait tout de suite agrafer.* "That little punk got nabbed right away." *Cf.* FRAPPE.

PETIT FRÈRE, *m.* Penis (lit. "little brother"). *Son petit frère ne supporte pas l'eau glacée.* "His dick doesn't like very cold water."

PETIT FRIPÉ, *m.* Anus (lit. "the little wrinkled one"). *Le roman de Burroughs met en valeur un petit fripé qui parle.* "Burrough's novel features a talking anus."

PETIT GUICHET, *m.* Anus (lit. "the little ticket window"). **Être du petit guichet = être de la pédale.**

(LE) PETIT JÉSUS EN CULOTTE DE VELOURS, *m.* Succulent food or drink (lit. "the baby Jesus in velvet britches"). *Le banquet était une succession de petits Jésus en culottes de velours.* "The banquet was a succession of exquisite dishes and drinks."

(AUX) PETITS OIGNONS. Excellent. *Votre soirée était aux petits oignons.* "Your party went off perfectly."

PÉTOCHE, *f.* Fear. **Avoir la pétoche.** To be afraid. *J'ai la pétoche quand il roule trop vite.* "It scares me when he drives too fast."

PÉTOUILLE = PÉTOCHE.

PETSEQUE = PÈTE-SEC.

PETZOUILLE = PEDZOUILLE.

PEUCLO = PECLO.

PÈZE, *m.* Money. *As-tu du pèze à me prêter?* "Got any bread to lend me?"

PHALLO, from **phallocrate.** Male chauvinist pig. *Il ne bande plus, mais il est toujours aussi phallo.* "He doesn't get it up anymore, but he's still as sexist as ever."

PHOQUE, *m.* **1.** Seal. **Les avoir à la phoque.** Work-shy individual (lit. "with turned-in flippers" or "hands"). *On ne peut compter sur lui; il les a à la phoque.* "There's no counting on him; he's a goldbrick." **2.** Homosexual; limp wrist (again, the connection is with "inversion" or "turning in"). *Notre fils se plaît au milieu des phoques.* "Our son likes to hang out with fags." See EN ÊTRE.

PHYSIQUE, *m.* Face. **N'avoir qu'un physique.** To be just a pretty face. *Faut pas croire que Line n'a qu'un physique; elle est très calée.* "Don't think that Line's just a looker; she's very knowledgeable. **Avoir le physique de l'emploi.** To look the part. *Ce croquemort est très marrant; il n'a pas du tout le physique de l'emploi.* "That undertaker's very jolly; he doesn't look at all like a gravedigger."

PIANO, *m.* Restaurant oven. *Le maître cuisinier tenait à l'œil son piano.* "The great chef kept an eye on his oven."

PIANO DU PAUVRE/PIANO À BRETELLES, *m.* Accordion. *Ce rameux est un virtuose du piano du pauvre.* "That strolling subway musician is an accordion virtuoso."

PIASSE, *f., Que.* = **PIASTRE.** *Ça ne coûte que 20 piasses.* "It costs only $20." (Note: **pièce de monnaie** = "coin," not "paper money").

PIASTRE, *f., Que.* (From the unit of currency once used in many countries. Piastres were in circulation before the introduction of the Canadian dollar. In the Fr. text of the Louisiana Purchase piastre is used for the U.S. dollar. Cajun sl. still uses it.) Canadian dollar. *Ce baise-la-piastre ne te les prêtera jamais, les 300 piastres.* "That tightwad will never lend you the $300."

PIAULE, *f.* Room. *C'est toujours le bordel dans sa piaule.* "His pad's always a mess."

PIAULER. To sleep; live. *Je ne piaule pas chez mes vioques.* "I don't live with my parents."

PICAILLON, *m.* Small change; cash. **Avoir des picaillons.** To be rich. *Je crois qu'elle a des picaillons.* "I think she's got big bucks."

PICHOUN = PITCHOUNET.

PICOLER. To tipple. *Ils picolent tous dur dans cette famille.* "They all hit the bottle in that family."

PICOUSE = PIQUOUSE.

PICRATE, *m.* Cheap wine. *Le prof les a bernés en versant un picrate dans une bouteille de Mouton-Rothschild.* "The prof fooled them by serving cheap wine in a Mouton-Rothschild bottle."

PIÈCE MONTÉE, *f.* Tiered wedding cake; deck of marked cards; scam. *La prétendue attaque n'était q'une pièce montée, inventée de toute pièces.* "The supposed attack was just a put-up job, made of whole cloth."

PIED, *m.* Foot. **Faire du pied à qn.** To play footsy/kneesies. *Son mari me faisait du pied sous la table.* "Her husband played footsy with me under the table." **Mettre le pied quelque part à qn.** To kick s.o. in the backside. *Tu vas avoir mon pied quelque part si tu continues à m'emmerder.* "I'll give you a kick in the ass if you keep bugging me."

See COMME UN PIED; COUP DE PIED EN VACHE; COUPS DE PIED AU CUL…; COUP DE PIED DE VÉNUS; PRENDRE SON PIED.

(C'EST) LE PIED! (That's) sensational; orgasmic; mindblowing!

PIED-DE-BICHE, *m.* Beggar; vagrant; door-to-door salesman (lit. "doe's foot"; "crowbar." May derive from a door knocker shaped liked a deer's foot.). *L'ancien PDG est devenu pied-de-biche.* "The former CEO's become a beggar." See TIRER…BICHE.

PIED DE GRUE, *m.* Crane's foot. **Faire le pied de grue.** To be kept waiting. *Tâche d'etre à l'heure; j'ai horreur de faire le pied de grue.* "Try to be on time; I hate to hang around for nothing."

PIED DE NEZ, *m.* Thumbing one's nose at s.o. *Quel impertinent, ce mouflet; il m'a fait un pied de nez.* "What an impudent brat; he thumbed his nose at me!"

PIEDS, *m., pl.* **Faire des pieds et des mains.** To go all out. *J'ai fait des pieds et des mains pour obtenir ce boulot.* "I moved heaven and earth to get that job." **Faire les pieds à qn.** To teach s.o. a lesson. *Il n'a rien foutu de l'année— s'il loupe son exam, ça lui fera les pieds!* "He goofed off all year—if he fails his exam it'll serve him right." See BÊTE…PIEDS; CASSE-PIEDS; CASSER LES PIEDS; CON COMME SES PIEDS; (S')EMMÊLER LES PIEDS.

PIEU, *m.* Bed (lit. "stake"). *Je rêvais d'un pieu au bord de la mer.* "I dreamed of a bed by the sea."

(SE) PIEUTER. To hit the sack. *J'adore me pieuter à la belle étoile.* "I love to sleep under the stars."

PIF. Nose; schnozz. **Au pif.** By a rough estimate. *Au pif, il a 100 mètres d'ici au garage.* "I'd say it was about 100 meters from here to the garage."

PIF(F)ER. To smell. **Ne pas pouvoir piffer qn.** To find s.o. unbearable. *Ce prof n'a jamais pu me piffer.* "That teacher could never stand me."

(AU) PIF(F)OMÈTRE = AU PIF.

PIFFRER = PIF(F)ER.

PIGE, *f.* Year. *Je me sens toujours jeune avec mes 80 piges.* "I still feel young at 80."

PIGEONNER. 1. to dupe. *Ils ont essayé de me pigeonner.* "They tried to make me their pigeon." **2. Faire pigeonner.** To lift and round breasts. *J'ai acheté ce bustier sexy pour faire pigeonner mes lolos.* "I bought this long-line sexy bra to push up my breasts."

PIGER. To understand. *Je te planque. Tu piges?* "I'm ditching you. Have you got that?"

(N'Y) PIGER QUE COUIC/DALLE/POUIC. To understand nothing at all. *Dans son argomuche je n'y ai pigé que couic.* "I couldn't make head or tail of his slang talk."

PIGNOLE, *f.* Masturbation. *Une petite pignole, ça te dit?* "Do you feel like a hand job?"

(SE) PIGNOLER. To masturbate. **Se pignoler à quatre mains.** To delude s.o. *Si tu crois que ça va marcher tu te pignoles à quatre mains!* "If you think that's going to work, you're kidding y.s. (lit. "jerking off with four hands")."

PIGNOUF, *m.* Boor. *Quelle bande de pignoufs!* "What a pack of louts."

PILIER, *m.* Pillar. **1. Pilier de bar.** Barfly. *Il n'est plus qu'un pilier de bar.* "All he does is hold up the bar now." **2. Pilier de cathédrale.** Churchy person. *Ma femme, pilier de cathédrale, ferait mieux de s'occuper de ma colonne.* "My wife, a staunch upholder of the church, ought to get my dick up instead." **3. Pilier de bordel.** Frequent brothel customer. *Si elle était plus obligeante je serais moins pilier de bordel.* "If she were more obliging I'd hang out less in whorehouses."

PILPOIL. Perfectly. *Ça me convient pilpoil.* "That suits me to a T."

PINAILLER. To nitpick. *Cesse de pinailler tout le temps.* "Stop splitting hairs all the time."

PINARD, *m.* Wine. *Il n'y a pas de bon pique-nique sans pinard.* "A picnic's not a picnic without wine."

PINCEAUX = PIED.

PINCE-CUL/PINCE-FESSES, *m.* Party; dance (lit. "pinch ass"). *Ils vont chaque samedi au pince-fesses.* "They go to the dance every Saturday."

PINCER. To arrest. *On l'a pincé sur le fait.* "They nabbed him red-handed."

(EN) PINCER POUR QN. To be infatuated with s.o. *Il en pince pour moi.* "He's taken a shine to me."

PINCES = PINCETTES 1.

(À) PINCES/PINCEAUX/PINGOTS. On foot. *Par ce froid je n'ai pas envie de rentrer à pinces.* "I don't feel like walking back in this cold."

PINCETTES, *f., pl.* **1.** Pair of tweezers; fire tongs. **Qn. pas à prendre avec des pincettes.** S.o. dirty or angry and thus not fit to go near. *Sa nana l'a quitté et il n'est pas à prendre avec des pincettes.* "His girl left him and there's no going near him (with a ten-foot pole)." **2.** Legs. **Remuer les pincettes.** To dance. *Pépé sait toujours bien remuer les pincettes.* "Gramps is still a good dancer."

PINE, *f.* Penis. *Molly Bloom se plaignait que les mecs ne se lavaient jamais la pine.* "Molly Bloom complained that guys never washed their dicks." See RENTRER…BRAS.

PINER. To have sexually. *Il ne pense qu'à piner.* "All he thinks about is getting laid."

PINGLOT/PINGOT = PIED.

PINOUZE = PINARD.

PINTER. To guzzle alcohol (from **pinte,** "pint," a measure no longer used in Fr.). *Tu ferais bien de pinter moins.* "It'd be a good idea for you to booze it up less."

PIOCRE, *m.* Louse. *Tous les gosses au bahut avaient des piocres.* "All the kids in school had lice."

PIOGER. To live. *Je n'y pioge plus.* "I don't live there anymore.

PIÔLE = PIAULE.

277

PION, -NNE, *m., f.* *adj.* and *n.* Drunk. *Ils étaient tous pions, sauf moi.* "They were all soused, except me."

PION(N)ARD, *m.* Drunk. *Je ne veux plus le voir, ce pionard.* "I don't want to see that drunk anymore."

PIONCER. To sleep. *Je pionce toujours au cours le lundi matin.* "I always get forty winks in school Monday morning."

(SE) PIONER/SE PIONARDER. To get drunk. *Je me suis pioné mais ça n'a pas aidé.* "I got drunk but it didn't help."

PIPE, *f.* **1.** Fellatio (lit. "pipe"). **Faire/tailler une pipe** (lit. "to do/trim a pipe"). To perform fellatio. *Je ne fais pas de pipe à des pines malpropres.* "I don't go down on dirty dicks." **2.** Head. See CASSE-PIPE; CASSER SA PIPE; (SE) FENDRE LA PIPE; NOM D'UNE PIPE; TÊTE DE PIPE.

PIPELETTE, *m.* Talkative person. **Quelle pipelette!** "What a chatterbox."

PIPER. To fellate. *Que tu sais piper! Tu m'as pompé.* "You give great head. You really drained my pipe." *Cf.* FAIRE UNE PIPE.

PIPEUR, -EUSE, *m., f.* Fellator/fellatrix. *Cette reine des pipeuses de la plage te fera un Cléopâtre craquant.* "That cocksucker queen of the beach will give you a mind-blowing blow job." *C'est un pipeur de première!* "He's a first-class cocksucker."

PIPI DE CHAT = PISSE D'ÂNE.

PIQUE-ASSIETTE, *m., f.* Sponger. *C'est un pique-assiette de première.* "He's a first-class freeloader."

PIQUE-FESSES, *f.* Nurse. *J'oublie le stress des piquouzes avec cette aguichante pique-fesses.* "That sexy nurse makes me forget the stress of the injections."

(PAS) PIQUÉ DES VERS/HANNETONS. Not half-bad at all. *Son soufflé n'était pas piqué des vers.* "Her soufflé was really excellent."

PIQUER. To take; swipe. *Shakespeare et Homer ont piqué leurs sujets à plusieurs sources.* "Shakespeare and Homer took their subjects from many sources."

PIQUER DU NEZ. To snooze. *Je piquais du nez au boulot, tellement j'étais crevée.* "I was so pooped I nodded off at work."

PIQUER DU ZEN = PIQUER DU NEZ. See ZEN **1.**

PIQUER UNE BÂCHE/UN ROUPILLON. See BÂCHE; ROUPILLON.

PIQUER UNE COLÈRE/CRISE. To fly off the handle. *Elle pique une colère chaque fois que sa frangine lui pique ses fringues.* "She hits the ceiling every time her sister pinches her clothes."

PIQUER UNE TÊTE. To dive. *Chaque jour il aimait piquer une tête dans la piscine.* "He liked to dive into the pool every day."

PIQUER UN FARD/SOLEIL. To blush. *Elle pique un fard pour un rien.* "She blushes for the slightest little thing."

PIQUETTE, *f.* **1.** Inferior wine. *Ils n'ont servi que de la piquette.* "All they served was cheap wine." **2.** Defeat. **Prendre/ramasser une piquette.** To get a real licking. *Il a pris une de ces piquettes au tennis.* "He was soundly beaten at tennis."

PIQUOUSE/PIQUOUZE, *f.* Injection; drug fix. *Il a la trouille des piquouses.* "He's afraid of injections."

PIQUOUSER/PIQUOUZER. To inject; shoot drugs. *Les flics ont vu qu'il se piquouzait.* "The cops saw that he was a mainliner."

PIRATE, *m.* **1.** Pirate. *Jean Bart et Surcouf étaient des corsaires, non des pirates.* "Jean Bart and Surcouf were government-sponsored privateers, not pirates." **2.** Computer hacker. *Les pirates de l'informatique lui ont volé ses données bancaires et son identité.* "Computer hackers stole her bank references and her identity."

PISSE-COPIE, *m.* Bad journalist. *Incroyable; ce pisse-copie a eu le prix Pulitzer!* "I don't believe it; that hack got the Pulitzer Prize."

PISSE D'ÂNE, *f.* Unsavory drink (lit. "donkey piss"). *Son café, c'est toujours de la pisse d'âne.* "Her coffee always tastes like dishwater."

PISSE-FROID, *m.* Cold fish. *Quel pisse-froid!* "What a wet blanket!"

PISSENLIT, *m.* Dandelion. **Bouffer/sucer les pissenlits par la racine.** To be dead and buried (lit. "to eat/suck the dandelions by the root"). *Il fumait trop! Maintenant il suce les pissenlits par la racine!* "He smoked too much. Now he's pushing up daisies!"

PISSE-MENU, *m.* Nonentity. *Ce pisse-menu se prend pour quelqu'un!* "That piddling jerk thinks he's somebody."

PISSE-PAROLE. Lawyer (lit. "word pisser"). *Le jury a avalé les boniments de son pisse-parole.* "The jury swallowed (fell for) his mouthpiece's line."

PISSE-VINAIGRE. Wet-blanket (lit. "piss vinegar"). *Ce pisse-vinaigre trouve le livre choquant.* "That kill-joy finds the book shocking." *Cf.* Eng. "sourpuss" with the Fr. idea of "sour piss."

PISSER. To urinate. **Ne plus se sentir pisser.** To be conceited (lit. "not to feel or notice o.s. pissing anymore"). *Il ne se sent plus pisser depuis qu'il habite un château.* "He thinks his shit doesn't stink anymore since moving into the castle." See LAISSE PISSER; LAISSER PISSER...; PLEUVOIR...PISSE.

PISSER AU CUL DE QN. To despise s.o (lit. "to piss on s.o.'s ass"). *Je te pisse au cul!* "Go fuck y.s.!"

PISSER DANS UN VIOLON/LA MER. To do s.t. useless (lit. "to piss into a violin/the sea"). *Essayer de le raisonner c'est comme pisser dans un violon.* "Trying to reason with him is like farting against the wind."

PISSER DES LAMES DE RASOIR. To have painful gonorrhea (lit. "to piss razor blades"). *Malgré la pénicilline, il pissait des lames de rasoir.* "Despite the penicillin, the clap hurt him like hell."

PISSER EN L'AIR = CRACHER EN L'AIR.

PISSER UN MÔME. See MÔME.

PISSETTE, *f.* **1.** A (small) pee. **Faire pissette.** To urinate. *Il faut que je fasse pissette.* "I've got to take a leak." **2.** Windshield wiper. *Fais marcher la pissette.* "Turn the windshield wiper on." **3.** Firehose nozzle. *L'eau ne sortait plus de la pissette.* "The water stopped running from the nozzle."

PISSEUX, -EUSE. Dingy (lit. "pissy"). *Je n'aime pas ce café pisseux.* "I don't like that dingy café."

PISSOIR, *m.* Men's room; urinal. *Plutôt pisser dans l'herbe que dans ce pissoir dégueu.* "I'd rather piss on the grass than use that filthy john."

PISSOIRE, *f.* = PISSOIR.

PISSOTIÈRE, *f.* Men's room; "tearoom" (homosexual). *La flicaille surveille toutes les pissotières du parc.* "The cops are watching all the tearooms in the park."

PISSOTTE, *f.* Vagina. *Elle avait la pissotte peu accueillante.* "Her pussy wasn't very hospitable."

PISTON, *m.* String pulling (lit. "piston"). *Il a eu son poste par piston.* "He got his job through pull."

PITCHOUNET, -TE. Tiny. *Son fils est beau mais pitchounet.* "Her son's handsome but tiny."

PITOUNE, *f., Que.* Flashy young girl. *Je me la farcirais bien, cette pitoune-là.* "I'd love to plug that chick."

PLANCHE, *f.* Board. **Planche à repasser; à pain** (lit. "ironing board; bread board"). Flat-chested woman. *Les mannequins sont souvent des planches à pain.* "Models are often flat-chested."

PLANCHER. 1. To work on s.t. for school. *J'ai planché deux heures sur un problème de maths.* "I sweated two hours over a math problem." **2.** To make a verbal presentation (from student slang for being "called to the blackboard"). *Au motel il va plancher sur l'immobilier.* "He's going to talk about real estate at the motel."

PLANER. To be high; stoned (lit. "to soar"). *Impossible de lui parler; il plane complet.* "Impossible to talk to him; he's totally spaced out."

PLAN-PLAN = **PLON-PLON.**

PLANQUARÈS. Hidden. *Le gangster est toujours plan-quarès.* "The gangster's still hiding out." See PLANQUER **1.**

PLANQUE, *f.* **1.** Easy job. *Son nouvel intérim c'est la planque!* "Her new temp job is really cushy." **2.** Hideout. *Les flics ont découvert leur planque.* "The cops discovered their hiding place."

PLANQUÉ, -E, *m., f.* S.o. with an easy job. *Ces planqués de fonctionnaires parlent de faire la grève.* "Those gold-bricking civil servants are talking about going on strike."

PLANQUER. 1. To hide. *Elle a planqué la came dans sa pissotte.* "She hid her stash in her twat." **2.** To keep under surveillance. *Les paparazzi ne cessaient de planquer la princesse.* "The paparazzi constantly kept tabs on the princess."

(SE) PLANQUER. To go into hiding. *Ils se sont planqués avec le butin.* "They went into hiding with the loot."

PLANQUOUSE = **PLANQUE.**

PLANTER SON PANAIS. See PANAIS.

(SE) PLANTER. 1. To have an accident. *Le skieur s'est planté en plein slalom.* "The skier crashed in full slalom." **2.** To make a mistake. *Tu vas te planter à nouveau.* "You're going to get it wrong again."

PLANTE VERTE. 1. Green plant. **Faire la plante verte.** To be decorative but useless. *Je n'a pas envie de faire la plante verte ici.* "I don't feel like just being a fixture/part of the furniture here." **2.** Guard stationed in one place. *Les plantes vertes gardent les ambassades.* "Guards are stationed in front of the embassies."

PLAQUER. To abandon. *Non seulement il a plaqué son job mais sa famille aussi.* "He not only quit his job, he walked out on his family too."

PLAT, *m.* Dish. **Faire du plat à qn.** To make advances to s.o. *Il me fait du plat mais je m'en fiche.* "He comes on to me but I'm not interested." **Faire (tout) un plat de qch.** To make a fuss about s.t. *Il ne faut pas en faire un plat.* "You don't have to make such a song and dance about it."

PLATES-BANDES, *f., pl.* Flower beds. **Marcher sur/ piétiner les plates-bandes de qn.** To encroach on s.o.'s territory. *J'insupporte qu'il marche sur mes plates-bandes!* "I won't have him trespassing on my turf."

(À) PLEINS TUBES. At maximum power. *Ils faisaient marcher leur télé à pleins tubes.* "They had their TV on full blast."

PLEURER. To weep. **Faire pleurer son aveugle/la fauvette/le colosse.** To urinate. *Le jogging me fait souvent pleurer le colosse.* "Jogging makes me take a leak often."

PLEUVOIR À BOIRE DEBOUT. *Que.* To rain buckets (lit. "to rain (so that) you can drink standing up"). *Pas besoin de mettre un récipient. Il pleut à boire debout.* "No need to set out a container. All you have to do is open your mouth."

PLEUVOIR COMME VACHE QUI PISSE. To rain cats and dogs. *Impossible de jouer au foot; il pleuvait comme vache qui pisse.* "Impossible to play football; it was raining buckets."

PLI, *m.* Fold. *Ça ne fait pas un pli!* **1.** That's just perfect! **2.** That's sure as shootin'. **3.** That's as good as done!

PLOMB DANS L'AILE. See AILE.

PLOMBE, *m.* **1.** Hour. *Il m'a raconté sa vie pendant des plombes.* "He spent hours telling me his life story."

PLOMBÉ, -E. Infected with VD. *Les filles de ce maq sont plombées.* "That pimp's whores are all clapped/syphed up."

PLOMBER. 1. To riddle with bullets. *Mon dab a été plombé lors de la St Valentin à Chicago.* "My father got a belly full of lead during the St. Valentine's Day massacre in

Chicago." **2.** To infect with VD. *Ce salaud m'a plombée et plaquée.* "That bastard gave me a dose and ditched me."

PLONGE, *f.* Dishwashing. *Étudiante, je faisais la plonge pour payer ma piaule.* "When I was a student I washed dishes to pay for my room."

PLONGEUR, -EUSE. *m., f.* Dishwasher (lit. "diver"). *Ce resto embauche des plongeurs.* "This restaurant is hiring dishwashers."

PLON-PLON. Easygoing. *Le prince est plon-plon, et assez populaire, mais la monarchie ne sera jamais restaurée.* "The prince is laid back, and popular enough, but the monarchy will never be restored."

PLOTTE, *f., Que.* Female; female genitalia. *Laisse ma plotte et chante-moi un peu la pomme.* "Leave my cunt alone and say sweet-nothings to me."

PLOUC. Unsophisticated. *Le marquis a l'air plouc.* "The marquess has a rough manner."

PLOUC/PLOUQUE, *m.* Country bumpkin. *Ce sont deux ploucs.* "They're a couple of yokels."

PLUMARD, *m.* Bed. *Mon plumard n'est pas trop petit pour nous deux.* "My bed isn't too small for the two of us."

PLUME, *f.* Feather. **Voler dans les plumes de qn.** To go after s.o. verbally and physically (lit. "to fly into s.o.'s feathers." Cf. Eng. "the fur will fly"). *Dès que je vois sa poufiasse j'ai envie de lui voler dans les plumes.* "Just the sight of his slut makes me want to pull her hair out/lay into her."

PLUMER. To steal (lit. "to pluck"). *Ils l'ont plumé, lui et son appart.* "They robbed him, and cleaned out his apartment."

POCHETRON, *m.* Drunk. *Ce pochetron m'a gerbé dessus!* "That drunken bum barfed all over me."

POÊLANT = POILANT.

(SE) POÊLER = SE POILER.

POGNE, *f.* Hand. **Être à la pogne de qn.** To be under s.o.'s thumb. *Il est à la pogne de sa regulière.* "He's under his wife's thumb." **Se faire une pogne.** To masturbate. *Je me sers des deux mains pour me faire une pogne.* "I use both hands to jerk off."

POGNER. 1. To grab; masturbate. *Et si je te pognais?* "Feel like a hand job?" **2.** *Que.* To understand, catch; get; be successful. *Je n'ai rien pogné à ta nouvelle chanson. Elle ne pognera pas.—Je m'étais pogné un rhume et je l'ai mal chantée.* "I didn't get anything in your new song. It won't catch on."—"I caught a cold and sang it badly." (The meanings "to seize, grab; masturbate" are still used in sl. in France. The idea has been expanded in Que. to mean "to grasp [literally or figuratively].")

POGNON, *f.* Money. *On m'a piqué mon pognon dans le métro.* "They stole my dough in the subway." See (SE) FAIRE DU POGNON.

POIGNER = POGNER.

POIL, *m.* Hair. **À poil.** Naked. *J'aime me baigner à poil.* "I like to skinny-dip." **Au (petit) poil; au quart de poil.** Perfect. *Ce resto est au poil.* "This restaurant is tops." **Au poil (du cul) près; à un poil (de grenouille) près.** Excellent to the last detail. *Ça me va au poil près.* "That suits me to a T." **D'un poil.** Barely. *Elle a loupé son vol d'un poil.* "She just missed her flight." **De bon/mauvais poil.** Good/bad mood. *Elle est toujours de mauvais poil le matin.* "She's always in a bad mood in the morning."

POILANT, -E. Hilarious. *Tout le film est poilant.* "The whole movie is a scream."

(SE) POILER. To laugh uproariously. *On s'est poilé avec ces comiques.* "We never stopped laughing with those comics."

POILU, -E. Courageous (lit. "hairy"). *Ces petits branleurs se veulent poilus.* "Those little jerks think they're spunky."

POILU, *m.,* homosexual slang. Hairy-chested hunk. *Cette tapette n'aime que les poilus.* "That queen only goes for hairy hunks."

POINT D'EAU, *m.* Bar. *Il y a un chouette point d'eau dans cette rue.* "There's a nice watering hole on this street."

POINTURE, *f.* Outstanding person (lit. "size"). *En saut à ski, c'est la grande pointure.* "She's a superstar in ski jumping."

POIRE, *f.* **1.** Face (lit. "pear"). *Il a une bonne poire.* "He has a friendly face." **2.** Individual. See RAMMENER SA POIRE. **3.** Naïve person; sucker. *Je suis trop bonne poire—c'est ça mon problème.* "I'm too much of a good egg—that's my problem."

POIREAU. 1. Penis (lit. "leek [vegetable]"). **Souffler dans le poireau.** To fellate. *Pourquoi tu ne me souffles pas un peu dans le poireau?* "Why won't you blow me a little?" *Cf.* ASPERGE **2**; PANAIS. **2.** Lone individual at a restaurant table. *C'est mort ce soir! Que quelques poireaux.* "It's dead tonight. Just a few loners."

(FAIRE LE) POIREAU, *m.* To wait around. *Elle m'a fait faire le poireau devant son appart.* "She kept me waiting in front of her apartment."

POIREAUTER. To let s.o. cool his or her heels. *J'ai poireauté deux heures en l'attendant.* "I was left to twiddle my thumbs for two hours while waiting for him."

(SE) POIRER = SE POILER.

POIROTTER = POIREAUTER.

POISCAILLE/POISSECAILLE, *m.* **1.** Fish. *Au port ça sent le poiscaille.* "The port smells of fish." **2.** Pimp. See POISSON **2**.

POISSON, *m.* **1.** Fish. **Engueuler comme du poisson pourri.** To yell and scream at s.o. *Je l'ai engueulé comme du poisson pourri quand il est rentré bourré.* "I really ripped into him when he came home drunk." **2.** Pimp. *Ce poisson l'a pourrie.* "That pimp corrupted her."

POIVROT, -E, *m., f.* Alcoholic. *La poivrote s'est fait désintoxiquer.* "The lush went to a drying-out tank."

POLAR, *m.* Detective story or movie. *Maman ne lit que des polars.* "Mom just reads whodunits."

POLAR, from **polarisé** (centered on). Eager beaver; workaholic. *Il est complètement polar.* "He just lives for his work."

POLICHINELLE, *m.* Punch(inello) [puppetry; theater]. **Avoir un polichinelle dans le tiroir.** To be pregnant. *À quatorze ans elle avait déjà un polichinelle dans le tiroir.* "Already at fourteen she had a bun in the oven." **C'est le secret de Polichinelle.** "It's an open secret."

(SE) POLIR LE CHINOIS. To masturbate (lit. "to polish the Chinaman"). *Nous nous polissons le chinois de concert.* "We beat the meat together."

POLITESSE, *f.* Politeness. **Faire une politesse.** To perform fellatio. *La femme de l'ambassadeur ne l'aimait pas, mais elle faisait souvent une politesse à son mari.* "The ambassador's wife didn't like it, but she often obliged her husband by going down on him."

POLTRON, *m.* Fart (lit. "coward"). *Qn. de la classe avait lâché un poltron.* "S.o. in the class let go a furtive fart."

POMME, *f.* **1.** Apple. **Tomber dans les pommes.** *À la vue du sang je suis tombé dans les pommes.* "I fainted at the sight of blood." **Chanter la pomme.** *Que.* To court. *Gil n'est pas le seul à lui chanter la pomme.* "Gil's not the only one courting her." **2. Ma/ta/sa pomme/nos pommes.** Individual (me/you, and so on). *D'abord ma pomme, ensuite vos pommes.* "I look out for number one, then you guys." **3.** Face. *Voici ma foto. J'espère que ma pomme te plaît.* "Here's my photo. I hope you like the kisser." See also (SE) SUCER.

POMPE, *f.* **1.** Shoe. **Être/marcher à côté de ses pompes.** Not to be with it (because one is daydreaming or mentally distraught). *Depuis son divorce il marche à côté des ses pompes.* "He's been beside h.s. since his divorce." See CIRER...POMPES; LÈCHE-POMPES. **2.** Pump. **Le/un coup de pompe.** Drained feeling. *Je crains les coups de pompe.* "I'm afraid of being overcome by attacks of fatigue."

POMPÉ -E. Exhausted. *Après le concours j'étais pompée.* "I was bushed after the competitive exam."

POMPER. 1. To pump. **Pomper l'air; les pomper.** To get on s.o.'s nerves. *Il me pompe l'air en se plaignant*
287

sans cesse. "He bugs me with his constant complaining."
2. To copy; plagiarize. *Pendant l'exam il a pompé sur son voison.* "He copied from his neighbor during the exam."

POMPER LE DARD/GLAND/NŒUD À QN. To fellate. *Je t'offrirai la lune si tu me pompes le gland.* "I'll give you anything you want if you'll suck me off."

POMPETTE. Slightly drunk. *Une coupe de champagne et la voilà pompette.* "She gets tipsy after just one glass of champagne."

POMPIER/POMPLARD, *m.* Fellatio (lit. "fireman"). **Faire/tailler un pompier.** To fellate. *Son maq exige qu'elle lui fasse des pompiers souvent.* "Her pimp insists that she give him head frequently."

PONTE, *m.* Big shot (from *Pontifex Maximus* [Chief Bridge Builder], a title of the Roman emperors and later of the popes). *Ce grand ponte de la cardio a loupé un triple pontage hier.* "That star cardiologist screwed up on a triple bypass yesterday." *Cf.* PONTIFE **1.**

PONTIFE, *m.* **1.** Big shot; pundit (lit. "pontiff [the Pope])." *Il se prend pour un pontife.* "He thinks he's a big shot." **2.** Penis. **Se faire tutoyer le pontife.** To get s.o. to give one a blow job (lit. "to have the Pope/penis addressed in the *tu* (intimate) form"). *Il se fait tutoyer le pontife chaque soir.* "He gets s.o. to blow him every evening." *Cf.* PAPE; PONTE.

PONTONNIÈRE, *f.* Prostitute who works on, under, or near bridges. *La vieille pontonnière est toujours fidèle au poste sur le Pont Neuf.* "The old hooker is always at her post on the Pont Neuf."

POPAUL, *m.* Penis. See EMMENER POPAUL…; MENER POPAUL.

POPOL = POPAUL.

POPOTE, *f.* Cooking. *J'en ai marre de faire la popote.* "I'm sick and tired of doing the cooking." See MARIE-POPOTE.

POPOTIN, *m.* Posterior. **Tortiller du popotin; se trémousser le popotin.** To wiggle one's hips when walking.

Elle les émoustille en tortillant du popotin. "She turns them on when she wiggles her fanny." See (SE) MAGNER LE POPOTIN.

POPULO, *m.* Crowd; riffraff. *Il y avait un des ces populos dans la rue.* "There was quite a mob in the street."

PORTE-COUILLES, *m.* **1.** Husband (lit. "balls carrier"). *Je déteste son porte-couilles.* "I don't like her husband." **2.** Proficient lover. *Elle est dingue de son nouveau porte-couilles.* "She's mad about her latest stud."

PORTÉ SUR LA BAGATELLE/CHOSE. See BAGATELLE; CHOSE.

PORTER LE CHAPEAU. To take the blame. *Les autres se sont sauvés et lui, il a porté le chapeau.* "The others took off and he was left holding the bag."

PORTILLON, *m.* Gate. **Se bousculer au portillon. 1.** To crowd in. *Lors des soldes ça bouscule au portillon.* "During the sales they knock t.s. out getting in." **2.** To fall over one's words. *J'étais très stressée et ça se bousculait au portillon.* "I was very tense and could hardly get my words out."

PORTO/PORTOCHE/PORTOS(S), *adj.* and *n.* Portuguese. *Les portoches foulent toujours les raisins du porto avec les pieds.* "The Portuguese still press the grapes for port wine with their feet."

PORTUGAISE, *f.* Ear (from the shape of oysters called **portugaises**). **Avoir les portugaises ensablées.** To be hard of hearing. *Après le match de boxe il avait les portugaises ensablées.* "After the boxing match he was half deaf."

POSER UN LAPIN À QN. To stand s.o. up. *Il m'a posé un lapin; je ne veux plus le revoir.* "He didn't show up; I don't want to see him again."

(SE) POSER LÀ. To be a prime example of. *Comme tombeur, il se pose là!* "He's one hell of a Don Juan."

POSTILLONER. To spray spittle as one speaks. *Arrête de me postilloner. J'suis pas une plante.* "Stop sprinkling me. I'm not a plant."

POT, *m.* **1.** Cooking pot. See TOURNER…POT. **2.** Drink. *Viens prendre un pot de beaujolpif!* "Come for a spot of Beaujolais!" **3.** Luck. **Avoir du pot.** To be lucky. *Elle n'a jamais eu de pot dans sa vie.* "She never had any luck in life." **4.** Posterior. **Avoir le pot près des talons.** (lit. "to have one's rump close to one's heels"). To be short. *Elle est une perche mais sa sœur a le pot près des talons.* "She's a giant but her sister's ass is very close to the ground." See DÉFONCER LE POT.

POT D'ÉCHAPPEMENT, (lit. "exhaust pipe; muffler") = **POT 4.**

POT-DE-VIN, *m.* Bribe. *Sans pots-de-vin, rien ne se fait.* "You get nowhere if you don't grease some palms."

POTE/POTEAU/POTO, *m., f.* Chum. *"Touche pas à mon pote!", disait le slogan.* " 'Keep your hands off my buddy,' said the slogan."

POUCAVE, *f.,* from Romany. Police informer. *C'était toi la sale poucave?* "Were you the stinking snitch?"

POUCAVE, *invar.* To inform. *Si tu me poucave aux poulets je te bute.* "If you fink on me to the pigs I'll kill you." *Cf.* BALANCER **4**; INDIC.

POUF, *m.* Brothel. *J'ai travaillé dans plusieurs poufs en province avant de monter à Paris.* "I worked in several provincial whorehouses before coming up to Paris."

POUFIASSE, *f.* **1.** Fat, slovenly woman. *J'ai pris quelques kilos mais c'est pas une raison de me traiter de poufiasse.* "I've gained a few pounds but that's no reason to call me a fat slob." **2.** Prostitute; bitch. *Je te plaque. Va baiser ta poufiasse.* "I'm dumping you. Go screw that slut of yours." *Cf.* GROGNASSE, PETASSE.

POUIC = COUIC.

POULAGA/POULARD/POULARDIN/POULMANN = POULET.

POULE, *f.* **1.** Young girl; chick (lit. "hen"). *Comment vas-tu, ma poule?* "How're you doin', my little chickadee?"

2. Prostitute. *À la Madeleine tu trouveras des poules de luxe.* "In the Madeleine district you'll find high-class whores."

POULE MOUILLÉE, *f.* Cowardly person (lit. "wet chicken"). *Ne fais pas la poule mouillée.* "Don't be chicken; a scared rabbit."

POULET, *m.* Policeman (lit. "chicken"). *Les poulets ont fait une descente dans le métro.* "The fuzz raided the subway station."

POULETTE = POULE 1.

POULICHE = POUFFIASSE.

POUPÉE = POULE 1.

POURLÉCHER. To lick one's lips. See BABINES.

POURRAVE. Rotten (from **pourri** with addition of Romany (Gypsy) **–ave**. *C'était total pourrave.* "It was really lousy."

POURRIEL, *m.* Spam, junk e-mail. (A play on pourri, "rotten" and COURRIEL, coined in Que. but appreciated by many elsewhere, even if they continue to say "*du spam*" and "*un mail.*") *L'anti-pourriel pourrait être plus performant.* "The spam blocker could be more effective."

POUSSE-CROTTE, *m.,* homosexual. **1.** Active homosexual; sodomizer (lit. "shit pusher"). *La tapette rêvait d'un pousse-crotte en sirotant son pousse-café.* "The old queen dreamed of a stud while sipping his after-dinner drink." **2.** Sodomy. *Je te ferai une pipe mais je n'aime pas le pousse-crotte.* "I'll blow you but I don't like browning."

POUSSE-MOULIN = CHÂTEAU-LAPOMPE.

POUSSER. To exaggerate. **Faut pas pousser mémé dans les orties!** Lit. "not necessary to shove granny into the nettles." "You don't have to go overboard." See (À LA) VA-COMME…POUSSE.

POUSSER LE BOUCHON (UN PEU/TROP LOIN). See BOUCHON **1.**

POUSSER UN COUP DE GUEULE/UNE GUEULANTE. To yell. *Il va pousser un coup de gueule quand il verra* *le gnion de sa voiture.* "He's gonna let out a holler when he sees the dent in his car."

POUVOIR (TOUJOURS) S'ALIGNER. See (s')ALIGNER **3.**

POUSSIÈRE, *f.* Dust. See ET DES POUSSIÈRES.

PQ = PAPIER-CUL.

PRALINE, *f.* **1.** Bullet; slug (lit. "sugar-coated almond"; "chocolate"). *Il aurait tué davantage mais il n'avait plus de pralines.* "He would have done more killing but he ran out of bullets." **2.** Clitoris. **Avoir la praline en délire.** To be very stimulated sexually. *Un seul baiser et j'avais la praline en délire.* "Just one kiss and I was hit by clitoral electricity."

PRÊCHI-PRÊCHA, *m.* Sermonizing. *Arrête ton prêchi-prêcha.* "Stop your preachifying."

PRÉCIEUSES, *f., pl.* Testicles. *Son zob est à peine visible et ses prècieuses sont ridicules.* "His dick's practically invisible and his family jewels are a joke."

(SE) PRÉLASSER. To lounge about, be lordly (from prélat, "prelate, ecclesiastical dignitary"). *Moi je bosse comme une cinglée et toi tu te prélasses comme un pacha.* "I'm working my head off and you loll about like a pasha."

(DE) PREMIÈRE. First-rate. *C'est un artiste de première.* "She's a top-notch artist."

(EN) PRENDRE DE LA GRAINE. To serve as an example. *Ton dab turbine; il faudrait que tu en prennes de la graine.* "Your dad's a hard worker; you should take a leaf from his book."

PRENDRE DE LA BOUTEILLE/DU BOUCHON/ CARAT. See BOUTEILLE.

PRENDRE DE L'AIR = CHANGER D'AIR.

PRENDRE DU CHOUETTE, *homosexual.* To sodomize. *Il prend souvent du chouette et se balade avec lubrifiant et présos.* "He has sex with lots of guys and walks around with a lubricant and rubbers."

PRENDRE DU GALON. To move up in the world (lit. "to get a military promotion"). *Depuis qu'elle a pris du galon elle ne se prend pas pour une petite merde.* "Ever since she's moved up in the world she thinks she's hot shit."

PRENDRE LA TÊTE (EN RAPPEL) À QN. To exasperate. *Et le prof et ses cours me prennent la tête.* "That teacher and his courses drive me nuts."

PRENDRE LE CAFÉ DU PAUVRE. To have sex (lit. "to have the poor man's coffee." Real coffee was scarce during wartime; sex was not). *On se console de toutes les tuiles en prenant le café du pauvre.* "We make up for all our hard luck by creating our own entertainment."

PRENDRE LE LARGE. To beat it (lit. "to head for the open sea"). *Trop de fumée ici; prenons le large!* "Too smoky here; let's blow this hole!"

PRENDRE LE THÉ. To be a sodomite; have anal sex (lit. "to have tea"). *Pendant la partouze à la bague on a tous pris le thé.* "During the daisy chain orgy we all buggered each other."

PRENDRE QCH. EN PLEINE GUEULE/SUR LE COIN DE LA GUEULE. To get hit in the face with s.t. *J'ai pris son parapluie en pleine gueule.* "His umbrella hit me right in the kisser."

PRENDRE SA PAUME. To sell securities at a loss. *Je savais que tu allais prendre ta paume avec ces titres.* "I knew you were going to take a beating on those stocks."

PRENDRE SON PANARD/PIED. 1. To experience orgasm. *Avec mon dernier jules je prenais mon pied à chaque fois.* "Every time I got it on with my last boyfriend, the earth moved." **2.** To experience pleasure. *Bill prend son pied en jouant du saxo.* "Bill gets off on saxophone playing."

PRENDRE UN COUP DE VIEUX. To age noticeably. *Il a pris un sacré coup de vieux, mais joue toujours les jeunes premiers.* "He's showing his age but still playing romantic leads."

PRENDRE UNE ARDOISE À L'EAU = MOUILLER UNE ARDOISE.

PRENDRE UNE CAISSE/CUITE. To get drunk. *Il s'est pris une bonne cuite ce week-end.* "He got thoroughly soused this weekend."

PRENDRE UNE CLAQUE. To suffer severe damages/ losses. *Il a pris une claque magistrale aux elections.* "He was soundly beaten in the elections."

PRENDRE UNE PIQUETTE. See PIQUETTE 2.

PRENDRE UNE RUE EN LEVRETTE. To use a one-way street illegally (lit. "to go in from the back"). *Si je prends une rue en levrette, j'aurai une contredanse salée.* "If I go the wrong way on a one-way street I'll get a stiff fine." See (EN) LEVRETTE.

PRENDRE UN GADIN/UNE BÛCHE/GAMELLE/ GAUFRE/PELLE. See RAMASSER…PELLE.

PRENDRE UN JETON (DE MATE). To see a sex show. *On a pris un jeton de mate de première.* "We saw a terrific sex show."

PRENDRE UN POT/VERRE. See POT 2; VERRE.

(SE) PRENDRE LA LOUCHE. To be self-important. *Depuis qu'il a gagné cette médaille, il se prend la louche.* "Ever since winning that medal, he's been swell-headed."

(SE) PRENDRE UNE BARRE. To split one's sides laughing. *On s'est pris une barre quand il a mimé le patron.* "We died laughing when he imitated the boss."

(SE) PRENDRE UNE (PEAU DE) BANANE. See BANANE 1.

PRÉSO, *m.* from **préservatif.** Condom. *Elle lui achète des présos de haute qualité.* "She buys high-quality rubbers for him."

PRIMO. Firstly. *Primo ça ne me plaît pas; deuxio je n'ai pas le temps.* "First of all I don't like it; second of all, I haven't the time."

PRINCESSE, *f.* Princess. **Aux frais de la princesse.** At s.o. else's expense. *Sa voiture est aux frais de la princesse.*

"His car is paid for by the company." *Le restaurateur déclarait que le gâteau d'anniversaire était aux frais de la princesse.* "The restaurant owner announced that the birthday cake was on the house."

PRISE, *f.* race track. High, last-minute bet. *La prise était une grosse perte et il s'est consolé avec une prise de cocaïne.* "The bet was no good and he consoled himself with a snort of coke."

PRISE DE BEC, *f.* Run-in. *On a eu une prise de bec avec le proprio.* "We had a row with the landlord."

PRIX D'ATTAQUE, *m.* Lowest price. See ATTAQUE **2.**

PROBLOC/PROBLOQUE = PROPRIO.

PROPRIO, *m., f., abbr.* of **propriétaire.** Proprietor; landlord; landlady. *La proprio nous a fait des facilités de paiement.* "The landlady arranged payment terms for us."

PROUT, *m.* Fart. *Ces flageolets me donnent des prouts.* "Those beans give me gas."

PROUT-PROUT!/PROUT-PROUT, MA CHÈRE!, homosexual. "Get you, Mary!" "My, you're such a lady!"

PROXÉMAC = PROXÉNÈTE/PROXO.

PROXO, *abbr.* of **proxénète.** Procurer. *Ce proxo fait travailler trois putes.* "That pimp has three hustlers working for him."

PRUNES, *f., pl.* Plums. **Des prunes!** "Not on your life!" "No way!" **Pour des prunes.** For nothing; practically nothing. *Je ne travaille pas pour des prunes.* "I don't work for peanuts."

PSY, *m., f. abbr.* of **psychonalyste.** Psychoanalyst. *Ça coûte cher, les psys.* "Psychiatrists are expensive."

PSY, *abbr.* of **psychiatrique.** Crazy. *Sa mère est un peu psy sur les bords.* "Her mother's a bit whacko."

PUCE, *f.* Flea; computer chip. See SAC À PUCES.

PUCIER = SAC À PUCES 1.

PUISSANT. Marvelous. *Puissant, ton blouson!* "Your jacket's stunning!"

PUNAISE, *f.* Thumbtack; insect; nasty woman. **Punaise de sacristie,** *pej.* Church lady (lit. "sacristy bug"). *Ce cureton lubrique a collé des morpions à la punaise de sacristie.* "That lascivious little priest gave the church lady crabs (pubic lice)." *Cf.* GRENOUILLE DE BÉNITIER; PILIER DE CATHÉDRALE.

PUNAISE! Damn it! (Euph. for **putain**). *Punaise! Elle m'a laissé une vaisselle dégueu.* "Damn it. She left me a pile of dirty dishes."

PURÉE! "For heaven's sake!"

PUTAIN, *adj.* Sycophantic. *Il est assez putain pour accepter ta proposition.* "He's enough of an ass-kisser to accept your proposition."

PUTAIN, *f.* Prostitute. *Cette rue grouille de putains.* "This street is swarming with hustlers."

PUTAIN! Damn it!

PUTAIN DE…! Filthy rotten! *Ralbol cette putain de pluie!* "I'm fed up with this goddamned rain!"

PUTAIN (DE BONDIEU) DE BORDEL (DE MERDE)! Holy fucking shit! *Putain de bordel—arrêtez vos conneries et foutez-moi le camp!* "Damn you all to hell—cut the crap and get the fuck out of here!"

PUTAIN DE MERDE! "God damn it!"

PUTASSE, *f.* Cheap whore. *Il m'a traité de putasse.* "He called me a low whore."

PUTASSIER = PUTAIN. *(adj.)*

PUTE = PUTAIN. *(adj. and n.)*

PV, *abbr.* of **procès-verbal.** Traffic ticket; fine. *Non seulement ils m'ont filé un PV, mais ils m'ont retiré mon permis.* "They didn't just give me a ticket; they took away my driver's license too."

(AU) QUART DE TOUR, *m.* At a quarter turn. **Comprendre/piger/biter au quart to tour.** To be quick on the uptake. *Elle a compris au quart de tour que c'était de la blague.* "She caught on right away that it was a joke." **Démarrer/partir au quart de tour.** To start right away. *La voiture a démarré au quart de tour.* "The car started right away."

QUARTIER CHAUD, *m.* Red-light district. *Il est chaud lapin et fréquente le quartier chaud.* "He's a horny guy and hangs out in the red-light district."

QUATRE-VINGT-HUIT, *m.* Kiss (lit. "88"). *Et pour moi un petit 88, vite fait, avant de prendre la route!* "And a nice little kiss for me before I get under way!" *Cf.* HUIT.

QUE COUIC = QUE DALLE.

QUE DAL(L)E. Nothing at all. *Ce problème de maths, je n'y pige que dalle.* "I understand zilch about that problem in math."

QUELLE CHIASSE! What a filthy mess!

QUELLE CHIERIE! What a bummer!

QUELQUE PART. Somewhere. **Aller quelque part,** *euph.* To go to the toilet. *Il faut que j'aile quelque part.* "I've got to wash my hands." **Se foutre/mettre qch. quelque part.** To stick s.t. you know where. *Ton cadeau, tu peux te le foutre quelque part.* "You can take your present and shove it."

QUENOTTES, *f., pl.* Teeth. *Elle a de belles quenottes.* "She has beautiful teeth."

QUÉQUETTE. Penis. *Les gosses s'amusaient à se montrer leurs quéquettes.* "The kids fooled around showing their peckers to each other."

QU'ES-ACO/QUÈS ACO? What on earth is that? *Tu me lâches pour ce p'tit con—qu'es-aco?* "You're leaving me for that jerk—what the hell's going on?"

QUÈS, *m.* Same. *C'est du quès.* "It's six of one, half a dozen of the other."

QUÉTAINE, *Que.* = KÉTAINE.

QUEUDE = QUE DALLE.

QUEUE, *f.* Penis (lit. "tail"). *"Con de Manon! Queue de des Grieux!," c'est un de ses jurons préférés.* "'Manon's cunt! Des Grieux's dick!'" That's one of his favorite cuss words." (Ref. to characters in the Abbé Prévost's novel *Manon Lescaut.*) See COUP DE QUEUE.

QUEUNER = QUEUTER.

QUEUTARD, -E, *m., f.* Person always out for sex. *C'est un queutard de première.* "He's a real sex fiend."

QUEUTER. 1. To fail. *Elle a queuté à son exam de conduite.* "She flunked her driving test." 2. To copulate. *Les soldats nous ont queutées nuit et jour.* "The soldiers ravished us night and day."

QUINCAILLE, *m.* Parisian outdoor bookseller who also offers cheap souvenirs. *Le quincaille du pont vend des tours Eiffel dorées.* "The bookseller by the bridge also sells gilded Eiffel Towers."

QUINCAILLERIE, *f.* 1. Computer hardware (lit. "hardware store"). *La quinquaillerie sur catalogue coûte moins cher.* "Hardware is cheaper by catalog." 2. Military decorations; cheap jewelry. *Au repas de famille les grand-dabes avaient sorti toute leur quincaillerie.* "At the family dinner, Grandpa and Grandma got out their military decorations and junk jewelry."

QUINQUETS, *m., pl.* Eyes (lit. "oil lamps") *Garde-les bien ouverts, tes quinquets!* "Keep your peepers peeled!"

QUIQUE/QUIQUETTE = QUÉQUETTE.

QUIQUI = KIKI 2.

R.A.B. See BRANLER **1.**

RAB, *m.* Second helping. *Oliver Twist réclamait du rab.* "Oliver Twist asked for more." **Faire du rab.** To work overtime. *Le patron nous a fait faire du rab.* "The boss made us work overtime."

(SE) RABIBOCHER. To reconcile. *Après six mois de séparation, ils se sont rabibochés.* "After a six-months separation, they kissed and made up."

RABIOT = RAB.

RABIOTER. To scrounge; wangle. *Il cherche toujours à rabioter qch.* "He's always trying to get s.t. extra on the side."

RABZA/RABZOUS = REUBEU

RACLÉE, *f.* Beating. *Le parti a pris une de ses raclées.* "The party was soundly defeated." See FILER UNE RACLÉE; FLANQUER UNE RACLÉE; FOUTRE UNE RACLÉE.

RACLI, *f.* Girl (from a Gypsy dialect). *Cette racli m'a ensorcelé.* "That chick's cast a spell on me."

RACLURE, *f.* Despicable person (lit. "scraping," as in s.t. you'd scrape up). *Pas la peine de me parler de cette raclure.* "No point talking to me about that sleazebag/ scuzzball."

RADADA, *m.* Posterior. **Aller au radada.** To have sex; a piece of ass. *Lili voulait aller au radada, mais Lulu venait de me pomper.* "Lily wanted us to make it, but I'd already given my all to Lulu." See RONDIBÉ.

300

RADAR, *m.* Radar. **Marcher au radar.** To function mechanically. *J'ai la gueule de bois et marche au radar.* "I've got a hangover and I'm walking around in a fog."

RADINER/SE RADINER. To show up fast. *Radine-toi, sinon je pars seul.* "Get over here fast or I'll leave without you."

RADIS, *m.* Cent (lit. "radish"). *Je suis partie sans un radis sur moi.* "I left without a cent in my pocket."

RAFFUT, *m.* Noise. **Faire du raffut.** To cause a commotion. *Ses révélations ont fait un de ces raffuts!* "Her revelations really made waves!"

RAGNAGNAS, *m., pl.* Menstrual period. *Elle a ses ragnagnas.* "She's got the rag on."

RAIDE. 1. Erect (lit. "stiff"). *Dès qu'elle s'approche de lui, il l'a raide.* "He gets a hard-on the minute she comes near him." **2.** Penniless. *Elle est toujours raide en fin de mois.* "She's always broke at the end of the month." **3.** Incredible. *Ses histoires sont un peu raides.* "His stories are a bit hard to swallow." **4.** Drunk. See RAIDE/RAIDE DEF/MORT.

RAIDE MORT. Stone-cold dead. *On les a trouvées raides mortes.* "They found them dead as a doornail."

RAIDE/RAIDE DEF/MORT. Dead drunk; drugged. *Ils était raides après le troisième sérieux.* "They were dead drunk after the third mug of beer."

RAISIN, *m.* Blood (lit. "grape"). See (SE) CAILLER LE RAISIN.

RALBOL, *m.* Exasperation. *Quel ralbol, cette grève des transports!* "What a crock of shit, this transportation (train/bus/air) strike!" *Cf.* RAS-LE-BOL.

RAMASSER LES BALAIS. To come in last in a race; fail. *J'ai ramassé les balais à cause d'une crampe.* "I came in last because of a cramp." *Cf.* VOITURE-BALAI.

RAMASSER UNE PIQUETTE. See PIQUETTE **2.**

RAMASSER UN GADIN/UNE BÛCHE/GAMELLE/ GAUFRE/PELLE. To fall down/fall flat on one's face.

Le même jour, j'ai ramassé un gadin dans le métro et une pelle au boulot. "On the same day, I had a fall in the subway and got egg on my face at work."

(SE) RAMASSER. To fall down (lit. "to pick o.s. up"). *Le premier de la classe s'est ramassé au concours.* "The star student fell flat on his face at the competitive exam."

RAMBOUR = RENCARD.

RAMDAM = RAFFUT.

RAME/RAMÉE, *f.* Oar. **Ne pas en ficher/foutre une rame.** Not to do a damned thing. *Dès que j'ai le dos tourné, ils n'en foutent pas une rame.* "As soon as my back is turned, they all goof off."

RAMENER SA FRAISE/POIRE. 1. To show up. See (SE) RAMENER. **2.** To put an oar in. *Il faut toujours qu'il ramène sa fraise.* "He always has to put in his two cents worth."

(SE) RAMENER. To show up. *On ne sait quand elle se ramènera.* "We don't know when she'll put in an appearance."

RAMER. To work hard (lit. "to row"). *Ça fait longtemps que nous ramons.* "We've been working away for months."

RAMEUX, -EUSE, *m., f.* Subway musician. *J'ai toujours de la monnaie pour les rameux.* "I always have a few coins for the music makers in the subway."

RAMONER (LA CHEMINÉE D') UNE FEMME. To have a woman sexually (lit. "to sweep a woman's fireplace/chimney"). *Son mari ferait bien de la ramoner plus souvent.* "Her husband ought to screw her more often."

RANCARD = RENCARD.

RANCART, *m.* Scrap. **Mettre au rancart.** To junk. *Il pense que nous sommes bons à mettre au rancart.* "He thinks we're ready for the glue factory."

RAOUSSE! "Get going!" "Get out!" (from Ger. **raus,** "out!").

RÂPÉ. Shredded. *C'est râpé!* "It's curtains!" "It's all over!"

RAPIDO/RAPIDOS. Very fast. *Il s'est taillé rapidos.* "He cleared out in a hurry."

RAPLAPLA(T). Exhausted. *Après le jogging elle était raplaplat.* "She was bushed after jogging."

RAPPER. To perform or dance to rap music. *Ils rappent mieux qu'ils ne chantent.* "They rap better than they sing."

RAPPEUR, -EUSE, *m., f.* Rap musician. *C'est devenu une mode pour les rappeurs d'employer le passé simple.* "It's become an in-thing for rappers to use the past definite tense."

RAQUER. To pay up. *Pour ne pas raquer, il est sorti avant qu'on présente la note.* "So as to not have to shell out (his share), he left before the check arrived."

RAS. Close-cropped; short. **En avoir ras le bol/cul/pot/la cale/caisse/patate/les couilles.** See BOL **3.**

RASE-BITE/RASE-BITUME, *m., f.* Short person (lit. "scrape pavement"). *Il est maigrichon et rase-bitume.* "He's a skinny half-pint."

RASER. To bore (lit. "to shave"). *Le cours de ce prof m'a rasée.* "That professor's course bored me stiff."

(SE) RASER (À CENT SOUS DE L'HEURE). To be bored to death. *Quand je vais chez eux je me rase à cent sous de l'heure.* "When I visit them I'm bored to death."

RASIBUS. Very short. *On s'est sauvé rasibus!* "We escaped just in the nick of time."

RAS-LE-BOL = RALBOL.

RAS LE BONBON/CRESSON/PÉTARD/PÈTE/LA TOUFFE. At pubic/pelvic level. *Les arpenteuses se fringuent ras le bonbon.* "Streetwalkers wear the miniest of skirts."

RASOIR. Boring. *Le film ce soir est rasoir au possible.* "Tonight's movie is excruciatingly boring."

RATE or **RATTE,** *f.* Hip chick; amoral slut (lit. "female rat"). *Cette rate chaude nous a tous allumés.* "That hot chick turned us all on."

RATÉ, -E, *m., f.* Failure. *Tu ne penses pas épouser ce raté?* "You're not thinking of marrying that deadbeat are you?"

RÂTELIER, *m.* **1.** Hayrack; trough. See MANGER…RÂTELIERS. **2.** False teeth. *Son râtelier a coûté bonbon mais il ne s'en sert pas.* "His dentures were expensive, but he doesn't use them."

RATER. To fail. **Ne pas en rater une.** To never fail to make a mistake. *Ce mec n'en rate pas une.* "That guy always puts his foot in it."

RATIBOISER. To clean out. *Il a été ratiboisé aux cartes.* "He was wiped out at cards." **Se faire ratiboiser (la colline).** To get scalped. *Il s'est fait ratiboiser.* "He got a baldie haircut."

RAYER LE CASQUE. To bite while fellating (lit. "to scratch the helmet"). *Elle te fera un pompier sans rayer le casque.* "She'll blow you without biting."

REBELOTE! Here we go again! *Et rebelote—j'ai encore oublié mes clefs!* "Just like me—I've forgotten my keys again!"

REBEU or **REUBEU,** backslang of **BEUR,** i.s. backslang of **arabe.**

RECHARGER LES ACCUS. To recharge one's batteries. See ACCUS.

RÉCHAUFFÉ. Reheated. **C'est du réchauffé.** "That's old news."

RECTIFIER. To kill (lit. "to correct"). *Il s'est fait rectifier par la pègre.* "He got sanctioned/bumped off by the mob."

REFILER DE LA BAGOUSE. See BAGOUSE **2.**

REFILER DE LA JAQUETTE. See JAQUETTE.

REFILER LE BÉBÉ À QN. To pass the buck (lit. "the baby"). *Il a foutu le camp en refilant le bébé à son pote.* "He beat it and left his buddy holding the bag."

REFILER UNE AVOINE. See AVOINE.

REGARDER LA FEUILLE À L'ENVERS. See FEUILLE.

REGARDER QN. AVEC DES YEUX DE MERLAN FRIT/DE CRAPAUD MORT D'AMOUR. To look at s.o. with lovesick eyes (lit. "with the eyes of a fried whiting [fish]/a toad that died of love"). *Ça me fait rire quand tu me regardes avec des yeux de merlan frit.* "I laugh when you look at me like a lovesick dog."

RÉGLO. Honest. *Confie-lui ce boulot; c'est un type réglo.* "Let him do the job; he's a regular guy."

RÉGULIER/RÉGULE = RÉGLO.

RÉGULIÈRE, *f.* Wife; steady girlfriend. *Aujourd'hui, il s'affiche avec sa régulière.* "Today he's out in public with his missus/mistress."

RELIGIEUSES, *pl.,* Testicles (lit. "nuns"). *Les pipeuses accomplies s'occupent pas seulement de Jésus mais aussi des religieuses.* "Accomplished cocksuckers don't just concentrate on Penis-Jesus but also on the sacred sisters." *Cf.* BURNES; CRÈCHE **2**; JÉSUS **2**; PONTIFE **2**; ROUBIGNOLLES; SERVICES TROIS PIÈCES.

RELUQUER. To observe. *As-tu fini de reluquer mes nichons?* "Have you finished staring at my breasts?"

REMBALLER SES OUTILS. To put one's pants on again (lit. "to rewrap one's tools"). *Vite fait, bien fait, il a remballé ses outils.* "In practically no time he hitched up his trousers again."

REMÈDE, *m.* Remedy. **Remède de cheval.** Drastic remedy. *L'entreprise a besoin d'un remède de cheval.* "The company needs a drastic overhaul." **Remède de bonne femme.** Old wives' cure. *Faut pas les mépriser les remèdes de bonne femme.* "You shouldn't look down on folk medicine."

REMPAS, *pl.* Backslang of "parents." *Ramper devant mes rempas? Jamais!* "Grovel before my parents? Never!" *Cf.* DARONS; REMPAS; VIOQUES.

REMPILER. To start; do over (lit. "to reenlist"). *Il a dû rempiler un an au bahut.* "He had to repeat a school year."

(SE) REMPLUMER. To recover health or finances. *Elle s'est remplumée en touchant l'héritage.* "Her finances improved when she came into the inheritance."

REMUER LES PINCETTES. See PINCETTES 2.

RENAUDER. To complain. *Cesse de renauder!* "Quit grousing!"

RENCARD, *m.* Date. *J'ai un rencard avec cette nana.* "I've got a date with that gal."

RENCARDER. To make a date. *Il m'a rencardée pour vingt heures au resto.* "He made a date with me for eight o'clock in the restaurant."

(SE) RENCARDER. To get information. *Tu peux me rencarder sur ce type?* "Can you give me the lowdown on that guy?"

RENCART = RANCART.

RENDÈVE, *m.,* from **rendez-vous.** *J'ai un rendève chez le dentiste.* "I've got a dental appointment."

RENIFLE. *f.* Cocaine; the police (from **renifler,** "to sniff"). *La renifle, surtout les stups, est en quête de renifle.* "The police, especially narcs, look for coke."

RENIFLETTE = RENIFLE.

RENOI, *m., f.,* backslang of **noir.** Black person. *Peu de renois assistaient à la conférence sur la négritude.* "Few blacks were present at the lecture on negritude." *Cf.* KARLOUCHE.

RENTRE-DEDANS, *m.* Heated confrontation (lit. "hand-to-hand combat"). *Hier au Sénat il y a eu du rentre-dedans.* "They went at it hot and heavy in the Senate yesterday." **Faire du rentre-dedans.** To make amorous advances. *Il m'a fait du rentre-dedans, mais je l'ai envoyé balader.* "He tried to get it on with me but I sent him packing."

RENTRER (AVEC) LA BITE/PINE SOUS LE BRAS. To not score with s.o. (lit. "to come back with one's dick under one's arm"). *Je me suis décarcassé pour coucher* *avec elle, mais je suis rentré la pine sous le bras.* "I knocked m.s. out trying to make her, but I didn't score."

RENTRER DEDANS. To beat to a pulp. *Je n'avais qu'une envie, c'était de lui rentrer dedans.* "All I wanted to do was knock his block off."

RENTRER DANS LE CHOU/LARD/MOU = RENTRER DEDANS.

REPOUTZÉ. Dressed-up (Swiss, from Ger. **putzen,** "to clean"). *Ce petit dandy est toujours endimanché, repoutzé, tiré à quatre épingles.* "That little dandy's always in his Sunday best, all spruced up, all dressed up."

RESTAU = RESTO.

(EN) RESTER BABA. See BABA, *adj.*

(EN) RESTER COMME DEUX RONDS DE FLAN. To be left speechless. *Pour une fois il était à l'heure; j'en suis resté comme deux ronds de flan.* "He was on time for once; I was dumbfounded."

(EN) RESTER SUR LE CUL. To be extremely astonished. *Quand j'ai appris qu'il avait violé sa fille, j'en suis restée sur le cul.* "When I learned he'd raped his daughter, it floored me."

RESTER EN CARAFE. To be left to wait. *Je suis resté en carafe à son rendève.* "I had a date with him but he stood me up."

RESTER LE BEC DANS L'EAU. To be left in the lurch. *Il m'a joué rip et je suis restée le bec dans l'eau.* "He ran off and I was left high and dry."

RESTIF = RESTO.

RESTO, *m.* Restaurant. *C'est une rue pleine de restos sympas.* "It's a street with many appealing restaurants."

RÉTAMER. To smash up. *Lui et sa voiture étaient rétamés après l'accident.* "He and his car were smashed up after the accident."

(SE) RÉTAMER. To get drunk. *Il se rétame à chaque fête.* "He gets smashed at every party."

RETAPE, *f.* Soliciting. **Faire de la retape.** To be a prostitute. *La veuve s'est mise à faire de la retape.* "The widow started hustling." **Faire de la retape pour.** To beat the drums for. *Il fait de la retape pour vendre sa camelote.* "To sell his junk he has to give it the hard sell."

RETOURNER QN. COMME UNE CRÊPE/UNE VIELLE CHAUSSETTE. To wind s.o. around one's little finger. *Sa nana sait le retourner comme une vieille chaussette.* "His woman can get him to do whatever she wants."

(SE) RETROUVER LE BEC DANS L'EAU = RESTER LE BEC DANS L'EAU.

REUCH, *youth,* backslang of **cher.** Expensive. *C'est pas reuch.* "It's not expensive."

REUF, REUM, REUP, REUS, *youth, cités,* backslang of "brother," "mother," "father," "sister." See MIFA.

REUS, *pl., youth, cités.* Euros. *File-moi 10 reus.* "Gimme 10 euros."

RICAIN, -E, *pej.* American. *Elle a surtout une clientèle de ricains.* "Most of her clients are Americans."

RIC-RAC/RIC ET RAC/RIC À RAC. 1. Precisely. *Sa facture est toujours ric-rac.* "His bill is always calculated down to the last detail/penny." **2.** Barely. *Elle a réussi à son exam, mais c'était ric-rac.* "She barely squeezed through on her exam."

RIFIFI, *m.* Fisticuffs. *Quel rififi quand les mecs se disputaient le cache-frifri de la strip-teaseuse Fifi la Fantastique!* "What a free-for-all when the guys brawled for stripper Fantastic Fifi's G-string!"

RIFLARD, *m.* Umbrella. *Ce riflard est riquiqui pour nous deux.* "This umbrella's too small for the two of us."

RIGOLADE, *f.* Fun. **C'est de la rigolade! 1.** That's as easy as pie! **2.** That's a lot of hogwash! See BOYAU.

RIGOLBOCHE = RIGOLO.

RIGOLER. 1. To laugh. *Ça me fait rigoler.* "That makes me laugh." **2.** To kid (around). *Mais tu rigoles!* "You must be joking!"

RIGOLO, -TE, *m., f.* **1.** Amusing person. *Elle est rigolote en travesti.* "She's a scream dressed like a man." **2.** Unreliable individual. *On ne peut pas se fier à ce rigolo.* "There's no trusting that jokester."

RIKIKI. Ridiculously small; measly. *Ta chemise fait rikiki.* "Your shirt looks undersized."

(SE) RINCER LA DALLE/LES AMYGDALES. To wet one's whistle. *J'ai une de ces envies de me rincer la dalle!* "Boy do I need a drink!"

(SE) RINCER L'ŒIL. To take a long/good look. *Il se rinçait l'œil quand elle se déshabillait.* "He got an eyeful when she undressed."

RINGARD, -E. Dated; corny. *Costumes et mise en scène étaient totalement ringards.* "The costumes and staging were definitely behind the times."

RINGARD, -E, *m., f.* **1.** Second-rate actor; has-been. *On me traite de ringard, mais j'ai toujours de l'espoir.* "They call me a has-been, but I still have hopes." **2.** Nonentity; fuddy-duddy. *Ce banquet était une réunion de ringards.* "That banquet was a convention of squares."

RIPA, backslang of **Paris.** *Quand irons-nous à Ripa?* "When are we going to Paris?" *Cf.* PANAME; PANTRUCHE.

RIPATON, *m.* Foot. *J'ai mal aux ripatons.* "My feet hurt."

RIPER. To scram. *Ils ont tous ripé à l'arrivée des flics.* "They all beat it when the cops arrived."

RIPOU. Crook; crooked cop. Backslang of **pourri.** *Il n'est pas le seul ripou du commissariat.* "He's not the only cop on the take at that station." *Cf.* BŒUF CAROTTES.

RITAL, -E, *m., f., pej.* Italian. *Ces ritals ne s'arrêtent pas de chanter.* "Those wops never stop singing."

ROBERTS, *m., pl.* Breasts (from the name of a manufacturer of baby bottles). *L'artiste aime peindre et sculpter*
309

les roberts de ses modèles. "The artist likes to paint and sculpt his models' breasts."

ROGNE, *f.* Anger. **Se foutre/mettre en rogne.** To hit the ceiling. *Il se met en rogne dès que je lui parle de fric.* "He blows his top every time I talk about money."

ROGNER LES AILES DE QN. To clip s.o.'s wings. *Il est temps de rogner les ailes de ce phallo.* "It's time to take that male chauvinist pig down a peg or two."

ROMBIÈRE, *f.* Old lady. *Cette une drôle de (vieille) rombière!* "She's a strange old bag."

ROND, RONDE. 1. Round. See TOURNER EN ROND; TOURNER ROND. **2.** Drunk. See ROND COMME UNE BARRIQUE.

ROND, *m.* **1.** Cent. **Avoir des ronds.** To be very rich. *Mes vioques ont des ronds; moi je n'ai pas un sou.* "My parents are loaded but I haven't got a red cent." **2.** Anus. *Il a le rond irrité.* "His ass is sore."

ROND COMME UNE BARRIQUE. To be rolling drunk (lit. "drunk as a barrel"). *Quand il sort du chai il est rond comme une barrique.* "When he leaves the wine storehouse he's high as a kite."

ROND COMME UNE BOULE/BILLE/QUEUE DE BILLARD = ROND COMME UNE BARRIQUE.

ROND DE FLAN. See (EN) RESTER...FLAN.

ROND DE JAMBE, *m.* Circular leg movement in ballet. **Faire des ronds de jambe.** To be excessively polite. *L'épicier du coin me fait des ronds de jambe pour que j'achète chez lui.* "The local grocer's sugar-sweet to me to get me to buy from him."

RONDELLE, *f.* Anus. See CASSER/DÉFONCER...RONDELLE; (SE) MAGNER LA RONDELLE.

RONDIBÉ (DU RADADA). Anus. **Espèce de rondibé du radada!** "You dumb asshole!"

RONDS DE CHAPEAU. See (EN) BAVER DES RONDS DE CHAPEAU.

ROPLOPLOS, *m., pl.* Breasts. *Avec de tels roploplos elle fera carrière.* "With jugs like that, her career is assured."

RORO, *m.* **1.** Gold (reduplicated backslang of **or**). *Tu l'aimes ma gourmette en roro?* "Do you like my gold chain bracelet?" **2.** Euro. *Ça m'a coûté 20 roros.* "That cost me 20 euros." *Cf.* REUS.

ROSE, *f.* Rose. **Ça sent la rose!,** ironic. "What a stench!" **Envoyer qn. sur les roses.** To tell s.o. where to get off. *Je l'ai envoyé sur les roses quand il m'a demandé des ronds.* "I told him where to go when he asked me for money."

ROSE DES VENTS, *f.,* homosexual. Anus (lit. "wind rose"). *Ta rose des vents doit être épuisée après tant de mecs.* "Your rosebud must be exhausted after so many guys."

ROSETTE, *f.* **1.** Rosette. **Avoir la rosette (de la Légion d'honneur).** To be an officer of the Legion of Honor. *Mon mari aura bientôt la rosette.* "My husband will soon be named an officer of the Legion of Honor." **2.** Anus. **Amateur de rosette; chevalier de la rosette.** Active homosexual (sodomizer). *La tapette rêvait de trouver un chevalier de la rosette.* "The fag dreamed of finding a knight to ride his rosebud."

ROSETTE DE LYON, *f.* Salami sausage. *La rosette de Lyon, quel délice!* "Lyon salami, how delicious!"

ROTOPLOS/ROTOTOS = ROPLOPLOS.

ROTULES, *f., pl.* Kneecaps. **Sur les rotules.** Exhausted. *La course de V.T.T. m'a mis sur les rotules.* "The mountain bike race really knocked me out."

ROUBIGNOLLES, *m., pl.* Testicles. *Ses roubignolles exècrent l'eau froide.* "His balls loathe cold water."

ROUGE. Red wine. *Buvons un coup de ce gros rouge qui tache.* "Let's light into this rough-and-ready red wine."

ROULÉ, -E, *m., f.* Well-built person. *J'aime les filles bien roulées.* "I like girls who are really stacked."

ROULER LA CAISSE/LES BISCOTOS/ MÉCANIQUES. To swagger. *Il aime les rouler, les mécaniques, devant les belles.* "He likes to strut his stuff in front of pretty girls."

ROULER SUR L'OR. To be very rich. *Ils ne roulent pas sur l'or mais ils ne manquent de rien.* "They haven't got money to burn, but they don't have to do without."

ROULER UN PALOT/PANTIN/SUSHI/UNE ESCALOPE/GALOCHE/PELLE. To tongue-kiss (lit. "to roll a spade/skate/sushi/cutlet/clog/shovel"). *Il m'a roulé une pelle en me tripotant.* "He French-kissed me as he felt me up." *Cf.* FRENCHER; GUÉLAN.

(SE) ROULER PAR TERRE. To laugh uproariously. *Ses histoires sont à se rouler par terre.* "Her stories are side-splittingly funny."

ROULURE, *f.* Slut. *Tu peux la sauter facilement; c'est une roulure.* "You can screw her easily; she's a tramp."

ROUPETTES = ROUBIGNOLLES.

ROUPILLER. To snooze. *Il roupille devant la télé.* "He nods off in front of the TV."

ROUPILLON, *m.* Nap. *Je piquerais bien un petit roupillon.* "I'd like to get a little shut-eye."

ROUSCAILLE = ROUSPÉTANCE.

ROUSCAILLER = ROUSPÉTER.

ROUSPÉTANCE, *f.* Complaining. *Retournez au boulot; pas de rouspétance!* "Get back to work; no bellyaching!"

ROUSPÉTER. To complain. *Dans ce resto il faut toujours rouspéter pour être bien servi.* "You always have to bitch to get good service in that restaurant."

ROUSTE/ROUSTÉE, *f.* Beating. *Tu l'auras, la roustée, si tu me casses ma bagnole.* "I'll knock your block off if you mess up my car."

ROUSTONS, *m., pl.* Testicles. *Il a reçu le ballon dans les roustons.* "The football hit him in the balls."

RUCHE, *f.* Nose (lit. "beehive"). **Se péter/se piquer la ruche.** To tipple. *On aime bien se piquer la ruche au vin.* "We like tying one on with wine."

RUP. High-class. *Cherchons un hôtel moins rup.* "Let's look for a less posh hotel."

RUPIN, -E = RUP.

RUPIN, *m., pej.* Very rich person; moneybags. *C'est un resto pour rupins.* "That's a ritzy restaurant."

RUSSCOF/RUSSKOFF/RUSSKI, *adj.* and *n.* Russian. *Si l'on allait bouffer ce soir chez les Russkoffs?* "How about eating in a Russian restaurant tonight?"

SABIR, *m.* Mumbo-jumbo; pidgin (a mixture of Fr., Sp., Ital. and Ar. From Sp. **saber,** "to know"). *Qui peut piger son sabir?* "Who can understand his gibberish?"

SABOT, *m.* Wooden shoe. See VENIR.

SABRE, *m.* Penis. **Filer un coup de sabre** (lit. "to make a saber thrust"). To copulate. *L'officier a eu juste le temps de lui filer un coup de sabre.* "The officer had just enough time to plug her."

SABRER. To fuck (lit. "to cut down with a sword"). *Le lieute était trop paf pour me sabrer.* "The lieutenant was too stewed to screw me."

SABRER LE CHAMPAGNE. To crack open a bottle of champagne (orig. by using a sword or knife). *Elle est toujours prête à sabrer le champagne.* "She's always ready to crack open a bottle of champagne."

SAC, *m.* Bag. **Vider son sac.** To confess; own up to (lit. "to empty one's bag"). *Vide enfin ton sac.* "Come on, spit it out now." See FAIRE UN SAC.

SAC À BITES, *m.* Prostitute (lit. "bag for dicks"). *Tu veux épouser ce sac à bites?* "You want to marry that super slut?"

SAC À PUCES, *m.* **1.** Bed, *dated* (lit. "fleabag"). *Il faut balancer ce sac à puces.* "We've got to throw out this bed." **2.** Computer (lit. "microchip bag"). *Il met une fortune dans ses sacs à puces.* "He spends a fortune on his computers."

SACARMENT!/SACRAMENT(E)!/SACRAMÈRE! *Que.,
euph. for* **sacrement.** See SACRE 2; SACREMENT; SAINT
SACREMENT.

SAC À SPERME, *m.* Easy lay. *Toute la bande est passée
sur ce sac à sperme.* "The whole gang's had her."

SACRANT. *Que.* **Au plus sacrant.** As fast as possible.
Il l'a fait au plus sacrant. "He did it pretty damned fast!"

SACRE, *m.* **1.** Rite, consecration. *"Le sacre du printemps"
fut accuelli par un sacré vacarme.* "There was quite
a hullabaloo when the *Rite of Spring* was premiered."
2. *Que.* Swear word; exclamation. *Les sacres québécois
ont souvent trait à la religion catholique.* "Quebec cuss
words often have to do with the Catholic religion." See
BAPTÊME!; CALICE!; CALVAIRE!; CIBOIRE!; CRISSE!; CHRIST!;
EUCHARASSE!; EUCHARISTIE!; (H)OSTIE!; OSTENSOIRE!; SACRA-
MENT!; SACRIFICE!; SIMONAC/SIMONAQUE!; TABERNAK!; TITI!;
TORRIEU!

SACRÉ, Remarkably good or bad (lit. "sacred"). *Notre
équipe a pris une sacrée décullotée.* "Our team was totally trounced." *Quelle sacrée bonne femme!* "That broad is
some piece of work!" **Sacré veinard.** Lucky devil. *Luc,
sacré veinard, a gagné gros à Las Vegas.* "Lucky devil
Luke won big in Las Vegas."

SACREMENT!/SACREMENT DE FESSES! *Que.* Goddamn it! (Lit. "sacrament, asshole sacrament"). Shit!,
Holy Hell! *Sacrement tu continues!* "Good Goddamn it,
you keep on!"

SACRÉMENT. Extremely. *Ana danse sacrément bien.*
"Ana's one hell of a dancer."

SACRER. 1. To consecrate (bishop); crown (king, competition winner). *Henri IV s'est fait sacrer à Chartres.* "Henry
IV had h.s. crowned at Chartres." *Line rêve d'être sacrée
Miss Monde.* "Line dreams of being crowned Miss
World." **2.** *Que.* To curse, blasphheme; inflict, give (as in
foutre 4). *Mamie n'aime pas que tu sacres comme ça. Si
tu persistes elle va te sacrer une sacrée claque.* "Granny

doesn't like your cussing like that. If you keep on she'll give you a whack you'll remember." (The meaning, "to curse" also existed in France but is no longer in current use there.)

SACREUR, *m., Que.* One who curses, blasphemer. *Criss! T'es en train de devenir un sacré sacreur!* "Jeez, you're becoming really foul-mouthed!"

SACRIFICE! *Que.* (from "sacrifice of the mass"). *Sacrifice! C'est toi qui as cassé le vase!* "God Almighty! You're the one who broke the vase." See SACRE **2.**

SACRIPANT! *Que., euph.* for **SACREMENT!**

SAINT, *m.* Saint. **Ne plus savoir à quel saint se vouer.** Not to know where to turn. *Nous ne savions plus à quel saint nous vouer.* "We were at our wits' end." *Il vaut mieux parler au bon dieu qu'à ses saints.* "It's better to talk to the boss man/lady rather than some underling."

SAINT CHRÊME!/SAINT CHRÊME DE CRISSE! *Que.* Holy oil used in several of the seven sacraments. No real equivalent in Eng. *Saint Chrême pourquoi t'as fait ça?* "Hell's Bells!/Holy (chrisming, jisming, creaming) Christ, why'd you do that?" Note: **Saint** can precede other Que. **sacres** as here and in **Saint Ciboire!** See SACRE **2.**

SAINTE-BARBE. See BARBE **2.**

SAINTE-NITOUCHE, *f.* Prudish woman. *Elle est baiseuse mais aime faire la Sainte-nitouche.* "She's a sexpot but likes to play the Puritan."

SAINT-ESPRIT, *m.* Holy Ghost. **Par l'opération du Saint-Esprit.** By divine intervention/by magic. *Grouille-toi et bosse! Ça ne se fera pas par l'opération du Saint-Esprit.* "Hurry up and hustle. It's not going to get done by magic." **Ne tenir que par le Saint-Esprit.** To hang by a thread. *Ça ne tient que par le Saint-Esprit.* "Only a whisper and a prayer hold it together." (Both uses illustrate the secularization of the spiritual.)

SAINTE TOUCHE, *f.* Payday (from **toucher,** "to get money"). *Ils célèbrent la Sainte-Touche au bistrot.* "They celebrate payday at the bistro."

SAINTE TRINITÉ PORTATIVE. Male genitalia (lit. "Portable Holy Trinity"). *Elle est très dévouée à la Sainte Trinité Portative, fête mâle mobile.* "She's very devoted to the Holy Trinity, a movable male feast!" *Cf.* JESUS **2**; SERVICE; SIÈGE.

SAINT-FRIC. Money. *Dans leur réligion on bénit Hermès, Mercure, Lakchmi, et le Saint-Fric.* "In their religion they bless Hermes, Mercury, Lakshmi, and Almighty Money."

SAINT-FRUSQUIN, *m.* **1.** The whole works. *Elle a vidé tout le saint-frusquin du grenier.* "She cleared everything out of the attic." **2.** Male genitalia. *Il est fier de son saint-frusquin.* "He's proud of his equipment."

SAINT-GLINGLIN. Indefinite date. **(Jusqu')à la Saint-Glinglin.** Never in a month of Sundays. *Tu peux attendre jusqu'à la Saint-Glinglin.* "You can wait till hell freezes over."

SAINT-JEAN, *f.* Midsummer. **En Saint-Jean.** Naked. *À Carnac, pour les feux de la Saint-Jean, les néo-druides dansaient en Saint-Jean.* "In Karnak, on Midsummer Eve, the neo-Druides danced in the all-together around the bonfires."

SAINT-LUNDI, *f.* **Faire/fêter la Saint-Lundi.** To take Monday off. *Fêtons la Saint-Lundi et partons à la campagne.* "Let's declare Monday a holiday and go to the country."

SAINT-PRIAPE, *f.* Sex (lit. "Saint-Priapus' day," after a Greco-Roman fertility God represented with a huge phallus). *Buvons et fêtons la Saint-Priape!* "Let's have a drink and a roll in the hay!"

SAINT SACREMENT, *m.* Something precious (lit. "Holy Sacrament"). *Tu portes cette bouteille de Château-Margaux comme si c'était le saint sacrement.* "You carry that bottle of Chateau Margaux as if it were the crown jewels/a holy idol/relic."

SAINT-TROU-DU-CUL, vulgar equivalent of SAINT-GLINGLIN.

SALADE, *f.* **1.** Stupid/untrue story; mess (lit. "salad"). *Ne nous emmerde pas avec toutes tes salades.* "Quit bugging us with all that bullshit." **2.** Fuss. **En faire toute une salade.** To make a fuss. *Il va en faire toute une salade.* "He's going to make a big to-do about that." See ARRÊTER.

SALADIER, *m.* **1.** Mouth (lit. "salad bowl"). See TAPER DU SALADIER. **2.** Fast talker. *Ce saladier devient de plus en plus chiant.* "That glib babbler bugs me more and more."

SALAMALECS, *m. pl.,* from Ar. for "peace be with you." Unctiousness. *Reçois-les sans faire de salamalecs.* "Greet them without fawning."

SALAMENT! *Que., euph.* for **SACREMENT!**

SALAUD, *m.* SOB. *Espèce de salaud!* "You bastard!"

SALÉ, -E. Excessive (lit. "salty"). *Dans ce resto la carte des vins est salée.* "In this restaurant the wine list is steep."

SALIGAUD = **SALAUD.**

SALOP/SALOPARD = **SALAUD.**

SALOPE, *f.* **1.** Bitch. *C'est la vraie salope!* "She's a real bitch!" See MARIE-SALOPE **1.** **2.** SOB. *Son mari est une sacrée salope!* "Her husband is a damned bastard!"

SALOPER. To botch. *Il ne sait rien faire sans saloper.* "He can't do anything without bungling it."

SALOPERIE, *f.* **1.** Bitchy comment. *Espèce de mal elevé, ravale tes saloperies.* "You boor, take back those nasty cracks!" **2.** Dirty trick. *Elle lui a fait une saloperie en couchant avec son frère.* "She played a dirty trick on him by sleeping with his brother." **3.** Trash. *Elle a acheté une saloperie comme souvenir.* "She bought a piece of junk as a souvenir."

SANDEC = **SANS DEC'.**

SANG, *m.* Blood. **Avoir du sang de navet.** To be gutless/a wimp (lit. "to have turnip's blood"). *Alors, tu y vas ou tu n'y vas pas? Tu as du sang de navet?* "Well are you going to or not? Are you chicken?" See (SE) CAILLER…SANG.

SANISETTE, *f.,* registered trademark in the sense of "toilet." Prostitute who works in toilets, alleys, hallways, and so on (lit. "public coin toilet"). *Impossible de pisser—les sanisettes sont au turbin.* "Impossible to take a piss—the working girls are at it."

SANS BLAGUE! No kidding!

SANS DÉBANDER. Nonstop (lit. "without losing an erection"). *On est parti faire la java trois jours sans débander.* "We partied three days nonstop."

SANS DEC', *abbr.* of **sans déconner.** No fooling. No kidding. *Tu l'as sautée, ta cousine? Sans dec'?* "You banged your cousin? No shit?"

SAPE, *f.* The garment industry. *Elle bosse pour la sape au Sentier.* "She works for the rag trade in the garment district."

SAPÉ, -E. Dressed. *Elle est toujours bien sapée.* "She's always well dressed."

SAPER. To sentence (lit. "to undermine"). *On l'a sapé à dix piges.* "He got sent away for ten years."

SAPES, *f., pl.* Clothes. *Tes sapes sont trempées.* "Your clothes are wet through."

(SE) SAPER. To dress; buy clothes. *Je me sape aux Puces de Clignancourt.* "I get my clothes at the Clignancourt flea market."

SAPERLIPOPETTE!/SAPERLOTTE!/SAPRISTI!, *euph. for* **SACREMENT!** Saints alive! Ye Gods! Holy Mackerel! (Mild oaths, now used whimsically.) *Cf.* BON DIEU DE BOIS.

SAQUER. 1. To give low marks. *Ils l'ont saqué à l'exam.* "They flunked him on the exam." **2.** To endure. *Sa gonzesse, je ne peux pas la saquer.* "I can't stand that broad of his."

SARDINE, *f.* Sardine. See ÉGOUTTER LA/SA SARDINE.

SATANÉ, -E! Damned. **Satanée pluie!** Damned rain!

SATURER. To be fed up (lit. "to saturate"). *Je sature sur les voisins.* "I've had it up to here with the neighbors."

SATYRE. Lecher; flasher. *Ce vieux satyre a son coin dans le bois de Boulogne.* "That old lecher's turf is in the Bois de Boulogne park."

SAUCE, *f.* **1.** Sauce. **Envoyer/mettre la sauce.** To go all out. *Ils ont mis toute la sauce pour gagner.* "They went all out to win." **2.** Sperm. *Après son rêve mouillé les draps étaient pleins de sauce.* "After his wet dream the sheets were full of sperm." **Balancer/envoyer la sauce.** To ejaculate. See LÂCHER LE JUS…; SEMOULE.

SAUCE, *m., youth, cités.* Chum. *Mes sauces et moi, nous sommes inséparables.* "My buddies and I are inseparable." (Influence of **associé,** "partner" and **sosie,** "double.") *Cf.* COUILLE **3.**

SAUCÉE, *f.* Downpour. *Mes sapes ont reçu la saucée.* "My clothes got drenched." *Cf.* DRACHE; FLOTTE.

SAUCER. 1. To copulate (lit. "to dunk in sauce"). *Messalina aimait se faire saucer.* "Messalina loved getting laid." **2.** To scold. *Je te l'ai saucé le gamin, après sa bêtise!* "I gave that kid a good dressing down after his mischief."

SAUCIFLARD, *m.* Sausage. *On n'a que du sauciflard à bouffer.* "Sausage is all there is to eat."

SAUCISSON, *m.* **1.** Sausage. See PEAU DE SAUSS. **2.** Golden oldie, music. *Il aime réécouter les mêmes saucissons.* "He likes to listen to the same old stuff."

SAUCISSONNÉ, -E. Bulging out of one's clothes. *Vise un peu comme elle est saucissonnée!* "Just look at how she's stuffed into her clothes!"

SAUDINE!/SAUDIT!/SAUDITES!, *Que., euph.* for **MAUDIT!**

SAUTE-AU-CRAC, *m.* Satyr (lit. "jumps to crack [vagina]"). *Ton pote, c'est un vrai saute-au-crac.* "Your buddy's a real gash hound."

SAUTE-AU-PAF, *f.* Nymphomaniac (lit. "jumps to penis"). *Trouver une saute-au-paf, c'était son rêve d'ado.* "Finding a nympho was the dream of his adolescence."

SAUTER. 1. To jump. **Et que ça saute!** "Jump to it!" "Step on it!" **2.** To copulate. *Au turbin, il l'a sautée aux WC.* "At work, he screwed her in the john."

SAUTERELLE, *f.* **1.** Tall person (lit. "grasshopper"). *Vise un peu les gambettes de cette sauterelle norvégienne!* "Take a look at that Norwegian gal's gams!" **2.** Female, sometimes *pej. J'ai vu ta sauterelle arpenter la rue Saint Denis.* "I think I saw your girlfriend working St. Denis Street."

SAUVAGE. Marvelous! (lit. "wild"). *Sauvage le concert rock!* "The rock concert was terrific!"

SAV = SAVONNETTE.

SAVON, *m.* Soap. **Passer un savon à qqn.** To tell s.o. off. *Elle lui a passé un de ces savons.* "She chewed him out good."

SAVONNER. To stammer (lit. "to soap up"). *Tu savonnes—explique-toi mieux.* "You're spluttering—explain yourself better." *Cf.* POSTILLONER.

SAVONNETTE, *f.* Cannabis (lit. "small bar of soap"). *Je n'ai plus qu'une savonnette.* "All I've left is a little stash of grass/hash."

SCAILLES = CHAILLES.

SCALPER. To arrest (lit. "to scalp"). *Les flics l'ont scalpé.* "The cops nabbed him."

SCAPHANDRE, *m.* Diving suit; space suit. **Scaphandre de poche.** Condom. *Elle lui a mis un scaphandre de poche.* "She put a rubber on him."

SCATO, *abbr.* of **scatologique.** Scatological. *Le prof de philo aime l'humour scato.* "The professor of philosophy loves bathroom humor."

321

SCHBEB, *m.* Homosexual (esp. in prison/the military [from Ar. for "pretty"]), *pej. Il était déjà schbeb à l'internat avant de faire de la tôle.* "He was already gay in boarding school before he did time."

SCHLAFFE/SCHLOF, *m.* Sleep (from Ger. **schlafen**). **Aller à/au schlof** or **faire schlof.** To go to bed. *C'est l'heure de faire schlof.* "It's time to hit the sack."

SCHLINGUER. To stink. *Ça schlingue la pisse de chat ici.* "It stinks of cat's piss here."

SCHNECK = CHNECK.

SCHNOC/SCHNOQUE, *m.* Idiot, "shnook." *C'est un vieux shnoque, ton tonton!* "Your uncle's an old fool."

SCHNOUF(FE), *f.* Heroin. (from Ger. for "snuff" and "sniff"). *Elle marche à la schnouffe.* "She's on big doses of the big H."

(SE) SCHNOUFFER. To shoot heroin. *Il ne se schnouffe plus.* "He no longer mainlines heroin."

SCHPROUM, *m.* Ruckus (from Ger. **Sprung,** "to jump"). **Aller au schproum.** To make a scene. *Pourqoui toujours aller au schproum?* "Why do you always make a scene?"

SCHTIB(E), *m.* Prison (either a variant of **Schtilibem** or from Ger. **Stübchen,** "little room"). *Il a appris à méditer au schtib.* "He learned how to meditate in the clink."

SCHTILIBEM, *m.* Prison (Gypsy parlance, with possible influence of Ger. **Stilleben** [still life]). *Le gitan chantait au schtilibem.* "The gypsy sang in the slammer."

SCHTOUILLE = CHTOUILLE.

SCHTUC, *m.* Little bit (from Ger. **Stück** [piece]). *Donne-m'en juste un schtuc.* "Give me just a smidgeon."

SCOTCHÉ. Stuck (from "Scotch tape®"). *Il a les yeux scotchés sur la télé.* "His eyes are glued to the TV."

SCOUZE! = SCUZMI.

SCRIBOUILLARD(E), *m., f., pej.* Journalist; pen pusher. *Ce scribouillard rêve d'écrire un grand roman.* "That journalist dreams of writing a great novel."

SCROGNEUGNEU, *m.* Old grouch; Col. Blimp. *Ce scrogneugneu fait la guerre à tous.* "That old grouch is hostile to everybody." *Cf.* PISSE-VINAIGRE.

SCROGNEUGNEU! Hell and damnation! Damn it!

SCROUM = SCHPROUM.

SCUZMI! Excuse me (from Eng. or It.) *Scuzmi, je suis à la bourre!* "Excuse me, I'm in a hurry!"

SEC, *adv.* Dryly. **Boire sec.** To drink a lot. *Elle boit sec, ta belle-doche!* "Your mother-in-law really puts it away!" See AUSSI SEC; CUL SEC!

SÉCATEUR, *m.* Pruning shears. **Baptiser au sécateur,** *pej.* To circumcise. *Avant de se convertir à l'Islam, il s'est fait baptiser au sécateur.* "Before converting to Islam, he was circumcised." **Baptisé au sécateur,** *pej.* Jewish. *On ne savait pas qu'il était baptisé au sécateur.* "We didn't know he was Jewish."

SECRET DE POLICHINELLE, *m.* See POLICHINELLE.

SEFFE, *f.,* backslang of **fesse.**

SEIGNEUR-TERRASSE, *m.* Person who spends much time but little money in a café (lit. "terrace lord"). *Plusieurs seigneurs-terrasse sirotaient leur café.* "Several table hogs sipped their coffee."

SÉMAPHORE, *m.* **1.** Traffic cop (lit. "semaphore"). *Ce sémaphore doit avoir les poumons noirs.* "That traffic cop's lungs must be black." **2.** Orchestra director. *On dit que les sémaphores vivent longtemps.* "They say conductors are long-lived."

SEMER QN. To shake s.o. off (lit. "to sow; scatter"). *Je ne sais pas pourquoi il m'a semée.* "I don't know why he ditched me." See ZIZANIE. *Cf.* LARGUER; PLAQUER.

SEMOULE, *f.* Semolina. **Être dans la semoule.** To be confused. *Je suis toujours dans la semoule pour remplir des formulaires.* "I'm always muddled when I have to fill out forms." See PÉDALER. **Balancer/envoyer la semoule.** To ejaculate. *Il avait du mal à balancer la semoule.* "He had a hard time coming." *Cf.* LÂCHER LE JUS.

SENTIR À PLEIN NEZ. To be obvious. *Ça sent à plein nez les accros.* "It's as plain as the nose on your face they're junkies."

(LE/LA) SENTIR PASSER. To experience s.t. unpleasant. *L'addition du Ritz, il l'a sentie passer.* "He won't forget the bill at the Ritz."

(SE) SENTIR PISSER. See PISSER.

SEQUINZOUIL, backslang of Louis Quinze. *Le poster montrait Nixon en Sequinzouil et lui attribuait les mots, "Après moi le déluge."* "The poster showed Nixon as Louis XV and attributed the words 'After me, the flood!' to him." *Cf.* BONBOUR.

SÉRIEUX, *m.* Liter glass of beer. *Il ne se prend pas au sérieux, peut-être parce qu'il aime la convivialité et s'envoie un sérieux chaque soir.* "He doesn't take h.s. very seriously, perhaps because he likes conviviality and belts down a big glass of beer every evening."

SERIN, *m.* Ninny (lit. "canary"). *Espèce de petit serin, change de disque!* "You nitwit, put on another record."

SERINETTE, *f.* Homosexual. *Je ne sais pas s'il en est, mais tous ses amis sont des serinettes.* "I don't know if he's 'one of them,' but all his friends are gay."

SERINGUER. To riddle with bullets (**seringue** = "syringe"). *Son mec l'a seringuée joliment.* "Her guy plugged her full of lead."

SERRER LA CUILER/LOUCHE/PINCE. To shake hands (lit. "the spoon/ladle/claw"). *En Europe on se serre la pince pour un oui, pour un non.* "In Europe people shake hands all the time."

SERRER LE KIKI. To strangle. *Si tu lui donnes encore du gin, je te serre le kiki.* "If you give him any more gin, I'll wring your neck."

SERRER LES FESSES. 1. To grit one's teeth (lit. "to squeeze one's buttocks together"). *Le toubib m'a dit de serrer les fesses avant de me charcuter.* "The doctor told me to grit my teeth before cutting me." **2.** To be afraid.

Je serre les fesses quand il roule trop vite. "I get all tensed up when he drives too fast."

SERVICE, *m.* Service. **Service trois pièces.** Male genitalia (lit. "three-piece dish set"). *Son service trois pièces—quelle sacrée trinité!* "His family jewels—what a trinity!" *Cf.* SAINTE TRINITÉ PORTATIVE.

SEUF, *f., youth.* Ass (backslang of **fesse**). *Grouille-toi, ramène ta seuf!* "Hurry it up. Get your ass over here."

SÉZIG(UE). Him; her. *C'est un cadeau de sézigue.* "It's a present from him."

SHIT, *m.* Hashish (from Eng.). *Passe-moi une boulette de shit.* "Pass me a hash pellet."

(SE) SHOOTER/SHOUTER. To inject o.s. with drugs. *Ils aiment se shouter ensemble.* "They enjoy shooting up together."

SHOOTEUSE/SHOUTEUSE, *f.* Drug needle. *Elle a toujours sa shooteuse avec elle.* "She's always got her syringe with her."

SIBLÈME!/SIBOL!, *Que., euph. for* **ciboire.**

SIDATEUX, -EUSE/SIDATIQUE, *m., f., pej.* Person with AIDS. *Il y a des centres pour aider les sidatiques.* "There are centers for helping people with AIDS."

SIDOUZE, *m.* AIDS. *Fais gaffe au sidouze!* "Be careful of AIDS." *Cf.* DASS(E).

SIÈGE, *m.* Seat. **Siège du pape.** Female genitalia. *Au bordel il adore s'agenouiller devant le siège du pape, siège sacrément saint pour lui.* "In the brothel he loves to kneel before the papal pussy throne, for him a truly holy seat." Note: **le Saint-Siège** = "The Holy Sea," originally "Seat." *Cf.* BÉNITIER; PAPE **2**, PONTIFE **2**.

SIFELLE = CIFELLE.

SIFFLER. To whistle. **Siffler un verre.** To belt down a drink. *Entre, juste le temps de siffler un verre.* "Come in for a quick drink."

SIFFLET, *m.* Throat (lit. "whistle"). See COUPER LE SIFFLET.

SINGE, *m.* **1.** Monkey. See PAYER EN MONNAIE DE SINGE. **2.** Corned beef. *À l'armée il bouffait du singe.* "In the army he ate corned beef." **3.** Boss. *Le singe nous a mis en chômage technique.* "The boss laid us off temporarily."

SINOC/SINOQUE/SINOQUET. Crazy. *Il est devenu complètement sinoc.* "He's gone completely around the bend."

SIPHONNÉ, -E. Crazy. *Ce type est siphonné; il m'a bousillé la voiture.* "That guy's bonkers; he screwed up my car."

SIX-À-NEUF = SOIXANTE-NEUF.

SMALA, *f.* Large family; entourage. *Il va venir avec toute sa smala.* "He'll come with his whole tribe."

SNIF, *m.* Cocaine. *Il trouve du snif pas cher.* "He gets inexpensive nose candy."

SNIFFER. To inhale cocaine and other things. *Il lui fallait sniffer de plus en plus.* "He grew more and more addicted to snow."

SNUFF = SNIF.

SŒUR, *f.* Sister. See ET TA SŒUR!

SŒURS, *f., pl.* Prostitutes who work for the same pimp, whom they call "husband." *Notre mari tient la bride haute à mes sœurs et à moi.* "Our husband keeps a tight rein on my sisters and me."

SOIE, *f.* Silk. **Péter dans la soie.** To live the life of Riley (lit. "to fart in silk [undies, etc.]"). *Après avoir pété dans la soie, il est tombé dans la misère.* "After having lived high on the hog, he fell on hard times."

SOIF, *f.* Thirst. **Il fait soif!** "I need a drink in this weather!" See COUPE-LA-SOIF.

SOIGNÉ, -E. Intense (lit. well-groomed). *J'avais un rhume soigné.* "I had a dirty rotten cold."

SOIGNER. To treat. **Il faut te faire soigner!** "You need to see a shrink!"

SOISSONAIS (ROSE), *m.* Clitoris (lit. "bean"). *Il m'a frotté le soissonais et j'ai senti un petit frisson.* "I felt a little thrill when he rubbed my clit." *Cf.* BONBON **3**; BOUTON **3**; HARICOT; PRALINE **2**.

SOIXANTE-NEUF, *m.* Simultaneous oral sex. *Elle est individualiste mais elle adore le soixante-neuf.* "She's an individualist but she loves 69."

SOLEIL, *m.* Sun. See PIQUER UN SOLEIL.

MADAME SOLEIL. Radio-TV astrologer, fortune-teller (who died in 1996 but lives on in popular speech.) *Si le dollar va remonter? J'en sais rien. J'suis pas Madame Soleil.* "Will the dollar go up? I have no idea. I haven't got a crystal ball." *Cf.* (LE) JEAN ROSSET; LUISANT; MAHOMET; MOULANA; PIQUER UN SOLEIL.

SONNÉ, -E. 1. Knocked out; groggy. *Après sa chute à ski elle était sonnée.* "She was dazed after her fall when skiing. **2.** Crazy. *Il est un peu sonné sur les bords.* "He's slightly cracked."

SONNER. To ring. *Elle a ses quarante ans bien sonnés.* "She's forty if she's a day."

SONNER LES CLOCHES À QN. To reprimand severely. *On lui a sonné les cloches pour avoir sécher l'école.* "They read him the riot act for having played hooky from school."

SONORGUE = SÉZIG(UE).

SORTIR PAR LES YEUX (ET LES OREILLES)/PAR LES TROUS DE NEZ. To leave (lit. "to be coming out of one's eyes (ears), nostrils"). To have a snoot/belly full of s.t. *Je l'évite car il me sort par les yeux.* "I avoid him because I've had as much of him as I can take."

SOT L'Y LAISSE. See BONNET D'ÉVÊQUE.

SOUDÉ. Jammed (said of traffic; lit. "welded"). *Le périf est archisoudé à 17 heures.* "The beltway is completely bottlenecked at 5:00 P.M."

SOUK, *m.* Disorder (from Ar. for "market"). *Sa chambre est devenue un souk invivable.* "His room's become a pigsty."

SOÛLARD, -E. *m., f.* Drunkard. *C'est un couple de soûlards.* "He and she are both lushes."

SOÛLAUD/SOÛLOT = SOÛLARD.

SOUPE À LA GRIMACE, *f.* A hostile reception. *Quand il rentre bourré, il a soupe à la grimace.* "He gets the cold shoulder when he comes home drunk."

SOUPE AU LAIT, *f.* Person quick to fly off the handle (milk added to boiling soup rises rapidly). *Il n'a aucune patience. Quelle soupe au lait!* "He has no patience. What a hothead!"

SOUPE DE LANGUES, *f.,* youth. Long Fr. kiss (lit. "tongue soup"). *Les ados sont friands de soupes de langues.* "Adolescents are fond of long wet kisses." *Cf.* FRENCHER; GUÉLAN; ROULER UN PALOT.

SOUPER. To have supper. **En avoir soupé.** To be fed up with s.t. *J'en ai soupé de faire le ménage après le boulot.* "I'm sick and tired of doing the housework after coming home from work."

SOURIS, *f.* Young girl (lit. "mouse"). *Il ne pense qu'aux souris.* "All he thinks about is chicks." *Cf.* RATE/RATTE.

SOURIS DE SACRISTIE, *f.* Sanctimonious church lady. *Ma grand-tante est une souris de sacristie.* "My great-aunt is a Holy Joe." *Cf.* PUNAISE.

SOUS-FIFRE/SOUS-FIFRESSE, *m., f.* Underling. *Le chirurgien fait sa ronde avec ses sous-fifres et sous-fifresses.* "The surgeon makes his rounds with his junior associates."

SOUS-PRÉFET, *m.* Subprefect. See AGACER…PRÉFET.

SOUTIF, *m.* Brassiere. *Elle ne porte jamais de soutif.* "She never wears a bra."

SPEEDÉ, -E. Hyper. *Ils étaient speedés lors du viol collectif.* "They were wired during the gang rape."

SPEEDER. To accelerate. *Je speede dès le matin.* "I've been going nonstop since morning."

SQUATTER. To occupy illegally. *La gare désaffectée est squattée.* "Squatters are occupying the former railroad station."

STARFORLAH!, *cités.* My God! Heavens! (from Ar. **ast-aghfiroullah,** "I ask pardon of God"). *Starforlah! J'ai encore perdu les clefs.* "Oh my God, I've lost my keys again." *Cf.* WALLAH.

STI! *Que.* See HOSTIE!; SACRE **2**.

STUP, *m., abbr.* of **stupéfiant.** Narcotic. *Il a fait de la taule pour un trafic de stup.* "He was in stir for drug dealing."

STUPS, *m., pl.,* from **Brigade des stups.** Narcotics squad. *Des stups américains et français devaient collaborer.* "American and French narcs were supposed to work together."

SUBITO(S)/SUBITO PRESTO. Suddenly; on the double. *Il nous a quitté subitos.* "He left us all of a sudden."

SUÇADE, *f.* Fellatio. *La suçade lui plaisait mieux avec la capote.* "She found frenching more pleasing with a rubber."

SUÇAGE, *m.* = **SUÇADE.**

SUCER LA POMME/LE MUSEAU. To kiss (lit. "to suck the face/muzzle"). *Le baisemain, c'est bien, mais j'aimerais mieux que tu me suces la pomme.* "A kiss on the hand is nice, but I'd rather you gave me a real kiss."

SUÇON, *m.* Kiss-mark. *Fais gaffe que ta femme ne voie pas ce suçon-là.* "Watch out your wife doesn't see that love bite."

SUCRE, *m.* Sugar. **Casser du sucre sur le dos de qn.** To speak ill of s.o. *Méfie-toi de cette garce qui ne cesse de casser du sucre sur ton dos!* "Be careful of that bitch who's always running you down."

SUCRER LES FRAISES. To have one foot in the grave (lit. "to sugar the strawberries"). *Heureusement nos parents ne sucrent pas encore les fraises.* "Fortunately our parents aren't on their last legs yet."

(SE) SUCRER. To feather one's nest. *L'agent immobilier s'est sucré en vendant ma boutique.* "The real estate agent lined his pockets in selling my boutique."

SUISSE, *m., f.* Swiss. **Faire le suisse.** To be ungregarious. *Fais pas le Suisse, viens nous rejoindre.* "Don't be standoffish, come join us." **En suisse.** On the sly; selfishly. *Suzanne fumait en suisse. C'était ça son secret.* "Suzanne sneaked smokes. That was her secret." **Boire en suisse.** To drink without standing a round for others. *Ce grippe-sou ne boit qu'en suisse.* "That tightwad only drinks alone."

SUPERBLIME. Marvelous (from **super** and **sublime**). *Le concert était superblime.* "The concert was fantabulous."

SURBOUM, *f.* Wild party. *On s'est bien pété la gueule à la dernière surboum.* "We all got smashed at the last big bash."

SURGÉ, *m.,* school, *abbr.* of **surveillant général.** Vice principal. *Le surgé est une peau de vache.* "The vice principal's a real SOB."

SURIN, *m.* Knife (from Gypsy **chouri**). *Jacques l'Eventreur savait filer les coups de surin.* "Jack the Ripper knew how to thrust in his knife."

SURINEUR, *m.* Knife-wielder. *Ce n'est qu' un film surineur de plus.* "It's just another slasher movie."

SURPATTE = SURBOUM.

SUSHI, *m.* Jap. fish dish. **Rouler/faire un sushi.** See ROULER UNE PELLE.

SYMPA. Pleasant. *Il nous a dégoté un coin sympa pour pique-niquer.* "He found a nice spot for our picnic."

SYPH/SYPHLOTTE, *f.,* from **syphilis.** *Fais gaffe, qu'il ne te colle pas la syphlotte aussi.* "See to it that he doesn't syph you up too."

SYSTÈME, *m.* System. **Courir/taper sur le système à qn.** To get on s.o.'s nerves (lit. "to run/hit on s.o.'s [nervous] system"). *L'entendre chanter faux me tape sur le système.* "Listening to his off-key singing grates on me."

SYSTÈME D (for **DÉBROUILLE/DÉMERDE**), *m.* Resourcefulness. *"Comment as-tu réussi à faire ça?" "Système D."* "How'd you manage that?" "Smarts!"

TAB, *f.,* drugs, *abbr.* of **tablette.** Amphetamine tablet. *Il avale tab sur tab.* "He pops speed constantly."

TABAC, *m.* **1.** Tobacco. **Passer à tabac.** To beat up. *La police l'a passé à tabac.* "The police worked him over." **2.** Success. **Faire un tabac.** To be very successful. *Cette diva a fait un tabac.* "That diva had a resounding success."

TABASSER. To beat up. *Ils l'ont tabassé à la sortie du match.* "They beat him up after the game."

TABERNAK! *Que.* (From **tabernacle,** place where the eucharist is kept.) Damn it! *Tabernak! Ce char de marde est à nouveau en panne!* "Shit! This goddamned car's broken down again." See SACRE **2.**

TABARNAME!/TABARNANE!/TABARNICHE!/ TABARNOUCHE!/TABAROUÈTE!/TABAROU-ETTE!/TABARSAK!/TABARSLAK!/TABER-NACHE!/TABOÎTE!/TORBINOUCHE! *Que.* Euph. for TABARNAK! See SACRE **2.**

TABOIRE! *Que., euph. for* TABERNAK! with influence of CIBOIRE! See SACRE **2.**

TACHE, *f.* **1.** Stain. **Faire tache.** To stick out like a sore thumb. *Dans sa robe rouge Jézabel faisait tache.* "Jezebel stuck out like a sore thumb in her red dress." **2.** Nonentity. *Pour moi, ce n'est qu'une tache.* "For me he's just a dud."

TAF, *m.* Job. *Au taf je taffe non-stop.* "When I'm on the job I work non-stop." **C'est pas mon taf.** "That's not my strong point/not my sort of thing." **Faire le taf.** To engage in prostitution. *J' fais plus le taf.* "I'm not a working girl anymore." *Cf.* TAPIN.

TAF-TAF = DARE DARE.

TAFANARD, *m.* Posterior. *En taule, il avait souvent le tafanard irrité.* "His ass often hurt in jail."

TAFFE = TOUFFE 2.

TAFIOLE/TARLOUZE = TAPETTE.

TAFLOUNE, *f., Que.* Cigarette; joint (marijuana). *T'as des taflounes?* "Got any smokes?"

TAG, *m.* Graffiti maker's signature; graffito. *Le bus était couvert de tags.* "The bus was covered with graffiti."

TAGGER = TAGUER.

TAGUER. To spray graffiti. *Ce petit morveux a tagué la maison.* "That little jerk has spray-painted the house."

TAGUEUR, -EUSE, *m., f.* Graffiti sprayer. *Le tagueur se balade avec sa bombe de peinture.* "The graffiti sprayer walks around with his can of spray paint."

TAILLER UNE BAVETTE. See BAVETTE.

TAILLER UNE PIPE. See PIPE.

TAILLER UNE PLUME. To fellate. *Il aime mieux tailler une plume, plutôt que de se faire turluter.* "He'd rather blow than be blown."

(SE) TAILLER. To beat it. *Dès que je le vois, je me taille.* "I split as soon as I see him."

TAISEUX. *Bel.* Silent, taciturn. *Line parle non-stop mais en pince pour les mecs costauds et taiseux.* "Line talks non-stop but goes for the strong silent types."

TAL, *m.* Money. *J'ai besoin de tal.* "I need money."

TALOCHE, *f.* Slap. See ALLONGER…TALOCHE.

TAMBOUILLE, *f.* Food. *Le resto du coin fait de la bonne tambouille.* "The local restaurant serves good food."

TAM-TAM ARABE = TÉLÉPHONE ARABE.

TANGEANTE, *f.* Tangent. **Prendre la tangeante.** To make o.s. scarce; to shirk s.t. *Ne pense pas à prendre la tangeante.* "Don't think of slipping off."

TANTE, *f.* Homosexual (lit. "aunt"). *C'est une belle brochette de tantes!* "What a bunch of fairies!"

TANTOUSE/TANTOUZE = TANTE.

TAPÉ, -E. Crazy (lit. "hit [in the head]"). *Il est bien tapé depuis qu'elle l'a quitté.* "He's been really bananas since she left him."

TAPE-À-L'ŒIL, *m.* Flashy stuff. *Chez eux le décor est très tape-à-l'œil.* "Their place is gaudily decorated."

TAPE-CUL, *m.* Rattletrap vehicle (lit. "ass hitter"). *Son bahut est un vrai tape-cul.* "His car's a real bone-shaker."

TAPÉE, *f.* A large amount. *Je ne supporte pas leur tapée de marmots.* "I can't stand their pack of brats."

TAPER. 1. To hit on; mooch (lit. "to hit; tap"). *Je peux te taper d'une clope?* "Can I bum a cigarette off you?" **2.** To stink. *Il adore les fromages qui tapent.* "He loves smelly cheeses."

TAPER DANS LA LUNE. To sodomize. *Il aime lui taper dans la lune.* "He likes to stick it up her ass."

TAPER DANS L'ŒIL. To impress. *Son diamant m'a tapé dans l'œil.* "Her diamond blew me away."

TAPER DES ARPIONS. To have smelly feet. *Mon mari tape toujours des arpions.* "My husband's feet are always smelly."

TAPER DU BEC/SALADIER. To have bad breath. *Elle le repousse parce qu'il tape du saladier.* "She keeps him distant because he's got bad breath."

TAPER L'AIL. To be a lesbian. See AIL.

TAPER L'INCRUSTE. To invite o.s.; be a gate-crasher. *Personne ne le soupçonnait d'avoir tapé l'incruste.* "Nobody knew he was a gate-crasher."

(SE) TAPER. 1. To treat o.s. to s.t. *On s'est tapé un resto trois étoiles.* "We treated ourselves to a three-star restaurant." **2.** To have sex. *Elle se tape un nouveau mec chaque soir.* "She bangs a different guy every night." **3.** To tackle s.t. difficult. *C'est moi qui me tape toujours la vaiselle.* "I'm the one who always gets stuck with the dishes."

(SE) TAPER LA CLOCHE. To eat a lot. *On s'est bien tapé la cloche chez mémé.* "We had a big feed at Grandma's."

(SE) TAPER LE CUL PAR TERRE. See ASTAP(E) **1.**

(SE) TAPER SUR LA LANTERNE. To be hungry. *Ça fait un moment que je me tape sur la lanterne.* "I've been hungry for some time now."

TAPETTE, *f.*, *pej.* Flaming faggot (lit. "flyswatter"). *Ce bar est un nid à tapettes.* "This bar is a home for flaming faggots." *Cf.* LUCIOLE; PÉDÉ COMME UN PHOQUE.

TAPIN, *m.* Prostitution. **Faire le tapin = Tapiner.**

TAPINER. To work as a prostitute. *Elle ne veut plus tapiner.* "She doesn't want to be a hooker anymore."

TARBOUIF, *m.* Nose. *Pour se sauver elle l'a cogné dans le tarbouif.* "To get away she hit him in the schnozz."

TARÉ, -E, *m., f.* Idiot. *C'est une famille de tarés.* "They're retards, that family."

TARIN = TARBOUIF.

TARPÉ, backslang of **pétard 4.**

TARTE, *adj.* Stupid. *Tu as l'air tarte avec ce chapeau.* "You look idiotic in that hat."

TARTE, *f.* **1.** Tart. **C'est pas de la tarte!** That's no picnic/piece of cake! **2.** Whack. See ALLONGER…TARTE.

TARTE AUX POILS, *f.* Female genitalia (lit. "fur pie"). *Elle peignait tous les matins sa tarte aux poils.* "She combed her hairy snatch every morning."

TARTEMPION, *m.* What's-his/her-name. *Monsieur et Madame Tartempion ont acheté l'appart d'en face.* "What's-their-name bought the facing apartment."

TARTIGNOLE = TARTE. (*adj.*)

TAS DE FERRAILLE, *m.* Old heap of a car (lit. "pile of scrap metal"). *Tu n'as acheté qu'un tas de ferraille qu'on devrait retirer de la circulation.* "All you bought was a pile of junk that should be taken off the road."

TASPÉ, *f.,* backslang of **pétasse.** Prostitute. *Il m'a taxée de taspé, mais j'suis une brave fille.* "He called me a whore, but I'm a good girl."

TASSE/TASSE À THÉ = THÉIÈRE 2.

(SE) TASSER LA CLOCHE = (SE) TAPER LA CLOCHE.

TATA = TANTE.

TATANE, *f.* Shoe; foot. **Filer un coup de tatane.** To kick. *Elle lui a filé un coup de tatane dans les roubignolles.* "She gave him a kick in the balls."

TAULARD, -E, *m., f.* Convict. *Elle fera une taularde si elle continue.* "She'll wind up a jailbird if she keeps on."

TAULE, *f.* **1.** Home; room. *Tu veux monter à ma taule?* "You want to come to my place?" **2.** Jail. *Il a fait deux ans de taule pour vol.* "He was in stir for two years for larceny."

TBM. 1. Very well hung (*abbr.* of **très bien monté**). *Elle m'a dans la peau car je suis TBM.* "She's nuts about me because I'm hung like a mule." **2.** Very good-looking guy (*abbr.* of **très beau mec**). *Elle n'a d'yeux que pour les TBM.* "She has eyes only for handsome guys."

TCHAO, phonetic rendering of Ital. **ciao.** "So long/ see you." Possibly from Ger. *Auf Wiederschauen* (See you).

TCHATCHER. 1. To gab; yak. *On tchatchait au café.* "We were shooting the breeze in the café." **2.** To smooth-talk; sweet-talk. *Ne me tchatche pas.* "Don't hand me a line."

TCHATCHEUR, -EUSE, *m., f.* Glib talker. *C'est un sacré tchatcheur.* "He's a real smooth talker."

TCHAVE, *m.* from Romany. Departure. **Se faire la tchave.** To shove off. *Faisons la tchave!* "Let's blow this hole!" *Cf.* NATCHAV!

TCHI/T'CHI, from Romany. Nothing. *Ton argot, je n'y pige que tchi!* "I don't understand a word of your slang."

TCHIN-TCHIN! A toast. "Cheers! Bottoms up!"

TCHÔ! Swiss equivalent of **TCHAO.** Popularized by the comic strip *Titeuf.* See TCHAO.

TCHOUCH, *m.,* street vendor slang. Free gift. *J'ai eu ce lapin en peluche en tchouch.* "I got this stuffed bunny as a freebie."

TDP, *m., abbr.* of **tour de poitrine.** Bust size. *Elle a donné son TDP dans son CV.* "She gave her bust size in her curriculum vitae."

TEBI/TÉBI = TEUBE.

TÉCÉ = TC.

TÉDÉPÉ = TDP.

TÉLÉMUCHE, *m.* Telephone. *Elle passe son temps au télémuche.* "She spends her time on the telephone."

TÉLÉPHONE ARABE, *m.* Grapevine. *Par le téléphone arabe j'arrive à tout savoir.* "I get to know everything through the grapevine."

TÉLÉPHONER AU PAPE. To go to the can; to defecate. *Au Vatican, je devais téléphoner au pape mais impossible de trouver les chiottes!* "At the Vatican I had to shit but it was impossible to find the can."

TÉLÉPHONER DANS LE VENTRE. To fellate. *Après lui avoir téléphoné dans le ventre, elle avait de l'amour dans la boudine.* "After giving him head, she had love in her belly."

TÉLOCHE = TÉLÉ.

TENIR. To hold. **En tenir une couche; en tenir.** To be really stupid. *Il en tient une couche; pas possible de discuter.* "He's as thick as a board; discussion is impossible."

TENIR LA JAMBE DE QN. To hold s.o. up by talking (lit. "to hold s.o.'s leg"). *Elle m'a tenu la jambe une heure.* "She buttonholed me for an hour."

TENIR LE COUP. To withstand. *Je craignais de ne pas pouvoir tenir le coup.* "I was afraid I wouldn't be able to stick it out."

(SE) TENIR À CARREAU. To watch one's step (from the Tarot cards). *Depuis sa dernière engueulade il se tient à carreau.* "Since his last chewing out he watches his step."

TÊTE, *f.* Head. **Être une tête.** To be brainy. *C'est une tête!* He's a brain! **Avoir la grosse tête.** To be swell-headed. *Depuis qu'il a hérité, il a la grosse tête.* "Since coming into money he's been on an ego trip." **Ça (ne) va pas la tête?** "Are you nuts?" **À la tête du client.** Depending on appearance. *Il fait son prix à la tête du client.* "He charges what the traffic will bear." See CASSE-TÊTE; CASSER/(SE) CASSER LA TÊTE; COUP DE TÊTE; (SE) CREUSER LA TÊTE.

TÊTE À CLAQUE, *m.,* police slang. Nighttime brothel customer. *Les keufs tenait ce tête à claque à l'œil.* "The cops kept an eye on the night owl brothel goer."

TÊTE À CLAQUES/À GIFLES, *f.* Repulsive face. *Ce mec a une tête à claques.* "That guy's got a mug that cries out for a whack in the mouth."

TÊTE DE COCHON/LARD/MULE, *f.* Stubborn person. *C'est une sacrée tête de lard; on ne peut pas raisonner avec lui.* "He's really pigheaded; there's no reasoning with him."

TÊTE DE NŒUD, *f.* Jackass. *Va te faire niquer, tête de nœud!* "Fuck off, asshole!" *Cf.* "dickhead" and "meathead."

TÉTER. To booze it up (lit. "to suck at"). *Il téte sans arrêt.* "He drinks like a fish, nonstop." **Va te faire téter!** Fuck/piss off!

TEUBE/TEUBI, *m.,* backslang of **bite.** Penis. *Son petit teube le complexe.* "He's self-conscious about his little dick."

TEUCH, *m.,* drugs, backslang of **shit.** Hashish. *Ils ont toujours du teuch sur eux.* "They've always got hashish on them."

TEUCHE, *f.,* backslang of **chatte.** Female genitalia. *Sa teuche est toujours prête.* "Her beaver is always eager."

TEUF, *f.,* backslang of **fête.** Party. *Ils aiment faire la teuf.* "They like to party."

TEUF-TEUF, *m.* **1.** Choo-choo train (children's language). *On va prendre le teuf-teuf.* "We're going to take the choo-choo." **2.** Rattling old car. *Il sortait tout courbaturé de son teuf-teuf.* "He was stiff all over when he got out of his old heap."

TEXTO or **TEXTUO** (from **textuellement**). Verbatim. *J'sais plus ce qu'il a dit texto mais je peux te le raconter grosso modo.* "I don't remember what he said word for word, but I can give you a rough idea."

TEXTO, *m.* Text message. *Notre petite n'a que 12 ans mais j'ai découvert des textos choquants sur son portable.* "Our little girl's only 12, but I discovered shocking text messages on her cell phone."

TÉZIG(UE). You. *J'aimerais danser avec tézigue.* "I'd like to dance with you."

TGV, *abbr.* of **train à grande vitesse** (high-speed train). **1.** Prostitute who turns tricks quickly. *Ce soir Marc a du temps, pas de TGV pour lui.* "Mark's got time tonight, and doesn't want a quickie." **2.** Really fast horse. *Il a misé sur un TGV.* "He bet on a fast horse." **3.** Amphetamine; cocaine. *Il se bourre de TGV.* "He loads up on speed."

THÉIÈRE, *f.* **1.** Head (lit. "teapot"). *Il n'a pas grand-chose dans la théière.* "He hasn't got much between the ears." **2.** Public urinal frequented by homosexuals (lit. "teapot"). *La tata trouvait la théière dégueu, mais y allait souvent quand même.* "The queen found the tearoom repulsive, but went there often anyway."

THUNE, *f.* Money (orig. a five-franc coin, then any coin, then money in general). *Je n'ai plus de thune.* "I don't have any more money."

THUNER. To beg. *Ça thune dans le métro!* "Lots of begging (goes on) in the subway!"

THURNE, *f.* Room; messy house. *Elle loue des thurnes à des étudiants.* "She rents rooms to students."

TIAGA or **TSIAGA,** *f.* Prostitute (from the Wolof lang. in Senegal). *Cette Séné c'est pas du tout une tiaga.* "That Senegalese woman's no hooker."

TICHE, *m.,* youth. T-shirt (from Eng.). *Elle vend des tiches dans la rue.* "She sells T-shirts on the street."

TICKSON/TICSON, *m.* Ticket. *Sans tickson, pas d'entrée.* "No tickee, no entry."

TIFS, *m., pl.* Hair. *Ses tifs ont à nouveau changé de couleur.* "Her hair's a different color again." See COUPE-TIFS.

TIFTIRE, *m.* Hairdresser. *Elle s'est fait tirer les tifs chez le tiftire.* "She had her hair done at the hairdresser's."

TIGE, *f.* **1.** Cigarette (lit. "stalk"). See GRILLER...TIGE. **2.** Penis. See BROUTER LA TIGE.

TIGIDOU! *Que.* OK! Fine! Okeydokey!

TIMBRÉ, -E. Crazy. *Il est timbré de rouler aussi vite.* "He's bonkers, driving that fast."

TINTIN! Nothing at all! No way!

(FAIRE) TINTIN. To have to do without. *Je voulais partir en vacances mais j'ai dû faire tintin.* "I wanted to leave on vacation but I had to give it up."

T'INQUIÈTE! from **ne t'inquiète pas.** "Don't sweat it!"

TIR, *m., abbr.* of **Transports Internationaux Routiers** (International Highway Shipments). Teamster who makes international trips. *Les tirs pensent faire la grève.* "The truckers are planning to strike."

TIRAVE, *invar.* To steal (from **tirer** with Gypsy suffix **–ave**). *Mon reuf a tirave neuf sacs hier. C'est un voleur* *à la tire de première.* "My brother snatched nine purses yesterday. He's a champion purse-snatcher." *Cf.* TIRER **2**; VOLEUR À L'ABORDAGE.

TIRE-AU-CUL/TIRE-AU-FLANC, *m.* S.o. who avoids work. *Ne compte pas sur lui; c'est un tire-au-flanc.* "Don't count on him; he's a lazy good-for-nothing."

TIRE-BOUTON, *m.* **La maison tire-bouton.** The world of lesbian sex, Dykeville. **Ménage tire-bouton.** Lesbian relationship. *Ma femme, mère et grand-mère, me quitte pour la maison tire-bouton. J'ai proposé un ménage à trois mais elle préfère le ménage tire-bouton total.* "My wife, a mother and grandmother, is leaving me for Lesbosland. I suggested a *ménage à trois* but the only songs she wants to sing are Sapphic." See BOUTON **3**.

(SE) TIREBOUTONNER. To engage in lesbian sex. *Ce micheton aime nous regarder nous tireboutonner mes sœurs et moi.* "That john (prostitute's client) likes to watch my sisters (other whores) and me loving each other."

TIRE-FESSES, *m.* Ski lift; ski tow. *Fais gaffe en prenant le tire-fesses.* "Be careful when you take the ski lift."

TIRE-GOSSE = TIRE-MÔME.

TIRE-JUS. Handkerchief; snot rag. *Il s'est branlé dans son tire-jus.* "He jerked off into his handkerchief."

(À) TIRE-LARIGOT. In quantity. *Il fume des clopes à tire-larigot.* "He smokes cigarettes like a chimney."

TIRELIRE or **TIRE-LIRE,** *f.* **1.** Piggy-bank. *Mon voyou de frère a cassé ma tirelire et volé toutes mes économies.* "My no-good brother busted my piggy-bank and stole all my savings." **2.** Mouth. *Enlève cette clope de ta tirelire!* "Take that cigarette out of your mouth!" **3.** Face. *Affiche un sourire à ta tirelire.* "Put a smile on your face." **4.** Head. See (SE) CREUSER LA CERVELLE. **5.** Stomach. *J'ai rien dans la tirelire depuis ce matin.* "I haven't had a thing to eat since this morning." **6.** Vagina. *Des tas de mecs ont déposé des masses de sauce dans ma tirelire. J'suis une* *vraie tirelire à foutre!* "So many guys have deposited so much come in my cunt. I'm a real sperm bank!"

TIRE-MOELLE = TIRE JUS.

TIRE-MÔME, *m., f.* Obstetrician; midwife. *C'est une tire-môme contre les faiseuses d'anges.* "She's a midwife hostile to back alley abortionists."

TIRE-MORVE = TIRE JUS.

TIRER. 1. To endure (lit. "to pull; shoot"). *Il y a encore deux moix à tirer devant les vacances.* "Still two months to get through before vacation." **2.** To steal. *On m'a tiré ma bécane.* "Somebody swiped my bike."

TIRER AU FLANC. To shirk. *Ne tirez pas au flanc avant la fin du boulot.* "No goldbricking before the job's done."

TIRER DANS LES JAMBES/PATTES DE QN. To make things difficult for s.o. *Cesse de me tirer dans les pattes.* "Quit giving me a hard time."

TIRER LA LANGUE. To be in need (such as financially) [lit. "to be panting"]. *Je tire la langue quand arrive le mois des impôts.* "I'm really strapped for money when it's tax-paying time."

TIRER LE PIED-DE-BICHE. To beg from house to house; sell from door to door. *C'est pas drôle, tirer le pied-de-biche quand il neige.* "It's no picnic, selling from door to door when it's snowing."

TIRER LES FICELLES. 1. To pull strings. *Il sait tirer les ficelles pour obtenir ce qu'il veut.* "He knows how to pull strings to get what he wants." **2.** To run the show. *C'est lui qui tire les ficelles.* "He's the power behind the scenes."

TIRER SA CRAMPE/CRAMPETTE = TIRER SON COUP.

TIRER SA FLEMME. To be idle. *J'aime tirer ma flemme le week-end.* "I like lazing about on weekends."

TIRER SON PETIT COUP. To have a quickie. *Moi, je cherche la tendresse, mais la plupart des mecs ne pensent* *qu'à tirer leur petit coup.* "I want tenderness, but with most guys it's just 'wham, bam, thank you ma'am'."

TIRER SUR LA FICELLE. To stretch too far (lit. "to pull on the thread"). *S'il te plaît, ne tire pas sur la ficelle.* "Come on now, don't push it."

TIRER UN/SON COUP. To have sexually; shoot a load. *Il aime tirer son coup avant de dormir.* "He likes to get his rocks off before going to sleep."

(SE) TIRER. To clear out. *J'ai hâte de me tirer d'ici.* "I'm in a hurry to get out of here."

(SE) TIRER DES ADJAS. See ADJA.

(SE) TIRER LA BOURRE/DES BOURRES. To compete fiercely. *Les lutteurs se tiraient la bourre.* "The wrestlers really battled it out."

TIREUR, *m.* Pickpocket (lit. "marksman"). *C'est un habile tireur.* "He's a skillful pickpocket."

TISANE, *f.* Fuel (lit. "herb tea"). *Ma meule bouffe beaucoup de tisane.* "My motorbike's a gas eater."

TITI, 1. *m.* Brash or resourceful kid. *Le titi parisien ne se plaisait pas à la cambrousse.* "The Paris urchin didn't like it in the country." **2.** *adj., Que. euph. for* **maudit** "cursed, damned." *Assez de tes frasques titis!* "Enough of your damned pranks."

TOC, *m.* Trashy, fake material. *C'est du toc.* "It's junk."

TOCANTE, *f.* Watch. *Ta tocante retarde.* "Your watch is slow."

TOCARD, -E. Cheap; tinselly; shoddy. *Il a des goûts tocards.* "He has trashy taste."

TOCCIN = TOQUANT.

T'OCCUPE! See OCCUPE.

TOF. Great, excellent (Bel. from Brit. sl. "swell, posh"). *La bouffe à l'hôtel était top. Tout le séjour etait tof.*

"Meals at the hotel were top quality. The whole stay was great."

TOGOS or **TOGOSSE,** *pl., youth, cités.* Money (from **nouchi,** Côte d'Ivoire sl.). *J'ai plus de togos.* "I don't have any more money." *Cf.* MAILLE; THUNES; ZÉYO.

TOILE, *f.* **1.** Canvas, painting. *Mamie trouve choquante* L'origine du monde, *magnifique toile de Courbet.* "Grandma finds Courbet's magnificent painting *The Origin of the World* shocking." **2.** Web. *Beaucoup disent "le Web" mais les puristes préfèrent "la Toile," et en discutent sur plusieurs sites Web.* "Many say the Web, but purists prefer "*la Toile*" and discuss it on several websites." **3.** Movie. **Se faire une toile.** To go to the movies. *Faisons-nous une toile ce soir.* "Let's go to the flicks tonight."

TOILES, *f., pl.* Sheets; bed. **Se mettre/se fourrer dans les toiles.** To go to bed. *Fourbu. Faut que je me fourre dans les toiles.* "Bushed. Got to hit the sack."

TÔLARD = TAULARD.

TÔLE = TAULE.

TOMATES, *f., pl.* Tomatoes. **Avoir ses tomates.** To have one's period. *J'avais mes tomates, mes j'ai quand même bien nagé.* "I was having my period but I swam well anyway."

TOMBER EN BOTTE(S)/COUILLE(S) = PARTIR EN COUILLE(S).

TOMBER EN CARAFE. To break down. *Je suis tombé en carafe en pleine nuit.* "My car broke down in the middle of the night."

TOMBER SUR UN BEC/OS. To hit a snag. *Je suis tombée sur un bec et j'ai pris du retard.* "I ran into a hitch and was delayed."

TOMBEUR, *m.* Seducer. *C'est un tombeur—méfie-toi!* "He's a Don Juan—be careful!"

TONDU, *m.* S.o. with close-cropped hair. See TROIS… TONDU.

TONNERRE DE BREST! Shiver my timbers! (Favorite oath of swaggering Captain Haddock in Hergé's comic book series *Les aventures de Tintin et Milou.* The *tonnerre* [thunder] is the noise made by the cannon fired twice daily to announce the opening and closing of the Brest Navy Yard. Variations on it include **Mille millions de mille sabords de tonnerre de Brest!**

TONNERRE DE DIEU! Thunderation! Hell's Bells! *Les 'Tonnerres de Dieu!' du fantôme Capitaine Gregg hantent toujours Mme Muir.* "The 'Damn and Blasts!' of Captain Gregg's ghost still haunt Mrs. Muir."

TONORGUE = TÉZIG(UE).

TOPO, *m.* Report; short talk. *Elle a bien travaillé son topo.* "She worked up a nice report." **C'est toujours le même topo.** "It's always the same old story/spiel."

TOQUANT, *m.* Heart. *Mon toquant fait tic-tac pour toi.* "My ticker ticks for you."

TOQUANTE = TOCANTE.

TOQUARD = TOCARD.

TOQUÉ, -E. 1. Slightly crazy. *Ton pépé est toqué.* "Your grandpa's a bit cracked." **2.** Smitten. *Il est vraiment toqué d'elle.* "He's really infatuated with her."

TORCHE-CUL, *m.* **1.** Toilet paper (lit. "ass wiper"). *Prends-moi du torche-cul triple épaisseur.* "Get me triple-ply toilet paper." **2.** Low-end newspaper. *Tu lis ce torche-cul?* "You read that rag?"

TORCHÉE, *f.* Beating. *Il a reçu une sacrée torchée.* "He was thoroughly beaten up."

(SE) TORCHER. To wipe o.s. **Se torcher (le cul) de qch.** To not give a damn. *Tous tes projets, je m'en torche!* "I don't give a shit about all your projects."

TORCHON, *m.* Theater curtain (lit. "cloth"). *Elle a eu beaucoup de levers de torchon aux rappels.* "She got many curtain calls after the performance."

TORCHONNER = TORCHER.

TORDANT, -E. Hilarious. *Elle est tordante dans ce sketch.* "She's a scream in that sketch."

TORD-BOYAUX, *m.* Rotgut alcohol. *Assez de ton tord-boyaux de fine!* "That's enough of your rotgut brandy."

(SE) TORDRE LES BOYAUX (DE RIRE)/SE TORDRE DE RIRE = (SE) BOYAUTER.

TORRIEU! *Que.* (Deformation of either **corps de Dieu,** "God's body" or **tort à Dieu,** "harm to God.") Jesus Christ! God Almighty! *Torrieu j'ai perdu mes clefs!* "Shit, I lost my keys!" See SACRE **2.**

TORRIEU, *m., Que.* Reprehensible person. *Si je t'attrape, sale torrieu, je te tue.* "I catch you, I kill you, no-good bastard!"

TOSCH = TEUCH.

TOSSER. To get high. *Il tossait dur.* "He was really high."

TOTOCHES = DOUDOUNES.

TOUBIB, *m.* Doctor (from Ar. **tbib**). *Son toubib va à domicile.* "Her doctor makes house calls." *Cf.* BABTOU.

TOUCHE, *m.* Key (on keyboard). **Faire une touche.** To make a hit with s.o. *Elle a fait une touche avec le facteur.* "She and the postman have hit it off." See SAINTE TOUCHE.

TOUCHE-PIPI. See JOUER À TOUCHE-PIPI.

(SE) TOUCHER. To masturbate. *Le curé demandait s'ils se touchaient.* "The priest kept asking them if they played with themselves."

TOUFFE, *f.* **1.** Female pubic hair (lit. "tuft"). *Elle se rase la touffe.* "She shaves her box." See RAS LA TOUFFE. **2.** Puff on a cigarette. *Passe-la moi pour tirer une touffe.* "Let me have a little drag on your cigarette."

TOUPET, *m.* Impudence. *Quel toupet!* "What nerve!"

TOURNANTE, *f.* Gang-rape. *Chacun son tour à la tournante avant de partir brûler les voitures.* "Everyone takes his turn at the gang-bang before leaving to burn cars."

TOURNER AUTOUR DU POT. To beat about the bush. *Cesse de tourner autour du pot et accouche!* "Quit beating about the bush and spit it out!"

TOURNER DE L'ŒIL. To faint. *Attendre longtemps debout la fait tourner de l'œil.* "She passes out if she has to wait on her feet for a long time."

TOURNÉE DES GRANDS-DUCS, *f.* Night on the town. *On s'est payé la tournée des grands-ducs pour nos noces d'or.* "We treated ourselves to a night on the town for our golden wedding anniversary."

TOURNER EN ROND. To go around in circles. *Depuis longtemps l'affaire tourne en rond.* "There's been no progress on the deal for some time." *Cf.* TOURNER ROND.

TOURNER LA PAGE. 1. To put an end to s.t. *Je ne veux plus le voir; j'ai tourné la page.* "I don't want to see him anymore; I've closed the book on him." **2.** To turn over for vaginal or anal penetration. *Elle avait ses règles et on a tourné la page.* "She had her period so I turned her over for sex."

TOURNER ROND. To run smoothly. *Enfin ça tourne rond au bureau.* "Finally, things are going right at the office." **Ne pas tourner rond.** To be a bit cracked. *Mes vioques ne tournent pas rond.* "My parents are a little nuts." *Cf.* TOURNER EN ROND.

TOUS AZIMUTS. See AZIMUT.

TOUS LES TRENTE-SIX DU MOIS. Once in a month of Sundays. *Mon fils ne vient me voir que tous les trente-six du mois.* "My son practically never comes to see me."

TOUT DE GO. Right away. *Elle a dit oui tout de go.* "She said yes right away."

(ET) TOUT LE BASTRINGUE/BATACLAN/FOURBI/ SAINT-FRUSQUIN/TRALALA; TREMBLEMENT. See BATACLAN; FOURBI; SAINT-FRUSQUIN; TOUTIM 2; TRALALA; TREMBLEMENT.

(À) TOUTE BARRE/BITURE. At full speed. *Le capitaine du* Titanic *a donné l'ordre d'avancer à toute barre.* "The captain of the *Titanic* gave the order to advance at full speed."

TOUTIM. 1. Short TV newscast on which an announcer is heard but not seen (from **toute-image**). *J'ai juste le temps de regarder les toutims.* "All I have time to watch are news briefs." **2. Tout le toutim.** The whole bunch. *Dans son camping-car il y a cousins, belles-doches, et tout le toutim.* "In his camper he's got his cousins, mothers-in-law, the whole kit and caboodle." *Cf.* TREMBLEMENT.

TOUTOU, *m.* **1.** Doggie. **Filer comme un toutou.** To be easily led. *Elle n'est pas du genre à filer comme un toutou.* "She's not the sort who can be dictated to." See (À LA) PEAU…TOUTOU. **2.** Prostitute (Fr. African). *Les tout-ous attendaient au bar.* "The prostitutes were waiting at the bar."

TOUTOUNE, *f., Que.* Fat female. *Luc n'aime que les bien enrobées, les toutounes.* "Luke just likes fat broads, full and fleshy."

TOUZEPAR, *f.,* backslang of **partouze.** Orgy. *La touzepar l'a fatigué.* "The orgy tired him out."

TOXICO, *m., f., abbr.* of **toxicomane.** Drug addict. *Je ne savais pas qu'il était toxico.* "I didn't know he was a junkie."

TOXIPUTE, *m., f.* Drug-addicted prostitute. *La toxipute faisait du yoyo pour racler du fric.* "The junkie whore turned lots of tricks to get money."

TRADALLE = TRADUC.

TRAFALGAR. See COUP DE TRAFALGAR.

TRAIN. Backside (lit. "train"). **Se magner/manier le train.** To get a move on. *Magne-toi le train, sinon tu loupes le bus.* "Move your butt or you'll miss the bus." See COLLER AU TRAIN.

TRAÎNER SES GROLLES. To go; frequent. *Où as tu encore traîné tes grolles pour être en retard?* "Where've you been hanging/gallivanting around so that you're late again?"

TRAITER QN. PAR-DESSOUS/PAR-DESSUS LA JAMBE. To treat s.o. in a shabby or offhanded manner. *Au boulot c'est stressant d'être traité par-dessus la jambe.* "It's stressful, being treated like a fifth wheel at work."

TRALALA, *m.* Frills; fuss. *Ils se sont mariés sans tralala.* "They had a simple wedding." **Et tout le tralala.** And all the rest. *Il me dit qu'il m'adore et tout le tralala.* "He tells me he adores me, and so on and so forth."

TRANCHE, *f.* Slice. **S'en payer une tranche.** To have a great time. *Eh dis, tu t'en es payé une tranche ce soir!* "Well, you're really having a ball tonight." See (S'EN) PAYER UNE TRANCHE.

TRAV = TRAVELO.

TRAVAILLER DU CHAPEAU/CHOU. To be a bit cracked. *Tu dis que ton tonton travaille de sa tête —moi, je dis qu'il travaille du chapeau!* "You say your uncle works with his head—I say he's off his rocker."

TRAVELO, *m.* Transvestite. *Vise la robe du travelo!* "Get a load of the drag queen's dress!"

(DE) TRAVIOLE. Lopsided. *Il marchait tout de traviole.* "He walked leaning to one side."

TRÈFLE/AS DE TRÈFLE. Posterior (lit. "clubs; ace of clubs"). *Il se grattait l'as de trèfle.* "He scratched his ass."

TREMBLEMENT, *m.* Trembling. **Et tout le tremblement.** The whole kit and caboodle. *Ils ont vidé le grenier, la cave et tout le tremblement.* "They emptied out the attic, cellar, the whole works." *Cf.* TOUTIM **2.**

TREMPE, *f.* Beating. *Il a reçu une bonne trempe.* "He got a real walloping." See FILER UNE TREMPE.

TREMPER SON BAIGNEUR/BISCUIT = TREMPER SON PANAIS.

TREMPER SON PANAIS. To have sexually (lit. "to dip one's parsnip"). See PANAIS.

TRENTE ET UN. Thirty one. **Se mettre sur son trente et un.** To get all dressed up. *Elle s'est mise sur son trente et un pour voir son jules.* "She dressed to kill to see her boyfriend."

TRENTE-SIXIÈME. Thirty sixth. **Être dans le trente-sixième dessous.** To be depressed; be at rock bottom financially. *Elle était dans le trente-sixième dessous après l'accident.* "She was really down after the accident."

TRIFOUILLER. To rummage around. *J'ai horreur que tu trifouilles dans mes papiers.* "I can't stand your messing around in my papers."

(SE) TRIMBALLER. To cart or drag around. *Je me trimballais toute la marmaille chaque dimanche.* "I had that bunch of kids on my neck every Sunday."

TRINGLE, *f.* Curtain rod. **Avoir la tringle.** To have or get an erection. *Il avait la tringle en visant du porno.* "He got a hard-on when looking at porn."

TRINGLER. To copulate. *Il l'a tringlée vite fait.* "He gave her a fast fuck."

TRINGLETTE, *f.* Nice little screw. *Une petite tringlette de temps en temps, ça fait du bien.* "A nice little screw now and then does you good."

TRINQUER. To take the rap (lit. "to clink glasses"). *Avec les flics c'est toujours les beurs qui trinquent.* "It's always the young Arabs who get the worst of it from the cops."

TRIQUE, *f.* Cudgel. **Avoir la trique.** To have an erection. *Il avait la trique en regardant les stripteaseuses.* "He got hard when looking at the strippers."

TRIQUETTE, *f.* Semierection. *Les sex-shops lui donnaient la triquette.* "The sex shops gave him a semierection."

TROGNE, *f.* Face, often *pej. "Quand je vois rougir ma trogne, je suis fier d'être Bourguignon,"* chante Papa. "'When I see my mug turn red (from drinking wine), I'm proud to be from Burgundy,' sings Dad."

350

TROIS PELÉS ET UN TONDU. Small/sparse audience (lit. "three peeled persons, and one shorn one"—the idea is sparse, as hair). *C'est dommage, il n'y avait que trois pelés et un tondu au concert.* "It's too bad there was only a handful at the concert."

TROIS PIÈCES. See SERVICE TROIS PIÈCES.

TROM'/TROMÉ, *m.* Subway (backslang of **métro**). *Prenons le tromé—Quoi? Le tramway?—Allons! Le tromé, c'est le verlan de métro.* "Let's take the tube."— "What? The tram (streetcar)?"—"Come on! The **tromé,** that's **métro** in backslang."

TRONCHE, *f., pej.* Face. **Faire la tronche.** To sulk. *Ne fais pas cette tronche.* "Don't pull a sour puss like that." See (SE) GRIFFER.

TRONCHE À CHIER DESSUS = GUEULE À CHIER DESSUS.

TRÔNER, youth. To astonish (lit. "to sit enthroned"). *Il m'a trônée en me montrant ses tatouages.* "He knocked me for a loop when he showed me his tattoos."

TROTTOIR, *m.* Sidewalk. **Faire le trottoir.** To solicit for prostitution. *Elle préfère faire le trottoir même en hiver.* "She prefers streetwalking even in the winter."

TROU DE BALLE (lit. "bullet hole") = **TROU DU CUL.**

TROU DE BITE/PINE. See YEUX EN.

TROU DU CUL, *m.* Asshole (lit. and fig., by metonymy [part for the whole], in this case "asshole," for the whole person). *Lui et ses copains, ce sont tous des trous du cul!* "He and his friends are all assholes." See SAINT...CUL.

TROUF/TROUFIGNARD/TROUFIGNON = TROU DU CUL.

TROUFION, *m.* Fool (lit. "private soldier"). *Ce ne sont que des troufions.* "They're all a bunch of assholes."

TROUILLARD, -E. Cowardly. *Ses copains le jugeaient trouillard.* "His friends thought him chicken."

TROUILLOMÈTRE, *m.* Fear indicator (hum. coinage. *Cf.* CONOMÉTRE; PIFOMÈTRE). **Avoir le trouillomètre à zéro.** To be scared stiff. *Quand j'ai vu les casseurs, j'avais le trouillomètre à zéro.* "When I saw the burglars I was scared stiff." *Cf.* ZÉRO **1.**

TROUSSER. To have intercourse quickly (lit. "to truss"). *Il l'a troussée sur l'herbe.* "He got it off with her on the grass."

TRUANDER. To swindle. *Ils se sont fait truander.* "They got swindled."

TRUC, *m.* **1.** Whatsit. *D'où sors-tu ce truc?* "Where'd you get that thing?" **2.** Thing. *La boxe, c'est pas mon truc.* "Boxing isn't my thing." See CHACUN.

TRUCMUCHE, *m.* Unidentified person or thing. *Tu as fourré ton trucmuche dans la sac de Trucmuche.* "You put that thingamajig in what's-his-name's bag."

TTBM = TBM with an extra **très.**

TUBAR, *m.* Connection. *C'est un boursier qui a de bons tubars.* "He's a stock market trader with good connections."

TUBE, *m.* Great success. *Cette chanson fera un tube.* "That song'll be a big hit." See (À) PLEINS TUBES.

TUER LE VER. To have a wake-up snorter (lit. "to kill the worm"). *Sa journée commence en tuant le ver.* "His day starts with a shot of alcohol."

TUILE, *f.* Unexpected hard luck (lit. "tile," that may drop on your head). *Quelle tuile!* "What a bummer!"

TUNE = THUNE.

TUNER = THUNER.

TURBIN, *m.* Daily grind. *C'est un vache de turbin!* "This is one rotten job!"

TURBINER. 1. To slave at a job. *Je turbine toute la journée.* "I slave away all day." **2.** To screw. *Oui, je les ai turbinées mais elles le voulaient.* "Yes, I plugged them, but they wanted it." *Cf.* BESOGNER.

TURLUPINER. To bother. *Les gosses me turlupinent sans cesse.* "The kids bug me constantly."

TURLUT(T)E, *f.* **1.** Fellatio (lit. "fishing rod," with probable influence of **turlurette** [small flute]). *Mon prix ne comprend pas la turlute.* "My price doesn't include a blow job." **2.** *Que.* Novelty song with vocalized syllables such as "tagadalaladi." *Cette Québécoise ne chante que des turluttes. J'aimerais plutôt qu'elle m'en fasse une.* "All that Quebec girl does is sing silly songs. I'd rather she sucked me off." *Cf.* JOUER…FLÛTE.

TURLUTER. To fellate (lit. "to tootle the flute"). *Laisse toutes ces histoires et viens me turluter.* "Forget all those stories and come blow me."

TURNE = **THURNE.**

TUTOYER. To use the familiar **tu** form. See PONTIFE **2.**

TUTU = **TOUTOU 2.**

TYPE, *m.* Guy. *Que penses-tu de ce type-là?* "What do you think of that guy?"

TYPESSE, *f., pej.* Female. *Je ne peux pas la blairer, cette typesse.* "I can't stand that broad."

U

-UCHE. Sl. suffix that imparts a sense of familiarity; for example, **galuche** = **Gauloise** (cigarette)**; loilpuche** = **à poil; Pantruche** = **Paris; paluche** = **patte.**

UNE, *f.* Front page (newspaper). *Ce scandale a fait la une.* "That scandal was front page news."

UNIF, *m.,* from **uniforme.** *Oui, il est beau en unif, mais même plus beau à poil.* "Yes he's handsome in uniform, but even more handsome in the all-together."

USINER. 1. To work long and hard (from **usine,** "factory"). *Elle usine chaque jour au zinc.* "She slaves away at the bar every day." **2.** To engage in sex. *Ne les dérange pas—ils usinent toujours.* "Don't disturb them—they're still screwing."

UTILITÉ, *f.* Theater. Minor part; small part (lit. "usefulness"). **Jouer les utilités.** To play bit parts; play second fiddle. *Avant de devenir une star, je jouais les utilités et bien sûr, je les ai jouées à merveille.* "Before becoming a star, I played minor parts and of course I played them perfectly."

VACANCES, *f., pl.,* drugs. Withdrawal time (lit. "vacation"). *L'accro a pris deux semaines de vacances.* "The junkie was clean for two weeks."

VACANT. Flat broke (lit. "vacant"). *À Las Vegas on était vacant.* "We were flat broke in Las Vegas."

VACCINÉ, -E. Impervious (lit. "vaccinated"). *Cesse tes lamentations; je suis vaccinée.* "Quit your groaning; I've heard it before."

VACCINÉ AU VINAIGRE (lit. "vaccinated with vinegar"). In a bad mood. *Il se lève toujours vacciné au vinaigre.* "He's always got a sour puss when he gets up."

VACHE, *adj.* Nasty. *Il a un côté vache, ce type là.* "That guy's got a mean streak."

VACHE, *f.* Cow. **Ah, la vache! 1.** That's incredible! (astonishment; admiration) *Ah, la vache! Notre équipe a gagné!* "Mind-blowing! Our team won!" **2.** Damn it! *(Ah) la vache, il a piqué ma bécane!* "Damn it, he's made off with my bike." See COUP...VACHE; PEAU DE VACHE; PLEUVOIR...PISSE.

VACHEMENT. Extremely. *Non seulement elle baise vachement bien mais elle est vachement intelligente.* "She's not only a terrific lay, but she's also super intelligent."

VACHER, *Que.* To loaf. *J'ai vaché tout le weekend.* "I wallowed the entire weekend."

355

VACHERIE, *f.* Nasty comment or deed. *Non seulement il me balance des vacheries, mais il m'en fait.* "Not only does he bad-mouth me, he also plays dirty tricks on me."

VACHETEMENT = VACHEMENT.

(À LA) VA-COMME-JE-TE-POUSSE. Any old way (lit. "like this is how I give you a little shove"). *Il a fait le boulot à la va-comme-je-te-pousse.* "He did a really sloppy job."

VACS, *f., pl.,* from **vacances.** Vacation. *Que de la flotte pendant les vacs.* "All it did was pour during our vacation."

VAGUER. 1. To go through s.o.'s pockets. *La police l'a vagué.* "The police frisked him." **2.** To wander; bum around. *Il vague dans la zone.* "He wanders around the shanty town."

VALDINGUER. To fall down. **Envoyer valdinguer.** To throw out; send packing. *J'ai tout envoyé valdinguer, lui et tout son foutoir.* "I threw him and all his junk out."

VALEUR, *f.* Value. **Valeur à la casse.** Scrap value. *Ce paumé? C'est une valeur à la casse.* "That bum? He's ready for skid row."

VALSE-HÉSITATION, *f.* Shilly-shallying. *Tu ne sais danser que la valse-hésitation. Tu viens, oui ou merde?* "All you can do is dilly-dally. Are you coming, yes or no?"

VALSEUR, *m.* Ass (lit. "waltzer"). *Son valseur est bien moulé dans sa robe.* "Her fanny is shapely in that dress." **Filer/onduler du valseur.** To wiggle one's bottom; mince (homosexual). *Tâche de moins onduler du valseur!* "Try not to shake your ass so much."

VALSEUSES, *f., pl.* Testicles (lit. "waltzers"). *Elle lui a foutu un coup dans les valseuses.* "She hit him in the balls."

VANNE, *f.* Sluice gate. **Balancer/envoyer une vanne/des vannes à qn.** To take verbal swipes at s.o; lash out at. *Il ne sait que balancer des vannes.* "All he can do is dump on people." (The idea is to let s.o. have it, like the sudden rush of water when a sluice gate is opened.)

VANNÉ, -E. Tired out (lit. "winnowed"). *En fin de journée on était tous vannés.* "At the end of the day we were all bushed."

VAPÉ, -E. Zonked; smashed. *Après l'accident, j'étais vapée.* "I was in a daze after the accident."

VAPES, *f., pl.,* from **vapeur** (vapor; steam). **Être dans les vapes.** To be dead to the world. *Avec tout cet alcool il sera demain dans les vapes.* "With all that alcohol, he'll be dead to the world tomorrow." Note: This expression, and the preceding one, are not arch or genteel, in the manner of vapid Victorian ladies who frequently had "the vapors," or "felt faint."

VASER. To rain. *Ça a vasé toute la journée.* "It's been pouring all day."

VASEUX, -EUSE. Woozy; hazy (lit. "muddy"). *Après cette bringue, nous étions tous vaseux.* "After that bash, we were all woozy."

VASOUILLARD, -E. Wishy-washy; unclear. *Ses explications sont vasouillardes.* "His explanations are as clear as mud."

VÉCÉS, *m., pl.* = **WC.**

VEINARD, -E. *m., f.* Lucky person. *Quel veinard! Il a décroché le job.* "What a lucky devil! He got the job."

VEINE, *f.* Luck (lit. "vein"). **Avoir de la veine.** *Elle n'a pas de veine avec sa bagnole toujours en panne.* "She's had no luck with her car that keeps breaking down." See COUP DE BOL/VEINE. *Cf.* DÉVEINE.

VENDRE DE L'AIL. To be a lesbian. See AIL.

VÉNÈRE, *invar.* To annoy, irritate. Backslang of **énerver.** *T'es toujours sur les nerfs et tu commences à me vénère.* "You're always edgy and you're getting on my nerves."

VENIN, *m.* Venom. **Cracher/filer/jeter/lâcher son venin** (lit. "to spit; hurl; leave one's venom"). To ejaculate. *Il a*

357

craché son venin et m'a quitté. "He got his rocks off and left me."*Cf.* LÂCHER LE JUS.

VENT, *m.* Wind. **Avoir du vent dans les voiles** (lit. "to have wind in one's sails"). To be drunk. *Les pompons rouges avaient du vent dans les voiles.* "The (Fr.) sailors were three sheets to the wind." **Être dans le vent.** To be fashionable (lit. "to be in the wind; air current, or **au courant**). *Elle est toujours dans le vent malgré son grand âge.* "She's always up-to-date despite her advanced years."

VENTRE, *m.* Abdomen. See TÉLÉPHONER…VENTRE.

VÉNUS. Venus. **Un coup de pied de Vénus.** Venereal disease (lit. "a kick from Venus"). *Lors du carnaval de Rio, Pol mettait toujours une chemise de Vénus. Malgré la capote, Vénus lui a donné a coup de pied.* "During carnival in Rio, Pol always Venus-sheathed his penis. Despite the rubber, he got an STD." *Cf.* CHEMISE DE VENUS.

VER, *m.* Worm. **Tirer les vers du nez à qn.** To worm s.t. out of s.o. *Les flics lui ont tiré les vers du nez et il a enfin avoué.* "The cops finally wormed a confession out of him." See (PAS) PIQUÉ…; TUER LE VER.

VERDURE, *f.* **1.** Greenery. **Faire de la verdure.** To look for sex; offer sex for sale in a park. *En été j'aime faire de la verdure.* "In the summer I enjoy soliciting in parks." **2.** Freshness; vigor. *Grand-dab a 80 piges mais la joie et la verdeur le caractérisent toujours.* "Grandpa is 80 but he's still joyous and vigorous."

VERJO = VERNI.

VERLAN (backslang of **l'envers**), *m.* Backslang, created by reversing or rearranging letters or syllables. Letters can be dropped or added, as in **barjo(t)/bargeot** (crazy) for **jobard** (crazy; gullible), **narca** from **canard** (newspaper).

VERNI, -E. Lucky (lit. "varnished; glazed"). *Qu'il est verni! Il a pu vendre son tas de ferraille.* "What a lucky devil! He was able to sell his old wreck of a car."

VERT, -E. Green. See LANGUE VERTE.

VERSAILLES. See OUVRIR…VERSAILLES; VICE-VERSAILLES.

VERSIGO = VERSAILLES.

VERT, -E. Slangy (lit. "green"). See LANGUE VERTE.

VESSE, *f.* Silent, foul-smelling fart. *Il accusait le chien d'avoir lâché une vesse.* "He alleged the dog cracked the sneaky, stinky fart." *Cf.* LÂCHER UN COLIS.

VESSER. To fart. **Vesser du bec.** To have bad breath. *Va voir le dentiste; tu vesses du bec.* "Go see the dentist; your breath stinks."

VESSIE, *f.* Bladder. **Prendre des vessies pour des lanternes.** To be very gullible and make blunders. *Ce n'est pas la première fois qu'il prend des vessies pour des lanternes.* "It's not the first time he's been sold the Brooklyn Bridge."

VÉTÉTEUX, *m.* Avid mountain biker. *Ils font partie d'une équipe de vététeux.* "They belong to a team of mountain biking fans." See VTT.

VÉTO, *m.* Veterinary. *Le véto a vacciné le chien contre la rage.* "The vet vaccinated the dog against rabies."

VEUVE, *f.* Widow. **Aller chez la Veuve Poignet.** To visit Mme Palm and her five daughters (lit. "to visit the Widow Wrist"). Masturbate. *Il est allé chez la Veuve Poignet car elle le repoussait.* "He jerked off because she rejected him."

VIARGE! *Que.* (*from* **vierge** "virgin," specifically the Virgin Mary). Holy Mary!, God Almighty!, Damn it! *Viarge, que tu m'emmardes!* "Jeez, you bug the shit outta me!" See SACRE **2.**

VICELARD, -E. *m., f.* Depraved individual. *Je me méfie de lui—c'est un vicelard.* "I don't trust him—he's a dirty old man."

VICE-VERSAILLES, *joc.* variation on **vice versa.** Reciprocally. *On s'est branlé, vice-versailles.* "We engaged in mutual masturbation." See VERSAILLES.

VIDÉ, -E. Exhausted (lit. "emptied"). *Après tant de nuits blanches, je suis vidée.* "After so many sleepless nights, I'm all played out."

VIDER. 1. To fire (lit. "to empty"). *Son patron l'a vidée.* "Her boss fired her." **2.** To throw out. *Il cherche la bagarre et se fait vider de tous les bars.* "He looks for trouble and gets thrown out of all the bars."

VIDEUR, *m.* Bouncer. *Parce qu'il est balèse on l'a pris comme videur.* "Because he's beefy they hired him as a bouncer."

VIEILLE CHAUSSETTE, *f.* Old sock. See LAISSER... CHAUSSETTE; RETOURNER...CHAUSSETTE.

VIEUX, *m., pl.* Parents (lit. "old people"). *Mes vieux ne me comprennent pas.* "My parents don't understand me." *Cf.* DABES; DARONS; REMPAS; VIOQUES.

VIF, *m.* The quick. **Couper/tailler/trancher dans le vif.** To take decisive action (lit. "to cut to the quick"). *Finies les valses-hésitations; il faut trancher dans le vif.* "That's enough shilly-shallying; we've got to come on strong now." See SUR LE VIF.

VIF-ARGENT, *m.* Quicksilver. *Ton pote, c'est du vif-argent.* "Your buddy's a real live wire."

VINAIGRE, *m.* Vinegar. **Faire vinaigre.** To hurry up. *Fais vinaigre ou tu seras en retard!* "Get a move on or you'll be late." See PISSE-VINAIGRE; VACCINÉ AU VINAIGRE.

VINASSE, *f.* Poor wine. *Ton grand cru, c'est de la vinasse.* "Your fine vintage wine is lousy."

VINGT-DEUX. Twenty-two. **Vingt-deux, v'la les flics!** "Watch out, here come the cops!"

VIOC = VIOQUE.

VIOLETTE, *f.* Tip; little extra (lit. "violet"). *Le serveur s'attendait à une violette.* "The waiter expected a tip." See DOIGTS DE PIEDS.

VIOLON, *m.* **1.** Violin. **Violon d'Ingres.** Artistic hobby. *Son violon d'Ingres, c'est la peinture.* "He's a Sunday painter." See PISSER…VIOLON. **2.** Jail. *Pris dans la manif, il a passé la nuit au violon.* "He was arrested during the demonstration and spent the night in the slammer."

VIOQUE, *m., f.* Old person; mother; father. *Il est de dab breton et de vioque parisienne.* "His father's a Breton, his mother a Parisian." *Cf.* DABE; DARON; DARONNE.

VIOQUES, *m., pl.* Parents. *Elle prend grand soin de ses vioques.* "She takes good care of her parents." *Cf.* DABES; DARONS; VIEUX.

VIPÈRE, *f.* Viper. **Vipère brousailleuse** (lit. "snake in the underbrush"). Penis. *Il lui courait après, la vipère brousailleuse à la main.* "He ran after her, holding his tool."

VIRÉE, *f.* **1.** Jaunt. *Elles font une petite virée au parc.* "They're on a little outing in the park." **2.** Barhop. *Les marins partaient en virée.* "The sailors went barhopping."

VIRER. To expel (lit. "to turn"). *Il s'est fait virer de tous les bahuts de la ville.* "He's been expelled from every school in town."

VISER. To look at (lit. "to aim at"). *Vise un peu la bath moto.* "Take a look at that cool (motor)bike."

VISU, *m.* Meeting; eyeballing. *Il faut qu'on fasse un visu.* "We've got to get a look at each other."

VITAMINE, *f.* Dope. **Vitamine A.** Acid; LSD. **Vitamine C.** Cocaine. **Vitamine E.** Ecstasy. *Il prenait des vitamines jusqu'à l'OD.* "He took lots of drugs until he OD'd."

VITE FAIT. In no time at all. *Avant le boulot elle prépare le déj vite fait.* "Before work she gets breakfast ready in a jiffy." **Tirer un coup vite fait.** To have a quickie (sexual). *Après avoir pris un pot vite fait, on a tiré un coup vite fait.* "After a quick snort, we had a quickie."

VITE FAIT, BIEN FAIT = preceding entry, but indicates that swift action was also smooth action.

VIVANT, *m.,* race track. Favorite (lit. "living being; live one"). *Il regrette d'avoir misé sur le vivant.* "He's sorry he bet on the favorite."

VIVRE À LA COLLE. To live together (**colle** = "glue; paste"). *Ils ont vécu à la colle dix ans avant de se marier.* "They shacked up together for ten years before getting married."

VOILE, *f.* Sail. **Être/aller/marcher à voile et à vapeur.** To be bisexual (the idea is to be both a "sailing ship" and a "steamship"). *Elle ne fréquente que les mecs qui marchent à voile et à vapeur.* "She dates only guys who swing both ways."

VOIR LES ANGES. To have an orgasm (lit. "to see the angels"). *Pour plaire à mon mari, je fais souvent semblant de voir les anges.* "To please my husband, I often pretend to have an orgasm."

VOITURE-BALAI, *f.* Last train; bus (lit. "broom vehicle," or one that "sweeps up" the latecomers). *Pour coucher avec moi tu as loupé exprès la voiture-balai.* "You missed the last bus deliberately so you could sleep with me." *Cf.* RAMMASER LES BALAIS.

VOL À L'ABORDAGE/À L'ARRACHÉ. Drive- or pass-by crime; mugging. *Il y a des vols à l'arraché sur les Bvds. de Paris.* "Purses get snatched on Paris boulevards."

VOL À LA TIRE = VOL À L'ABORDAGE/ ACCROCHAGE.

VOLAILLE, *f.* 1. Girl, esp. bar girl (lit. "poultry"). *Les étrangers cherchent la volaille de Pigalle.* "Foreigners seek out the B-girls of Pigalle." *Cf.* POULE; POULETTE; VOLIÈRE. 2. Police. *La volaille est à la sortie du métro Les Halles.* "The cops are at the Les Halles subway station exit." *Cf.* POULAGA….; POULET.

VOLANT, *m.* Steering wheel (car). See AS DU VOLANT.

VOLÉE, *f.* Beating (lit. "flight"). *Rentré trop tard il a reçu une sacrée volée.* "Because he came back too late, he got a real thrashing."

VOLEUR, *m.,* race track. Horse likely to "steal" the race (lit. "thief"). *Les initiés parieront sur ce voleur.* "Insiders will bet on that dark horse."

VOLEUR À LA TIRE. Pickpocket, purse-snatcher. See TIRAVE; TIRER.

VOLIÈRE, *f.* Whorehouse (lit. "aviary"). *Cette poulette finira à la volière.* "That chick's gonna wind up in the cathouse." Note the avian connection in "chick" and "bird" (Brit. slang for "girl," although some say "bird" in the sense "girl" derives from "burd," an obsolete word for "girl"). *Cf.* also VOLAILLE **1.**

VOLO, *f., abbr.* of **volonté. À volo.** Unlimited. *Le prix du repas comprend le vin à volo.* "The price of the meal includes all the wine you want."

VOLUME, *m.* Volume. **Faire du volume.** To throw one's weight around (lit. "to be bulky"). *Il ne se prend pas pour de la petite bière et aime faire du volume.* "He's conceited and likes to throw his weight around."

VOUZAILLES = VOZIQUE.

VO(S)ZIG(UE)S/VOZIGUE. You. *J'ai pris ceci pour vozigue.* "I bought this for you."

VRAI, -E DE VRAI, -E, *m., f.* The real thing; the real McCoy. *C'est un breton, un vrai de vrai.* "He's a Breton, through and through."

VRILLE, 1. Homosexual; dominant lesbian (lit. "gimlet" [tool for boring holes]). *J'suis vrille, mais j'ai pas du tout une allure virile.* "I'm a bull dyke but I don't look at all butch. **2.** Spiral; tailspin (aviation). **Partir en vrille.** To go off the deep end. *Pourquoi tu pars en vrille pour qch. d'anodin?* "Why're you going overboard for s.t. trivial?"

VTT, *m., abbr.* of **vélo tout terrain** (mountain bike). *Le vététeux prend soin de son VTT.* "The mountain biking enthusiast takes care of his bike." *Cf.* VÉTÉTEUX.

(À) VUE DE NEZ = AU PIF.

VULGOS, from **vulgaire.** Vulgar. *Il y en a qui l'ont trouvé innovateur son film; d'autres qui l'ont jugé vulgos.* "Some found her movie innovative; others thought it coarse."

VURDON, *m.* Gypsy caravan of trailers. *Je rêve de partir en vurdon avec un violoneux gitan.* "I dream of going off in a trailer with the gypsies and a gypsy violinist."

WAGON, *m.* Wagon; railroad car. **Raccrocher les wagons.** To put things right again (lit. "to hook the rail cars together again"). *L'affaire s'est faite car j'ai pu raccrocher les wagons.* "The deal went through because I was able to smooth things over."

WAGONNIÈRE, *f.* Prostitute who solicits on trains. *Les wagonnières voyageaient à tarif réduit.* "The train trollops rode at reduced rates."

WALLAH! *cités.* God! (Ar.). **Dis Wallah!,** lit. "Say 'By God!'." Swear it by God! *Tu me prêtes le zéyo? Dis Wallah!* "You'll lend me the money? Swear it by God!"

WATERLOO, *m.* Catastrophe; bad luck (from the famous battle). *Je n'ai connu qu'une kyrielle de waterloos.* "All I've had is a string of rotten luck." *Cf.* COUP DE TRAFALGAR.

WATERS, *m., pl.* Toilet. *S'il vous plaît, où sont les waters?* "Where's the john, please?"

WC, *abbr.* of "Water Closet." *Les WC du bar sont dégueulasses.* "The bar's toilets are revolting."

WESH! *youth, cités.* From Ar. "what." **1.** Hi! Greetings! What's doing? *Wesh, mon poto, ça va?* "Ho, bro, how's it going, what's goin' down?" **2.** What. *Tu veux ou wesh? Décide-toi.* "Ya wanna or what? Make up your mind." *Cf.* WESHKEN.

WESHKEN, *f., cités.* Old lady; gossip (from Ar. "What's going on?"). *La weshken sait tout.* "That busybody knows everything." *Cf.* MAQUERELLE **2.**

WICHE, *f.* Penis (Bel., NE France). *Lors du Carnaval de Dunkerque mon wiche était content de trouver une koukelour accueillante.* "During Carnival in Dunkirk my cock was happy to find a receptive pussy."

X, *m.* X. **Avoir les jambes en x.** To be knock-kneed. *Elle les trouve belles, les jambes en x de son mari.* "She thinks her husband's knock-knees are attractive."

X, *f.,* pronounced either as in Fr. *(eeks)* or as in Eng. Ecstasy (the drug). *Il dépense tout son fric pour l'X.* "He spends all his money on ecstasy."

XÉROX®, *m., f.* Unoriginal or robotic individual. *Au bureau ils sont tous des xérox.* "They're all just ciphers at the office."

Y ALLER AU BÉGUIN. See BÉGUIN **2.**

(N')Y ALLER QUE D'UNE FESSE. To undertake s.t. half-heartedly. *Si tu n'y vas que d'une fesse, tu saloperas le boulot.* "If you go at it half-heartedly, you'll do a half-assed job."

Y ÊTRE. To understand. *Tu y es? Oui, j'y suis!* "You get it? "Yes, I see." See ÇA Y EST!

Y ÊTRE POUR QCH. To have s.t. to do with. *J'ai fait carrière dans la musique et mon mari y est pour qch.* "I made a career in music and it's partially my husband's doing." **Ne pas y être pour rien.** Not to be responsible for. *Mais je n'y suis pour rien; c'est ton talent qui a triomphé.* "But I had nothing to do with it; it's your talent that triumphed."

YAOURT, *m.* **1.** Yoghurt. See PÉDALER…YAOURT. **2.** Gobbledygook. *Il croyait chanter en anglais, mais c'était du yaourt!* "He thought he was singing in English, but it was gibberish."

YEUX, *m., pl.* **Ne pas avoir les yeux en face des trous.** To not see the obvious; not feel up to par. *Tu n'avais pas les yeux en face des trous pour faire une connerie pareille.* "You must have been asleep; sick; dreaming to do s.t. so stupid." See COÛTER LES YEUX DE LA TÊTE; SORTIR…YEUX.

YEUX EN TROU DE BITE/PINE, *m., pl.* Tiny, deep-set eyes (not "cockeyed" but lit. "eyes like the meatus [opening] of the penis"). *Il me regardait, médusé, avec ses yeux en trou de bite.* "He looked at me dumbfounded, with his beady little eyes."

YÉYÉ, *m.* **1.** Sixties rock (from Eng. "yeah, yeah"). *Ils écoutent toujours le yéyé.* "They still listen to sixties rock." **2.** Sixties' rock fan. "My parents were sixties rockers."

YIÈCHE = IÈCHE.

YOMBER, *youth, cités.* To annoy (from repetitive, acquiescent **bon, bon** in response to an interlocutor's assertions). *Tu me yombes avec toutes tes histoires connes.* "You bug me with all your stupid stories." *Cf.* VÉNÈR.

YOUDE/YOUDI = YOUPIN.

YOUPIN, -E, *m., f., pej.* Jew. *Il bouffait du youpin avant d'apprendre qu'il etait juif lui-même.* "He used to be violently antisemitic before finding out that he was Jewish h.s."

YOUVOI, *m.* backslang of **voyou.** Hooligan. *Il est devenu youvoi.* "He's become a thug."

YOYO, *m.* Yo-yo®. **Faire du yoyo.** To turn a succession of tricks. *Pour plaire à mon mac je fais du yoyo.* "To please my pimp I turn lots of tricks." *Cf.* COCOTTE-MINUTE.

ZAPPER. 1. To change TV channels; zap. *Elle zappait avant de se coucher.* "She channel-surfed before going to bed." **Zapper qn.** To shut s.o. out (shut off like a TV channel). *Après toutes ses vacheries je l'ai zappé.* "I dumped him after all his dirty tricks." **2.** To go away. *On reste ou on zappe?* "Do we stay or blow this hole?"

ZAPPETTE, *f.* Remote control. *Je paume souvent la zappette.* "I often misplace the remote."

ZAPPEUR, -EUSE, *m., f.* Inveterate channel surfer. *Les zappeurs suivent plusieurs films à la fois.* "Zappers follow several movies at once."

ZAP-ZAP, *m.* = **ZAPPETTE.**

ZARB/ZARBI. Weird (backslang of **bizarre**). *C'qu'il est zarb, ce gus!* "That guy's a real weirdo!"

ZAUDIT! *Que., euph. for* **MAUDIT!**

ZEB, = **ZOB.**

ZÉBER, backslang of **baiser.** To fuck. *Il ne pense qu'à zéber.* "All he thinks about is screwing."

ZÉBI = **ZOB.** See PEAU…ZÉBI.

ZÈBRE, *m.* Guy. *C'est un drôle de zèbre!* "He's an odd one."

ZARMAZONE, *f.* Feminist. *Les zarmazones du IXème arrondissement sont militantes et intellos.* "The feminists in the 9th district (Paris) are militant and intelligent."

ZEF, *m.,* from **zéphyr.** Wind; fart. *Que vous ayez toujours le zef dans le dos, et qu'il ne soit jamais le vôtre.* "May the wind always be at your back, and may it never be your own." *Cf.* LÂCHER UN COLIS….; VESSE.

ZEN, *m.* **1.** Nose (backslang of **nez**). **Piquer du zen.** To nod off. *Papa piquait du zen devant la TV.* "Pop nodded off in front of the TV." **2.** Zen (Buddhism). **Rester zen.** To stay calm. *Elle restait zen en toute circonstance.* "She kept her cool in all circumstances."

ZEPPELIN, *m.* Huge cigarette of *cannabis. Le zeppelin était la star de la noce.* "The huge joint was the star of the wedding party."

ZÉRO, *m.* **1.** Zero. **C'est un zéro fini!** "He's a total zero." **Les avoir à zéro.** To be very afraid. *En conduisant en montagne je les avais à zéro.* "When driving in the mountains I was very afraid." *Cf.* TROUILLOMÈTRE. **2.** High-grade hashish. *Il est accro au zéro.* "He's hooked on quality hash."

ZETOUPAR, *f.,* backslang of **partouze.** Orgy. *Puritaine que je suis, j'ai refusé de participer à leurs zetoupars.* "Puritan that I am, I refused to take part in their group sex parties."

ZÉYO, *m., youth, cités.* Money. Modified backslang of **OSEILLE.**

ZGUEG, *m.* Penis. *Il ne se lave jamais le zgueg.* "He never washes his dick."

ZIB, *m.* Penis. *Il prétend que son zib a sa propre volonté.* "He claims his dick's got a will of its own."

ZIC/ZICMU/ZIQUE, *f.* Music. *J'adore ta zic.* "I love your music."

ZIEUTER = ZYEUTER.

ZIEUTISTE, *m., f.* Ophthalmologist. *C'est aujourd'hui le dentiste. Demain le zieutiste.* "It's the dentist today. The eye-doctor tomorrow."

-ZIG(UE). Suffix used to create slang forms of the peronal pronouns. See MÉZIG(UE)/MÉZIGO.

ZIGOMAR/ZIGOTO/ZIGUE, *m.* Guy. *Que fout-il, ce zigomar?* "What's that guy doing?" **Faire le zigoto.** To act the fool. *Arrête de faire le zigoto!* "Quit horsing around." *Cf.* ZOUAVE.

ZIGON(N)ER. 1. To waste time, horse around. *Tu ne fais que zigoner.* "All you do is goof off." **2.** To fuck. *Ça fait longtemps que je l'ai zigounée.* "I had her long ago."

ZIGOUIGUI, *m.* **1.** Female genitalia. *J'essaye d'approfondir les grands mystères de son zigouigui.* "I'm trying to get to the bottom of the great mysteries of her box." **2.** Penis. *Il n'a pas de zigougui dont je peux me vanter.* "He hasn't got a cock I can brag about." **3.** Thingamajig. *À quoi ça sert, tous ces zigouiguis?* "What are all those thingama-bobs for?"

ZIGOUILLER. To kill. *Le casseur a zigouillé le gardien.* "The burglar knocked off the security guard."

ZIG-ZIG, *m.* Sex. **Faire zig-zig.** To have sex. *Veux-tu faire zig-zig avec moi?* "You wanna get it on with me?"

ZINC, *m.* Counter in a bar; café. *Il est chaque soir au zinc.* "He's at the bar every night."

ZINZIN. Crazy. *C'est lui le plus zinzin.* "He's the zaniest of them."

ZINZIN, *m.* **1.** Whatsit. *Voilà un drôle de zinzin.* "That's an odd little object." **2.** Noise. *Arrête enfin ton zinzin!* "Quit that racket, will you."

ZINZINS, *m., pl.,* stock market. Institutional investors (from the liaisons in **les investisseurs institutionnels**). *Les zinzins boudent les nouvelles actions.* "The institutional investors aren't buying the new stocks."

ZIZANIE, *f.* **1.** Rye grass (a weed). **2.** Discord. **Mettre/semer la zizanie.** To create ill feeling. Zizanie de Fragonard *était son parfum préféré, mais elle n'a jamais semé la zizanie.* "Zizanie de Fragonard was her favorite perfume, but she never stirred up trouble."

ZIZETTE, *f.* Female genitalia. *Ma zizette est presque prête.* "My pussy's almost ready." *Cf.* FOUFOUNE; NOUNE; ZIGUIGUI **1**; ZIZOUNETTE.

ZIZI, *m.* **1.** Child's penis. *Les gamins comparaient leurs zizis en chantant* Le zizi de Pierre Perret. "The kids compared their dicks as they sang *The Willy* by Pierre Perret. *Cf.* ZGUEG; ZIB; ZIGUIGUI **2**; ZOB. **2.** Vagina (rarely. See **ZIZETTE).**

ZIZIQUE, *f.* Music. *Coupe ta zizique—je veux dormir.* "Shut off your music—I want to sleep." *Cf.* ZIC.

ZIZOUNETTE, *f.* Female genitalia. *Fais voir ton zoune et je te ferai voir ma zizounette.* "Lemme see your dick an' I'll letcha see my snatch."

ZOB, *m.* Penis (from Ar.). **Mon zob!** My eye! My ass! See PEAU…ZOB.

ZOMBLOU, *m.,* backslang of **blouson.** Jacket. *Il s'est acheté un zomblou d'aviateur.* "He bought a bomber jacket."

ZONARD, *m.* **1.** Vagrant. *Elle a créé un foyer pour zonards.* "She founded a shelter for the homeless." **2.** Punk; tough. *Il ne fréquente que des zonards.* "He just hangs out with hooligans."

ZONER. 1. To hang out. *Il a zoné tout l'été.* "He just loafed all summer." **2.** To size s.o. up. *Je l'ai zonée au premier coup d'œil.* "I sized her up at first sight."

ZOUAVE, *m.* Guy; clown (orig. a soldier in military units formed in Algeria in 1831). **Faire le zouave.** Act the fool; waste time. *Il s'amusait à faire le zouave.* "He enjoyed horsing around."

ZOUNE, *f., Que.* Penis. *Gil a une zoune zarbi.* "Gil's got a funny lookin' dick." *Cf.* ZGUEG; ZIB; ZIGUIGUI **2**; ZOB.

ZOUZOUNE, *f.* Female genitalia. *Je ne rêve qu'à ses doudounes et sa zouzoune.* "All I dream of are her knockers and bush." *Cf.* FOUFOUNE; NOUNE; ZIGUIGUI **1**; ZIZOUNETTE.

ZOZORES, *f., pl.* Ears. *Ouvre tes zozores et écoute-moi.* "Open your ears and listen to me."

ZUT!/ZUT ALORS! Darn it! Damn it! Hang it!

ZUT POUR VOUS! Go to the devil! Nuts to you!

ZYEUTARD or **ZYEUTEUR,** *m.* **1.** Peeping Tom. *Elle aime s'exhiber aux zyeutards.* "She likes to exhibit h.s. to peeping Toms." **2.** Non-paying spectator of streetwalkers (prostitutes). *Dans les quartiers chauds y a souvent plus de zyeuteurs que de michetons.* "In the red-light districts there are often more voyeurs/tourists than clients."

ZYEUTER. To scrutinize. *Il ne cesse de me zyeuter.* "He keeps staring at me."

ZYGOMATIQUE, *m.* Zygomatic (facial muscle). **Titiller le zygomatique de qn.** To make s.o. laugh. *Le comique a titillé le zygomatique de tous.* "The comic tickled everyone's funny bone."

ZYGOS/ZYGOSSES, *m., pl.,* from **zygomatique.** *J'ai mal aux zygos d'avoir tant ri.* "My face aches from laughing so much."